WOOI
Ship-Building

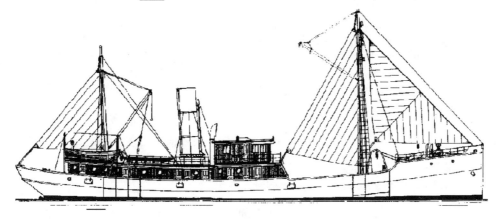

Charles Desmond

Vestal Press

VESTAL PRESS, Inc.

Published in the United States of America
by Vestal Press, Inc.
4720 Boston Way
Lanham, Maryland 20706

British Library Cataloguing in Publication Information Available

Library of Congress Cataloging-in-Publication Data

Desmond, Charles.
  Wooden ship-building.

  Reprint. Originally published: New York : Rudder Pub. Co., c1919.
  Includes indexes.
  1. Ships, Wooden. 2. Ship-building. I. Title.
 VM144.D4 1984   623.8'207   84-7577
 ISBN 0-911572-37-6

ISBN 0-911572-37-6

∞™ The paper used in this publication meets the minimum requirements of
American National Standard for Information Sciences—Permanence of
Paper for Printed Library Materials, ANSI Z39.48–1984.
Manufactured in the United States of America.

Introduction

THE object of this book is to place at the disposal of builders of wood ships some much needed information about construction and equipment. Each principal part of a vessel's construction is explained, the information being arranged in such a manner that the reader can either use the book for reference purposes and quickly obtain from it desired information about any selected part of hull or equipment, or he can read the book as one continuous story covering the construction and equipment of a vessel.

If it is desired to make use of the book for reference purposes, turn to indexed name of part or piece you desire information about. (The headings are arranged alphabetically.)

CONTENTS

Chapter I

Classification and Insurance

In almost every instance kinds and dimensions of materials to use for constructing a ship are determined by the designer, or builder, in accordance with rules laid down by the classification society that will classify the vessel for insurance purposes.

1a. CLASSIFICATION FOR INSURANCE EXPLAINED

Seagoing vessels are classified for insurance because unless this is done insurance rates for vessel and for cargo carried cannot be fixed with any degree of certainty.

When a ship owner contracts with a builder for a new vessel he generally stipulates that the vessel shall be built to conform with the classification rules of a known classification society, and selects the class he desires vessel to enter; and the builder, knowing these things, obtains a copy of building rules and dimensions of material tables issued by the named classification society and constructs the vessel to conform to the rules.

These rules stipulate the kinds and dimensions of materials that must be used for each principal part of hull and equipment, and also the manner in which the parts should be put together; and as the rules are based upon results of actual tests made by practical shipbuilders and owners all over the world, it is evident that both builder and owner have every reason to adhere to them.

The Classification Societies' rules most generally used are:

Lloyd's rules and regulations for the classification and construction of vessels. (British.)

American Lloyd's (Bureau of American Shipping) rules for classification and construction.

Bureau Veritas (French) rules for construction and classification.

British Corporation rules.

Though methods of measuring and determining necessary dimensions of material to use are not alike, somewhat similar results are obtained by the four classification societies' rules mentioned, therefore a vessel built to conform to a certain class in one society will be granted a corresponding classification in any other society.

As I have mentioned classification of vessels for insurance, perhaps I had better explain its meaning a little more fully. The majority of seagoing vessels are insured by their owners, and the cargo carried is also separately insured by its owners. The amount of "risk" or danger of vessel and cargo being lost or damaged depends very largely upon strength and seaworthiness of vessel and her equipment, therefore it is imperative that people who insure, and people who desire to ship cargo, have some ready

means for determining (a) the condition of the vessel and her equipment, and (b) the proper amount of risk involved by shipping cargo. If a vessel is sound and has proper equipment the risk is necessarily very much less than if a vessel is old, or badly constructed, or poorly equipped, and of course the smaller the risk of loss or damage the lower the premium will be for both vessel and cargo carried.

You can therefore readily understand that a well-found, properly constructed vessel will seldom have to wait for cargo. The means employed for determining condition of a vessel and for letting all shippers of cargo know her condition is to have a vessel classified by a known and competent authority and to have this classification done while vessel is being constructed and at certain periods after launching.

The classification is done by skilled surveyors, employed by classification society, who designates the class that vessel's construction and equipment entitles her to receive. Under Lloyd's rules a vessel will be classed "A" provided it is found to be in a fit and efficient condition for its contemplated employment. If a vessel is being built for any particular trade, there will be affixed to the letter the name of trade, such as "A" for coast service only.

If vessel is built properly and in accordance with material and dimension rules, the number 100 will be prefixed to the letter, thus: A 100; and if the equipment, such as anchor, chains, rigging, etc., is as specified in tables, the figure (1) is placed immediately after the letter designating class. Thus a vessel classed as 100 A 1 is known to be in fit condition, to be built of materials that are proper in strength and put together in a proper manner, and to have equipment, rigging, etc., that is proper in amount, dimensions and quality. If a vessel's construction is not quite up to the standard called for by rules, the numeral 100 is replaced by one of lesser value (95 or 90).

In the American Lloyd's (Bureau of American Shipping) classification the character assigned to vessels is expressed by number from 1 to 3, A 1 standing for highest class and A 3 for lowest. Intermediate numbers (1½, 1¾, 2, 2½) being assigned to vessels that, while not as good as A 1, are superior to A 3.

In general new wooden ships built in accordance with Lloyd's building rules can obtain classification in Class A for a designated number of years, and can have this classification continued on the termination of the named period if, after survey, the ship is found to be in proper condition for a continuation of the classification.

Class A ships are entitled to carry all kinds of cargoes in any waters.

Ships that have passed out of Class A and are not in condition to be continued in it and ships not built in accordance with rule are generally classed in Class A, in red.

Ships which are found on survey fit for carrying dry and perishable cargoes on short voyages are classed AE, and ships which are not safe for carrying perishable cargoes but perfectly safe for carrying cargoes not likely to be damaged by salt water are classed E.

These classification rules are mentioned because it is necessary that you have some knowledge of the underlying principles of the rules for classifying vessels.

To get a class, or get a vessel classified, a written application must be made to a properly authorized agent, or surveyor, of the classification society, and the established fee paid. It is usual to apply for classification before work on a vessel is commenced, because the rules of classification societies stipulate that their surveyor shall inspect hull during construction and specify the stages of construction when each inspection shall be made.

Inspections are usually made:

1st.—When keel is laid and frames are up.

2d.—When planking is being wrought.

3d.—When planking is completed and caulked, but before deck is laid.

4th.—When decks and ceiling are laid and vessel is ready for launching.

5th.—When vessel is completed, outfitted and ready for sea.

When a class is assigned to a vessel it is assigned for a certain stated number of years and upon the condition that vessel is to be kept in good repair and properly equipped during the whole of named period; and it is also stipulated that whenever a vessel is being repaired, or whenever she is damaged, a surveyor must be notified and vessel be inspected. In addition to this all vessels must be submitted for resurvey at the expiration of a named number of years. These rules not only insure that a vessel shall be properly built, but they also insure that all classified vessels shall be kept in good repair under penalty of withdrawal of certificate or lowering of class. Having thus briefly explained the meaning of classification and the reason for classifying vessels, I will tell you about the kinds of materials used in ship-building and the proper dimensions of materials to use in each principal part of a vessel's construction.

Chapter II

Information About Woods

The substance named *wood* is, for the most part, elastic, tenacious, durable, and easily fashioned. The part that is characterized as *timber* is obtained from the body of trees, or that part of those which grow with a thick stem, rising high, and little encumbered with branches or leaves, which is called the *trunk*. The *head* of the tree consists of the branches, which are adorned with leaves; these attain their full development in the Summer, and then, in the great majority of species, fall in the Autumn.

In ship carpentry, the wood of the trunk and largest branches alone is used; and only that of the commoner species of trees.

Some of the timber trees attain an immense size when they are allowed to come to full maturity of growth. Oaks and beeches are found to attain the height of 120 feet; the larch, the pine, the fir grow to the height of 135 feet. Other kinds, as the elm, the maple, the walnut, the poplar, and the cypress, reach sometimes a great elevation.

Botanists classify trees according to their physiological and structural peculiarities; and in this way trees are divided into two great classes,—Monocotyledonous, or Endogenous, and Dicotyledonous, or Exogenous trees.

The terms Monocotyledonous and Dicotyledonous, belong to the Jussieuan system of nomenclature, and are descriptive of the organization of the seeds. Endogenous and Exogenous are the terms used by modern botanists, and are descriptive of the manner of growth or development of the woody matter of the tree, which is, in the endogens, from the outside inwards towards the interior, and in the exogens, outwards to the exterior.

The monocotyledonous or endogenous trees have no branches: their stems, nearly cylindrical, rise to a surprising height, and are crowned by a vast bunch of leaves, in the midst of which grow their flowers and fruits. In this class are the palm trees, growing only in tropical climes, where they are of paramount importance, yielding to the people of those countries meat, drink, and raiment, and timber for the construction of their habitations.

The palm tree will serve as a type of the endogenous structure. Dicotyledonous or exogenous trees, which form the second class, are in much greater variety, and much more widely spread over the globe, than trees of the first class. The form of their trunks is generally conical, tapering from the root to the summit: the summit or head of the tree is formed by the prolongation of the trunk, which divides into sundry primary branches; these again ramify into innumerable secondary branches; and these throw out small twigs, to which the leaves are attached by foot-stalks, larger or smaller. At first sight it appears as if the leaves grew by chance, but an order, regular and constant in each species, presides in their distribution.

On making a transverse section of a dicotyledonous tree, we see that it is composed of three parts, easily distinguished—the bark which envelops, the pith which forms the core or center, and the woody substance which lies between the bark and the pith.

In the woody substance we distinguish two thicknesses: the one which envelops the pith is the greatest, and is of a harder nature than that which adjoins the bark. The former is termed perfect wood, the latter *alburnum*. The inner layer of bark next the alburnum is called the *liber,* a name given from its being used to form the books (*libri*) of the ancients. Between the liber and the alburnum there is a substance partaking of the qualities of both, and called *cambium*. This is developed in the Spring and Autumn, when its internal portion changes insensibly into alburnum, and the exterior into liber. The liber never becomes wood: it is expanded continually by the process of growth in the tree, and forms the bark, which rends and exfoliates externally, because of its drying; and the layer of liber, in growing old, cannot extend in proportion to the augmentation in the circumference of the tree.

Duhamel and Buffon long since proved that alburnum, in process of time, became perfect wood; and there is now no doubt in regard to the manner in which the tree grows and produces its wood.

Exogens, or outward growers, are so called because, as long as they continue to grow, they add new wood to the outside of that formed in the previous year; in which respect they differ essentially from endogens.

The only respects in which the growth of exogens corresponds with that of endogens are, that in both classes the woody matter is connected with the leaves, and in both, a cellular substance is the foundation of the whole structure.

As new layers of alburnum are produced, they form concentric circles, which can be easily seen on cutting through the tree; and by the number of these circles one can determine the age of the tree. Some authors assert that this is not so, since a tree may produce in one year several concentric layers of alburnum, and in another year only one. Nevertheless, the commonly received opinion is, that the number of concentric circles in the cross section of the wood, called annual layers, indicates the time it has taken to reach its size. Although a layer of alburnum is deposited each year, the process of transformation of it into perfect wood, otherwise *heart-wood,* is slow, and, consequently, the alburnum, or *sap-wood,* comprehends many annual layers.

The annual layers become more dense as the tree grows aged; and when there is a great number in a tree of small diameter, the wood is heavy, and generally hard also. In wood which is either remarkably hard or remarkably soft, the annual layers can scarcely be distinguished. They cannot, for example, be distinguished in ebony, and other tropical woods, nor in the poplar, and other soft white woods of our climate. In the case of the softer woods in our climate, the layers are frequently thinner and more dense on the Northern side than on the opposite. In a transverse section of a box tree, about 7 inches diameter, we reckoned one hundred and forty annual layers.

The roots of a tree, although buried in the soil, have, as we have seen, an organization resembling that of the trunk and branches. The roots of several trees are employed in the arts and in ship-building, but as these are fully described in another chapter I need not dilate on the subject: I shall only remark, that as the branches of a tree divide into smaller branches and twigs, expanding to form a head, so the roots divide also into branches, which expand in every direction in the ground, and these branches again divide, their ultimate division being into filaments, commonly called fibres, which appear to be to the roots what the leaves are to the branches.

It has been remarked that there is a sympathy between the branches and the roots in their development. Thus, when several considerable branches of a tree are lopped off, the corresponding roots suffer, and often perish.

2a. Cultivation of Trees

Trees are the produce of forests, planted spontaneously, and consequently very ancient, or of forests and plantations created by man since he has engaged in this kind of culture.

The reproduction of trees, their culture, and the felling of timber, belong more to the management of forests; but I shall remark briefly on some qualities which are derived from growth.

The size and fine growth of a tree is not an infallible sign of goodness of quality in the wood. The connection of the age of a tree with its development, and the nature of the soil in which it grew, ought to be inquired into to enable a judgment to be formed of the quality of the wood.

In general, boggy or swampy grounds bear only trees of which the wood is free and spongy, compared with the wood of trees of the same species grown in good soil at greater elevations. The water, too abundant in low-lying argillaceous land, where the roots are nearly always drowned, does not give to the natural juices of the tree the qualities essential to the production of good wood. The oak, for example, raised in a humid soil, is more proper for the works of the cabinet-maker than for those of the ship-carpenter; because it is less strong and stiff, and is softer and more easy to work than the same wood raised in a dry soil and elevated situation: it is also less liable to cleave and split. Its strength, compared with that raised in a drier soil, is about as 4 to 5, and its specific gravity as 5 to 7.

Wet lands are only proper for alders, poplars, cypress, and willows. Several other species incline to land which is moist or wholly wet; but the oak, the chestnut, the elm, thrive only in dry situations, where the soil is good, and where the water does not stagnate after rain, but is retained only in sufficient quantity to enable the ground to furnish aliment for the vegetation. Resinous trees, too, do not always thrive in the soils and situations proper to the other kinds of timber, and especially in marshy soils: sandy soils are in general the best for their production; and several species affect the neighborhood of the sea, such as the maritime pine, not less useful for its resin than for its timber.

In fine, trees which grow in poor and stony soils, and generally in all such soils as oppose the spreading of their roots, and do not furnish a supply of their proper sap, are slow and stunted in their growth, and produce wood often knotty and difficult to work, and which is mostly used as veneers for ornamenting furniture.

The surest tokens of good wood are the beauty, clearness, and firmness of the bark, and the small quantity of alburnum.

It has been remarked that timber on the margin of a wood is larger, more healthy, and of better quality than that which grows in the interior, the effect of the action of the sun and air being less obstructed.

2b. Timber for Ship-Building

The qualities which fit woods for use by shipbuilders are durability, uniformity of substance, straightness of fibre, strength and elasticity. The good quality of a wood is known by uniformity and depth of color peculiar to its species. When color varies much from heart to circumference it is safe to assume that the tree from which the timber was cut was affected by disease.

Knotty and cross-grained wood is difficult to work and should be rejected especially for use in pieces subjected to great strains. The knots are always a source of weakness because the straightness of fibres which gives strength is interrupted.

Knots are the prolongation of branches across the perfect wood of the trunk of the tree. If the branches have grown with the tree to the time it was cut down the knots will be perfect wood and the fibres of the trunk will only be slightly turned from their straightness, but if the branch forming the knot ceased to grow before tree was cut down the knot will be "dead" and will not only greatly weaken the timber but may have caused some of the surrounding wood to decay. In all woods of a given species the heavier the specimens are the stronger and more durable. Timber cut from the butt of a tree is always the heaviest and strongest, and for this reason all pieces of timber that have to be steam bent should be cut from butt ends of logs.

Among resinous woods those which have the least resin in their pores, and among non-resinous woods those which have the least sap, or gum, in them are generally the strongest and most durable.

The tenacity of wood when strained along the grain depends on the tenacity of the fibres, and tenacity when strained across the grain depends upon the adhesion of the fibres to each other.

Timber used for ship-building should be free from cracks radiating from the center (called "clefts"), from cracks which partially separate the layers (called shakes), and from sap-wood (the light-colored wood nearest the bark), and should be properly and thoroughly air seasoned.

2c. Care of Timber

If timber be exposed to great changes of temperature, to alternations of wetness and drought, to a humid and hot atmosphere, it will inevitably suffer a deterioration of those qualities which render it serviceable for the ship-carpenter.

Timber, when too suddenly dried, is liable to split: when exposed to too high a temperature in a close atmosphere, its juices are liable to fermentation, followed by a loss of tenacity and a tendency to rot and become worm-eaten. The greater the quantity of timber thus kept together, the more rapidly is it impaired, which is made sensible to the smell by a peculiar odor emitted from it.

When timber is exposed to injury from the weather, and lying long exposed on a damp soil, it is attacked by wet rot. The alternations, too, of drought and rain, of frosts and of heat, disorganize the woody fibre, which breaks, and a species of rottenness ensues resembling the decay of growing timber. The means of defending the timber from these various causes of waste, and preserving it in a state fit and proper to be used in construction, we now propose to describe.

When the timber is squared and cut up, care must be bestowed on it; not alone on the ground that it is then so much the more valuable by the labor which it has cost, but because, by its being divided, it is more easily affected by deteriorating causes; and by its surface being augmented, these causes have also a larger field to operate on.

Timber of the same scantling should be piled together; and there should not be mingled in one pile wood of different species.

The first layer of the pile should be elevated above the soil on sleepers, the higher the better, as securing a freer circulation of air, and preventing the growth of fungi. The most perfect security, however, is obtained by paving the site of the pile, and building dwarf walls or piers, with strong girders, to form the foundation for the first tier.

Where the space will admit of it, and the timbers are square, they should be laid in tiers crossing each other alternately at right angles, and at least their own width apart. This method will not do for thin planks, because it would not allow a sufficient circulation of air. These are better when piled so that in the alternate tiers there are only planks sufficient to keep the other tiers from bending. Where space can be afforded, it is well to pile square timber in this way. The diagram (Fig. 1) will best explain this mode.

After timber is erected as part of a ship it will rapidly deteriorate unless protected against the causes of

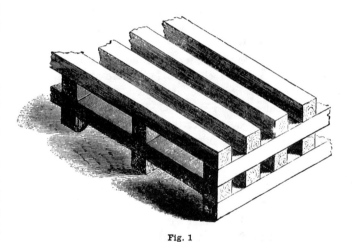

Fig. 1

decay, which are principally: (a) imperfect seasoning, (b) improper ventilation and presence of impure air in holds of a ship, (c) changes in temperature and presence of moisture in holds and around joints of the ship's structure, (d) dirt in holds and around the framing.

In the present day very little shipbuilding timber is properly seasoned and for this reason it is expedient to close up every rend, shake, and opening, and the surfaces of joints that cannot be reached after the pieces are assembled, with some substance that will act as a preservative by resisting the action of water and prevent moisture getting into the pores of the wood. The ventilation of holds and circulation of air around the timbers of the frame should be properly planned because it is in the hold of a ship, more than in any other part, that decay starts; here the greatest degree of moisture collects and the greatest amount of impure air accumulates, especially if holds are not properly cleaned when a cargo is removed, or if through some damage to ceiling of a hold dirt or decaying refuse from cargo is allowed to accumulate around the frames and in places where it cannot be readily removed from.

Timbers that are found to be decayed at the lower part of the extremities of a ship, and in which the decay proceeds from the center, will usually be found upon examination to have some surface defect, such as a shake or fissure, through which air and moisture have been admitted to the heart, and in the case of joints that have decayed it will generally be found that air and moisture has had access to the center of joint through some defect or opening in joint.

Without air and moisture decay in timber cannot begin. Decay in timber is a fungus that requires air to stimulate its growth, as can be easily proved by admitting moist air to the heart of timbers that are apparently sound. With the admission of air and moisture the growth of fungus of decay is almost immediately started.

2d. Of the Bending of Timber

Curved forms require that the ship-carpenter should obtain the timber naturally curved, or should possess the power of bending it. Trees which yield timber naturally curved are generally used for the constructions of the naval architect. If, where curved timber is required, it should be attempted to be formed by hewing it out of straight timber, two evils would ensue: the first, a loss of wood; the second, and greater, the destruction of its strength by the necessary cross-cutting of its fibres. Hence, to maintain the fibres parallel among themselves, and to the curve, recourse is had to curving or bending the timber artificially. This process may be performed on the timber after it is squared or cut up.

The process of bending timber artificially is founded on the property which water and heat have of penetrating into the woody substance, rendering it supple and soft, and fitting it to receive forms which it retains after cooling.

Bending timber is effected in the five following ways:

1. By using the heat of a naked fire.
2. By the softening influence of boiling water.
3. By softening it by vapor.
4. By softening it in heated sand.
5. By vapor under high pressure.

The first method of operation is only applicable to timbers of small scantling.

In the second method, the timber is immersed in water, which is heated until it boils, and is kept boiling until the timber is wholly saturated and softened. The timber being then withdrawn, is immediately forced to assume the required curvature, and is secured by nails or bolts. This proceeding has the defect of weakening the timber, and lessening its durability. It should, therefore, be used only in such cases as do not require the qualities of strength and durability.

In the third process, the timber is submitted to the action of the steam of boiling water. For this purpose it is inclosed in a box made perfectly air-tight. The box has a series of grated horizontal partitions or shelves on which the timbers are laid. From a steam boiler conveniently situated, a pipe is carried to the box. The steam acts on the timber, and in time softens it and renders it pliant. The time allowed for the action of the steam to produce this effect is generally one hour for every inch of thickness in the planks.

The fourth method of preparing the wood for bending, is by applying heat and moisture to it through the medium of the sand bath. The apparatus for this purpose is a furnace with flues, traversing the stone on which the sand is laid, in the manner of hothouse flues. There is also provided a boiler in which water is heated. On the stone a couch of sand is laid: in this the timbers are immersed, being set edgeways on a bed of sand about 6 inches thick, and having a layer of sand of the same thickness separating them, and being also covered over with sand. The fire is then lighted in the furnace, and after a time, the sand is thoroughly moistened with boiling water from the boiler before mentioned. This watering is kept up all the time that the timber is in the stove. Thin planks require, as in the preceding case, an hour for each inch of thickness; but for thick scantlings the time requires to be increased; for instance, a 6-inch timber should remain in the stove eight hours.

The fifth mode, by means of high-pressure steam, only differs from the third process described in this, that the apparatus requires to be more perfect. The box, therefore, is generally made of cast-iron, and all its parts are

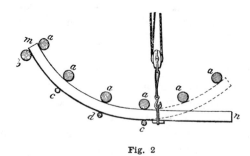

Fig. 2

strengthened to resist the pressure to be employed. When the steam has a pressure of several atmospheres, the softening of the wood is very rapid; and it is very effectually done by this method.

After the timber is properly softened and rendered pliable, it is bent on a mould having a contour of the form which the timber is required to assume.

The simplest method of doing this is shown in outline in Fig. 2. A series of stout posts, *a a a*, are driven into the ground, on a line representing the desired curve. The piece of wood *m n*, when softened, is inserted between two posts at the point where the curvature is to begin, as at *a b,* and by means of a tackle, applied near that point, it is brought up to the next post, *a,* where it is fixed by driving a picket, *c,* on the opposite side. The tackle is shifted successively from point to point; and the pickets, *c, d, e,* are driven in as the timber is brought up to the posts. It is left in this condition until it is cold and dried; and then it is removed to make way for another piece. But if the balk is required to be more accurately bent, and out of winding in its breadth, squared sleepers, *a a a* (Fig. 3, Nos. 1 and 2), are laid truly level across the line of curvature, and the posts *b b* are also accurately squared on the side next the balk.

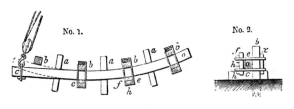

Fig. 3

An iron strap *c,* which is made to slide freely, is used for attaching the tackle, and as the balk is brought up to the curve, it is secured to the posts *b, b* by two iron straps, *e e, e e* (seen better in the vertical section, No. 2), which embrace the pieces *f,* on the opposite side, and are wedged up tight by the wedges *h h.*

In operating in either of the ways described, only one piece of timber can be bent at a time. By the following method several pieces may be bent together:

Fig. 4 is a vertical projection, and a transverse vertical section, of the apparatus. It consists of the horizontal pieces *a a,* arranged with their upper surface in the contour of the curve. They are sustained by strong framing *b b, c c, d d.* The timber is laid with its center on the middle of the frame, and by means of purchases applied at both sides of the center, and carried successively along to different points towards each end, it is curved, and secured by iron straps and wedges as before. The frame may be made wide enough to serve for the bending of other pieces, as *m, n;* or for a greater number, by increasing the length of the pieces *a a,* and supporting them properly.

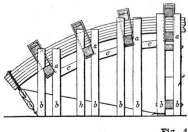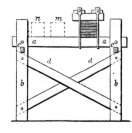

Fig. 4

These methods are not quite perfect; for in place of the timber assuming a regular curvature, it will obviously be rather a portion of a polygonal contour. To insure

perfect regularity in the curve, it is necessary to make a continuous template, in place of the several pieces *a a a.*

Care must be taken that the curvature given to the timber is such as will not too greatly extend, and, perhaps, rupture the fibres of the convex side, and so render it useless.

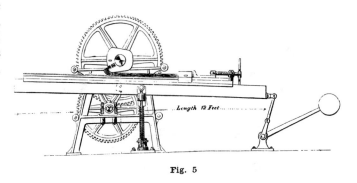

Fig. 5

The process of bending timber which we have described, is, as will be seen, restricted to very narrow limits. The effect, when the curve is small, is to cripple the fibres of the inner circumference, and to extend those of the exterior, and the result is, of course, a weakening of the timber. Bending, effected by end pressure, is not only not attended with injurious effects, but on the contrary, gives to the timber qualities which it did not before possess.

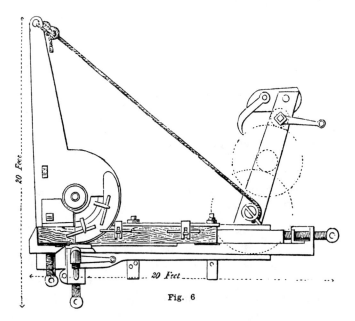

Fig. 6

Wood can be more easily compressed than expanded; therefore, it is plain that a process which induces a greater closeness in the component parts of the piece under operation—which, as it were, locks up the whole mass by knitting the fibres together—must augment the degree of hardness and power of resistance.

Another of the good results of this method is, that the wood is seasoned by the same process as affects the bending. The seasoning of wood is simply the drying of the juices and the reduction of the mass to the minimum size before it is employed, so that there should be no future warping. But, as the compression resorted to

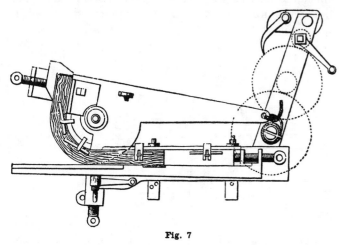

Fig. 7

in the system at once expels the sap, a few hours are sufficient to convert green timber into thoroughly seasoned wood.

Fig. 5 shows the form of the machine for timbers under 6 inches square. Figs. 6 and 7 show the machine for heavy timbers above that scantling.

The principle, as has been stated, is the application of end pressure; but another characteristic feature is, that the timber, during the process, is subjected to pressure on all sides, by which its fibres are prevented from bursting or from being crippled; and, in short, the timber is prevented from altering its form in any other than the desired manner. The *set* imparted to it becomes permanent after a few hours, during which time it is kept to its form by an enveloping band and a holding bolt, as shown in Fig. 8.

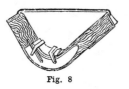

Fig. 8

2e. Seasoning of Timber, and the Means Employed to Increase Its Durability

Seasoning timber consists in expelling, or drying up as far as possible, the moisture (sap) which is contained in the pores. Air, or natural, seasoning is best and consists in simply exposing the timber freely to air in a dry place sheltered from sunshine and rain. Air seasoning of hard wood cannot be completed in less than two years. To immerse the logs in water for a few weeks before they are sawed into plank will hasten the seasoning because the water expels the sap.

Timber can be artificially seasoned by placing it in a tight chamber, called a dry kiln, and exposing it to a current of hot air which is forced into the compartment by fans. The temperature of the air should vary with kind of wood:

For oak it should not exceed	105°
For hard woods in general, in thick planks, about	100°
For pine woods in thick pieces, about	180°
For pine timbers	200°
For mahogany	260°

The current of air being freely circulated around the planks, which should be piled, with spaces between them, for not over 12 hours a day.

The drying should be gradual; for if the moisture be carried off too rapidly the fibres of the wood will collapse or lose their power of adhering to one another and the timber will split along the grain. One reason why kiln-dried timber is not advocated for use in ships is the tendency of kiln-dried timber to imbibe moisture from the atmosphere and thus induce decay.

An attempt to fix a time for air seasoning timber would be utterly useless because time required to season timber will vary with kind and quality, and also with conditions of climate, piling, etc.

In general it can be said that timber for ship-building should not be used sooner than three years after felling. If timber is squared, cut to scantling, and placed in a situation where air can pass freely over each piece, pieces 6 inches square will season sufficiently to be usable in six months; pieces 12 inches square will require from *twelve* to *fifteen* months; and pieces over 12 inches square will require from *twenty* to *twenty-four* months. But this period of seasoning will not thoroughly dry the timber; it will only put it into condition to be used for parts that do not require thoroughly air-dried timber.

Timber in seasoning loses from 6 to 40% in weight, and from 2 to 8% in transverse measurement (through shrinkage).

Immersion in hot water effects the same purpose much more rapidly; but as the wood has to be submitted to the action of the water for ten or twelve days, the expense is prohibitive of the process, unless in cases where the condensing water of a steam engine in constant operation can be made available. As we have before remarked, when speaking of the bending of timber, the action of the hot water impairs its strength, and should not be used where strength is an object.

Immersion in salt water is a means of adding to the durability of timber. It increases its weight, and adds greatly to its hardness. It is attended, however, by the grave inconvenience of increasing its capacity for moisture, which renders this kind of seasoning inapplicable for timber to be employed in the ordinary practice of the carpenter.

The water seasoning of which we have been speaking has many objectors; but numerous experiments prove, beyond contradiction, that timber immersed in water immediately after being felled and squared, is less subject to cleave and to decay, and that it dries more quickly and more completely; which proves that the water evaporates more readily than the sap, of which it has taken the place. The immersion, however, impairs, to some extent, the strength of the timber; and this consideration indicates the applicability or non-applicability of the process. When the timber is required for purposes for which dryness and easiness of working are essential, then the water seasoning may be employed with advantage; but when for purposes in which strength alone is the great requisite, it should not be used.

2f. Loss of Weight and Shrinkage of Timber in Seasoning

While seasoning timber will lose a considerable portion of its original (green) weight and it will also shrink in width and in thickness. The amount of loss of weight and dimensions in seasoning varies considerably, being much greater in some kinds of timber than in others. On the accompanying Table 1 (page 17) I give figures obtained by carefully weighing and measuring a number of experimental pieces of timber. The figures are for thorough seasoning during a period of over *three* years. You will note that there is some variation in shrinkage between butt and top planks of same timber.

Among the insects whose attacks are most fatally injurious to the wood are the white ant, the *Teredo navalis,* a kind of *Pholas,* and the *Limnoria terebrans.*

The white ant devours the heart of the timber, reducing it to powder, while the surface remains unbroken, and affords no indication of the ravages beneath.

The *teredo* and *pholas* attack wood when submerged in the sea. The *teredo,* its head armed with a casque or shell in the shape of an auger, insinuates itself into the wood through an almost imperceptible hole; it then in its boring operations follows the line of the fibre of the wood, the hole enlarging as the worm increases in size. It forms thus a tube, extending from the lowest part of the timber to the level of the surface of the water, which it lines with a calcareous secretion. A piece of timber, such as a pile in a marine structure, may be perforated from the ground to the water level by a multitude of these creatures, and yet no indications of their destructive work appear on the exterior.

The *pholas* does not attack timber so frequently as the *teredo;* and its ravages are more slowly carried on. Its presence in the wood, therefore, though very dangerous, is not so pernicious as the other.

For the protection of timber from disease, decay, and the ravages of insects, various means are employed. These may be classed as internal and external applications.

I. *Preservation of Wood by impregnating it with Chemical Solutions.*

The chemicals usually employed in solution are the deutochloride of mercury (corrosive sublimate), the protoxide of iron, the chloride of zinc, the pyrolignite of iron, arsenic, muriate of lime, and creosote. They are either used as baths, in which the timber is steeped, or they are injected into the wood by mechanical means; or the air is exhausted from the cells of the wood, and the solutions being then admitted, fill completely every vacuum.

All of these processes are advantageous under certain circumstances; but it cannot be said that any of them is infallible.

But it is to be feared that against the attacks of the marine pests—the *teredo,* the *pholas,* and the *Limnoria terebrans*—the protection these processes afford is at the best doubtful. An exception to this may probably be taken in favor of the creosote process. The soluble salts are supposed to act as preservatives of the timber, by coagulating its albumen; thus the very quality of combining with the albumen destroys the activity of the salts as poisons, and hence although preservatives against decay, they may, when thus combined, be eaten by an insect with impunity. With creosote, however, the case is different. It fills the vessels of the wood, and its smell is so nauseous that no animal or insect can bear it. It is also insoluble in water, and cannot be washed out. It is thus a protection to the wood against the ravages of insects, and also a preservative from decay. The base of many of the marine preservative and, so-called, anti-fouling bottom paints is creosote.

Previous to the application of any of these substances, however, and as a preparative for it, it is essential that the timber be thoroughly deprived of its moisture.

II. *Preservation by Paints and other Surface Applications.*

Timber, when wrought, and either before it is framed, or when in its place, is coated with various preparations, the object of which is to prevent the access of humidity to its pores. In the application of such surface coatings, it is essential that the timber be thoroughly dry; for if it is not, the coating, in place of preserving it, will hasten its destruction, as any moisture contained in it will be prevented from being evaporated, and will engender internal decay. This result will be more speedily developed as the color of the coating is more or less absorbent of heat.

One of the most common applications to timber constructions of large size is a mixture of tar, pitch, and tallow. The mixture is made in a pot over a fire, and applied boiling hot.

But the most universally applicable protective coating is good oil paint. It is necessary that the oil should be good, the paint insoluble in water, and thoroughly ground with the oil, and that in its application it should be well brushed with the end, and not with the side of the brush. Such a coating has not the disadvantage of weight, like the painting with sand; nor does it, like it, alter the form of the object to which it is applied.

The timber to be painted in oil should be planed smooth; and it is essentially requisite that it be dry. It is usual to submit it to the action of the air for some time before painting, and then to take advantage of a dry season to apply the paint.

To render effectual any of the surface coatings we have mentioned, it is necessary to take care that the joints of framing are also coated before the work is put together. If this be neglected, it will happen that although any water which may fall on the work will evaporate from the surface, some small portions may insinuate themselves into the joints, and these remaining, will be absorbed by the pores of the wood, and become the cause of rot. The joints of all exposed work should, therefore, be well coated with the protective covering before it is put together.

Besides these fluid compositions, timber exposed to the action of marine insects is often covered with a sheathing of metal, usually copper.

I will now give a brief description of each kind of wood used by shipbuilders in the U. S. A., the average weights of each, and the strength compared with that of oak.

2g. Description of Woods—Hard Woods

Oak.—The oak is one of the strongest and most durable of shipbuilding woods that grow in the U. S. A., but all of the oaks are not equally durable and valuable.

The most durable and valuable of the oaks is the *live oak.* This is a fine-grained, compact and heavy wood obtained from trees that only grow near the sea-coast of some of the Southern States. The trees are rarely found more than 15 miles from the coast and are most abundant along the shores of creeks and bays. It is the most durable and strongest of the oaks that grow in the U. S. A., but is difficult to procure in large quantities because the trees seldom attain large dimensions and are never found in forests.

Next in value to the live oak is the *white oak.* This is a light-colored, hard and durable species of oak that grows in great abundance in the Eastern half of the U. S. A. The wood is very durable both in and out of water and possesses great strength. Experiments on samples of white oak gave these results:

Specific gravity, about .... .934
Weight of cubic feet in ℔ (nearly dry) 58.37
Comparative strength, or weight necessary to bend .... 149.
Comparative strength .... 350.
Cohesive force per square inch ....℔ 13,316.
Comparative toughness .... 108.

Red oaks and other varieties of *common oaks,* of which there are several, are less durable and do not possess the strength of white oak and for these reasons should not be used when white oak can be obtained. For interior finish the red oak is preferable to the white because it is a softer wood and has a much finer grain, or figure, when quarter-sawed.

Chestnut is a soft coarse-grained wood, somewhat similar in color to white oak. It is found in the Eastern part of the U. S. A., and while not nearly as strong as oak its lasting qualities are excellent. For this reason a certain percentage of chestnut can be used in the frames of vessels without loss of class. The average cohesive force of chestnut is about 9,700.

Its stiffness to that of oak is as 54 to 100.
Its strength to that of oak is as 48 to 100.
Its toughness to that of oak is as 85 to 100.

Rock Elm.—The elm is a large tree, common in the U. S. A. There are about fifteen species, of which the rock elm is the most valuable for ship-building. Its wood is ruddy brown, very fibrous and flexible, subject to warp, tough, and difficult to work. It is not liable to split and bears the driving of nails or bolts better than any other wood. When kept constantly wet it is exceedingly durable, and is, therefore, much used for keels of vessels and in wet places.

The weight of a cubic foot when green is about 60 ℔ and when dry about 43 ℔.

Its strength to that of white oak is as 82 to 100.
Its stiffness to that of white oak is as 78 to 100.
Its toughness to that of white oak is as 86 to 100.
Its absolute cohesive strength is about 13,000 ℔.

Soft elm is the worst of all the species and is absolutely useless for shipbuilding use.

Ash is an excellent wood for oars, blocks, handspikes, etc., because its toughness and elasticity fit it for resisting sudden and heavy shocks. It is of little use for other shipbuilding purposes because of its liability to rot when exposed to dampness or used in places where it will be alternately wet and dry.

The weight of a cubic foot of green ash is about 60 ℔ and of dry wood about 49 ℔. Its cohesive strength is about 17,000 ℔.

Its strength to that of white oak is as 119 to 100.
Its stiffness to that of white oak is as 89 to 100.
Its toughness to that of white oak is as 100 to 100.

Teak.—While not a native U. S. wood, teak is extensively used in ship-building and is, in fact, one of, if not the most valuable of all shipbuilding woods. It is a native wood of India, and is one of the few woods that can withstand the ravages of white ants. The wood is light brown in color, is durable both in and out of water, and possesses very nearly the strength of white oak. Its tenacity is about 13,000 ℔ per square inch.

Teak is largely used for deck plank in yachts, for rails, for joinerwork, and in places where great durability is desired.

In countries where it is plentiful it is used for keels, frames, and planking of vessels, and when so used the vessels are practically indestructible through decay.

There are two descriptions of teak used in ship-building; one of which is brought from Moulmein and the other from Malabar. The former of these is in various respects superior to the latter; in India, where the opportunities of comparing them have been more ample than in this country, it is stated to be of less specific gravity, of greater flexibility, and freer from knots and rindgalls than the teak of Malabar; it is also of a lighter color.

It grows to an immense size in the forest, and trees are sometimes cut of 8 or 9 feet in diameter; but most of such trees are unsound; smaller trees are therefore preferred, ranging down to 18 inches in diameter. The largest pieces of this teak run to about 85 feet in length, and are about 8 or 9 feet in girt; keel-pieces range from 38 to 50 feet in length, squaring from 15 to 24 inches.

This timber is killed before it is felled: the trees are girdled all round through the sap about 3 feet above the ground, just before the rainy season begins, and when the sap is low. The vitality of the trees being thus destroyed, they are left in that state to season, for two or even three years before they are felled. The trees are considered to arrive at perfection in about seventy years; a transverse section of some trees exhibits the periodical rings of the stem at half an inch or even three-quarters of an inch asunder, while in other specimens of the same timber these rings can hardly be distinguished. Some butts are of a close and even texture; and the same feature of the wood extends the whole length of the log though it be 60 feet: other butts are soft for several inches round the heart.

Maple.—Maple is a hard, heavy, strong and close-grained wood of light color. The hard maple is extensively used for launching ways and for planking of slipways. The wood is durable when fully covered with water but is not very durable when alternately wet and dry. When green it weighs about 62 ℔, and when dry about 51 ℔. Its tenacity is about 10,586 ℔.

Locust.—The timber of the acacia is called locust wood. In color it is yellow. It is an extremely durable wood of great strength. Experiments have shown that it is heavier, harder, stronger and more rigid than the best white oak. Its use, however, is almost entirely confined to treenails, because the trees from which the timber is cut are always very small, and for this reason locust is seldom used except for pieces that can be made out of small timbers. For treenails it is far superior to all other woods.

Its strength compared with oak is as ....135 to 100.
Its weight is about 45 ℔ a cu. ft. and its tenacity is ℔ 16,000.
Locust wood shrinks very little indeed in seasoning.

Birch.—There are two kinds of birch used in ship construction, the black and the yellow. The black is the most durable and is the one preferred by shipbuilders. It is moderately hard wood, weighs when green about 60 ℔, and when dry about 45 ℔. Its tenacity is 15,000 ℔ a square inch. The yellow birch is not a very durable wood.

Mahogany.—This wood is extensively used for ship joinerwork and planking of small boats. It is a native of the West Indies and Central America. The mahogany tree is one of the most beautiful and majestic of trees. Its trunk is often 50 feet high, and 12 feet diameter. It takes probably not less than two hundred years to arrive at maturity.

The mahogany tree abounds the most and is in greatest perfection between latitudes 11° and 23° 10′ N., including within these limits the islands of the Caribbean Sea, Cuba, St. Domingo, and Porto Rico, and in these the timber is superior in quality to that of the adjacent continent of America, owing, it is to be supposed, in some measure, to its growing at greater elevations and on poorer soils.

Mahogany timber was used at an early period by the Spaniards in ship-building. In 1597 it was used in the repairs of Sir Walter Raleigh's ships in the West Indies.

The finest mahogany is obtained from St. Domingo, the next in quality from Cuba, and the next from Honduras.

In the island of Cuba the tree is felled at the wane of the moon from October to June. The trunks are dragged by oxen to the river, and then, tied together in threes, they are floated down to the rapids. At the rapids they are separated and passed singly, then, collected in rafts, they are floated down to the wharves for shipment. It is considered essential to the preservation of the color and texture of the wood that it should be felled when the moon is in the wane.

The Honduras mahogany is commonly called bay wood, and is that most used for the purposes of carpentry. It recommends itself for these purposes by its possessing, in an eminent degree, most of the good and few of the bad qualities of other timber. It works freely; it does not shrink; it is free from acids which act on metals; it is nearly if not altogether exempt from dry rot; and it resists changes of temperature without alteration. It holds glue well; and it does not require paint to disguise its appearance. It is less combustible than most woods. The weight of a cubic foot is 50 ℔, and its tenacity is given by Barlow at 8,000 ℔.

Its strength compared with oak is as 96 to 100.
Its stiffness compared with oak is as 93 to 100.
Its toughness compared with oak is as 99 to 100.

Sabicu.—The wood of a beautiful tree which grows in Cuba. It is used in the government yards for beams and planking. The weight of a cubic foot is from 57 to 65 ℔.

Greenheart (Nectandra rodiœi).—This wood is a native of Guiana, where it is in great abundance. The trees square from 18 to 24 inches, and can be procured from 60 to 70 feet long. It is a fine but not even-grained wood. Its heart-wood is deep brown in color, and the alburnum pale yellow. It is adapted for all purposes where great strength and durability are required. The weight of a cubic foot is from 51.15 to 61.13, and its specific gravity from 831 to 989.

Poplar (Populus).—The wood of the poplar is soft, light, and generally white, or of a pale yellow. It has the property of being only indented and not splintered by a blow.

It is adapted for purposes which require lightness and moderate strength, and when kept dry it is tolerably durable. It weighs when green 48 ℔ 3 oz. per cubic foot, and from 24 to 28 ℔ 7 oz. when dry. It shrinks and cracks in drying, and loses about a quarter of its bulk. When seasoned it does not warp, and takes fire with difficulty. Its tenacity is 6,016.

2h. Resinous and Soft Woods

Of the timber of the resin-producing trees, belonging to the natural order Coniferæ, many varieties are used. The white pine of America, which is the *Pinus Strobus;* the yellow pine of America, *Pinus variabilis;* the pitch pine, *Pinus resinosa;* the silver fir, *Pinus Picea;* and the various white firs, or deals, the produce of the *Pinus Abies,* or spruce fir; and also the larch, are all used in almost every kind of construction.

No other kind of tree produces timber at once so long and straight, so light, and yet so strong and stiff; and no other timber is so much in demand for all purposes.

From the growing trees are obtained turpentine, liquid balsam, and the common yellow and black rosin. Tar is obtained by cutting the wood and roots into small pieces, and charring them, or distilling them in a close oven, or in a heap covered with turf. The lampblack of commerce is the soot collected during this process. Fortunately, the trees of the pine and fir tribe, so useful to man, are found in great abundance in America and Europe.

White or Northern Pine.—This wood grows in the Northern States of the U. S. A. and in Canada. It is a light, soft, straight-grained wood of a light yellowish color, and is one of the most reliable of woods for staying in place after it is fastened, because it does not warp. It is extensively used for patterns, for deck plank, for joinerwork that will be painted, and for planking of small craft of all types.

> Its strength to that of oak is as 90 to 190.
> Its stiffness to that of oak is as 95 to 100.
> Its toughness to that of oak is as 103 to 100.
> Its weight when green is about....... 36 ℔.
> Its weight when dry about.......... 28 ℔.

Georgia Pine.—Also known as pitch pine, as *yellow pine,* and as *"longleaf pine"*, is a strong, close-grained, durable wood extensively used in ship-building. This pine grows in Southern States from Virginia to Texas, and can be obtained in lengths up to at least 60 feet and dimensions up to about 14 by 14 inches. Yellow pine is largely used for planking, for decking, for a large portion of the longitudinal framework, for keels and keelsons and for spars.

> Its strength as compared with that of oak is as 90 to 100.
> Its toughness as compared with that of oak is as 96 to 100.
> Its weight when green is about .... 56 ℔.
> Its weight when dry about .... 45 ℔.

Spruce.—There are four kinds of spruce in U. S. A., of which only two are suitable for shipbuilding use, viz., the *black* and the white spruce. These are tough, light woods that are fairly durable when used in wet and damp places. For this reason it is used for floors, for keelsons and for longitudinal members of vessels' framework. Its strength is about the same as that of white pine. Bear in mind that it is the color of the bark and not the wood that gives the name to each kind. The woods cannot be distinguished after bark is removed.

Oregon Pine.—This is a species of pine that grows on the Western Coast; its texture is somewhat like that of the Eastern white pine but the wood is slightly harder and contains more rosin. The wood is extensively used for shipbuilding purposes and rates next to yellow pine for durability and strength. It is an excellent wood for masts and spars. Oregon pine can be obtained in lengths of 100 feet and over, and some of the timbers of this length are almost clear of knots. Oregon pine is also called Douglas fir.

White Cedar.—This is a soft, white, fine-grained wood in great demand for planking small boats and yachts. The wood is a native of Virginia, where it grows in swampy land. Species of white cedar are also found in Canada, in Michigan, in New Jersey and in Florida. The wood is exceedingly durable, is tough and is extremely light in weight, some of the Canadian cedars weighing only 15 ℔ per cubic foot. The weight of an average Virginian white cedar log is about 20 ℔ per cubic foot.

Red Cypress.—This is another Southern wood in great demand for small boat and yacht construction work. Its color is reddish yellow and the wood is one of the most durable of woods, either in or out of water.

Cypress has, however, this defect: it soaks up water very readily, and for this reason it must be kept well covered with paint or varnish. The wood is soft and bends readily.

As cypress trees grow to heights of over 100 feet, the wood can be obtained in long lengths and almost free from knots and defects. The red cypress is the name given to the dark-colored wood cut from trees that grow near the coast—the lowland cypress. The upland light-colored cypress is worthless for boatbuilding purposes and is not at all durable. In color the lowland cypress is yellowish and for this reason it is called yellow cypress.

The most valuable woods in the U. S. A. for shipbuilding purposes are teak, live oak, white oak, common oak, chestnut, elm, hackmatack, yellow pine, spruce, Douglas fir or Oregon pine, red cypress, white cedar, Washington cedar, and white pine.

Lignum Vitæ.—This is one of the hardest and heaviest species of wood; and owing to its valuable peculiarities it is applied to uses in which the greatest strain has to be borne, and chiefly for the sheaves of blocks and lining of shaft bearings. In this use it endures a vast amount of friction, and bears the strain of enormous weights. When the wood is used for sheaves, care should be taken so to cut it that a band of the sap may be preserved all round; as this preserves the sheaves from splitting from the outside inwardly towards the center, which they would do if they consisted of the perfectly elaborated wood alone.

As the sap of this wood is so important, care should be taken to preserve it from the depredations of worms; and also to protect the wood generally from too much draught, especially when it is newly cut.

The Havana Cedar (*Cedrela odorata*) belongs to the same natural order as mahogany, which it resembles, although it is much softer and of a paler color. It is imported from the island of Cuba, and is much used both in cabinet work and in boat-building.

The New South Wales Cedar (*Cedrela toona*) somewhat resembles the Havana cedar, but is of a coarser grain and of a darker color. It grows in the East Indies as well as in New South Wales. Most of the cedars are used in boat-building.

TABLE 1

TABLE OF TRANSVERSE SHRINKAGE AND LOSS OF WEIGHT IN SEASONING TIMBER

Kind of Timber	12-Inch Boards Shrunk to These Widths in Seasoning		Weights of Cubic Foot of Timber	
	Butt Plank	Top Plank	Green State	When Seasoned
White oak	11.75	11.60	58—64	53—58
Common oak	11.60	11.50	56	47
Common oak	11.50	11.35	54	42
Canadian oak	11.60	11.45	57—60	54
Larch	11.55	11.40	37—40	32—35
Hackmatack	11.60	11.50	43	36—38
Elm, American	11.70	11.45	60	46
Elm, Canadian	11.55	11.30	56	42
Fir	11.80	11.70	46	36
Fir, Douglas	11.90	11.80	43	34
Pine, white	11.80	11.65	36	28
Pine, long leaf	11.95	11.85	56	42—45
Pine, yellow	11.75	11.65	50	39
Cedar, white	11.40	11.30	32	28
Ash	11.55	11.45	56	44—46
Spruce, Eastern	11.85	11.75	40	29—31
Cypress, red	11.50	11.30	38	27—29

TABLE 2
TABLE OF THE PROPERTIES OF TIMBER

	1.	2.	3.	4.	5.	6.	7.	8.	9.	Tredgold's Formulæ		Barlow's Formulæ	
										10.	11.	12.	13.
	Specific Gravity, Water being 1.0	Weight of a foot, Dry, in lbs.	Weight of a Bar, 1 ft. long, 1 in. sq., in lbs.	Absolute Tenacity of a sq. in. Average, in lbs.	Tenacity of a sq. in without injury, in lbs.	Modulus of Elasticity, in lbs.	Modulus of Elasticity, in feet	Crushing force per sq. inch, in lbs.	Constants for Posts, and value of e	Value of a	Value of C	Value of S	Value of E
Acacia	.710	44.37	.30	18,290	......	1,152,000	373,900	......	......		.621	.1867	......
	.690	43.12											
Ash	.845	53.81		17,200	3,540	1,644,800	4,970,000	8,683	.00168	.0105	.677	.2036	.244
	.760	47.5	.33			1,640,000		9,363					
Bay tree	.822	51.37	.35	12,396				7,158					
Beech	.690	43.						7,733					
to	.854	53.37	.315	14,720	2,360	1,353,600	4,600,000	9,363	.00195	.0127	.552	.1556	.195
Birch	.792	49.5	.34	15,000			5,406,000	6,402		.0141	.643	.1881	.240
" American	.648	40.5	.28	11,663		1,257,600	3,388,000	11,663			.605	.1834	.256
Box	.960	60.	.41	19,891									
Bullet tree	1.029	64.31	.446			2,601,600	5,878,000				.882	.2646	
Cedar, white	.450	28.		10,293		700,000		5,674					
" red	.560	47.06	.32	9,000		650,000		4,912					
Chestnut	.657	41.06	.285	11,900		1,000,000				.0187			
Crab tree	.765	47.81	.33	......				{ 7,148 / 6,499 }					
Cypress	.441	27.60		6,000	1,500	900,000		6,000					
Elder	.695	43.43	.30	10,230				{ 9,973 / 8,467 }					
Elm	.671	42.	.236		3,240	1,340,000	5,680,000		.00184	.017	.372	.1115	.101
	.748	46.75		13,489		699,840		10,331					
Fir, Riga	.753	47.06	.32	{ 11,549 / 12,776 }		{ 1,328,800 / 869,600 }	4,080,000	{ 5,748 / 6,819 }	.00152	.00115	.369	.1108	.167
" Red													
" Douglas	.560	35.	.30	12,000			2,797,000			.0233	.380	.1144	.94
Hornbeam	.76	47.5	.32	20,240									
Hackmatack	.590	37.00		14,000	3,000	1,200,000		7,289					
Lance	1.022	63.87	.44	23,400									
Larch	.522	32.62		10,220		10,740,000	4,415,000	5,568	.0019	.0128	.284	.853	.120
	.560	35.	.243	8,900	2,065	1,052,800							
Lignum-vitae	1.22	76.25	.53	11,800									
Lime tree	.760	47.50	.32	23,500						.0152			
Mahogany, Spanish	.800	50.	.34	16,500				8,198	.00205	.0137			
" Honduras	.560	35.	.243	18,950	3,800	1,596,300	6,570,000		.00161	.0109			
Maple	.793	49.56		10,584						.0197			
Oak, white	.830	52.	.36		3,960	1,700,000	4,730,000	{ 4,684 / 9,509 / 10,058 }	.0015	.0124	.553	.1658	.210
	.934	58.37		13,316		1,451,220							
" Canadian	.872	54.50	.378	10,253		2,148,800	5,674,000	{ 4,231 / 9,509 }		.009	.588	.1766	.310
" common	.756	47.24	.327	12,780		1,191,200	3,607,000	7,731		.0087	.560	.1457	.149
" African	.972	60.75	.42			2,282,300	5,583,000						
Pear tree	.661	41.31	.283	9,861				7,518		.0215			
Pine, Pitch	.660	41.25	.283	7,818		1,225,600	4,364,000	{ 6,790 / 5,445 }		.0166	.544	.1632	.177
" Red	.607	41.06	.26	10,000		1,840,000	6,423,000	{ 5,375 / 7,518 }		.0109	.447	.1341	.272
" American white	.461	28.81	.20	7,000	2,900	1,000,000	8,700,000	5,445		.0112			
" (N. C.) yellow	.612	38.40		16,000		1,200,000		5,445	.0110				
" (long leaf) yellow	.698	43.62		20,000		1,700,000		9,000					
" (Oregon)	.544	34.00		13,800		1,400,000		7,000					
" Red wood	.419	26.23		8,000		700,000		2,500					
Plane tree	.640	40.	.28	11,700						.0128			
Plum tree	.786	49.06	.338	11,351				{ 10,493 / 9,367 / 3,657 wet }					
Poplar	.383	23.93	.164	6,016				{ 3,107 / 5,124 }		.0224			
Spruce, Oregon	.590	36.87	.25			1,536,200	6,268,000			.0089	.577	.1731	.190
" Norway	.340	21.25	.147	17,600				7,293	.00142	.0124			
" white	.470	29.37	.20	14,000		1,200,000				.0124			
Sycamore	.69	43.1	.296	13,000						.0168			
Teak	.657	41.06	.282	12,460		2,414,400	7,417,000	12,101	.00118	.0076	.820	.2462	.349
Walnut	.671	41.93	.288	8,465				7,227		.020			
Willow	.390	24.37	.167	14,000				6,128		.031			
Yew, Spanish	.807	50.43	.347	8,000									

Chapter III

Kinds and Dimensions of Material to Use

The relative value of each wood for shipbuilding purposes has been carefully considered and classified by the vessel insurance companies for durability and strength. This classification is in the form of *years* of *service* assigned to each wood when utilized for each principal part of a vessel's construction, for you must bear in mind that while one wood may give excellent service when used for planking, it may not be at all suitable for the framework.

Below I give a table of years of service assigned by insurance companies to each wood when it is used for designated parts of a vessel.

This table must be used in conjunction with one that designates the dimensions of materials to use; because sometimes, by increasing dimensions of a less valuable wood the years of that wood for a designated part will be increased.

3a. EXPLANATION OF TABLE 3

Table 3 gives years assigned to different kinds of timber, when used in the construction of a vessel built under Lloyd's rules for classification of wooden vessels.

3b. DIMENSIONS OF MATERIALS TO USE

The specifications of both *Lloyd's* and the *Bureau of American Shipping* construction rules cover workmanship, as well as quality and dimensions of timbers and fastenings.

Tonnage is the base used for determining all scantlings of hull, the tonnage for Lloyd's being, in flush deck vessels having one, two or three decks, the tonnage under upper deck, without abatement for space used by crew or for propelling power; and in vessels having raised quarter deck, or top-gallant forecastle, or deck houses, the total tonnage below the tonnage deck.

In Bureau of American Shipping the tonnage for scantlings is determined by using this formula:

$$\frac{L \times B \times D \times .75}{100} = \text{Tonnage.}$$

L = Length from after part of stem to fore side of stern post.

B = Breadth over all at widest part.

D = Depth from top of ceiling alongside keelson to

TABLE 3

LLOYD'S TABLE OF YEARS ASSIGNED TO EACH KIND OF WOOD

Kind of Timber	Keel	Stem and Stern Post	Apron, Etc.	Deadwoods, Transom	Floors	Timbers				Keelsons	Knight H'ds.	Ceiling				Beams	Knees	Hooks	Plank			Deck				Bitts	Rudder
						1st Foot Hooks	2nd Foot Hooks	3rd Foot Hooks	Top Timbers			In Flat	Bilge	Side	Clamps				Garboards	Bottom	Side	Covering B.	Locks	Upper	Lower		
1. East India Teak	16	16	16	16	16	16	16	16	16	16	16	16	16	16	16	16	16	16	16	16	16	16	16	16	16	16	16
2. English, African and Live Oak Greenheart, iron bark	12	12	12	12	12	12	12	12	12	12	12	12	12	12	12	12	12	12	12	12	12	12	12	12	12	12	12
3. Sabien, Jarrah, Kurrie, Blue Gum, Red Gum, Pencil Cedar	10	10	10	10	10	10	10	10	10	10	10	12	12	12	12	12	12	12	12	12	10	10	10	10	10	10	10
4. Second Hand English, Oak Greenheart	8	7	7	7	8	8	7	7	7	7	7	7	7	7	7	7	7	7				7	7	7	7	7	7
5. Red Cedar, Philippine Island Cedar		7	7	7	8	8	7	7	7	8	7	8	8	8	8	7	7	7	12	12	8	7	7	7	7	8	8
6. Danish Oak, Mahogany (hard)	9	9	9	9	9	9	9	9	9	9	9	10	10	10	10	9	9	9	12	10	10	10	10	10	10	9	9
7. North American White Oak	8	8	8	8	8	8	8	8	8	8	8	8	8	8	8	8	7	8	12	12	8	8	8	8	8	9	9
8. Pitch Pine, Oregon Pine, Kauria Pine, Larch, Hackmatack, Juniper	9	9	9	9	9	9	9	9	9	9	9	9	9	9	9	9	9	9	12	12	10	10	10	10	10	9	9
9. Danzie, French, Red Pine	9	9	9	9	9	9	9	9	9	9	9	9	9	9	9	9	9	9	9	9	9	9	9	9	9	6	6
10. English Ash		4	4	4	8	6	5	5	5	5	5					5	5	5	10	10	5					5	5
11. Rock Maple	10				8							5	5	5		5	5	5	8	.8	6	6	6	6			
12. Rock Elm	10		6	6	6	6	6	6	6	7						7	6	7	12	12	7					7	7
13. Grey Elm		6	6	6	6	6	6	6	6	6						6	6	6	12	12	6						
14. Black Birch	10				7	6													10	10	6					6	6
15. Spruce, Fir	8	8	8	8	8	8	8	8	8	8	8					8	8	8	8	8	8	8	8	8	8		
16. Beech					7	6													12	12	6					6	6
17. Yellow Pine	8	4	4	4				4	4	4						4	4	4	6	6	5	5	5	5	5		

underside of main deck, to be measured at fore end of main hatchway.

In both rules the scantlings as listed are correct for use in vessels that are properly designed, have normal shape, and have not over a certain named proportion of length to breadth and of length to depth. In cases when proportion of length to breadth is in excess, or when the proportion of depth to length is below requirements, some addition to structural strength is required, this additional strength being obtained partly by the use of diagonal steel straps and partly by increasing scantlings.

In all cases, workmanship must be first class and the kinds of materials used must not have a lower rating for durability and strength than those named in list. The number, kind and size of fastening must also be as listed in rules. In cases when a weaker or less durable kind of material is used for a part some addition to dimension of part must be made. Below I give a brief synopsis of building rules and scantling tables.

3c. Lloyd's Rules and Dimension of Material Tables

The number of years assigned to a new vessel is determined with reference to construction and quality of vessel, the materials employed and mode of building.

Defects in workmanship or quality of timber will involve a reduction in class.

Ships built with mixed timber materials below the 14-year grade, and in which high class materials and extra fastenings have been judiciously employed may be allowed a period, not to exceed two years, exceeding that to which the material of the lowest class used would otherwise entitle them, providing workmanship is high class thoroughout.

All timber must be of good quality, properly seasoned, and of the descriptions and scantlings shown on tables.

Should the timber and space (spacing of frames) be increased, the siding of timbers must be increased in proportion.

In ships claiming to stand for twelve or fourteen years, timber materials must be entirely free from sap and all defects.

If a ship is properly salted during her construction, one year will be added to her term for classification.

Workmanship is to be well executed for all grades; (a) timbers to be frame bolted together throughout their entire length; (b) the butts to be close fitted; (c) scarphs are to be of proper length.

In all ships *air courses* must be left, either immediately below or one strake below the clamps of each tier of beams, and one or two air courses must be left in hold, between the keelson and hold beam clamps.

All ships of 600 tons and up, the frames of which are

TABLE 3B—LLOYD'S SCANTLING TABLE

Minimum Dimensions in Inches, of Timbers, Keelson, Keel, Planking, Etc.

TONNAGE	100	200	300	400	500	600	700	800	900	1050	1150	1250	1350	1500	1750	2000
Timber and Space—Inches	19	21½	24¼	27¼	30	30½	31¼	31¾	32½	33¼	33½	33½	33¾	34	34½	35
Floors, S & M at Keelson, if Squared	7½	8¾	10¼	11¾	13	13¼	13½	13¾	14	14½	14¾	15	15¼	15¼	15½	15¾
Double Floors, S & M at Keelson, if Squared	6½	7¾	9¼	10½	12	12¼	12½	12¾	13	13½	13¾	14	14¼	14¼	14½	14¾
1st Futtocks, S & M at Floorheads, if Squared	6½	7¾	8¾	10	11	11½	11¾	12¼	12½	13¼	13½	13¾	14¼	14¼	14½	14¾
2nd Futtocks, Sided, if Squared	6	7	8	9	10	10½	10¾	11¼	11½	12¼	12½	12¾	13¼	13¼	13½	13¾
3rd Futtocks, Sided, if Squared	5¾	6½	7¼	8¼	9	9½	9¾	10¼	10½	11¼	11½	11¾	12¼	12¼	12½	12¾
Top Timbers (Short), Sided, if Squared	.....	.....	.....	.....	9	9¼	9½	9½	9¾	10	10¼	10½	10¾	10¾	11	11¼
Top Timbers, Moulded at Heads, if Squared	4½	5	5¼	5¾	6	6¼	6½	6¾	7	7¼	7½	7¾	8½	8½	8¾	9
Breast Hooks and Wing Transom, S & M in Middle	8½	9¾	10¾	12	13	13¼	13½	13¾	14	14½	14¾	15	15¼	15¼	15½	16
Keel, Stem, Apron, and Sternpost, S & M	9	10¾	11¾	13	14	14¼	14½	14¾	15	15½	15¾	16	16¼	16½	16¾	17
Keelson, S & M	10	11¾	12¾	14	15	15¼	15½	15¾	16	16½	16¾	17	17¼	17½	17¾	18
Wales	3½	4¼	4½	4¾	5	5	5¼	5½	5½	6	6	6	6¼	6½	6¾	7
(e) Bottom Plank, from Keel to Wales	2¼	2¾	3¼	3¾	4	4	4	4¼	4¼	4½	4½	4½	4½	4½	4¾	5
Sheer Strakes, Top Sides, Upper Deck Clamp (No Shelf); Lower Deck, Clamp with Shelf	2½	3¼	3½	3¾	4	4	4¼	4¼	4¼	4½	4¾	4¾	5	5¼	5½	5½
Ceiling Below Hold Beam Clamp	1¾	2¼	2¾	2¾	3	3¼	3¼	3½	3½	3¾	3¾	4	4	4¼	4½	4½
Waterway:																
Hardwood	4	5	5½	6	6½	6½	7	7	7½	7½	7½	8	8	8½	8½	9
Fir	4½	5½	6½	7	8	8	8½	8½	9	9	9	9½	9½	9½	9½	10
Ceiling Betwixt Decks	1¾	2	2¼	2½	2½	2½	2¾	2¾	2¾	2¾	3	3	3	3¼	3½	3½
Bilge Plank, Inside, Thick Strakes and Limber Strake	3	3¾	4	4¼	4½	4½	4½	4¾	5	5½	5¾	6	6¼	6¼	6½	7
Lower Deck Clamp (No Shelf) and Spirketting	3	3¼	3¾	4	4½	4¾	4¾	4¾	5	5¼	5¼	5½	5½	5½	5¾	6
Upper Deck Clamp (With Shelf)	2¼	2½	2¾	2¾	3	3¼	3¼	3½	3½	3¾	3¾	4	4	4¼	4½	5
Planksheer	2¼	2¾	3¼	3¾	4	4	4	4	4	4	4	4	4	4¼	4½	5
Flat of Upper Deck	2½	3	3	3	3½	3½	3½	3½	4	4	4	4	4	4	4	4
Scarphs of Keelson Without Rider	4′9″	5′3″	5′10″	6′6″	7′	7′	7′	7′3″	7′3″	7′6″	7′9″	7′9″	8′	8′	8′	8′
Scarphs, where Rider Keelson is added, also Scarphs of Keel	4′3″	4′9″	5′2″	5′6″	6′	6′	6′	6′3″	6′3″	6′6″	6′9″	6′9″	7′	7′	7′	7′
Main Piece of Windlass—Inches	14	15	15	16	17	18	19	21	22	23	23	24	24	25	25	27

composed of fir, and all ships the length of which shall exceed five times the extreme breadth, or eight times and under nine times their depth, shall have diagonal steel straps inserted outside the frame, the straps to extend from upper side of upper tier of beams to first futtock head.

The dimensions of straps to be not less than as follows:

TABLE 3a

In ships from 100 to 200 tons.....3½" × 7/16"
200 to 400 " .....4" × ½"
400 to 700 " .....4½" × 5/8"
700 to 1000 " .....5" × ¾"
1000 to 1500 " .....5½" × 13/16"
1500 to 2000 " .....6" × 7/8"
2000 and above .....6½" × 7/8"

Straps to be placed diagonally at not less than 45 degrees and to be fastened with bolts, one at each alternate timber, not of less diameter than given for through butt bolts. The number of straps to be in the proportion of not less than one pair for every 12 feet of ship's length.

In vessels exceeding six breadths, or nine and under ten depths in length, the number of diagonal straps must be not less than one pair to every 10 feet of the ship's length. And in addition to the requirements for ships of five times their breadth in length, such ships must be fitted with rider keelson, or with a pair of sister keelsons properly fastened with through bolts.

Spacing of deck and hold beams is regulated by depth of hold, and ships having extreme depth must be fitted with riders, or with orlop deck beams properly secured.

Methods of fastening, dimensions of fastenings, and in fact particulars of every important detail of construction are fully explained in the building rules, and in my description of each part of a vessel's construction.

TABLE 3C—LLOYD'S PLANKING TABLE

For the Thickness of Inside Plank, and in the Construction of Ships in the British North American Colonies and All Fir Ships Wherever Built

TONNAGE—Tons	100	200	300	400	500	600	700	800	900	1050	1150	1250
Thick Waterway—Inches.	5¼	6	6½	7½	8	8½	9	9½	10	11	11½	12
Spirketting.	3	3¼	3¾	4	4½	4¾	4¾	5	5½	5¾	6	6¼
Ceiling Below Hold Beam Clamp and Between Decks.	2	2½	3	3½	3¾	4	4¼	4½	4¾	5	5¼	5½
Bilge Plank (inside).	3	3¾	4¼	4¾	5½	6½	7	8	9	10½	11½	12
Thickstuff Over Long and Short Floorheads and Limber Strakes.	2¾	3¼	3½	4	4½	5	5½	6	6½	7	7¼	7½
Main Keelson (Rider Keelsons may be two-thirds that of main ditto).	10	11¾	12¾	14	15	15½	15½	15¾	16	16½	16¾	17

TABLE 3D—LLOYD'S FASTENING DIMENSIONS

Sizes of Bolts, Pintles of Rudder, and Treenails

TONNAGE	100	150	200	250	300	350	400	450	5 0	700	900	1350
Heel-Knee, Stemson and Deadwood Bolts ....Inches	15/16	1	1	1 1/16	1 2/16	1 2/16	1 3/16	1 4/16	1 4/16	1 5/16	1 6/16	1 8/16
Bolts in Sister Keelsons, Scarphs of Keel (a), Breast Hooks, Pointers, Crutches, Riders, Knees to Hold or Lower Deck Beams, Shelf, Clamp and Waterway Throat Bolts of Upper Deck Hanging Knees.	12/16	12/16	12/16	13/16	14/16	14/16	15/16	15/16	1	1 2/16	1 3/16	1 4/16
Keelson Bolts, Throats of Transoms, Throats of Breast Hooks, and Throats of Hanging Knees to Hold or Lower Deck Beams.	13/16	14/16	14/16	15/16	1	1	1 1/16	1 2/16	1 2/16	1 3/16	1 4/16	1 6/16
Bilge, Limber Strake, and Through Butt Bolts.	10/16	10/16	11/16	11/16	12/16	12/16	13/16	13/16	14/16	14/16	15/16	1
Other Butt Bolts.	10/16	10/16	10/16	11/16	11/16	11/16	12/16	12/16	12/16	12/16	13/16	14/16
Bolts through Heels of Cant Timbers, Bolts of Upper Deck Waterway, Shelf and Clamp, Arms of Hanging and Lodging Knees.	11/16	11/16	11/16	12/16	13/16	13/16	14/16	14/16	14/16	15/16	1	1 2/16
Pintles of Rudder.	2	2	2¼	2⅜	2½	2⅝	2¾	3	3	3¼	3½	3½
Hardwood Treenails.	1	1	1⅛	1⅛	1⅛	1¼	1¼	1¼	1⅜	1⅜	1⅜	1½

(a) Number of Bolts in Scarphs of Keel:
In ships of 150 tons and under ....6 Bolts
" " above 150 tons and under 500 tons. 7 Bolts } These bolts to be of Copper or Yellow
" " 500 tons and above.............8 Bolts } Metal in all cases

N.B. Bolts to be through and clenched, and to be of good quality, well made with suitable heads and be tightly driven.

TABLE OF DIMENSIONS OF PARTS TAKEN FOR SHIPS NOW UNDER CONSTRUCTION

TABLE 3E

DIMENSIONS OF TIMBER FOR SHIPS (Inches)

Approximate length between perpendiculars	.....	.....	145	145	168	175	200	200	225	214	226	235	240	282	300
Breadth, extreme	.....	.....	25	33	35	37	38	40	40	43	44	45	46	48	48
Depth, hold	.....	.....	13	13	14′ 3″	15	16	17	18	20	21	22	23	24	25
Ship's Tonnage	150	250	350	450	600	750	900	1050	1200	1400	1600	1800	2000	2500	2750
Name of Part	S M	S M	S M	S M	S M	S M	S M	S M	S M	S M	S M	S M	S M	S M	S M
Keel	10x12	10x14	11x14	12x15	14x16	14x18	15x18	15x19	15x20	16x20	17x20	17x21	18x22	19x23	20x24
Scarphs of keel length	52	60	66	69	72	78	81	84	90	93	93	96	96	102	102
Deadwoods	10	10	11	12	14	14	15	15	15	16	17	17	18	19	20
Stem and Stern Post	10x12	10x14	11x14	12x15	14x16	14x18	15x18	15x19	15x20	16x20	17x20	17x21	17x22	18x23	18x24
Apron						Sid	ed mea	sure to	suit						
Transom or counter timbers	10x12	11x12	12x13	13x14	15x15	15x16	16x16	16x17	17x18	17x18	18x18	18x18	18x18	18x19	18x20
Spacing of frames, timber and space	20	23	25	28	30	31	32	33	33	33	34	34	35	36	36
Floor timbers (double)	8x10	9x11	9x12	10x12	11x13	11x14	11x15	12x15	12x15	13x16	13x17	13x17	13x18	14x18	15x19
Top timbers (double)	5x5	6x6	7x6	7x7	8x7	8x7	8x7	9x7	9x7	9x8	9x8	10x8	10x8	11x9	11x10
Keelson	10x15	11x24	12x26	12x30	14x32	15x36	16x40	16x46	17x52	17x56	17x58	17x60	18x60	19x60	20x60
Scarphs of keelson	60	66	72	78	80	84	87	90	93	96	96	96	96	102	102
Ceiling on flat thick	2½	3	3	3	3½	3½	4	4	4	4	5	5	5	5	5
Ceiling at bilge	3½	5½	6	6½	7	7½	9	9½	10	10	10½	11	11½	12	12
Ceiling above bilge, thick	3	3½	4	4½	5	5	5½	6	6½	6½	6½	7	7	7½	8
Rider keelson	10x15	11x24	12x26	12x30	14x32	15x36	16x40	16x46	17x52	17x56	17x58	17x60	18x60	19x60	20x60
Diagonal straps (steel)						See	dimen	sions o	f strap	s					
Garboards 1	4	5	5½	6	6½	7	8	8	8	8½	8½	8½	9	10	11
Garboards 2	.....	4	4½	4½	5	5	6	6	6	7	7	7	7	8	9
Garboards 3	.....	.....	.....	.....	.....	.....	5	5	5	5	6	6	6	7	7
Planking garboard to Wales	3	3	3½	3½	3½	3½	4	4	4	4	4½	4½	4¾	5	5½
Wales	3½	4	4	4	4	4½	5	5	5½	6	6	6	6	7	7½
Top planking	3	3	3	3	3	3½	3½	3½	3¾	4	4	4½	4½	5	5½
Plank Sheer	3	3½	4	4½	5	5	5	5	5½	5½	5½	6	6	7	7½
Clamps, main deck	4x12	4½x12	5x12	6x12	6x14	6½x14	6½x14	6½x14	6½x14	6½x14½	7x15	7x15	7x15	7x15	7x16
Clamps, lower deck	4x12	4x12	5x12	6x12	6x14	6½x14	6½x14	6½x14	6½x14	6½x14	7x15	7x15	7x15	7x15	7x16
Shelf	4x10	5x10	6x10	6x12	7x12	7x14	7x14	8x14	8x14	8x15	9x14	9x14	9x15	10x15	10x16
Deck beams, main					Acco	rding t	o brea	dth of	vessel	—see t	able				
Deck beams, lower					Acco	rding t	o brea	dth of	vessel	—see t	able				
Hold beams					Acco	rding t	o brea	dth of	vessel	—see t	able				
Spacing of deck beams (inches)	20	23	25	28	30	31	32	33	33	33	33	34	35	36	36
Hanging knees, main deck	1½	1¾	2	2½	2½	2¾	2¾	3	3	3	3¼	3¼	3½	3¾	4
Hanging knees, lower deck	2½	2¾	3	3¼	3½	4	4¼	4½	4½	4¾	5	5¼	5½	6	6
Waterways	5x8	6x10	7x10	8x10	9x11	9x12	9x13	10x13	10x13	10x14	10x15	11x15	11x15	12x16	12x18
Deck plank, main deck	2½	3	3	3	3½	3½	4	4	4	4	4	4	4	5	5
Deck plank, lower deck	.....	.....	.....	.....	3	3	3	3	3	3	3	3½	3½	4	4
Pointers					Sa	me sid	ed dim	ensions	as dec	k bea	ms				
Rudder stock, dia	12	13	14	15	16	16	16½	17	18	18½	19	19	19	20	20

TABLE OF DIAMETERS OF FASTENINGS USED IN SHIPS NOW BEING CONSTRUCTED

TABLE 3F

SIZES OF FASTENINGS

Approximate:
Length..........
Breadth..........
Depth..........

Name of Part	150 Dia.	250 Dia.	350 Dia.	450 Dia.	600 Dia.	750 Dia.	900 Dia.	1050 Dia.	1200 Dia.	1400 Dia.	1600 Dia.	1800 Dia.	2000 Dia.	2500 Dia.	2750 Dia.
Keel	7/8	1	1 1/8	1 1/8	1 1/8	1 1/4	1 1/4	1 1/4	1 1/4	1 3/8	1 3/8	1 3/8	1 3/8	1 3/8	1 1/2
Deadwood	7/8	1	1 1/8	1 1/4	1 1/4	1 1/4	1 1/4	1 1/4	1 1/4	1 3/8	1 3/8	1 3/8	1 3/8	1 3/8	1 1/2
Keel Scarphs	3/4	7/8	7/8	7/8	1 1/4	1 3/8	1 1/8	1 1/4	1 1/4	1 3/8	1 3/8	1 3/8	1 3/8	1 3/8	1 1/2
Stem and Stern Post															
Aprons	3/4	7/8	7/8	7/8	1	1 1/8	1 1/8	1 1/4	1 1/4	1 1/4	1 1/4	1 1/4	1 3/8	1 3/8	1 3/8
Transoms	3/4	7/8	7/8	7/8	1	1	1 1/8	1 1/4	1 1/4	1 1/4	1 3/8	1 1/4	1 3/8	1 3/8	1 3/8
Frames and Futtocks together	3/4	7/8	7/8	7/8	1		1 1/8	1 1/4	1 1/4	1 1/4	1 1/4	1 1/4	1 3/8	1 3/8	1 3/8
Floor Timbers to Keel	3/4	7/8	7/8	7/8	1	1 1/8	1 1/8	1 1/4	1 1/4	1 1/4	1 1/4	1 3/8	1 3/8	1 3/8	1 1/2
Keelson	7/8	7/8	1 1/8	1 1/8	1 1/8	1 1/4	1 1/4	1 1/4	1 1/4	1 3/8	1 3/8	1 3/8	1 3/8	1 3/8	1 1/2
Keelson Scarphs	7/8	7/8	1 1/8	7/8	1	1 1/4	1 1/4	1 1/4	1 1/4	1 3/8	1 3/8	1 3/8	1 3/8	1 3/8	1 3/8
Ceiling	3/4	3/4	3/4	3/4	3/4	3/4	3/4	7/8	7/8	7/8	7/8	15/16	15/16	15/16	1 1/2
Rider Keelson	7/8	1	1 1/8	1 1/8	1 1/8	1 1/4	1 1/4	1 1/4	1 1/4	1 3/8	1 3/8	1 3/8	1 3/8	1 3/8	1 1/8
Garboards	7/8	3/4	3/4	3/4	3/4	3/4	3/4	3/4	7/8	1	1	7/8	15/16	1 1/8	1
Pointers	3/4	3/4	7/8	7/8	3/4	3/4	7/8	7/8	7/8	1	1	15/16	15/16	1 1/8	
Planking Fastenings	3/4	3/4	3/4	3/4	3/4	3/4	3/4	7/8	7/8	7/8	7/8	15/16	15/16	15/16	1 1/2
Planking Butts	5/8	5/8	3/4	3/4	3/4	3/4	3/4	7/8	7/8	7/8	7/8	15/16	15/16	15/16	
Treenails of Planking	1 1/8	1 1/8	1 1/8	1 1/8	15/16	1 1/8	1 1/8	1 1/8	1 1/4	1 1/4	1 3/8	1 3/8	1 3/8	1 3/8	1 1/2
Clamps	3/4	7/8	7/8	7/8	15/16	1	1 1/16	1 1/16	1 1/8	1 1/8	1 3/16	1 3/16	1 3/16	1 1/4	1 3/8
Scarphs of Clamps	3/4	7/8	7/8	7/8	15/16		1 1/16	1 1/16	1 1/8	1 1/8	1 3/16	1 3/16	1 3/16	1 1/4	1 3/8
Shelf	3/4	7/8	7/8	7/8	15/16	1	1 1/16	1 1/16	1 1/8	1 1/8	1 3/16	1 3/16	1 3/16	1 1/4	1 3/8
Deck Beams, main and lower	3/4	7/8	7/8	7/8	15/16	1	1 1/16	1 1/16	1 1/8	1 1/8	1 3/16	1 3/16	1 3/16	1 1/4	1 3/8
Hold Beams	3/4	7/8	7/8	7/8	15/16	1	1 1/16	1 1/16	1 1/8	1 1/8	1 3/16	1 3/16	1 3/16	1 1/4	1 3/8
Throat Bolts of Wood knees, clinched	7/8	7/8	7/8	1	1	1 1/8	1 3/16	1 1/4	1 1/4	1 3/8	1 3/8	1 3/8	1 3/8	1 1/2	
Lodge Knees } arms	3/4	3/4	7/8	7/8	7/8	1 1/8	1	1 1/4	1 1/16	1 1/8	1 1/8	1 1/4	1 1/4	1 1/4	1 3/8
Hanging Knees } arms	3/4	3/4	7/8	7/8	7/8	1 1/8	1	1 1/4	1 1/16	1 1/8	1 1/8	1 1/4	1 1/4	1 1/4	1 3/8
Deck Plank	5/8	5/8	5/8	5/8	5/8	5/8	5/8	3/4	3/4	3/4	3/4	3/4	3/4	3/4	1
Rudder	7/8	1	1 1/8	1 1/4	1 1/4	1 1/4	1 1/4	1 1/4	1 1/4	1 3/8	1 3/8	1 3/8	1 3/8	1 3/8	1 1/2

3d. General Remarks

While building rules specify dimensions of materials that should be used for each part of a vessel's construction it is not necessary to use materials of exact dimensions named, providing scantlings used are not *less* than those specified in tables. Thus it is permitted to use heavier frame timbers spaced a greater distance apart, or to use keel, keelson and other longitudinal timbers having sided and moulded dimensions differing from those specified but in all cases the alteration in dimensions must not lessen strength of the whole structure and, of course, the actual strength of each assemblage of timbers must be equivalent to strength of timbers having dimensions specified by rules.

In addition to this, improvements in construction details likely to increase strength of whole structure, or to make a vessel constructed of lighter scantlings equal or superior in strength to one constructed of materials having specified scantlings are permitted by all classification rules providing the plans of construction are submitted to classification society before vessel is built and construction as shown on plans is approved.

Originally a wooden vessel was entirely a timber product, shaped and assembled by hand-labor, and being such the required construction strength was obtained by using an exceedingly large amount of first-quality material. In other words, dimensions of material were excessive.

With the advent of machinery and larger use of iron and steel it became possible to reduce the amount of material used for many parts of construction and by substituting iron and steel for other parts, or combinng the proper amounts of these metals with the wood, to obtain greater strength with lessened weight.

Today, many labor-saving machines are used in shipyards, thus methods of assembling timbers and combining them with steel and wood that could not be used in the old days, because of excessive cost, are now available and it has become possible to construct wooden vessels that have greater strength than any turned out in the old days.

The successful wooden vessel of the future will be one in which parts composed of wood will be composed of a minimum of material fitted together in such a manner that a maximum amount of strength will be obtained, and a certain proportion of steel will be used in combination with the wood. Thus, in place of an all wood solid keelson it is likely that all wood trussed keelsons will be used, or all steel trussed keelhons, or a combination of a steel trused nelson with wood members.

It is also likely that there will be an increased use of diagonal steel bracing both outside and inside of the frames, and very likely steel knees will be substituted for wooden ones. In addition to this, it will be found advantageous to substitute steel waterways and sheer strakes for the present wood ones.

FORMULA FOR ASCERTAINING DIMENSIONS OF MATERIALS TO USE

Rule—If the moulded breadth of vessel is multiplied by the decimal entered against each principal part of construction the proper dimension of material to use will be ascertained, approximately.

Name of Part	Decimal Multiplier
Keel Siding	.40—.42
Keel Moulded	.45—.50
Keelson Main	.40—.42
Frame Siding	.25—.28
Frame Moulded at Floors	.40—.42
Frame Moulded at Top	.16—.20
Main Deck Beams	.30—.35
Planking Thickness, Bottom	.1
Planking Thickness, Wales	.12
Planking Thickness, Top Planking	.15
Ceiling at Bottom	.15—.20
Ceiling at Bilge	.25
Clamps	.25—.30
Deck Planking	.1
Coamings	.15—.20
Stanchions Between Decks	.20—.22
Lodge Knees	.15—.18
Hanging Knees	.20—.25

Chapter IV

Tonnage

In the early days of commercial intercourse between France and England, a large portion of the cargo carried in vessels consisted of wine in large casks, called *tuns.* As trade increased it was found that it would be a great convenience to have some generally understood and simple method for determining the carrying capacity of each vessel, and very naturally it became a practice for vessel owners to state, when a question regarding size of a vessel was asked, that the capacity was so many tuns of wine, and as the tun was a standard of measure known to all who owned vessels and shipped goods in them, a knowledge of capacity in tuns enabled both to accurately estimate capacity for carrying in other trades. Thus the tun became a standard of a vessel's capacity to carry cargo of all kinds.

The word *tun* ultimately became corrupted to *ton* and tunnage to *tonnage,* and no doubt the fact that the actual weight of a *tun* filled with wine approximated 2,000 ℔ tended to preserve the name even after the necessity for doing so ceased.

Note.—The capacity of a *tun* was equal to 252 gallons of 231 cubic inches.

The *tonnage* of a ship is the capacity which the body, or hull, has for carrying cargo, or weights.

4a. TONNAGE. EXPLAINED

In these days the word *tonnage,* when referring to a vessel, should never be used without expressly stating the kind of tonnage meant. Unless this is done confusion results, because any one of five different tonnage weights or measurements can be meant. These are:

1st.—The builders', or classification societies' tonnage measurement, sometimes used when calculating dimensions of materials required to insure proper strength of construction.

2d.—The Gross registered tonnage, or *total* internal capacity of vessel as measured by a government surveyor for the purpose of registration.

3d.—The Net registered tonnage, or tonnage measurement ascertained by deducting from gross tonnage the measurement (capacity) of space occupied by engines, steering apparatus and certain designated spaces that cannot be used for the storage of cargo. This measurement is also made by a government surveyor.

4th.—The Light displacement (in tons), ascertained when vessel is designed by actually calculating the displacement weight to water-line vessel will float

when ready for sea with clear swept holds, empty bunkers and tanks.

5th.—The Heavy displacement, or loaded displacement (in tons), also ascertained by designer calculating displacement weight when vessel is floating to the deepest water-line she can safely be loaded to.

4b. METHOD OF CALCULATING BUILDERS' OR CLASSIFICATION SOCIETIES' TONNAGE

The length, breadth and depth of vessel is measured.

Length measurement being taken from after side of stem to fore side of stern-post. This measure is taken along center line of deck.

Breadth measure is taken over all at widest part.

Depth measure is taken from top of ceiling of hold alongside keelson, to underside of main deck. This measure is made at forward end of main hatch.

Then the tonnage is ascertained by multiplying dimensions, taken as above, into each other, and dividing the product by 100. Three-quarters of quotient will be the tonnage.

$$\frac{L \times B \times D \times 0.75}{100} = \text{Tonnage.}$$

Note.—In the above formula the divisor 100 represents the average number of cubic feet of bulk allowed for one ton of cargo when vessel is measured in manner stated. The coefficient 0.75 indicates the assumed fineness of form (block coefficient) of the average vessel.

4c. MEANING OF GROSS TONNAGE AND METHOD OF CALCULATING IT

The Gross tonnage of a vessel is its internal capacity, as calculated by method of measurement in use in the country where vessel is being measured. There are several methods of measuring tonnage—U. S. A., British, Panama Canal, Suez Canal, Italian, etc.—and while each country uses a different method, the underlying principle of each rule is to ascertain as accurately as possible the actual internal capacity of vessel.

The United States and British rules are very similar, and as they are the ones most frequently used, I will explain method of measuring a vessel by using these rules.

Gross tonnage in U. S. A. is measured in this manner:

The length of vessel is measured in a straight line from inside of plank at side of stem to inside of plank at stern timbers, deducting from this length what is due to rake of bow and of stern timber in the thickness of deck, and also what is due to rake of stern timber due to round of beam; the length thus ascertained is divided into equal parts, the number depending upon length of vessel:

Vessels 50 feet and under in length are divided into six parts;

Vessels over 50 and up to 100 are divided into eight parts;

Vessels over 100 and up to 150 are divided into ten parts;

Vessels over 150 and up to 200 are divided into twelve parts;

Vessels over 200 and up to 250 are divided into fourteen parts;

Vessels above 250 feet are divided into sixteen parts.

Then at each point of division of length measure the transverse area is ascertained in this manner:

The depth of vessel at each point of division is measured from top of ceiling to the underside of tonnage deck and from this measure is deducted one-third of the round of tonnage deck beam. If the depth measure at midship point of division does not exceed 16 feet, each depth measure is divided into four equal parts and the *inside* horizontal breadth at each depth point of division including the upper and lower points is ascertained (five measures in all at each depth measure). The points of division are numbered from 1 at deck to 5 at ceiling, then the second and fourth breadth measures are multiplied by four, and the third by two; these products are added together and to the sum is added the breadth measure of first and fifth; the quantity thus obtained, when multiplied by one-third the common interval between breadth measurement lines, will give the transverse area. In cases when depth measure at midship point of division exceeds 16 feet, depth must be divided into six parts (seven lines for measuring), the multipliers for second, fourth and sixth measurement is four, and the third and fifth is two. Products are added and the calculation made in exactly the same manner as explained for the smaller depth.

When transverse area at each point of division is ascertained, the Gross registered tonnage is calculated in this manner:

The areas are numbered successively, beginning with 1 at extreme bow. (There will be an odd number of areas in every instance.) All *even*-numbered area measures are added and product multiplied by *four*, then all even numbered area measures, *except first and last*, are added and product multiplied by *two;* the two products are added and to the sum the area measures of first and last is added. When the total thus obtained is multiplied by one-third the common interval between points of length division, the cubical contents of vessel below tonnage deck will be ascertained. This tonnage measurement is subject to these additions:

If there is a break, a poop, or any other *permanent* closed-in space on upper deck available for cargo, or stores, or the accommodation of passengers or crew, the cubical contents of such spaces must be ascertained in a similar manner to the one explained and added to total already ascertained, and if a vessel has a spar deck the cubical contents of the space between it and the tonnage deck must also be measured in the manner already explained and total added to other totals. The sum of all these totals is the cubical measurement of vessel's internal space and if this sum is divided by 100 the *gross registered tonnage of the vessel will be ascertained.*

4d. MEANING OF NET REGISTERED TONNAGE AND METHOD OF CALCULATING IT

The *net* tonnage is the internal capacity of space available for carrying cargo and passengers, and is ascertained by deducting from the *gross* internal capacity, as ascertained by the rule, the capacity of spaces that are *exempt* from measurement.

These spaces are:

(a) Spaces occupied by or appropriated to use of crew of vessel.

Note the regulations of U. S. require that each member of crew have a space of not less than 12 superficial feet and 75 cubic feet allotted to him.

(b) A reasonable and proper amount of space exclusively for use of the Master.

(c) Space used exclusively for working of helm, the capstan, the anchor gear, and for the keeping of charts, signals, and other instruments of navigation.

(d) Space occupied by donkey engine if same is connected to main pumps of vessel.

(e) In sailing vessels, space used exclusively for storage of sails, tonnage of said space not to exceed 2½% of gross tonnage.

(f) In vessels propelled by steam, the deduction for space occupied by propelling machinery is as follows:

If propelled by paddle wheels, and the space occupied by machinery and for the proper working of boilers and machinery is above 20% and under 30% of gross tonnage, a deduction of 37% from gross tonnage is allowed; in vessels propelled by screws, if space is over 13% and is under 20%, the deduction shall be 32%. In all cases the space occupied by shaft alleys shall be deemed a space occupied by machinery.

(g) In cases when the actual space occupied by machinery amounts to under 20% of gross tonnage in the case of paddle vessels, and under 13% of gross tonnage in case of screw vessels, the deduction shall be 1½ times the actual space in the case of paddle vessels and 1¾ times space in cases of screw vessels.

vessel, but there is for every vessel a water-line beyond which it is not safe to immerse a vessel, and this maximum safe water-line is the Heavy displacement water-line.

This heavy displacement water-line is always fixed, when vessel is built, by the classification society that surveys the vessel for classification and is indicated by marking on side of vessel near its midship section an identifying freeboard mark somewhat similar to the one shown by Fig. 10.

4j. EXPLANATION OF FREEBOARD MARK

The long horizontal mark indicated by letter *S* is placed on line to which vessel may load in salt water during the summer months. The upper short line marked *FW* is placed on line to which vessel may be loaded when in service in fresh water.

The lower short line marked *W* is placed on line to which vessel may load when in service on salt water during the winter months.

The long line is placed through center of a circle and all marks including circle are permanently graved or marked on hull plating or planking and then painted a color that will be clearly distinguishable.

Both light and heavy displacement water-lines and weight required to immerse a vessel to these lines is known and fixed, but suppose a vessel is loaded to a line between these two and that it is desired to ascertain the displacement weight to the intermediate line, how can this be done? It is done in this manner:

4k. DISPLACEMENT CURVE AND DEADWEIGHT SCALE

When a vessel is designed, the designer calculates the displacement weight to a number of equally spaced parallel water-lines between the heavy and light ones, and having done this he lays out a curve of displacement and vertical deadweight scale, from which the owner of vessel can quickly ascertain displacement weight of vessel to any intermediate water-line, the cargo weight necessary to immerse vessel to any draught of water between light and heavy L.W.L. draughts, and amount of freeboard when vessel is immersed to any water-line.

On Fig. 11 I show displacement curve and deadweight vertical scale of cargo vessel No. 8 (See page 28.)

EXPLANATION OF FIG. 11

The vertical scale on left is divided into equally spaced intervals, each interval representing 100 tons of displacement, the 0 of displacement scale beginning at intersection point of the two scales.

The curved line that begins at bottom of vertical scale

and extends diagonally to horizontal scale is the displacement curve of vessel plotted by calculating displacement of vessel at several evenly spaced water-lines, marking points where the ascertained tonnage and draught lines will intersect and drawing a curved line to cut the points. Thus as the light displacement draught is 7 feet and the displacement at that draught is 690 tons, a horizontal line is drawn from named draught and a vertical line down from ascertained tonnage for that draught, and the point of intersection found. The displacement curve passes through this point, and others found in a like manner.

On the right of curve is shown the deadweight scale. This is divided into four columns, the first being marked in tons displacement, the second in feet of draught from keel up, the third in deadweight tons beginning with 0 at the light displacement draught, and the fourth in freeboard measures beginning with 0 at sheer and progressing downwards to the light displacement line.

To make the explanation clearer, I have marked at left of scale an outline of cross-section with light and heavy water-lines marked. The portion of section that is diagonally cross lines in one direction is the portion immersed when vessel is floating to her light displacement line (without cargo, stores and equipment), the portion cross lines in two directions is the portion immersed by putting cargo, stores, etc., on board, and the portion that is not lined is the part of vessel that is out of water (freeboard) when she is loaded to her deepest draught.

4l. VOLUME OF INTERNAL BODY OR ROOM IN A SHIP

This is very different from the displacement which measures the whole space a ship occupies in the water, and the weight of both vessel and everything on board. The volume of internal room in a ship is measurement of the empty space left inside of hull.

On Table 4a is given the approximate thickness of sides of wood cargo vessels and the percentage of difference between internal and external capacity.

TABLE 4A

Internal Capacity in Tons	External Capacity Increased Per Cent in Wood Ships	Thickness of Sides of Wood Ships in Inches
100	0.28	11
200	0.27	12½
300	0.26	14
400	0.25	15½
500	0.24	16
1000	0.20	20
2000	0.16	24

The proportions above are for ordinary sailing vessel and will hold good for ships that are similar.

If the designer fails to accurately determine beforehand the relative proportions that internal capacity available for cargo bears to displacement it may happen that a vessel will not have enough displacement of underwater body to enable her to carry a full weight of cargo and it may also happen that she has plenty of displacement to carry more cargo without having room to store it.

Chapter V

Strains Experienced by a Ship's Structure

The chief strains to which a ship's structure is subjected are:

1st.—Strains tending to produce longitudinal bending of the whole structure.

2d.—Strains tending to alter the transverse shape.

3d.—Local affecting some particular part and tending to produce local changes in shape or damage.

4th.—Strains due to propulsion by steam or sail.

The first and second items mentioned are strains that affect the structure as a whole, and therefore must be taken care of and overcome by an intelligent design of the whole structure and a proper use of materials. The effects of third and fourth items being local can be readily overcome by giving ample strength to parts of structure likely to be affected by the strains.

5a. Longitudinal Bending Strains When a Ship Is Afloat in Still Water

These are partly due to uneven distribution of weight of hull structure and the fact that this distribution does not coincide with the longitudinal distribution of upward pressure due to buoyancy of water, and partly to weight of cargo and its uneven weight distribution.

When a ship is afloat in still water the down pressure due to weight of hull is exactly the same as the up pressure due to buoyancy of water, and the longitudinal center points of these two forces always exactly coincide. Considered in this manner it would naturally seem that the two forces being equal and acting in opposite directions, there is an absence of strain; but this is not really the case as will appear when I analyze the problem.

A ship placed in water will sink until it displaces a volume of water having a weight exactly equal to the weight of ship and all on board, the bulk of immersed portion of ship and bulk of water displaced will be identical, the longitudinal center point of bulk of water displaced and of weight of ship will be located exactly over each other, and ship will float to a straight water-line. This condition exists because the pieces of which ship is built being rigidly connected, the structure has become a single object and must be considered as such.

Fig. 12 is a longitudinal view of a ship afloat and on

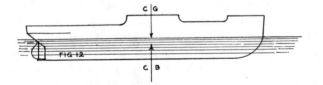

FIG 12

it I have marked the center points of bulk of water displaced and of weight of ship with arrows pointing in direction of line of action of strain due to buoyancy up force and weight down force.

That the up and down forces are equal, and that the center of these forces are located the same distance from bow, is known, because these are fundamental laws of flotation, but until the longitudinal immersed form of a ship and the longitudinal distribution of weights of construction are analyzed and compared, it will not be known whether the longitudinal distribution of bulk and of weight coincide at points of length other than at the ones marked (the center points). Unless they do coincide at all points there will be a permanent strain put on structure, the amount depending upon the difference between bulk and weight distribution throughout ship's length.

To explain this more fully I have drawn illustration Fig. 13.

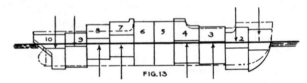

FIG. 13

Fig. 13 shows longitudinal view of Fig. 12 ship afloat, but in place of its being one rigidly connected structure, I have assumed that the structure has been divided into ten parts, that each part has been made watertight without increasing weight, and the parts connected in such a manner that while free to move up and down, they cannot separate or move sideways.

If the ten-part connected-together ship is now placed in water instead of floating to a longitudinally one level water-line as shown in Fig. 12, it will float somewhat in the manner shown on Fig. 13, the reason being:

While the total weight of ship has not changed and it displaces exactly the same bulk and weight of water as before, the separation of ship enables each part to act in accordance with the law of displacement, which is—*weight and bulk of object immersed and weight and bulk of water displaced must be identical.*

In other words, each part accommodates itself to a water-line that equalizes weight and immersed bulk, which it cannot do when whole ship is one rigidly connected structure.

Thus Nos. 1, 2, 9, 10 portions of structure (bow and stern) have a greater proportion of weight than buoyancy below marked water-line requires, and therefore being free to immerse independent of other portions, they sink until marked water-line is some distance below water level.

The Nos. 3, 4, 7, 8 portions have varying degrees of greater buoyancy below marked water-line than their weights require, therefore these portions float with marked water-line well above water level.

The Nos. 5, 6 portions have weight and bulk below marked water-line very nearly equalized, therefore these portions float with marked water-line nearly corresponding with water level.

It therefore can be said that if the ten separated parts, when floating as shown in Fig. 13, were rigidly connected together again both longitudinal weight and bulk strains would be equalized for the entire length of ship and there would be an absence of structural strain due to unequal distribution of weight and bulk, and it can also be said that if the ten parts are rigidly connected in any other position weight and bulk will not be equally distributed throughout length, and consequently there must be some degree of structural strain due to this unequal distribution.

As a ship cannot float in the manner shown by Fig. 13, and as in all ships the longitudinal distribution of bulk below L.W.L. does not coincide with longitudinal distribution of weight of construction, etc., it is evident that the hull structure of every ship is under strain when afloat. Bear in mind that this strain is always present, but is never noticeable and does not have any permanent effect on hull unless the longitudinal structure is too weak to withstand it.

5b. Hogging Strains Explained

If strength of hull structure is not sufficient to withstand the strain the ends of ship will drop, relative to center, and hull will ultimately change its form and become "hogged".

The dotted lines on Fig. 14 show shape when ship shown by heavy lines become hogged.

Hogging strains are nearly always present when a ship is floating without cargo in still water, but if it should happen that condition of weight and buoyancy are such that there is an excess of buoyancy at ends and an excess of weight near middle, the middle would drop relative to ends and change of form, if hull is weak, would occur near middle length. A change in this kind is known as sagging.

5c. Sagging Strains Explained

Sagging strains are seldom present throughout the whole length of a ship's structure when ship is without cargo and is floating in still water. In loaded condition and when moving among waves, the conditions are frequently such as to produce sagging strains at every part

of the length. (Fig. 14a dotted lines, show shape of ship that has sagged.)

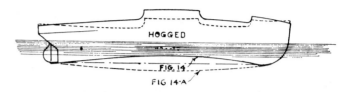

Before it is possible to accurately determine the effect longitudinal strains will have on hull structure of a ship it is necessary to ascertain the relative positions and magnitude of each kind of strain throughout the length of ship and to calculate their effect when coupled as one.

Perhaps you will more clearly understand my explanations of strains and bending moments if I first explain a few simple problems, such as strains on weighted and supported beams.

Fig. 15 shows a beam supported at its center and loaded at both ends, the weights W and W W being equal and placed at equal distances from support. A beam loaded and supported in this manner is under a strain similar to that experienced by a ship afloat in still water and having an excess of weight at ends and buoyancy and weight equalized at middle.

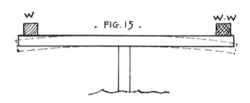

Fig. 15a shows the same beam loaded at center and supported at ends, a condition of loading that puts a sagging strain at center of beam. A beam loaded in this manner is under a strain similar to that experienced by a ship afloat in still water and having an excess of weight at center and buoyancy and weight equal at ends.

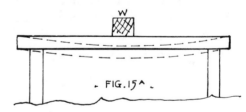

Fig. 15b shows the same beam supported near ends and loaded at ends and at center—a condition of loading that puts both sagging and hogging strains on beam, the magnitude of each depending upon weight and distance from the supports.

If $W2$ weight is greater than W-$W1$ weights there will be a sagging moment at center of beam, but the portion of beam between ends and supports will be subjected to hogging strains and so also will be some portion

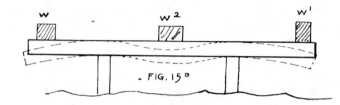

of beam lying between the supports and middle. On the illustration a dotted outline shows general lines of direction of strain. But if the moment of the W-W_1 weight × distance weights are from nearest support, is greater than moment of W_2 weight × distance, there will be a hogging strain at middle of beam and no portion of beam will be subjected to a sagging strain.

As bending moment = weight × length or leverage, you can readily understand that before it is possible to determine the strains on a weighted beam, it is essential that the longitudinal distribution of both weight and supports be known.

The weighted and supported beam conditions mentioned above are similar to those for a ship, therefore, it is an easy matter to estimate the bending moment or strain a ship's structure must withstand when the longitudinal distribution of weight and buoyancy (support of water surrounding ship) is known.

5d. Curves of Buoyancy Distribution

The longitudinal distribution of the buoyancy of a ship floating at rest in still water may readily be determined when the lines of vessel are available, and a curve of buoyancy can be plotted by marking a base line to represent length of ship and on this base line erecting ordinates at right angles to it and spaced the same distance apart that cross-sections used for displacement calculations are.

Then if along each ordinate line there is measured a distance equal to cross-section area of ship at that point a series of points will be obtained and a line drawn to cut these points will be curve of buoyancy of ship when floating to the water-line cross-section areas are taken from.

On Fig. 16 I show curves of buoyancy of a ship.

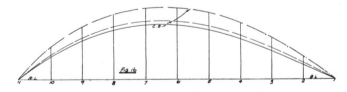

B. L.=Base Line.

1, 2, 3, etc., are ordinate lines spaced the distance apart that cross-section lines drawing are.

C. B. curve of buoyancy drawn through points laid off on ordinate line, the solid lines curve being curve of buoyancy for ship when floating to her light W.L. without coal, stores or cargo on board, and the dash line curve is curve of buoyancy to line ship floats to when everything is on board and ship is fully loaded with cargo.

Each curve clearly represents the longitudinal distribution of buoyancy of ship floating to a different W.L. and the area enclosed within each curve represents the total buoyancy or displacement volume to water-line measurements are taken from.

The buoyancy weight of portion of ship lying between any two ordinates can be ascertained by measuring areas enclosed between the selected lines and converting it into its equivalent displacement volume. The light displacement volume of ship to which curve belongs is 47,250 cubic feet, the area enclosed within solid line curve is 47,250 square feet, and therefore each square foot of area represents one cubic foot displacement volume, or if expressed in terms of weight—64 lb (salt water), and if the number of square feet area enclosed between any two ordinates is multiplied by 64 the actual buoyancy of portion of ship between the selected ordinates is expressed in weight terms. Similar conditions prevail for all buoyancy curves.

5e. Curves of Weight Distribution

The longitudinal distribution of construction, equipment, lading and other weights of ship can be graphically illustrated by means of a curve, or curves, laid out in a similar manner, but in place of using cross-section areas measures for curve points on ordinates, the weights of construction, lading, equipment, etc., of portion of hull between each two ordinates is determined. The weight is then converted into its equivalent volume (by dividing by 64) and the volume measure used as a point for curve of weight.

Thus the weight of construction, etc., of portion of hull enclosed between No. 1 and No. 2 ordinates is converted and measurement point marked on ordinate erected midway between No. 1 and No. 2; the weight of construction, etc., of portion between No. 2 and No. 3 is converted and point marked on an ordinate erected midway between No. 2 and No. 3, and so on for the whole length. A series of points for laying out curve of weight is thus obtained, and a curved line drawn to cut all points will graphically illustrate the longitudinal distribution of weights, just as the buoyancy curve graphically illustrates the longitudinal distribution of buoyancy. Of course as weight and buoyancy must always be equal, the area enclosed within weight curve must be exactly the same as that enclosed within buoyancy curve.

It is usual to lay out two, or three, curves of buoyancy and of weight, one being for ship in light condition without cargo, coal or stores, another being for ship with everything on board except cargo, and the third being for ship when fully loaded with cargo. If only two sets of curves are laid out, omit the second.

On Fig. 17 I show the Fig. 16 curves of buoyancy and on same base line is laid out two corresponding weight curves, the solid-lined curves being one pair, the dash-lined ones another.

By laying out the curves in this manner it is an easy

Fig. 17

matter to compare the longitudinal distribution of buoyancy with that of weight and determine with exactness the points where buoyancy or weight is in excess.

Where the curve of buoyancy line of a pair is outside the weight curve buoyancy is in excess; where the two lines cross weight and buoyancy are equal and where weight lines is outside buoyancy line weight is in excess.

And knowing the points where buoyancy or weight is in excess a curve of loads can be laid out and the value of the longitudinal bending moment at any cross-section determined.

5f. Curve of Loads

A curve of loads is laid out in this manner:

The same length of base line and ordinate spacing used for weight and buoyancy curves is marked off and then the *distance between* each line (buoyancy and weight curve lines) of a pair is measured at each ordinate and transferred to base line, measurements taken where buoyancy is in excess being transferred *above* the base line and those where weight is in excess *below*.

On Fig. 18 illustration is shown the curve of loads (two) laid out from measurements taken from Fig. 17 illustration.

When the curve of loads for any ship floating to a certain water-line and loaded in a certain manner is plotted, it is an easy matter to calculate the longitudinal bending moment or strain at any part of the hull by ascertaining the excess buoyancy or weight at the designated location and multiplying it by the longitudinal distance this excess is from the point the strain is being calculated from. For ships afloat in still water the point generally selected for this calculation is either midship section, bow, or stern.

The light load figures for ship that curves of loads laid out on Fig. 18 belong are as follows:

For first 80 feet from bow, weight is in excess 400 tons.

For the 70 feet nearest stern, weight is in excess 450 tons.

For 150 feet amidships, buoyancy is 850 tons in excess.

This condition parallels that of the loaded beam illustrated by Fig. 15b.

While the loading of a ship with cargo increases weight it does not always increase strains, as you will see by referring to the dash-lined curve of loads, which shows that by loading the ship strain has actually diminished.

5g. Longitudinal Strains Among Waves

When a ship passes into disturbed water, the movement of the waves will cause ship to rise and fall continually and this up-and-down movement will affect both the size and character of bending moments and will also cause rapid changes in direction of strain in certain parts of ship.

To illustrate the effect that movement of waves has on a ship, I will take two extreme positions, the first being a condition in which wave has immersed the middle portion of ship more deeply and has left the ends partially unsupported, and the second being a condition where waves have been more deeply immersed the ends and left middle portion partially unsupported.

Figs. 19 and 20 illustrate these two conditions.

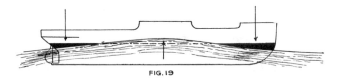

FIG. 19

An examination of the Fig. 19 illustration will show the great change that takes place in longitudinal distribution of weight and buoyancy when a wave lifts a ship on its crest, or when a ship falls into a hollow between two waves. In general, when a ship is supported on the crest of a wave of its own length there is a hogging strain on the whole structure, the maximum hogging moment being at, or near to, midship section and being, approximately, between three and four times the maximum experienced in still water. On the other hand, when a ship is in the condition shown on Fig. 20 the whole structure is under a sagging strain largely in excess of still-water maximum, the point of maximum strain being at, or near to, midship section, and in addition to this it must be remembered that these excessive hogging and sagging strains alternate at intervals of a few seconds. (In a 360-foot ship the intervals between extremes of rising and falling when waves are 17 feet high is approximately 4½ seconds.)

Fig. 18

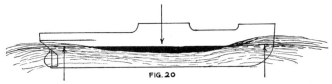

FIG. 20

While in every instance strain varies with height and length of waves it is safe to assume, for the purpose of calculation, that the maximum longitudinal bending moment is experienced when wave length is equal to length of ship and wave height between one-twelfth and one-fifteenth of length.

When longitudinal distribution of weight and buoyancy of a ship is known the maximum hogging or sagging bending moment at any point for still water, on a wave crest, or in a wave hollow can be determined with reasonable accuracy by using this formula:

$$\frac{\text{Weight} \times \text{Length}}{\text{Numeral for length of ship and type}} = \begin{array}{l}\text{Maximum} \\ \text{bending moment} \\ \text{in foot-tons.}\end{array}$$

Weight being total excess, buoyancy or weight, at selected point.

Length being distance excess is from point of support, or from point where buoyancy and weight is equalized.

Numerals vary with size of ship and conditions of loading. For cargo steamers from 250 to 350 feet in length and loaded with miscellaneous cargo in all holds the numerals are:

Still water ....From 110 to 150
On wave crest ....From 25 to 40
In wave hollow . . . . From 30 to 50

(These figures are approximate.)

When longitudinal distribution of weight and buoyancy is not known a reasonably accurate formula to use for computing maximum bending moment in foot-tons, among waves, for ships of ordinary form loaded with miscellaneous cargo properly stowed throughout length, wave height being about 1/15th of length, is

$$\frac{L \times W}{20} = \text{Bending moment in foot-tons.}$$

L = length of ship.
W = weight of ship.

When making calculations for longitudinal strains it is assumed that the ship remains upright. We, of course, know that this condition is not possible when ship is in a sea because both rolling and pitching occur simultaneously; but to calculate strains for any assigned transverse inclination, or variation between upright and a named degree, would entail a large amount of labor and results obtained would be of very little practical value providing calculations for both direct transverse and longitudinal strains are made.

It must, however, be kept in mind that when a ship is poised upon the crest of a wave and inclined transversely by the wave forcing one side of stern down and supporting the opposite side at bow, there is a twisting strain put on structure and this strain must be resisted

by making the parts affected sufficiently strong and fastening them securely. In a very large number of wooden ships structural weakness, especially when twisting, is largely due to improper or weak fastening.

5h. Transverse Strains When a Ship is Afloat

Strains of this kind tend to produce a change in transverse form and are largely caused by oscillations and rolling movements when ship is in a sea, and by unequal pressure of water on underwater body. Fig. 21 is for the purpose of explaining this transverse water pressure.

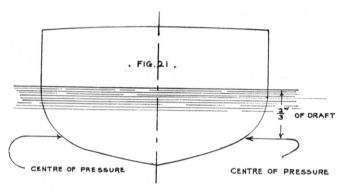

Fig. 21 shows cross-section of a ship floating upright in still water. When afloat in this condition weight pressure acts down through the C.G. point and upbuoyancy pressure acts upwards through the C.B. point and as both pressures are equal and act along the same vertical line the ship is at rest.

There is, however, another pressure, or strain, that must now be considered—i.e., the horizontal water pressure acting on opposite sides of ship along horizontal lines and having the center of pressure located about two-thirds of mean draught below the L.W.L. This horizontal pressure tends to compress the hull, or change, the transverse form of ship along its whole length being greatest at ends where sides of ship are nearly vertical and where transverse area is smallest.

The ordinary framing (transverse) of a ship is generally strong enough to withstand this pressure, except at bow, where it is usual and necessary to add structural strength to prevent the pressure causing leaks in wood ships and "panting" (in-and-out movement of plating) in steel ones.

In wood ships the forward end is strengthened by means of knees and pointers, and in steel ships by means of additional frames called panting frames or beams.

So long as a ship remains upright and in still water, transverse pressure strains, while much greater than longitudinal pressure ones (they are about eight times greater), are not excessive, but just as soon as the ship inclines, moves ahead, or pitches and rolls in a sea, transverse water pressure and the forces tending to alter transverse shape greatly increase. The strain when a ship is in any one of the named conditions is very largely a racking one that is continually striving to alter both the transverse and longitudinal form, and unless the framing, especially at connections between deck beams and side framing, is amply strong and properly fastened there will be some change of form or loosening of knees and framing of decks and bilges.

When a ship's righting moment is known the approximate racking strain at any transverse inclination can be ascertained by making use of this rule:

$$\frac{D^2}{D^2 + B^2} \times \text{Righting moment for inclination} = \text{Moment of racking force in foot-tons.}$$

D standing for depth of ship from upper deck to keel.
B standing for breadth of ship from outside to outside.

The period of oscillation, or time required for a ship to make one complete roll from port to starboard, has a very great influence upon total strain that a ship's structure has to withstand. The more rapid the oscillations are the greater the number of times the racking strain changes its direction in a named period (such as one minute), and as each change of direction (from port to starboard and vice-versa) tends to produce changes in transverse form, it is advantageous to have a long period of oscillation. A deep-rolling and quick-acting ship always requires greatest strength of hull structure to withstand strains. So also does one in which the proportion of length to depth is excessive.

5i. Local Strains

By local strains is meant strains that affect some particular portion of the hull structure and which are due to that part of the structure being subjected to some strain that is local in its effect. For instance, if a heavy or unusual load is concentrated upon some part of the hull structure (a deck winch, for instance), the strain due to this load will be local.

Thrust of a screw propeller produces a local strain on that part of the ship to which the thrust block foundation is attached.

The downward thrust of a mast produces a considerable local strain at and near to part of hull where mast is stepped.

Wind pressure on sails is transferred to spars and rigging and then to hull structure where masts are supported and rigging fastened.

Chain plates produce local strains on parts of structure where they are fastened.

Engines and boiler weights are concentrated along a short portion of ship's length and cause local strains of great importance. One of the most effective methods of overcoming strains of this kind is to distribute these permanent weights over as large a portion of hull as possible by extending the foundation structure over a much greater (length and width) area than weight occupies.

5j. Strains Due to Propulsion by Sails or Steam

In nearly every instance strains due to propulsion are local and can best be overcome by adding strength to the parts of structure in the locality where strains are greatest.

When a ship is propelled by sail power the effective wind pressure acts both longitudinally and transversely, the longitudinal thrust acting principally in driving the ship ahead and the transverse thrust acting largely upon the structure of ship and tending to rack the structure, especially at points where masts are stepped and rigging secured to hull.

It is therefore necessary to strengthen any part of hull where a mast is secured or supported, or where any standing rigging is fastened.

In the case of propulsion by a screw propeller the thrust is delivered in the direction ship will travel and therefore there will be no transverse strain, except in cases when hull vibrations are set up by unbalanced moving parts of machinery or by the period of engine vibration not being properly tuned to hull vibration period.

Every structure has a natural period of vibration and in a ship this period is governed by the structural arrangement, weight and distribution of material. In an engine the period of vibration is governed by the balancing of moving parts, and the period of revolution. If the revolution period of engine approximates in regularity to the hull structural vibration period, hull vibrations will be very noticeable; it is therefore necessary to determine the natural period of hull vibration and then have engine revolutions fixed at a number that will not be a multiple of the hull period. This can nearly always be done by selecting a propeller that will allow engine to turn at a number of revolutions that will not be a multiple of the hull revolution period.

Unbalanced propellers will set up vibrations similar to those produced by unbalanced moving parts of engine.

Chapter VI

Estimating and Converting

6a. BILLS OF MATERIAL

The usual procedure in a modern shipyard is to first prepare detailed bills of materials on which is specified these things:

> The names of principal parts of ship.
>
> The kind, quantity, quality and dimensions of materials needed for each part.
>
> The order in which materials are needed and date they should be delivered.

On the bills of material is listed all lumber, fastenings, fittings, equipment, rigging, machinery, etc., required for the job, and in every case quantities named should include a proper allowance for wastage during converting or manufacturing.

I say bills of material, because it is more satisfactory to make up a separate bill of material for each principal division of the work or for each production department. Thus one bill would cover lumber, fastenings, fittings, etc., for the hull construction department; another would cover materials and equipment for pipefitting and plumbing department; another material for engineering department; another materials required by rigging and sailmakers' department; another materials for painting department.

Specifying each department's materials separately simplifies checking quantities and keeping track of deliveries.

Quantities are generally calculated from plans, specifications and mould loft measurements, and as the work must be very accurately done the man assigned to the job should be a competent estimator and have a fair knowledge of ship construction work.

The usual practice is for the estimator to enter on his estimating sheets every needed item of material piece by piece. The sheets then go to stock keeper, who checks off items that can be supplied from stock and then passes the sheets along to purchasing department, where items that cannot be supplied from stock are listed and ordered.

In the next column I give headings of a very satisfactory estimating sheet for use in a large shipyard.

A filled-in copy of Sheet No. 1 is attached to each department's material list and to it is attached filled-in sheets having headings as given in Sheet No. 2.

Copies of estimates should be sent to stock keepers, to purchasing department and to the head of each department, and it should be the duty of each department head to report when any item of material is not delivered on date wanted, and of the purchasing and stock keeping departments to enter dates ordered and received on all

---

Sheet No. 1 .... Date ....
Name of Firm ....
Quantity estimating sheet for ship No.....Designed by........
Contract No..................... Signed on.................
Date set for delivery ....

The following dates have been set for the named divisions of work to be completed:

Keel laid ....Framed up ....
Planked ....and caulked ....
Deck laid ....and caulked ....
Joiner work completed ....
Engines and boilers in place.........Condensers in place........
Auxiliary machinery in place............Tanks in place........
Pipe fitting completed.........and covered ....
Electric wiring completed ....and tested ....
Plumbing completed ....and tested ....
Deck fittings and equipment in place.........................
Spars, booms and rigging completed ....
Steering gear and navigation equipment in place.............
Painting completed ....
Sails bent ....
Vessel will be launched on ....
Trial trip will be run on.................................
Delivery will be made .... At...............

As these dates have been set after consultation with heads of departments, they must be adhered to unless changed by written authority of the President of Company.

Sheet No. 2...........Ship No. ....Date ....
Material estimate for ....Department

Date Ordered	Date Wanted	Quantity	Description	Used for	Remarks	Date Received

Checked by .... Estimator

---

department copies of estimates. Thus a very satisfactory cross check is kept of delays, should any occur.

In all cases the estimated wanted date should be fixed several days ahead of actual requirements.

6b. SELECTING TIMBER REQUIRED FOR THE CONSTRUCTION OF A SHIP

The first work of the shipbuilder is to "lay down" the lines and construction details full size, and make the full-sized templates (moulds) required by the converters, ship-carpenters, and erectors, and while this work is going on the necessary timber can be selected and got ready. Selecting timber should be done with care and by men who are thoroughly familiar with ship construction and the grading of lumber.

Timber used in a modern shipyard is usually delivered in these conditions:

(a) In pieces squared on four sides to dimensions named. This is termed squared material (dimension stock) and is principally used for keels, keelsons, deadwood, and pieces that can be advantageously got out of heavy straight dimension material. When ordering material of this kind, it is necessary to state length, width and thickness of each piece and quality, or grade of material desired.

Shipyards usually keep a stock of standard dimension squared material on hand—yellow pine, fir, oak.

(b) In pieces, or planks, sawed to named thickness, the edges of pieces being left with the natural taper or curve of tree intact. Material of this kind is called "flitch cut" and it is very advantageous to have such material for frames, floors, futtocks, stem, planking, and pieces that have to be got out to some curved shape, because the natural taper or curve will materially reduce waste and enable the shipbuilder to avoid a great deal of short grain (cross grain) that is always present when a curved piece is got out of a straight plank. Material of this kind is generally ordered "log run" and therefore it is not graded for quality.

(c) Planks edged and cut to named thickness. Useful for planking, ceiling, decking and in places where long straight planks are needed. Material of this kind is cut to specifications as to thickness, width, length and grade, or quality.

(d) In pieces planed and finished ready for use. Under this heading is included flooring, joinerwork material, matched material, etc.

(e) In pieces sawed to designated thickness and having the natural curve of roots and butt portion of tree intact. Material of this kind is termed natural knees, and is usually either oak, spruce, pine or hackmatack. Knees are usually ordered by thickness and as each piece has curve of root and butt of tree intact, it is necessary to designate the approximate angle of knee required. Thus if knees having less than a right angle is desired, "*in*" angle knees is designated. Knees having more than a right angle are termed "*out*" angle knees.

Wooden ship-building is naturally a wasteful industry, because of the large number of pieces that have to be cut with some curvature, or taper. Therefore, it naturally follows that the man in charge of the selection of material holds a most responsible and important position, because upon the judgment and skill with which his selection is made depends, to a considerable extent, strength, and durability of the ship, and economy of ma-

terial. A good converter can save material, reduce cost of labor and thus add many dollars to a firm's profit, while a bad converter can so increase cost of material and labor that profits will vanish. I mention this because I know of instances in which yard managers have, through mistaken economy, looked upon the selection of material for the various parts of a ship as being of secondary importance, and a matter that can be properly attended to by an ordinary yard foreman or sawmill leading man. It is false economy to do this, and I know through experience that it pays to have a man in charge of this work who has a good knowledge of ship construction, a fair knowledge of mould loft work, and a thorough knowledge of timber and sawmill work.

6c. Converting

By converting timber is meant selecting the timber and planks for each piece and part of ship, marking out shape and form of the pieces, and getting them sawed, or machined, as near as possible to required shape. Therefore, the material has to pass through three different departments before it is ready for the ship-carpenters.

1st.—The men who select the materials.

2d.—The men who mark out the materials to required shape.

3d.—The men who actually machine or saw the material to shape.

Here are a few things that should always be kept in mind by the men who select and convert timber:

Waste material should be kept to a minimum by selecting logs and planks as near as possible of the required dimensions, and by carefully considering *before* a log or plank is cut whether the waste from it can, or cannot be used for some other part.

Every log, or plank, should be carefully inspected for defects *before* any work is done on it, and if defects exist the templates should be laid out on the material in such a manner that the more serious ones are cut out or left in a position on completed piece that will not detract from strength or durability.

In all cases when it is practicable, timber should be so converted that the end of a log or plank that was nearest the top of tree will be placed in ship at the part in which decay starts quickest; as, for instance, the top of the log from which stern-post is sawed should be placed uppermost, as the butt will be better preserved when entirely immersed in water.

In converting timber, particular care should be taken to avoid, as far as possible, an excessive amount of cross grain located where it will detract from strength, or where it will not be supported or reinforced by other adjoining pieces of material.

In getting out futtocks of frame timbers cross grain of one piece can nearly always be strengthened and reinforced by straight grain of adjoining piece.

Scarphs should never be cut until it is ascertained that

the piece of timber is fit for the intended use. It is therefore advisable to cut each piece of material to shape before cutting or forming a scarph.

No heart shake, check or knot should be located at or near to a scarph unless fastenings are located in such a manner that they will tend to close the defect and prevent it detracting from strength of the finished piece.

In a modern shipyard every effort should be made to reduce the amount of hand labor to a minimum by using power and labor-saving machines. The handling of heavy timber should be done by means of electric timber trucks and self-propelling hoists, and the shaping of the many pieces that enter into the construction of a vessel should be very largely done by means of machinery. Nearly every piece of the transverse frame of a vessel can be sawed, shaped and beveled by machinery. Planking, decking, ceiling and nearly every longitudinal piece of material can also be shaped and beveled by machinery, all joinerwork material can be machined ready for assembling, fastening holes can be drilled with the aid of machinery, and in addition to this the actual caulking of planking and deck seams can be largely done with the aid of caulking machines.

Chapter VII

Joints and Scarphs

In ship construction it is necessary to join together a number of pieces of wood in such a manner that the strength of joints will at least equal the strength of material used.

The meeting place of two pieces of wood is called the *joint* and the joint is circumscribed by the lines which mark the intersection of the faces of one piece with the other.

The simplest and easiest joints to make are those in which the bearing faces are planes of the same size and shape in relation to the planes of the axes.

The putting together of two pieces of wood may be done in three ways:

1st.—They may meet and form an angle.

2d.—Two pieces may be joined in a right line by lapping and indenting the meeting ends on each other. This is called *scarphing*.

3d.—The two pieces may be joined longitudinally, the joint being secured by covering it on opposite sides by pieces of wood, or metal, bolted to both beams. This is called *fishing*.

7a. Joints That Form an Angle

Should two pieces of wood that meet and form an angle be joined by simple contact of the end of one piece with its bed on the other, the pieces are said to abut, and the joint is called a plain joint. This method of joining does not prevent one piece sliding on the other, unless it is fastened with nails or bolts, and even when these are used the joint will be a very insecure one.

Plate VIIa Illustrations

Fig. 1 shows the simplest means of obtaining resistance to sliding by inserting the piece *C* in notches cut in both pieces. On the upper view of joint is shown the proper mode of securing joint by a bolt. A stronger but more costly method of joining is the mortise and tenon, and as this is the principle of a large number of joints, I will describe it at length.

The simplest case of a mortise and tenon joint is when two pieces of wood meet at right angles. Such a joint is shown on Fig. 2.

The tenon is formed at the end of one piece in the direction of its fibres and a mortise of exactly the same size and form as the tenon is hollowed in the face of the other piece. The sides of the mortise are called the cheeks, and the square parts of the piece from which the tenon projects, and which rest on the cheeks, are called the shoulders. As the cheeks of the mortise and the tenon are exposed to the same amount of strain, it follows that each should be equal to one-third the thickness of timbers in which they are made.

The length of a tenon should equal the depth of the mortise, so that its end will press on bottom of mortise

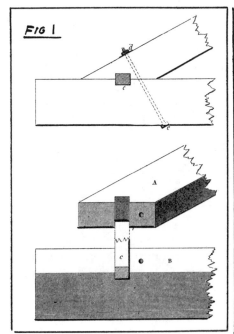

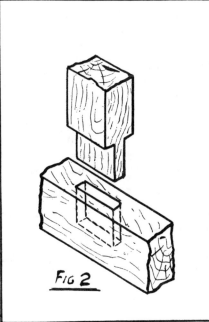

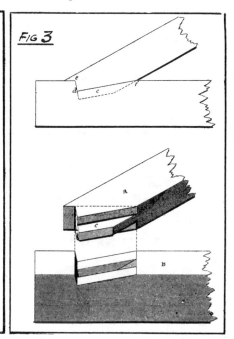

Plate VIIa

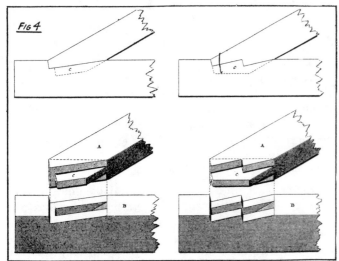

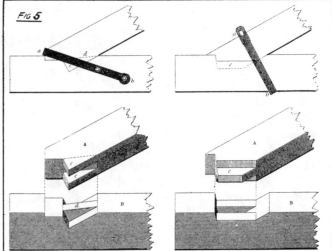

Plate VIIb

when shoulders bear on the cheeks. In practice this perfection of joining cannot be obtained, so the tenon is generally made slightly shorter than depth of mortise, thus enabling the shoulders to press closely upon cheeks.

When a mortise and tenon joint is cut and put together, the pieces are generally secured by a key or treenail. The key is generally a round one having a diameter equal to about one-fourth the thickness of the tenon and it is usually inserted at a distance of about one-third the length of tenon from the shoulder.

The key, however, is never depended upon as a means of securing the joint, because joints of this kind should be so closely fitted that they will hold together without the aid of key.

The foregoing describes a simple tenoned joint when the pieces to the joint are at right angles to each other.

When the pieces to be joined are not at right angles, a more complicated method of tenoning must be used.

This method is shown on Fig. 3.

You will note that the cheeks of mortise are cut down to form an abutment or notch, thus increasing the bearing surface and adding to the resistance to slipping.

PLATE VIIb ILLUSTRATIONS

Fig. 4 shows other forms of this kind of joint, and on Fig. 5 I show methods of adding to resistance to slippage by using straps and bolts. Note that a steel wedge is inserted into opening of strap (*a*).

7b. SCARPHS

In ship-building it is often necessary to join timbers in the direction of their length in order to secure scantlings of sufficient longitudinal dimensions. When it is necessary to maintain the same depth and width in the lengthened beam, the mode of joining is called scarphing. Scarphing can be performed in a number of different ways, but in all cases it is very necessary to consider the direction of strain to which the lengthened beam will be subjected, whether longitudinal or transverse, and to select the method that will give the maximum resistance in the direction from which the strain comes.

The following illustrations will serve to explain a number of excellent methods of scarphing and lengthening beams.

PLATE VIIc ILLUSTRATIONS

Fig. 6 illustrates a plain scarphed joint. The ends of each piece of timber are cut obliquely and lapped and then secured by bolts that pass through plates or washers to prevent the screwing up of the nuts injuring the wood.

The strength of a scarph of this kind depends entirely upon the holding power of the bolts and the resistance to slipping is very slight.

Fig. 7 shows a similar scarph, but as the ends are indented and a key is inserted through opening cut in timbers midway from ends of scarph, the resistance to

Fig. 1.

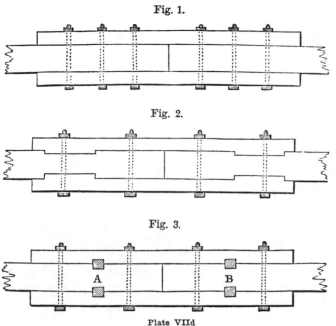

Fig. 2.

Fig. 3.

Plate VIId

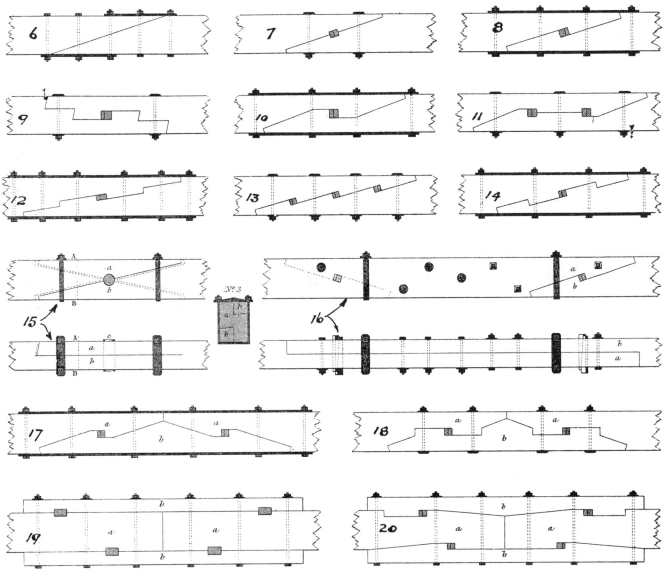

Plate VIIc

slipping is very greatly increased. This scarph is an improvement over Fig. 6.

Fig. 8 illustrates a scarph that is stronger than Fig. 7. Here the indentions are placed at ends and center and key is also used. With number of fastenings shown on illustrations the relative strength of the three scarphs is:

Fig. 7 is one and one-quarter times the strength of Fig. 6.

Fig. 8 is two and one-half times the strength of Fig. 6.

Figs. 9 to 14 show other, more complicated, methods of scarphing that can be used when maximum strength of scarph is desired.

Figs. 15 and 16 show two views of combined vertical and horizontal scarphs, and Figs. 17 and 18 illustrate methods of lengthening beams by inserting a short piece between two longer pieces.

When a beam does not have to be same thickness throughout, the lengthening can be done by simply butting the pieces and lacing pieces of timber each side, bolting and keying the four pieces together.

PLATE VIID ILLUSTRATIONS

Fig. 1 shows a plain fished joint.

Fig. 2 shows an indented fished joint.

Fig. 3 shows a keyed fished joint. *A, B* are keys.

This method of joining timbers is called *fishing*.

The timber used for the deck framing of a ship is seldom of sufficient length to permit the use of one-piece beams, so each beam and timber is generally composed of two or more pieces scarphed together.

PLATE VIIE ILLUSTRATIONS

On Plate VIIe is shown methods of scarphing deck beams.

Figs. 21 to 23 show accepted methods of scarphing beams used for deck framing of vessels.

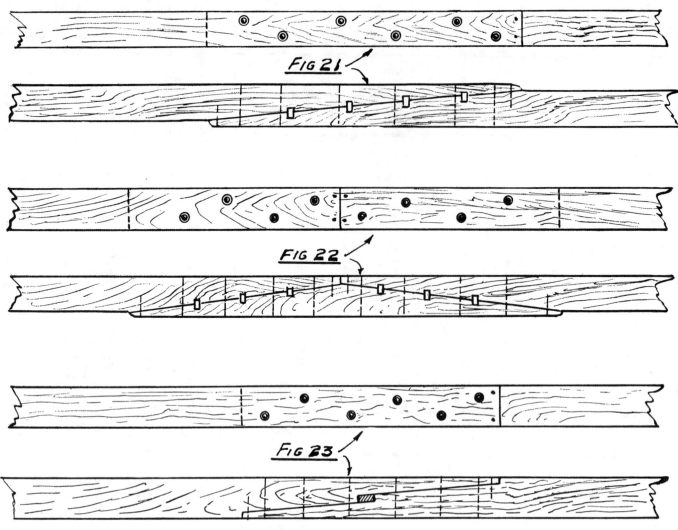

FIG 21

FIG 22

FIG 23

Plate VIIe

Fig. 21 illustrates how a two-piece beam is put together, the upper view being a side or moulded view and the lower one a view as seen from above. A scarph of this kind is usually made one-third the length of the whole beam.

In cases where it is necessary to make the beam out of three pieces, the scarph is made in the manner shown by Fig. 22. The length of scarph is usually about one-fourth the length of beam.

Fig. 23 shows an exceptionally strong method of scarphing beams. The keys in a scarph of this kind are of iron or steel and must be tapered and fitted snugly, and the lips of scarph must be cut square to the moulded edge of beam. The length of this kind of scarph need not be more than one-fifth or one-sixth length of beam.

7c. Dovetailing, Halving

Fig. 16 (Plate VIIf) shows two pieces of timber joined together at right angles by a dovetailed notch. As to dovetails in general, it is necessary to remark that they should never be depended upon for joints exposed to a strain, as a very small degree of shrinkage will allow the joint to draw considerably.

Figs. 17 and 18 (Plate VIIf) show modes of mortising wherein the tenon has one side dovetailed or notched, and the corresponding side of the mortise also dovetailed or notched. The mortise is made of sufficient width to admit the tenon, and the dovetailed or notched faces are brought in contact by driving home a wedge c. Of these, Fig. 18 is the best.

Fig. 19 (Plate VIIf) shows the halving of the timbers crossing each other. Fig. 20 shows a joint similar to those in Nos. 17 and 18, but where the one timber b is oblique to the other a.

Fig. 21 (Plate VIIf).—Nos. 1 and 2 show a mode of notching a horizontal beam into the side of an inclined one by a dovetailed joint. The general remark as to dovetailed joints applies with especial force to this example.

7d. An Explanation of Coaked Scarphs

The word coaked refers to a method of increasing strength of scarphs by preventing the joint from moving sideways or endways. A coak is a rectangular or round piece of hard wood laid into the surface of the two pieces of timber that are scarphed together in such a manner that one-half of depth of coak will be in each piece of timber. On Fig. 33 (page 49) is shown a properly coaked keel scarph, and you will note that by the addition of coaks the resistance to sliding has been greatly increased and the holding strength of bolts has also been increased.

In the days when wooden ships were built in large numbers all the principal keel, stem, stern, keelsons and frame scarphs were coaked, but in these days coaking is seldom used, and in ignoring the advantages of coaking a scarph I believe the shipbuilders are making a serious error. Round coaks are used up to 3 inches in diameter and rectangular ones up to 3 inch × 6 inch.

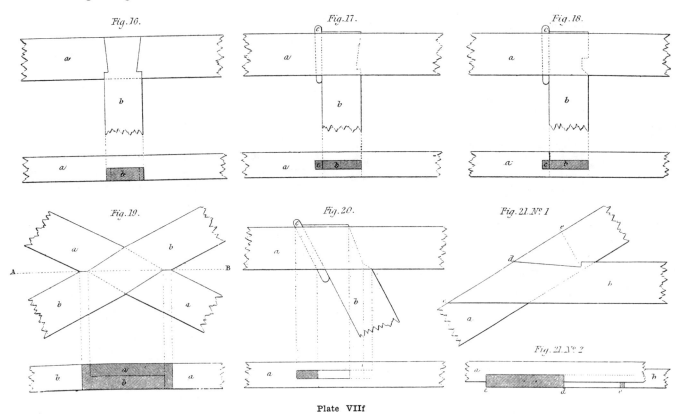

Plate VIIf

Chapter VIII

Describing the Different Parts of a Ship Constructed of Wood

In this chapter I shall describe and illustrate the principal parts of a wooden ship's construction, explaining the position each occupies, its duty, and how it is shaped and fastened.

8a. EXPLANATORY

The longitudinal form of a vessel is determined by timbers called the keel, the stem and the stern-post. The stem, which is at the foremost extremity, is supported by its combination with the keel, which is the lowest part of the structure, by other timbers lying in its concave part, called the apron, and the stemson; the apron and stemson unite with timbers called the deadwood and with the keelson, which timbers strengthen and give support to the keel; the stern-post, which is at the aftermost extremity, is supported by timbers called the inner stern-post and the sternson; and these timbers likewise form a junction with the keelson, deadwood, and keel, so that a mutual connection is kept up by them, to preserve the longitudinal form.

Transversely, the form is given by assemblages of timbers placed vertically, called frames. The lowest timbers of the frames, called floors, lie between the keel and keelson, extending equally on each side; the other timbers of the frames, called futtocks and top-timbers, connect keel to the timbers that form the upper boundary of the structure, which are called gunwales and plank-sheers.

The longitudinal form is further maintained, and strengthened, by exterior and interior linings, called planking, and by interior binders, called shelf-pieces, which are united to the frames. The exterior lining or planking which is connected with, and covers the whole surface of the frame, is made watertight, to preserve the buoyancy of the body. The two sides are connected and sustained at their proper distance apart by timbers lying horizontally, called beams; these are firmly united to the sides of the ship. Platforms, called decks, are laid on the beams, on which the cabins for the accommodation of officers and ship's company are placed.

The beams are so disposed on the different decks that their sides may form the hatchways and ladderways, which are the communications from one deck to another, and to the hold; and to give support to pieces fixed to them, called mast partners, for wedging and securing the masts. The beams on the different decks are placed immediately over one another, in order that pillars may be placed between them, to continue to the upper decks the support given to lower beams by pillars resting on keelson.

The deck beams are secured to the side by large timbers, called shelf-pieces, on which the beams lie, and to other large timbers called waterways, lying on ends of the beams, both well fastened to the ship's side. Knees under the beams, and steel plates bolted to the side, give additional security.

Below the lower deck, in two-decked ships and upwards, upon the inside planking, were formerly placed interior frames, in the full part of the body, extending from the keelson upwards to lower deck beams, called bends or riders; the lowest timber, called the floor rider, extended equally on each side of the middle; the other timbers, according to their position with this, were called, first, second, and third futtock riders. These timbers were intended to support the body against the upward pressure should the ship ground.

These riders are in some cases omitted, diagonal frames being introduced on the inside of frame timbers, forming a system of braces and trusses, that takes their place. The diagonal framing was brought into use to prevent ships hogging through the unequal vertical pressures of the weights downwards, and of water upwards, in different parts of a ship's length.

At the present time, a greatly improved method of diagonal framing is used. This method calls for the use of flat steel straps on the *outside* of frames, the straps being let in flush and placed to cross the frames and each other at an inclination of about 45° from the perpendicular. In addition to this, steel plate riders and a

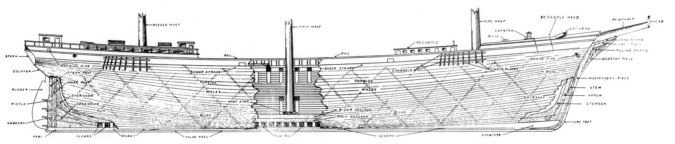

Fig. 25

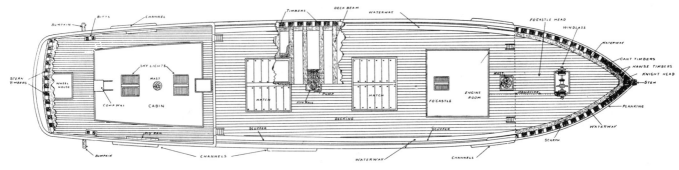

Fig. 26

steel arch are worked on inside of frames, the arch extending from near deadwood forward up to main deck beams amidships and to stern-post near deadwood aft. This arch is securely fastened to all the frames it crosses.

Figs. 25, 26, 27 and 28 show construction details of a wooden ship, the principal parts being marked for identification.

8b. KEEL. DESCRIPTION

The keel is the principal longitudinal timber of a ship and is the first construction timber to set on the building slip blocks. A ship's keel is usually parallel sided except for a short distance near the forward and after ends, where the sided dimension is reduced to that of stem and stern post.

The sided and moulded (S. & M.) dimensions of keel required for a ship can be ascertained, when ship's tonnage is known, by referring to Table of Dimensions issued by classification society under whose rules the ship is being built, (see Tables 3b to 3f) or it can be calculated, when dimensions of ship are known, by using formula at end of Chapter III.

8b¹. *Material For Keels*

The keel of a ship should be made of selected straight-grained, well-seasoned timber of a kind that is durable when immersed in water, and that has sufficient tensile strength to withstand the maximum keel strain.

The relative durability and strength of different kinds of woods used for keels is given in Tables 2 and 3.

In U. S. A. at present time, Douglas fir, and long-leaf yellow pine, are the two most readily procurable woods suitable for keels of large ships. Timbers of these trees can be obtained in long lengths and of better quality than other more highly rated (by insurance companies) woods, and in addition to this these woods do not shrink

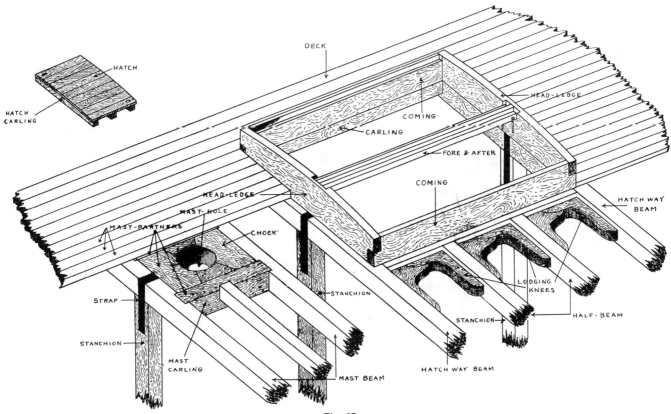

Fig. 27

very much while seasoning and for this reason, if partially seasoned timber is used, the danger of seams of scarphs opening through wood shrinking is greatly reduced.

Fig. 29 is a photograph of a ship's keel being set on building blocks; Fig. 30 shows photograph of keel, stem and stern post of a shallow draught hull set on building blocks, and Fig. 31 shows drawings of construction details of which keel forms a part.

8b². *Scarphing Keels*

As timber long enough to make a keel of a ship is difficult to obtain, it is very often necessary to join two or more pieces lengthways by scarphing and bolting or riveting. Keel scarphs should always be either nibbed or hooked, because a plain scarph lacks strength and cannot be held in place under the strain a keel is subjected to. On Plate VIIc, 6, 7, 8, I show details of plain, nibbed and hooked scarphs, the relative strength of each

being: The nibbed scarph has one and one-quarter times the strength of the plain one, and the hooked scarph has two and one-half times the strength of the plain one. While scarphs can be cut either vertically or horizontally, meaning by this cut on a vertical plane parallel to moulded surface (side) of keel, or cut on a horizontal plane parallel with sided surface (top) of keel, horizontal scarphs are generally used when scarphing keels because they are easier to cut, fasten and keep tight; but no matter which kind of scarph is used, it is very important to make it of sufficient length to permit the proper number of fastenings to be driven. Length of scarphs should vary with dimensions of material and size of ship, but it is safe to adhere to this rule: *Make keel scarph extend under at least four frames (three frame spaces).*

In some cases, especially if ship is a large one, it is necessary in addition to scarphing two or more timbers

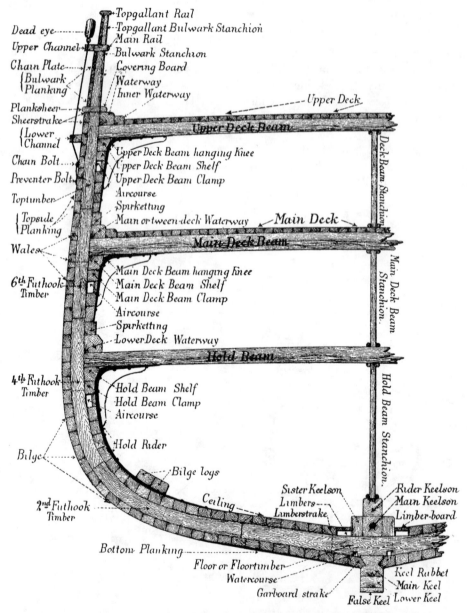

Fig. 28. Cross-Section of Ship, Showing Construction Details, Marked For Identification

Fig. 29. Laying the Keel of Another Ship as Soon as the Accoma Left the Ways at the Foundation Company's Yard

together to make the required length of keel, to also fasten two or more timbers on top of each other to get the required moulded (depth) size.

In such cases the scarphs must be located longitudinally, so that there is a considerable distance between the location of a scarph on top keel timber and that of scarph on piece of timber immediately below. By doing this each scarph is supported and strengthened against hogging and sagging strains by the solid timber immediately below or above.

8b³. *An Explanation of Coaked Keel Scarphs*

The word "coaked" refers to a method of increasing strength of scarphs by preventing the joint from moving sideways or endways. A coak is a rectangular or round piece of hard wood laid into the surface of two pieces of timber, that are scarphed together, in such a manner that one-half the depth of coak is in each piece of timber. On Fig. 33 is shown a properly coaked keel scarph and it is apparent that, by the addition of coaks, the resistance to sliding and holding strength of bolts has been greatly increased. In the days when wooden ships were built in large numbers, all principal keel, stem, stern, keelson and frame scarphs were coaked, but in these days coaking is seldom used, and in ignoring the advantages

of coaking a scarph I believe the shipbuilders are making a serious error. With modern machinery now available every scarph could be coaked without seriously increasing cost.

8b⁴. *Fastening Scarphs of Keels*

Next in importance to cutting and fitting is method of securing, because the strength and number of fastenings must be proper to withstand all strains put upon joint or scarph. Fig. 33, drawing of keel, shows two pieces of timber scarphed and fastened, the scarph being a longitudinal nibbed and coaked one. Fastenings are clearly indicated on drawing. Note there is a clench ring under the head and also under riveted end of each fastening, and that one-half the fastenings are driven from each side (top and bottom) of keel. Below I mention a few good rules to adhere to when laying out keel scarph fastenings.

(*a*) Make the diameter of fastenings in accordance with size laid down by classification society, and bore holes for fastenings with an auger that is at least one-eighth inch smaller than bolt.

(*b*) At extreme ends of scarph let there be double fastenings.

(*c*) Space intermediate fastenings equally and locate each fastening a sufficient distance inside edge of keel to bring both the fastenings and washers well inside and clear of rabbet.

(*d*) Locate all keel scarphs fastenings in positions that will not interfere with the driving of frame to keel fastenings, and keelson to frame and keel fastenings.

On Fig. 33 is shown frames and keelson in position and fastened to keel.

8b⁵. *Stopwaters in Keel Scarphs*

I will next call attention to the method of keeping water from leaking through a horizontal keel scarph. Before the scarph is put together for fastening, it is usual to either paint or treat the surfaces that go together with some wood preservative and, of course, the scarph is accurately fitted before it is fastened. But these precautions do not prevent the wood shrinking and the joint opening. So it is necessary to use some methods of preventing water from passing inside the ship should a scarph joint open. The most satisfactory method of doing this is to put one or more stopwaters through the seam of a scarph in such a location that the stopwater will prevent water that passes along scarph getting inside the ship.

A stopwater is a well-seasoned soft-wood dowel or plug that is driven into a slightly smaller hole bored edgeways along the seam of a scarph in such a manner that one-half of hole will be each side of joint.

Of course the stopwater must be located in the proper position, which is, in a keel scarph like the one I am

Fig. 30.   Keel Set Up

referring to, in rabbet of keel. When located in this position the caulking of garboard covers end of stopwater and prevents water from passing back of it. Holes for keel stopwaters should never be bored or stopwater driven until ship is ready for planking.

On Fig. 34 I have shown keel stopwater in place; note it is in such a position that garboard will cover it.

Fig. 31.   As Soon as the Congaree Was Launched From the Foundation Company's Yard Workmen Laid the Keel For Another Vessel

8b⁶.   *Keel Rabbet*

In paragraph above I mentioned rabbet of keel, so perhaps I had better explain how a keel rabbet is cut.

The rabbet extends from end to end of keel and merges into rabbet of stem and stern; it is sometimes a groove cut at proper angle and width for plank to fit into and sometimes is formed by beveling the upper corners of keel in such a manner that garboard will fit square against keel. On cross-section construction view (Fig. 28) a grooved rabbet cut near to top of keel is shown, and on Fig. 29 (photo of keel) the beveled upper corner rabbet can clearly be seen. Note that rabbet at ends of keel is never cut until after stem and stern post is set up and fastened in place. As regards value the advantage lies with grooved rabbet, because the wood back of groove forms a backing for caulking, while the groove tends to add support to garboard along its lower edge, and in addition to this the small amount of keel wood above rabbet is sufficient to necessitate the notching of floor timbers over keel and thus they are strengthened against side thrust. As regards labor to construct the advantage lies with the beveled-edge rabbet.

8b⁷.   *Edge-Bolting a Keel*

In the days when wood was the principal shipbuilding material, keels were nearly always edge-bolted, the bolts being driven from alternate side of keel and spaced the distance alternate frames were apart, all bolts being placed some distance below garboard, as edge-bolts through garboard into keel were considered sufficient to strengthen the upper edge of keel.

Without doubt edge-bolting a keel is advantageous because it tends to prevent keel being split by driving the large number of vertical bolts that pass through it, and by the working of these bolts when ship is afloat; and in addition to this edge-bolting will oftentimes prevent a keel splitting should the ship go aground.

8b³. *False Keel, or Shoe*

This is a relatively thin piece of timber 2 inches to 4 inches in thickness, that is fastened below keel for the purpose of protecting its lower portion from damage should a ship go aground. On Figs. 25 and 28 the false keel is plainly marked.

The false keel extends the whole length of keel and is fastened with independent fastenings that do not pass entirely through keel, their number and strength being sufficient to secure the keel under normal conditions, but not sufficient to hold it in place should ship go aground. The false keel is always fastened in place after ship is built, and when keel timber is relatively soft material, such as Douglas fir, or long-leaf yellow pine, false keel is made of some durable wood, oak, hard maple or beech.

8c. THE STEM

The stem is the extreme forward construction timber of a hull and is the timber to which the ends of planking are fastened. The stem is attached to forward end of keel by scarphing and is reinforced and held in place by knees or timbers riveted or bolted to both keel and stem; these timbers are clearly shown on Fig. 35, which is a reproduction of the drawing of keel, stem and stemknee construction of a modern wood ship.

The Fig. 35 construction details are the simplest that it is possible to design, and in simplifying the construction strength has not been sacrificed.

For the purpose of enabling a comparison to be made between the older and more modern methods of constructing a stem I have shown on Fig. 36 stem construction of a wood ship built in 1876.

Compare Fig. 35 with Fig. 36 and the more complicated construction is noticeable.

When scarphing a stem to keel it must be remembered that the scarph will have to withstand strains coming from ahead, and therefore the scarph must be nibbed, or hooked, in such a manner that it will add strength to fastenings should the stem receive a direct blow from ahead, as would be the case should ship hit another vessel or take the ground head on.

On Fig. 35 and 36 the scarph fastenings are clearly shown.

You should also note that on Fig. 36 stem construction names of principal pieces are marked.

One thing should be kept in mind when laying out a stem, and that is, to have the grain of wood run lengthways of all pieces of timber. It is, of course, impossible to have full-length grain in all pieces, but if the shape of stem is such that a great deal of cross-grained wood must be used, if stem is gotten out of straight planks or timbers it is better to make use of some knees or material that has a certain amount of natural bend of grain or fibres.

Every piece of short grain should be supported or backed by a piece having straight grain and the fastenings should be spaced and located in such a manner that the several pieces of timber will be rigidly fastened together and to keel.

A stem receives the ends of outside planking and therefore it must have a rabbet. This rabbet is cut either upon the after edge, or along the stem a little distance inside of its after edge, but in either case the rabbet extends from stem head to keel and is backed up by apron piece into which a number of the plank end fastenings will be driven.

Ahead of rabbet the stem is beveled to take the approximate shape of longitudinal lines of ship, and after this beveling is completed the front of stem is frequently protected by a piece of steel, called a stem band, that extends from above the heavy load water-line down to fore-foot.

8d. THE APRON

The apron is the piece of timber that is fitted to after side of stem and extends from stem head down to forward deadwood. In fact, the apron can be considered as a continuation of forward deadwood. The apron forms a support for stem and for the fastenings that hold the forward ends of planking in place in stem rabbet. On Figs. 35 and 36, the apron is clearly indicated, as well as method of fastening it to stem. Some shipbuilders make it a practice to allow apron piece to extend to forward ends of planking, and thus the whole of rabbet is cut in apron, and stem only forms a protection for the ends of planking. This method is largely resorted to when constructing smaller craft and it has the advantage of allowing replacing a stem, should it be damaged, with the minimum of labor. This method, however, has the disadvantage of reducing strength of construction.

In large vessels the rabbet for plank is cut in stem and therefore joint between stem and apron is along a line cut a short distance inside of bearding line of rabbet.

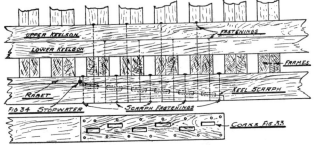

Coaked Keel Scarph and Stopwater

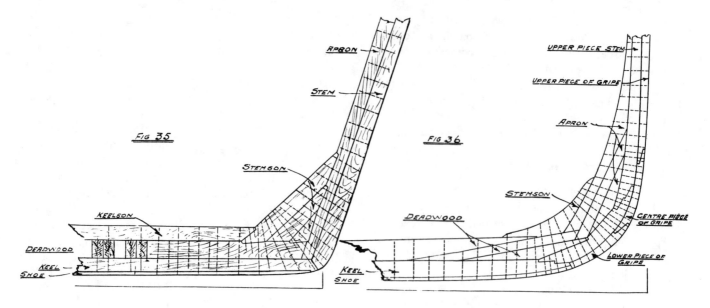

It is usual to make apron the same width as stem, but if it is impossible to get proper bearing for planking end fastenings without increasing width of apron, the apron is made of material considerably wider than stem. In fastening apron to stem, through bolts are usually employed, and care should be taken to space them in such a manner that they will not interfere with bolts of cant timbers or breasthook fastenings. In a number of cases I have noticed that shipyards are driving apron and stem fastenings parallel to each other. This is not good practice, and much better results, so far as resistance to pulling apart or damage is concerned, will be obtained by driving fastenings at varying angles to each other. Tests of the holding power of fastenings driven parallel to each other and fastenings driven at various angles show that "various angle" fastenings have a holding power 60% greater than parallel fastenings. This test was made with 1-inch diameter fastenings connecting together two 12-inch pieces of yellow pine. The power used was applied for the purpose of separating the joint.

Hard wood is the best material to use for stem and apron, and even if stem is made of a resinous wood, such as fir or yellow pine, the apron should be of oak, or a hard wood of similar strength and durability. Apron is shown on Figs. 25, 35 and 36 illustrations.

8e. The Knightheads

Knightheads are timbers placed on each side of apron when the rabbet is on after edge of stem, and partly on stem and partly on apron when rabbet is cut along stem and apron. These timbers give support to bowsprit, and add strength to the foremost extremities of outside planking (called hooding ends.)

Knightheads should extend a sufficient height above bowsprit to receive the fastenings of bowsprit chock, and a sufficient distance below deck to give necessary added strength to the structure around the bowsprit.

When the diameter of bowsprit exceeds siding of stem at head, so that knightheads would have to be cut considerably to allow bowsprit to pass between them, pieces of timber, called stem pieces, sufficiently thick to give necessary increase of width to stem and apron, are fastened to sides of stem and apron.

Knightheads and stem pieces are made to conform to scantling of frame, and are bolted to stem. When the bow of vessel is not too acute the bolts should pass through both knightheads and stem; but when too acute the bolts can be driven from each side through one knighthead and stem only.

On Fig. 26 the knightheads are indicated.

8f. Forward Deadwood

This is the piece of timber placed on top of keel, immediately aft of stem, for the purpose of making depth of wood at forward end of keel sufficient to allow a solid backing for the frames.

In most vessels, as stem is approached the lines narrow to such an extent that the frames assume a "V"-like appearance and this, of course, will increase the distance between rabbet and bearding line, and from bearding to cutting down line, or line where top edge of timbers leave side of keel, stem or deadwood. On Figs. 25, 35 and 36 the forward deadwood is clearly shown.

Fig. 35 shows modern method of forward deadwood construction when straight material is used, and Fig. 36 shows method of construction that was in use before the advent of steel ships. The old method is more complicated but it has the advantage of being more durable and stronger than the more modern method.

In constructing forward deadwood it is essential that fastenings be properly driven and correct in size and

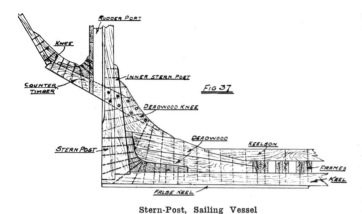

Stern-Post, Sailing Vessel

number. It is advantageous and advisable to nib the ends of deadwood into keel and stem, and to use coaks when deadwood is built of straight material.

The size of dimensions of deadwood is usually the same as keel.

8g. STERN-POST

Stern-post is the perpendicular piece of timber fastened to after end of keel. The stern-post forms a portion of the after boundary of the framework of ship and is the timber to which after ends of all lower planks fasten.

The stern-post is usually constructed of material of same sided dimensions as keel and is rabbeted to receive the ends (after hoods) of all planks that terminate at stern-post. It is usual to secure stern-post to keel by tenoning it into mortises cut into keel, and securing the tenoned lower end against rupture by placing dove-tail plates (let in flush) on each side and securing them with through bolts. In addition to this the stern-post is supported and fastened to the after deadwood and to shaft log if there is one.

In vessel propelled by sail only the after end of stern-post is grooved in such a manner that forward edge of rudder post will lay close against it, and by closing the opening between stern-post and rudder eddies at this point are eliminated. In such vessels the stern-post must have a sufficient width and strength to receive the fastenings of rudder gudgeon and pintle straps.

On Fig. 37 is shown details of sternpost construction of sailing vessel, and you will note that the stern-post is composed of two pieces of material fastened together. This is done when width of available material is not sufficient, or when additional strength of stern-post is needed. The forward piece of the two is named the inner stern-post.

On Fig. 39 is shown the modern method of construction at after end of keel.

In vessels that have a screw propeller located along center line the stern-post is shaped to receive the outboard bearing of propeller shaft, and rudder is hung some distance aft of stern-post on a frame erected to receive

Fig. 38. Side Counter Timbers

it. Of course a hole for propeller shaft to pass through must be bored through stern-post.

On Fig. 38 I show construction of stern-post of a screw-propelled vessel.

8h. AFTER DEADWOOD

The after deadwood bears the same relation to stern-post that forward deadwood does to stem. It is fitted on top of keel and against stern-post, and is sufficiently deep to permit the heels of after frames to be secured to it. The after deadwood is generally made of timber having the same siding as keel and stern-post.

In screw-propelled vessels the upper edge of deadwood timbers forms a bearing for shaft log or box, and after shaft log is in place the sternson knee is fastened in place and adds strength to the whole assemblage of pieces.

It is advantageous to use coaks in deadwood timbers and to drive the fastenings at varying angles.

On Fig. 39 construction of screw-propelled vessel's after deadwood is shown, and Fig. 37 shows construction of a sailing vessel's after deadwood; compare the two types of construction.

On Fig. 36 is shown after deadwood construction of vessel built in 1868.

8i. COUNTER TIMBERS—ON COUNTER AND ELLIPTICAL STERNS

Counter timbers extend aft from stern-post in all round and elliptical stern vessels to form the rake of stern. There are in reality three counter timbers, two *side* counter timbers and one *center* counter timber.

The side counter timbers are placed each side of stern-post, extend aft at rake that lower portion of counter must have, are set into grooves cut each side of stern-post, and securely bolted to stern-post, to deadwood, to

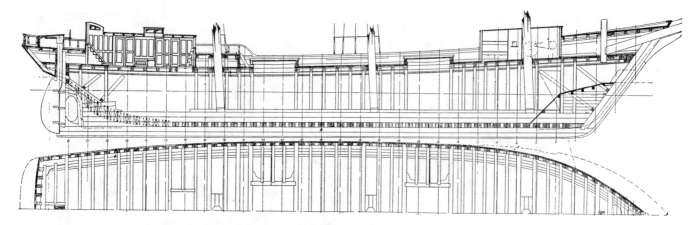

Fig. 39.   Construction Plan of Three-Masted Auxiliary Schooner, Which Will Carry 700 Tons Dead Weight

each other, and to deadwood, sternson knee and shaft log (if there is a shaft log) ahead of stern-post.

On Fig. 38 the side counter timbers of an elliptical stern vessel are shown in place, and on Fig. 37 the method of fastening them to deadwood and stern-post is shown.

The center counter timber must be large enough to fill the space between side counter timbers, and as rudder-post opening is cut through the center counter timber the distance from inside of one counter timber to inside of the other one must be at least equal to diameter of rudder post.

A rudder port is constructed around rudder-post opening. After the three counter timbers are bolted together a rabbet to receive edge of planking that terminates along counter is cut along the lower outer edge of outside counter timbers.

Fig. 40 illustrates modern elliptical stern construction details.

8k. THE FRAME

This is the name given to the transverse timbers that are shaped to the form of vessel and placed at stated distances apart from stem to stern.

Along the center portion of a vessel, where the shape does not change very much, the frame timbers are placed square to the longitudinal plane and for this reason are named *square* frames. But at the ends (bow and stern) where shape changes considerably the frame timbers are placed obliquely to longitudinal vertical plane and for this reason are named *cant* frames. (They are canted or inclined from the perpendicular.) In addition to the frame of a vessel being composed of a number of timbers, placed as stated above, each separate frame is composed of several pieces assembled and fastened together, and each of these pieces (called timbers of the frame) has a distinguishing name, viz., first, second, third, fourth, fifth and sixth futtocks; and long and short top timbers. Of course you will understand that the number of futtocks will vary with size of vessel.

In addition to this each frame of the square body is fastened to a floor timber that scores over and lays across

the keel. The cant frames do not generally have floor timbers but have their lower ends mortised directly into the deadwood or other piece of material against which they rest.

The sided and moulded dimensions of frames and also distance center of one frame is from center of next one, called timber and space, is specified for all sizes of

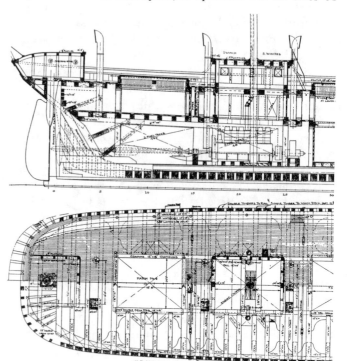

Fig. 40

vessels (see Table 3b), and Fig. 41 defines the meaning of terms Sided, Moulded, and Timber and *Space*.

Explanation of Terms

The *sided* measure of a frame is width or thickness of material of which it is composed measured on fore-and-aft line when frame is in position in vessel.

Moulded measure of a frame is width or breadth of material of which frame is composed measured along a transverse line when frame is in position in a vessel. The term means the measurement of side on which the mould of shape of frame is placed.

Timber and space means the longitudinal space, or room, occupied by the timber of one frame added to the space between it and the next frame.

On Fig. 28 I show a transverse view of an assembled square frame, each piece of which is identified.

Beginning at the lower (keel) end of a frame I will describe each piece and explain how the various pieces are shaped and fastened together.

8k¹. *The Floor or Floor Timber*

This is the name of the piece of timber that crosses keel and serves to tie a frame on one side of keel with one on the other. On the illustration the floor is clearly marked.

The floors of the midship frame usually, in flat-floored ships, extend out to about one-fourth the breadth on each

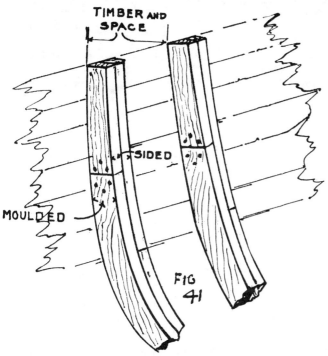

FIG 41

side of keel, but it must be remembered that if the floors are *doubled* (two floors placed alongside of each other) each will have a long and a short arm, the long arm of one floor being on side of keel that the short arm of adjacent one is. The reason for this is explained in description of frame timbers.

Floors are secured to keel with bolts, and if notched over keel their lowest points must exactly reach to bearding line of rabbet. The distance from bearding line of rabbet of keel to the upper part of floors, at their center line, is called the cutting down, or throating.

Dimensions of floors and their fastenings are given in Tables 3b and 3d.

8k². *The Frame Timbers*

The pieces of timber of which a frame is composed

must be disposed in such a manner that they can be fastened together securely. This is done by shifting the butts and bolting the pieces together in the manner illustrated on Figs. 28 and 42a and explained below.

The floor on illustration is a double one, the dash line marked near keel across it indicating the end of a short arm, and the full line a little further out indicating end of a long arm.

The first futtock is butted against the end of short arm of floor and the upper end of this futtock extends to dotted line next above the full line that indicates end of long arm of floor. This permits lower portion of first futtock to be bolted to portion of long-arm floor that extends beyond the short arm of adjacent floor. The lower end of second futtock butts against long-arm end of floor and upper end of this futtock extends some distance above upper end of first futtock. The lower end of second futtock is fastened to portion of upper end of first futtock that extends beyond end of long arm of floor. In this manner each succeeding futtock overlaps and is bolted to the one below, and thus any short grain of wood at the end of a futtock is strengthened by the long grain of piece that overlaps it. On illustration the even numbered futtocks are marked for identification, and location of odd numbered ones is indicated by dash lines and numbers only.

Bolts are used to fasten the futtocks to floor arms and to each other, and if maximum strength is desired round coaks are inserted between the overlapping portions of futtocks.

All fastenings of futtocks should be located in positions that will keep them clear of knee and waterway fastenings, and if filling frames are to be used the heads and ends of bolts that are located where filling frames will be must be countersunk flush with surface of wood.

8k³. *Filling Frames*

This is the name given to short frames located between the frames proper and extending from keel to about the turn of bilge. Their use is to strengthen the transverse bottom framing of vessel, but originally they were used in conjunction with caulking to make the whole of bottom of a vessel's transverse framing watertight.

The old method of using filling frames was to make these frames extend from keel to orlop deck location and to completely fill spaces between frames proper. Thus the whole of bottom and bilges of a vessel was made one solid mass of wood, and when the seams between the various frames and filling frames were caulked with oakum the whole bottom framing of vessel was made watertight. Construction of this kind requires a very large amount of material, and the weight of a vessel constructed in this manner is much greater than that of a vessel constructed in accordance with modern ideas of what is proper and necessary. In present-day construction of large vessels one filling frame, or at most two,

Fig. 42. The Dimensions Are: L. O. A. 200 Ft., Length on Deck 177 Ft., Breadth 36 Ft. 8 In.   She Is to be Rigged With Four Masts

is placed between each two regular frames, the filling frames extending out to about turn of bilge.

In small and moderate sized vessels the filling frames are frequently omitted entirely.

In addition to these filling frames, filling pieces are placed in the wake of fore, main, and mizzen rigging, wherever a valve connection passes through the bottom or side of vessel, where a knee will not coincide with a regular frame, and wherever an opening of any kind is cut through side or bottom.

8k⁴. *Cant Frames*

I have already mentioned that some of the frames are canted out of perpendicular. I will now explain the reason for doing this.

When referring to the transverse framing a vessel is considered as being divided into two principal parts, one part being named the square body frame and the other the cant body frame. Along the square body (the part of a vessel where the shape of cross-section changes very little) the frames stand perpendicular at right angles to center line of keel, and parallel to each other; and along the portions of a vessel where cant frames are located the frames are canted, or swung around to an angle, thus increasing the distance they are apart at deck line. Cant frames are canted forward at bow, and aft at stern, the number of cant frames varying in each vessel and depending upon fullness at deck relative to fullness along deadwood at stem and stern. The reason that forward and aft frames of a wooden vessel are canted is, that in the

parts where deck outline merges into stem, and around the curve of an elliptical stern square timbers would have to be beveled to an excessive degree to make planking lay against the frames for their full width, and this excessive beveling would greatly weaken frames; or if frames were a sufficient width to allow for beveling an excessive amount of material would be wasted.

By inclining, or canting, each frame so that its outer face parallels, as near as possible, the deck outline the amount of bevel necessary to make plank fit against a frame for its full width is greatly reduced and additional strength of frame is obtained without adding to the material. Cant frames at bow always cant forward and those at stern cant aft.

On Fig. 42 I show views of forward cant frames in position. You will note by referring to illustration that no change is made in spacing of lower ends of cant frames, but by canting the actual interval (space) between upper ends of frames increases, and as outer face of frames more nearly follows shape of vessel's outline, they offer a greater resistance to pressure of waves at bow and at stern.

The lower ends of cant frames are always "boxed" into deadwood about 1½ inches deep, except in range of a shaft hole, and each cant frame is bolted through deadwood.

Before the days of steel ships it was usual to cant all frames ahead and aft of the middle body, but modern wooden shipbuilders do not consider it necessary to cant

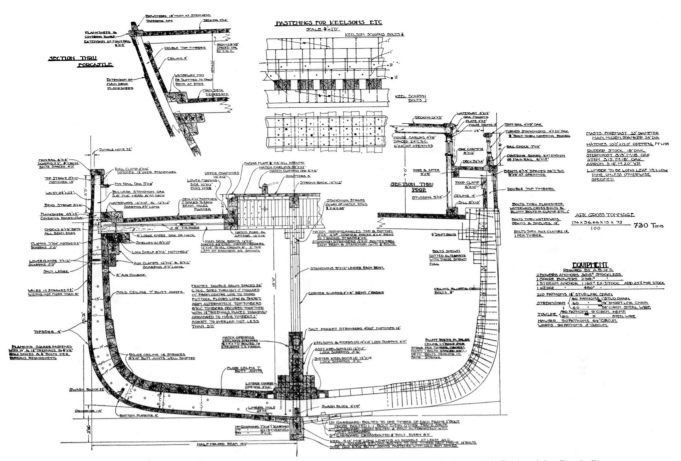

Fig. 42a. Midship Construction Plan of Four-Masted Schooner Building For J. W. Somerville, Designed by Cox & Stevens

more than a few frames at extreme bow and a few at extreme stern.

The old method is certainly the best but it entails a greater amount of work both in the mould loft and when erecting the frame.

81. HAWSE PIECES

Hawse pieces are pieces of timber used to fill in between the knightheads and the foremost cant frames. Their use is to give solid wood for the hawse pipe to pass through and fasten to.

In reality hawse pieces are cant frames that close the openings between forward cant frames from the knightheads aft as far as necessary to give good solid fastening for hawse-pipe flanges. The lower ends of hawse timbers are bolted to the apron and the several hawse timbers are edge-bolted together, care being taken to keep bolts clear of positions where breasthooks and hawse holes are located. On Figs. 25 and 26 hawse pieces are marked and on Fig. 42 they are very clearly shown.

8m. KEELSONS

8m¹. Main

The keelson is a timber placed immediately over keel on top of the floors, over which it is sometimes notched, and extending from forward deadwood to after dead-

wood. It unites in one solid structure the keel, floors and deadwoods.

The main keelson is usually built up of a number of pieces scarphed together, and when laying out a keelson it is necessary to locate the scarphs in positions that will not bring them immediately over a keel scarph. The scarphs are usually nibbed and have a length equal to at least two frame intervals (double the room and space). Some of the fastenings of scarphs must pass through both floors and keel, and if the maximum strength of construction is desired two or three circular coaks should be fitted into each scarph. The lips of scarphs are fastened with two short bolts that do not pass through keel.

At forward end of vessel the main keelson usually scarphs into deadwood and is then secured to apron by means of a stemson knee. Aft the main keelson scarphs into deadwood and in some vessels the sternson knee rests upon main keelson and serves to fasten its after end to stern-post.

The main keelson is fastened in place with bolts that pass through floors and into keel, and in vessels that are well constructed additional strength is given to the whole structure by coaking the lower piece of main keelson to each floor and filling that it crosses: 3-inch diameter coaks are used for doing this.

If the main keelson is built up of two or more timbers placed on top of each other the pieces should be coaked together with square coaks before the through floor and keel fastenings are driven.

On Figs. 25, 28, 35 a main keelson is shown in its proper position in a vessel.

8m². *Sister Keelsons*

Sister keelsons are generally placed each side of and close to main keelson, extending fore-and-aft parallel with main keelson to where the reduction in width of floor of vessel reduces their depth to about 6 inches.

These keelsons, in properly constructed vessels, are coaked to floors and filling timbers with circular coaks, then bolted to floors and fillings and edge-bolted to main keelson. Scarphs of sister keelsons are cut and fastened the same as main keelson scarphs. On Fig. 28 sister keelsons are shown in place.

8m³. *Boiler or Bilge Keelsons*

In all vessels having machinery, two or more boiler or bilge keelsons are run parallel with sister keelsons and sufficiently apart to form the lower timber of engine and boiler foundations. These keelsons are coaked and fastened to all frames and filling they cross, and are always extended as far as possible forward and aft, because by doing this the strain caused by weight of machinery, as well as the local vibrations caused by the rotation of engine crank are spread over a wide extent of the structure.

8m⁴. *Rider Keelsons*

Rider keelsons are placed on top of main keelsons for the purpose of giving additional strength to the whole longitudinal structure of a vessel. In Chapter V on Strains I explained that hogging and sagging strains can best be resisted by adding strength to the longitudinal members of a vessel's structure, and this the rider keelson does.

On Fig. 28 a rider keelson is shown in position.

Rider keelson scarphs and fastenings are similar to those in keelsons, and of course scarphs must be properly located so as not to coincide with keelson or keel scarphs.

Power of resistance against hogging and sagging strains is increased when rider keelson fastenings are diagonally driven at varying angles from the perpendicular.

8n. STEMSON

The stemson is the piece of material, a natural knee, placed in angle formed by apron, upper piece of deadwood and forward end of keelson. It acts as an additional support for stem and serves to properly tie keelson and forward deadwood to stem and apron.

The fastenings go through stem, apron and stemson at one end, and keel, deadwood, keelson and stemson at the other.

It is advantageous to use coaks in addition to the metal fastenings, and of course all fastenings should be through bolts clenched on rings.

On Fig. 25 the stemson is clearly indicated.

8o. STERNSON

The sternson bears the same relation to stern-post that stemson does to stem. It is used to strengthen stern-post and is, in the case of vessels having a shaft log, placed on top of log and serves to hold log in position.

On Fig. 25 a sternson knee is shown, but in present-day practice stemson and sternson knees are now seldom used, as an examination of illustrations and construction details shown in this book will indicate.

8p. DIAGONAL STEEL BRACING OF FRAME

Steel straps are fastened diagonally across outside of the frame of a vessel for the purpose of strengthening vessel against strains that tend to change its shape longitudinally. (Hogging or sagging strains.) These straps are let into frames flush, cross frames at about 45° inclination, and are fastened with at least one bolt through each strap into each frame, and to each other with rivets wherever two straps cross. The dimensions of straps, their number and location varies with the size of the vessel. (See Table 3a in Chapter III.)

On Fig. 25 is shown by dotted lines the general direction of diagonal straps. In large vessels, in addition to diagonal straps, it is usual to insert a steel strap arch on inside of frames. This arch begins at stem near to deadwood, rises in a curve to lower side of upper deck beams at about midships, and from these descends in a curve to near deadwood at stern-post. This strap is let into frames flush and is fastened in place with one bolt into each frame. Bear in mind that these and the diagonal straps are supplemented later by one or more of the planking fastenings at each frame going through both strap and frame.

8q. PLANKING

Planking is the name given to outer covering of the transverse frame. It is put on in strakes that run from stem to stern, each strake being properly proportioned in width from bow to midship and from midship to stern. In other words, the planks are not parallel for their entire length but have their widths graduated in such a manner that the number of planks required to fill space at stem, which is the narrowest space to fill, will also fill space at midship section, which is the widest space to fill. A single plank that runs from stem to stern is called a strake of planking. Below I give names and description of principal planks.

8q¹. *Garboard*

The plank next to keel is named the garboard. The lower edge of this plank is fitted into rabbet of keel, stem, and stern-post, and it is usual to edge-bolt this plank to keel, in addition to fastening it in the usual manner to all frames at crosses. The garboard is generally made of thicker material than rest of planking, as you will note by referring to Fig. 42a.

In a large vessel there may be two or three thick strakes next to garboard proper. In such cases each strake is slightly thinner than garboard proper, and it is correct to refer to all these thick strakes as being garboard strakes. Technically there can be only one garboard strake, but as it is impossible to obtain one plank sufficiently wide to cover the space that thick strake next to keel should cover, the term garboard is used when referring to all thick strakes next to keel.

On Fig. 42a three thick strakes are shown and you will note how each succeeding plank is slightly thinner than the last one put on. When planking a vessel the garboard is the first bottom plank put in position, and after vessel is planked the excess thickness is "dubbed off" for a few feet at bow and stern.

8q². *Sheer Strake*

The top strake of planking is called the sheer. This is usually the first strake of planking put on.

As this plank is an important one in the assemblage of planks that aid in resisting longitudinal strains its strength should be at a maximum, and for this reason butts of sheer strake should also be scarphed and edge-bolted instead of being butted in the manner that planks

of other strakes are joined. On Fig. 43 is shown a proper method of scarphing and fastening a sheer strake.

The scarph, as you will note, is a nibbed one that extends across three frames and after planks are fastened in position the scarph is edge-bolted between frames, the edge-bolts passing through sheer and into next plank below.

8q³. *The Wales (an old term)*

This name applies to an assemblage of planks that covers the frame from immediately below sheer strakes (the three or four top strakes used to be termed sheer planking) to bilge planking, which commences at or near to bilge. The term is seldom used by shipbuilders of the new school.

The wales were always somewhat thicker than the rest of planking and it was usual to designate wale strakes according to their location. Thus the wale strakes located where channel fastenings are, were named *channel wales*. The planks below were named the *main wales*, and below these again were the *diminishing strakes,* so called because it was here the planks began to be diminished in thickness and merge into bottom planks located immediately below the diminishing strakes and which filled space between them and garboard strakes.

On Fig. 28 I have identified the various assemblages of planks by marking names against them.

New Planking Names

The present-day method of planking is similar to the old in many respects, but as all planks between sheer and garboard strakes are alike in thickness and method of fastening, the old distinguishing names for the thicker planks have become obsolete and now all planks between top of garboard and bilge are known as bottom planking, and that from bilge to under side of sheer as topside planking, or side planking.

On Fig. 42a illustration shows the new planking method with names of assemblage of planks marked for identification.

8q⁴. *Caulking*

Caulking is the operation of making seams of planking watertight by forcing oakum into the seams by means of a caulking iron and mallet. In caulking the thickness of plank regulates the quantity of oakum that should be driven into each seam or butt joint. The following table gives number of threads of oakum for planks from 10 inches down to 1 inch thick.

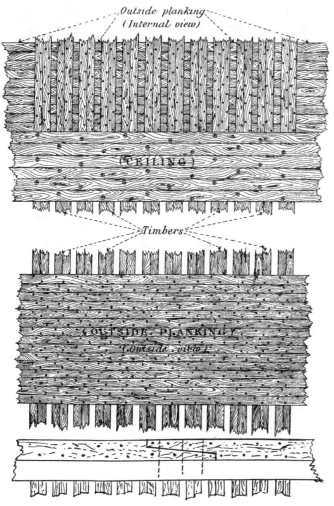

Outside planking
(Internal view)

(CEILING)

Timbers

OUTSIDE PLANKING
(Outside view)

Fig. 43

Thickness of Plank		Number of Double Threads of Oakum	Number of Single Threads of Spunyarn	
Wales and bottom planks.	10 inches	13	2	Seldom used now
	9 "	12	2	
	8 "	11	2	
	7 "	10	2	
	6 "	8	2	
	5 "	6	2	
	4 "	5	2	
	3 "	4	1	
	2½ "	3	—	
	2 "	2	—	
	1 "	1	—	

Topsides and Waterways.		Double Threads, Black Oakum	Double Threads, White Oakum or Cotton
	9 inches	11	—
	8 "	10	—
	7 "	9	—
	6 "	7	—
	5 "	5	1
	4 "	4	1
	3 "	3	1
	2½ "	2	1

Deck.		Single Threads, Black Oakum	Single Threads, White Oakum or Cotton
	4 inches	3	1
	3 "	2	1
	2½ inches	2	1
	2 "	1	1

In order that the proper quantity of oakum may be driven all seams to be caulked are made tight at the bottom and open at surface. This is called allowing the seam.

The necessary seam for plank of any thickness may be found by drawing two lines, 10 inches long, so that they meet at one end, and are ½ inch apart at the other; if the thickness of plank be set off from the point where lines meet, the distance lines are apart at this place will be the open seam that must be allowed. The progressive manner of caulking is, by first driving wedge-like irons into the seams to open them on the surface. This operation is called raiming or reeming. After this, the spunyarn, white oakum or cotton, is driven, if any, and then the number of black threads, which are then hardened, or what is called horsed up; this is done by one man holding, in the seam upon the oakum, an iron, fixed in a handle, called the horse iron, and another driving upon it with a large mallet, called a beetle, that the oakum may be made as firm as possible and be below the outer surface of the plank. It is of importance, in order to give firmness to the caulking, and to prevent decay, that the threads be driven into the seam as far as possible, or driven home, and not choked, as is sometimes the case. The whole of the oakum driven should form a wedge and be what is called, well bottomed.

On Fig. 44 are shown men engaged in caulking outside planking seams of a vessel's bottom.

Inside Planking of a Vessel

8q⁵. *Ceiling*

This is the name given to planking that covers *inside* of the frames of a vessel. It begins below clamps and covers the entire inside of frames from clamps to keelson.

On Figs. 28, 43 and 43a methods of fastening the ceiling are clearly shown and on Fig. 42a is shown present-day method of ceiling a vessel which I will now describe.

Immediately next to keelson is laid the *limber strake,* which is a strake of ceiling placed in such a position that by removing portions of it access to limber chains or watercourses can be obtained. (See Fig. 28.)

Immediately next to limber strake begins the ceiling

Fig. 44

proper and this extends to just below turn of bilge where the bilge ceiling begins. The bilge ceiling is of thicker material than ceiling proper and extends up until curve of bilge is passed, when the thinner ceiling again begins and extends up to air course left directly under clamps.

Ceiling extends from bow to stern, is put on in strakes that fit tightly against one another, and is securely fastened to frames and filling, some of the fastenings going through both frames and outside planking. On Fig. 43b is shown interior view of a vessel with bottom ceiling in place.

8q⁶. *Fastening the Planking*

It is necessary to describe the fastenings both outside and inside (ceiling) planking at one time because many of the fastenings go through outer plank, frame, and inner plank. Correct fastening of planking is essential for strength, and not only must the fastenings be ample in number and of proper size, but they must be properly located and driven.

First I will call your attention to a most important detail of fastening frequently overlooked by shipbuilders of the present-day.

All plank fastenings are driven through holes bored with an auger. Up to within the last year or so these fastening holes were bored with hand-operated augers, and the regulations for proper sizes of holes (based upon experience) stipulated that holes should be bored ⅛ inch

Fig 43a. Laying Ceiling

(for 1-inch fastening) *smaller* than fastening. This insured that fastening would fit tightly into hole and hold properly after it was driven. This regulation for *hand-bored* fastening holes is absolutely sound and correct, but when it is applied to *machine-drilled* holes it is *incorrect* and results in fastenings being loose and insecure.

When a fastening hole is drilled with an auger attached to an air-driven tool *the auger should be one or two sizes SMALLER than the one used for boring for same sized fastening by hand.* The smaller size auger is necessary when a machine is used because the higher speed of rotation, coupled with the difficulty of holding auger perfectly vertical and steady, nearly always causes the hole to assume an oblong shape and to become slightly larger than size of auger.

Whenever a fastening hole is to be bored with a machine-operated auger use an auger one size smaller than is specified for hand-operated augers.

Two kinds of fastenings are used for connecting planking to the frame; *wood* (called treenails) and *metal* (copper, composition metal, or iron), and the fastenings can be spaced either single, double, or alternate single and double.

By single fastening is meant each strake having one fastening of each kind into each frame; by double fastening is meant each strake having two fastenings of each kind into each frame, and by alternate fastening is meant each strake having one fastening of each kind in every other frame and two fastenings of each kind into each frame between single fastened frames.

On Fig. 45 is shown sections of planking with single, double, and alternate fastenings through each strake. Before the advent of steel ships the larger wooden vessels were nearly always double fastened, medium-sized ones were double fastened above water and alternate fastened below, and the smaller ones were alternate fastened above water and single fastened below. This

practice was an excellent one and with this modification should be followed in these days: *Wherever fastenings of knees, clamps, shelf, pointers, or riders pass through frame and outer planking the planking fastenings should be only sufficient in number to draw planking to its position against frames.*

The reason for this modification is: The through fastenings of parts mentioned must have a clear passageway through frames and must have proper amount of solid wood surrounding them. If double fastenings of planking are driven in places where other fastenings must pass through, one of two things may happen,—either the additional fastenings will cut an excessive amount of wood from frames and thus weaken the frame, or else the fastenings of planking will interfere with knee and other additional fastenings.

It is well to bear in mind this important fact—*treenail* fastenings resist transverse strains better than metal, but the metal will better resist direct separation strains. It therefore is apparent that a wise combination of the two kinds of fastenings is most desirable.

As the inside planking (ceiling) is not laid at the same time that outside planking is a certain proportion of both outer and inner planking fastenings must be driven into frames only.

The usual manner of fastening is somewhat along these lines: The outer planking is first fastened with a certain number of metal fastenings that pass through

Fig. 43b. Edge Bolting Ceiling

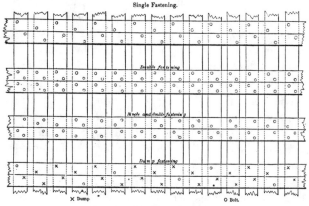

Fig. 45. Planking Fastenings

planking and into frames for about two-thirds of their depth, a certain number of treenail fastenings are then driven through outer planking and frames and wedged tight. These fastenings are only sufficient in number to securely hold planking in position until inner planking (ceiling) is wrought.

The ceiling is first fastened with a minimum number of short fastenings that only pass through ceiling and into frames. After ceiling is in place the planking fastenings that go through outer and inner planking and frame are put in, the metal ones being clenched and the wood ones wedged.

To fasten butts through bolts, treenails and short welts are used. Butts are usually cut upon the middle of a timber and are fastened with one treenail and one short bolt through the butt of each plank into butt timber (timber butt is cut on) and one through bolt, called a butt bolt, in timbers nearest to butt timber.

On Fig. 46 is shown a properly cut and fastened butt and below the illustration are given rules for spacing butts.

Now a few words about wedging treenails.

After treenails are driven their ends are cut off flush and wedged with hardwood wedges, the wedges serving the double purpose of expanding ends of treenails and thus increasing resistance to separation of the two or three pieces of material that the treenails fasten together; and of caulking the ends.

Very large treenails used to be caulked with three wedges forming a triangle, and small ones with two wedges crossing each other at right angles, but in these days the practice is to use the cross wedges on very large treenails and a single wedge on the smaller ones. Treenails *must* drive tight, meaning by this, be driven through holes that are somewhat smaller than the treenail. On Fig. 47 are shown a number of treenails ready to drive.

8r. The Clamps

The clamps are two or three thick planks extending the whole length of frame and located immediately under each tier of deck beams, their use being to help support

deck beams and add strength to the structure along point of joining of a deck with side framing.

In sailing vessels the deck beams very often rest directly upon clamps and are fastened to them and to frame of vessel with hanging knees. These knees are shown in outline on Fig. 28.

In ships driven by steam and in many of the larger sailing crafts the clamps form a backing for shelf on which the deck beams rest.

Each tier of beams has its clamps and shelf. (See Fig. 28.)

The upper edge of each set of clamps is usually located at proper height to allow deck beams to be let in about one inch, or if it is not intended to let beams in, the upper edge is placed high enough for beams to have a full bearing.

If maximum strength is desired clamps should be coaked to frames, each assemblage of clamps should be edge-bolted between timbers and butts should be scarphed; the scarphs being sufficiently long to extend over and fasten to three frames. All scarphs should be properly edge-bolted.

Clamps are usually first fastened to frames only, and after they are firmly set in their proper position additional fastenings that go through outer planking, frame and clamp, are driven from outside and clenched on clamp.

8r¹. *Air Course*

This is an opening left immediately under lowest clamp plank for the purpose of allowing air to circulate freely around the frames. (See Fig. 28.)

8s. The Shelf

This is the name given to a heavy continuous timber, or a combination of two or more timbers, that extends from bow to stern at each tier of deck beams and is fastened to inner face of upper clamps in a position that will allow deck beams to have a full width bearing on upper face of shelf.

On Fig. 42a the shelf is shown in position under a deck beam. Shelf timbers are usually scarphed in the same manner that clamps are, and are securely fastened to clamps, frames and outer planking.

The duty of a shelf is to resist strains tending to extend the vessel, to support deck beams and form a secure base for securing them to.

8s¹. *Shelf Fastenings*

Shelves are fastened in the same manner that clamps are and, in addition, they are fastened to clamps with metal fastenings driven through shelf and into at least two of the clamp timbers. (See Fig. 42a.)

8t. Deck Beams

Deck beams are horizontal timbers that extend across a vessel and support the decking. The ends of deck

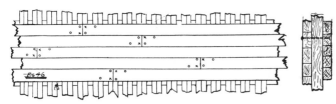

Fig. 46. Butt Fastenings

Name	Orlop Deck Beams	Lower Deck Beams	Upper Deck Beams	Quart'd Deck and Forec'tle Beams
Length of scarph	8 feet	7—8 ft.	7—8 ft.	8—7 ft.
Depth of lip	3 inches	3 inches	3 inches	3 inches
Bolts in lip	2 of 7/8"	2 of 7/8"	2 of 3/4"	2 of 5/8"
Bolts in middle	3 of 1¼"	3 of 1¼"	3 of 1"	3 of 7/8"
Through Ends	4 of 1½"	4 of 1¾"	4 of 1¼"	4 of 1¼"

beams rest upon shelf and clamps and are strengthened by means of hanging knees (vertical knees), one end of which fastens to beams and the other to clamps, ceiling, and frames at side. In addition to these hanging knees a certain number of horizontal ones, called *lodge knees,* are fastened at designated positions throughout length of vessel. On Fig. 28 the vertical knees are shown in place, and on Fig. 27 is shown some lodge knees.

Along center line of vessel the deck beams are supported by pillars or stanchions that have their lower ends firmly resting on and secured to keelson and their upper ends secured to a longitudinal deck stringer and to the beams. Separate longitudinal stringers and stanchions are fitted between each tier of beams, and the stanchions of each tier are always located immediately over one another. Thus the whole center line of deck framing is supported and tied longitudinally and to the keel structure.

In some vessels the ends of stanchions are kneed to deck frames and to keelson, and in others they are secured with deck straps. (See Fig. 50 for method of using strap at upper end and knee at keelson.)

Sometimes a system of supports and diagonal fore-and-aft bracing, or trussing, is used between orlop deck beams and keelson, and sometimes a fore-and-aft longitudinal bulkhead with openings through it, at stated intervals, extends from keelson to orlop deck beams. The supports above orlop deck are in both these methods of construction stanchions fitted as already described.

In some steam-driven vessels longitudinal stringers are located in line with the outboard sides of hatch openings and practically form a part of hatch framing. In vessels constructed in this manner it is usual to place sister keelsons immediately below these side stringers and to erect stanchions between the sister keelsons and longitudinal stringers.

In many cases it is necessary to join two or more pieces of timber together to form a deck beam. When this is done the beam is termed a two or three-piece beam and the scarphing is done in one of the ways shown on Plate VIIe.

When laying out a scarph for a deck beam it is essential that length of scarph be sufficient to insure that joint (scarph) has ample strength when fastenings are in place.

Below I give a brief list of suitable dimensions for beam scarphs and fastenings of beams about 40 feet in length.

8t¹. *Fastening the Knees and Deck Beams*

Deck beams are fastened to shelf with bolts that pass through beams into shelf and are riveted along underside of shelf.

The hanging knees are fitted to underside of beams and to side of vessel and fastened with through rivets driven at varying angles. On Fig. 50 knee fastenings are clearly shown. When designating parts of hanging knees the proper terms to use are:

The Arm.—Meaning by this the end of knee fitted against beam.

The Body.—Meaning the portion of end of knee fitted against clamps and side of vessel.

Lodge or lodging knees usually have their arms fitted against side of beam and body fitted against clamp. The fastenings of lodge knee arms are bolts that pass through arm of knee and beams, and of body bolts that pass through knee, clamp and frame.

Fastenings of knees are designated as being either in-and-out, or fore-and-aft, depending upon whether they are driven through side of vessel or through the beam. Those used to fasten body of knee to side are termed in-and-out bolts and those used to fasten arm of knee to beams are termed fore-and-aft.

There are usually from five to seven in-and-out bolts

Fig. 47. Treenails Ready to Drive Into Ceiling Frame and Planking

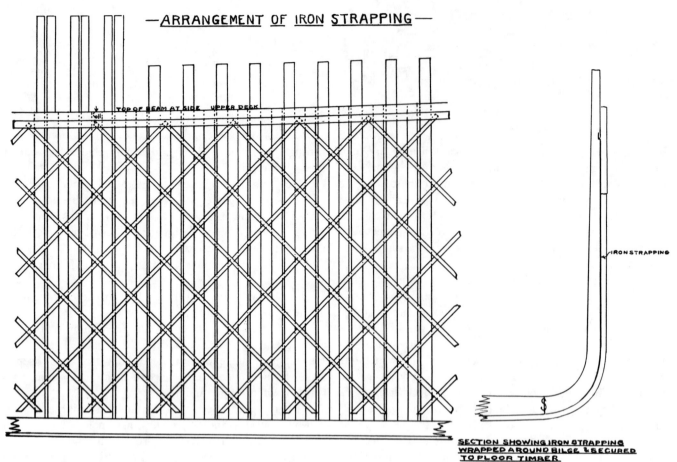

Fig. 49. Diagonal Straps

used in a hanging knee, each bolt being driven at an angle that will cause it to take the *shortest* distance between knee and outside of planking. All but one or two of these bolts are driven from the outside and clenched on inside, and all in-and-out fastenings are driven, and knee secured to side of vessel, before the fore-and-aft fastenings are driven and secured. This is done to insure that knee fits snug against side of vessel.

The fore-and-aft fastenings should consist of from three to five bolts passing through both knee and beam.

The in-and-out bolts in lodging knees should never be fewer than one in each timber, and the knees should be sufficiently long to cross at least four timbers. If an exceptionally strong job of work is desired the fore-and-aft bolt fastenings should be reinforced by using circular coaks. On Table VIII[1] is entered the minimum number of pairs of hanging knees to use in vessels of named tonnage.

TABLE VIII[1]

NUMBER OF HANGING KNEES

Tons	To Hold Beams Pairs	To Upper Deck Beams Pairs	Tons	To Hold Beams Pairs	To Upper Deck Beams Pairs
150	—	4	600	10	14
200	4	6	650	10	15
250	5	7	700	11	16
300	6	8	750	11	17
350	7	9	800	12	18
400	8	10	900	13	20
450	8	11	1000	14	22
500	9	12	1100	15	24
550	9	13	1350	17	26

8t[2]. *The Framing of Decks*

The framing of deck consists of athwartships beams, half-beams, longitudinal carlings and ledges. Dimensions of beams vary with their length. On Table VIII[2] is given dimensions of beams, and method of framing is clearly shown on Figs. 27, 28, 42a and 50.

In general one half-sized beam is placed between each two main beams except in spaces between beams that form the hatchways and around masts, where there are generally two half-beams placed between each two beams.

All deck beams should be crowned, those of the upper decks having the greatest amount of crown.

Deck beams are crowned because the crown causes water to quickly flow to the waterways, where it passes clear through the scuppers and in addition to this transverse strength is increased by crowning beams, especially if, as is sometimes done, the beams are crowned while being placed in position.

It is advantageous to let ends of beams into shelf in the manner shown on Fig. 42a.

8t[3]. *Framing of a Hatchway*

Fig. 27 clearly illustrates the proper way to frame a hatchway of a medium-sized vessel. In larger vessels the center line longitudinal deck stringer mentioned in paragraph 8th extends longitudinally across hatchway

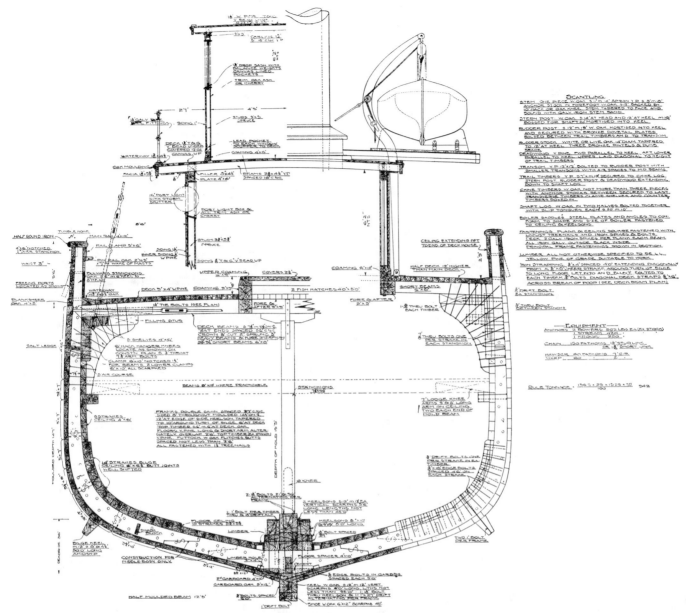

Fig. 50. Construction Plan of Section of Steam Trawler by Cox & Stevens

practically dividing it into two portions, and when the side longitudinal stringers are used they form a support for the coaming.

8t⁴. *Framing of Mast Partners*

Mast partners is the name given to the framing around hole in deck through which mast passes. The framing must be strong and solid because it has to withstand the strains of both mast and bitts that are generally placed close to a mast in sailing vessels.

On Fig. 27 is shown the usual method of framing a mast partner of a sailing vessel.

8t⁵. *Framing of Decks Around Stem and Stern*

At stem the deck framing of each deck terminates in a solid block of wood, or a natural knee, called a breasthook. This breasthook is securely fastened to stem and apron and to the clamps it rests against, the fastenings

through clamps passing through knightheads, frame and planking. The tops of breasthooks are rounded to the same crown that has been given to deck beams.

On Fig. 51 is shown details of forward deck framing and on Fig. 52 is shown some wood and steel knees used when framing a vessel.

Around the stern it is necessary to have solid wood to receive the deck and fastening. If the vessel has a transom stern the upper transom is always shaped and rabbeted to receive ends of deck planks and their fastenings. If an elliptical stern the upper piece of stern framing is shaped to receive deck ends and their fastenings.

8t⁶. *Framing of Decks under Deck Winches, Capstans and Anchor Engine*

It is always necessary to strengthen the deck frame at and around locations of deck winches, anchor windlass and capstans. This is done by filling in between the deck

beams and supporting this filling by bolting longitudinal
planks to the deck beams it crosses. The filling and
planks should extend some distance outside the space that
will be occupied by deck windlass or other piece of equipment, and of course the filling must cover the entire
space between under side of deck and upper surface of
the supporting planks. The deck is laid on this filling
and after deck is finished and caulked wood foundation
timbers are fitted on deck, the upper surface of these being
arranged to receive the holding down bolts of windlass
or other piece of equipment.

When the piece of equipment is very heavy supporting
stanchions are added under the deck beams.

8u. THE WATERWAYS

The waterways are pieces of timber that rest on deck
beams and fit in angle made by deck beams and side of
vessel. Waterways extend from forward to after ends
of each deck, are worked to the shape of inside of vessel
and are securely fastened to deck beams and shelf or
clamps beneath the beams; they should be edge-bolted into
frames.

In some vessels filling-in pieces are fitted to fill the
space between shelf and top of beams and from side of
ship to where inner edge of waterway will be located.
When this is done the waterways can be fastened to shelf
between beams and thus additional strength is gained.

Waterways are always made of thicker material than
the deck, and scarphs of waterways should always be
vertical, have nibbed ends, or be hooked, and be edge-
bolted.

On Fig. 28 is shown a detail of waterway construc-

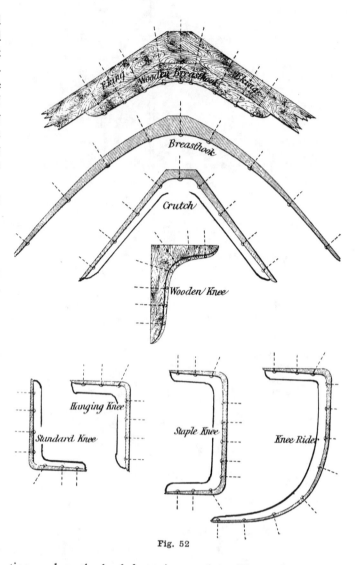

Fig. 52

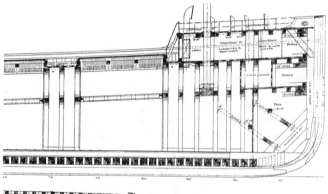

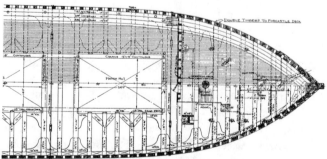

Fig. 51. Bow Framing

tion and method of fastening, and on Figs. 26, 53, and
54 waterways are shown fitted in place alongside frames.

8u¹. *Lock or Thick Strakes*

These are strakes of decking that adjoin the waterways. They are thicker than deck proper and are joggled
over beams. This joggle is clearly shown on Fig. 42a.
These strakes extend from bow to stern and are fastened
vertically with two fastenings through every beam, and
horizontally with one bolt in every second timber. (Note
it is usual to leave room for these fastenings by omitting
a fastening from every frame to which thick strakes will
be fastened.)

8u². *Decking*

The upper or main deck planking should be composed
of clear straight-grained material put on in greatest
obtainable lengths. Deck planks are usually worked fore-
and-aft and the laying is begun at or near to center line
of vessel. The ends of deck planks that butt against
thick or lock strakes of waterways should be let into
thick strake about 2 inches, thus eliminating a feather
edge and giving a good seam for caulking. On Fig. 55
the ends of deck planks are shown let into thick strake

Fig. 53. Deck Framing and Waterways

of waterway. Deck planks are laid with seams for caulking and are fastened to beams with at least two spikes into each beam.

Butts are square cut on center of a beam and should

Fig. 54. Showing Waterways in Main Deck Forward of Auxiliary Schooner

be bolted. Rules for spacing butts of deck planks and caulking seams conform to those laid down for outer planking of frames.

TABLE VIII[2]

SIDING AND MOULDING OF BEAMS

Length of Beam Amidships Ft.	Hold Beams		Deck Beams	
	Sided and Moulded In.	Moulded at Ends In.	Sided and Moulded In.	Moulded at Ends In.
10	....	....	4½	3¾
11	....	....	5	4
12	....	....	5¼	4¼
13	....	....	5½	4½
14	....	....	5¾	4¾
15	8	6¾	6¼	5¼
16	8½	7	6½	5½
17	8¾	7½	6¾	5½
18	9¼	7¾	7	5¾
19	9½	8	7¼	6
20	10	8½	7½	6¼
21	10¼	8¾	7¾	6½
22	10½	9	8	6½
23	11	9¼	8¼	6¾
24	11¼	9½	8½	7
25	11¾	9¾	8½	7¼
26	12	10	8¾	7¼
27	12¼	10¼	9	7½
28	12½	10½	9	7½
29	12¾	10¾	9¼	7¾
30	13	11	9½	8
31	13¼	11¼	9½	8
32	13½	11½	9¾	8¼
33	13¾	11½	10	8¼
34	14	11¾	10	8½
35	14¼	12	10¼	8½
36	14½	12¼	10¼	8½
37	14¾	12½	10½	8¾
38	15	12½	10½	8¾
39	15¼	12¾	10½	9
40	15½	13	10¾	9

WATERWAY

DECKING

FIG. 55

Fig. 55. Ends of Deck Let Into Waterways

Chapter IX
Building Slips and Launching Ways

9a. BUILDING SLIP FOUNDATION

The ground upon which a vessel is built is termed the building *slip,* or *berth,* and the fixed timbers that carry vessel from building slip into the water are called *launching ways*.

Both building slip and ways must have a firm foundation and be laid at proper inclinations; and one of the most important details in connection with laying out a shipyard is correct planning and construction of building slips and ways.

The first essential is that the foundation be sufficiently solid to bear the maximum load that will have to be carried, and this solidity must be *alike* for the entire length and width of building slip and ways.

The universally adopted and most practical method of getting the necessary solidity of foundation in a small shipyard is to drive a sufficient number of rows of piles into the ground at proper locations to support keel blocking, ways and staging, spacing them as close as necessary to attain the desired end. The tops of the piles are then cut off at proper height and capped with timbers, placed at right angles to launching direction, extending sufficiently far out each side of keel position to cover keel and launching way piles and allow all bilge, bottom, and staging supports to be placed on them.

When constructing a building slip of this kind the ground is leveled to some desirable inclination and piles driven and cut off to inclination selected for slip, then the athwartships caps are placed over piles and fastened and slip filled in with cinders, or other suitable material, to a proper height to make a good platform for the men working under vessel during construction.

Very often the portion of slip from land end down to where stern of vessel will be when being built is filled in level with top of caps, then from this point to a little below the low-water level the slip is floored over for about three-quarters of its width. From the low-water level the slip extends into water a sufficient distance to give the required launching depth of water over ends of launching ways, this portion of slip consisting of rows of piles, to act as bearers for launching ways, cut off at proper inclination and height and capped longitudinally. Cross capping is not generally used here, because it is likely to interfere with launching of vessel. Fig. 56 shows plan of such a building slip.

9b. INCLINATION OF SLIP

While the contour of ground upon which a building slip is placed, the length of ground available for the land

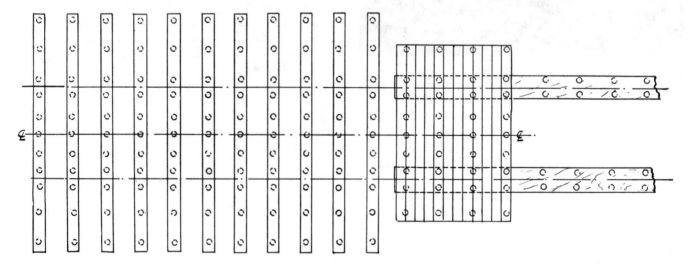

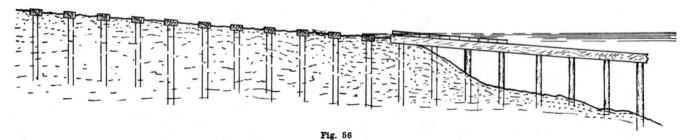

Fig. 56

Fig. 57. Steel and Concrete Building Slips, N. Y. Shipbuilding Comp any, Camden, N. J

end of slip, depth of water at end of slipway, and width of channel available for free launching purposes, are things that must be carefully considered when selecting the most suitable inclination for building slip, the inclination that keel will be laid at, and inclination of launching ways necessary to insure a successful launching of the largest and smallest vessels likely to be built upon the slip must also be considered as a part of the problem.

The nearer the longitudinal inclination of slip is to the average inclination of launching ways the better. An inclination of about 4° to the horizon seems to be excellent for slips that are used for the construction of vessels of moderate tonnage and length.

In reality the inclination of slip floor is a matter of minor importance so long as the inclination is one that will give a good working platform for men and permit proper shoring and securing of keel blocks and launching ways.

On slips constructed in manner described, the keel blocking and launching ways are set up for vessel and arranged at inclinations that are considered most suitable.

A more costly kind of building slip is constructed in this manner:

After the ground is piled in manner already explained the piles are cut off at, or near to, the average launching inclination and sufficiently low down to bring top of cap timbers a few inches below the desired level of building slip floor. The cap timbers are then used as supports for a flooring which is laid, longitudinally, over that portion of slip, except its center where keel will come, that is above the low-water level.

The longitudinal planking of slip floor that comes near places where launching ways will be laid is generally made out of much heavier material than floor proper and forms a permanent longitudinal stringer, or foundation, on which the launching ways can be laid.

The portion of slip below low-water point is constructed in manner already described.

A still more costly and permanent style of building slip is one constructed on concrete foundations set on piles cut off some distance below the level of ground.

Slips constructed in this manner are generally covered with a steel structure and fitted with traveling overhead crane for handling material used in the construction of vessels.

Fig. 57 is an excellent illustration of a slip of this kind.

Thousands of Piles Are Driven Into the Marsh on Which to Build the Piers. The Picture on the Left Shows the Piling For Pier and That on the Right Shows Pier Completed and Ready For Use

In all cases when laying out a building slip it is very necessary to carefully plan for economical moving and placing of construction material in position on vessel.

For a small shipyard one of the most economical methods of doing this is to lay rails on one or both sides of slip and from slip to places in yard where the material will be converted and got ready for erection. Then by using a traveling hoist of sufficient capacity the heaviest piece of material can be moved and lifted into position without having to use costly hand labor. If a method of this kind is used, level runways for the rails on which hoist will travel must be erected each side of slip and sufficient space allowed between adjacent slips to permit hoist to pass between the vessels and be properly operated.

The number of piles required for a slip will vary with nature of ground and weight of vessel to be carried and should be carefully calculated before commencing work.

9c. Information About Piles

Piles are made from trunks of trees and should be straight and not less than 6 inches in diameter for light foundation or 9 inches for heavy ones. The woods generally used for piles in the Northern States are oak, spruce, hemlock, Norway pine, Georgia pine, and occasionally elm, gum and bass wood. In Southern States oak, Georgia pine and cypress is extensively used. While there does not appear to be much difference in the durability of these woods under water, oak makes the most satisfactory piles and next to it the ones made of the hardest wood. This is especially so if the ground is hard and driving is difficult.

All piles should be cut from growing timber, should be butt cuts and only have bark peeled and knots trimmed. It is probably best to remove the bark though there is some difference of opinion on this point. The specified sizes are diameters at stated distance from ends, and length. Oak piles should be of either white, burr or post oaks; they should not have over 2 inches of sap wood and should be at least 9 inches in diameter at 6 feet from butt for piles less than 28 feet and 12 inches in diameter for piles 30 feet and over and the taper should be uniform and gradual from butt to top, the top being not less than five-eighths of greatest diameter.

Norway and tamarack piles should not be less than 10 inches diameter for a 30 foot, 14 inches for a 36 foot, and 16 inches for a 40 foot at butt.

Cedar piles 30 feet long should not be less than 14 inches in diameter at butt.

Piles are prepared for driving by sawing ends square and pointing the lower end, or by capping the upper end and shoeing the lower should the hardness of ground and length of piles warrant doing this.

In soft ground a square-ended pile seems to drive better and straighter than one that has been pointed.

When driving into compact soil, such as gravel or stiff clay, the lower end of pile should be pointed and shod with iron.

And in cases when the ground is so hard that pile drives less than 6 inches at each blow the head should be capped with a ring of iron to prevent its splitting.

The usual method of driving piles is by a succession of blows given with a block of cast iron which slides up and down between long uprights mounted on a machine called a pile driver. The machine is moved over the place where pile is to be driven, the pile is placed under hammer, small end down, and held there while the machine lifts the weight (called the hammer) to required distance above pile and then lets it drop on pile. The hammer is raised by steam power and dropped by releasing a catch when it has reached the desired height.

The weight of hammers used for driving piles for slipways is between 1,200 and 2,000 ℔ and the fall varies from 5 feet to 20 feet or over.

When driving piles care must be taken to keep them plumb and to regulate the drop of hammer to suit nature of soil. When soil is mud penetration becomes small. the

The Picture on the Left Shows the Ground on Which Shipways Now Stand, That on the Right Shows the Shipways Completed.

fall should be lessened and blows given in rapid succession. When a pile refuses to drive before it has reached the required depth it should be cut off and another pile driven close alongside.

A pile that has been driven to a depth of 20 feet over and then refuses to move under several blows of the hammer falling about 15 feet can be considered satisfactory.

The most reliable way to ascertain the carrying power of piles is by actual experiment with piles driven into the ground where the slip is to be built. This experiment can be made by driving about two piles a selected distance apart, connecting them together and building a rigid platform on top. Then by loading platform until the weight begins to sink piles further into the ground the maximum carrying weight per square foot of surface, or per pile, will be ascertained. This carrying weight must be in excess of the requirements.

The carrying weight value of piling can be determined with a sufficient degree of accuracy for ordinary conditions by making use of this formula:

$$\text{Safe carrying load in pounds} = \frac{2\,W\,H}{S + 1}$$

W = Weight of hammer in pounds.

H = fall of hammer in feet.

S = average penetration of pile in ground during last five blows.

Assuming that a 1,000-℔ hammer is used and that average penetration for last five blows is 6 inches and fall is 15 feet, the safe load for pile is 4,286 ℔.

$$\frac{2 \times 1,000 \times 15}{6 + 1} = \frac{30,000}{7} = 4,286 \text{ ℔.}$$

This rule is a fairly accurate one to use when average conditions prevail, but it must be recognized that nature of soil largely determines length of pile necessary.

The following table of bearing value of piles in various kinds of soils will prove of value as a guide:

Nature of Soil	Length of Pile in Feet	Average Dia. in Inches Whole Length. Inches	Average Penetration in In. Last Five Blows. Inches	Load in Tons Pile Carried. Tons
Mud	30	8	2	6
Soft earth	30	8	1½	7
Soft clay	30	8	1	9
Quicksand	30	8	½	12
Firm earth	30	8	½	12
Sand	20	8	Solid	18
Gravel	15	8	Solid	18

It is safe to say this: No pile should be less than 5 inches in diameter at small end and 10 inches at large for 20 feet length of driving, or 12 inches for 30 feet, and no pile should be expected to carry more than 18 tons, even under the best conditions of ground and location.

Piles for foundations of building slips should not be spaced closer than 2 feet 6 inches. If spaced closer than this there is danger of the ground being broken up and holding power of adjacent piles lessened. A good plan is to use two, three, or four rows of piles under center of slip to act as supports for keel blocks; two, three, or four more closely spaced rows each side to form supports for launching ways, and additional intermediate and outside piles if ground is soft and weight to be carried is excessive.

Of course the cross caps will connect these rows of piles and make a level and evenly supported athwartships bearing surface for keel blocks and launching ways.

The longitudinal spacing will depend somewhat upon weight to be carried and length of vessel that will be built on ship, but it should always be remembered that spacing must be sufficiently close to allow two cross caps to be used as supports for the lower pieces of each keel block in cases where blocking has to be sufficiently high to warrant cribbing it.

9d. LENGTH AND WIDTH OF BUILDING SLIPS

The length of that portion of the building slip that is above high-water mark should be at least one and a half times the length of longest vessel that will be constructed on slip; and there must always be sufficient dis-

Fig. 58.   Three Wooden Ships That Were Launched From the L. H. Shattuck, Inc., Yard at Portsmouth, N. H.

Another View of the Shattuck-Built Ships and the Long Line of Building Ways at Portsmouth, N. H.

tance between stern-post and water to allow vessel to attain a safe launching velocity before it reaches a depth of water sufficient to reduce speed to a point where the slightest obstruction might cause vessel to stick on ways. The distance that longitudinal underwater portion of slip extends out must be sufficient to give firm support to launching ways until vessel becomes water-borne, or "tips." Therefore determine launching draught of the largest vessel likely to be built on slip, and have the ends of slipway extend out a sufficient distance from shore to give more than the required depth of water when tipping occurs. The tipping can be considered to occur when the longitudinal center of vessel is over ends of way. Fig. 56 outer end of landing ways.

The width of building slip must be sufficient to permit the building of the widest vessel, the erection of proper staging, and the handling of material on each side.

Four important width measures must be selected.

1st.—The width of blocking necessary to support keel.

2d.—The width required for launching ways and distance the center of ways will be out from center line of keel.

3d.—The extreme width of slip necessary for erecting staging around vessel.

4th.—The additional width required for handling material along sides of slip.

The first can be considered to be about 4 feet, therefore, piles should be sufficiently closely spaced throughout the whole length of slip, for 2 feet each side of its center line, to carry all the weight that must be supported on keel blocks during construction.

Launching ways are generally placed about one-third extreme breadth of a vessel apart. So consider that one-sixth the width of widest vessel likely to be built on slip as distance that center of launching ways supporting piles must be out from center line of slip and have one line of piles driven along this line, two lines of piles outside of it, and three or four lines inside of it. This will give six or seven lines of piles for supporting launching ways and a sufficiently wide support to take care of ordinary variations of width of launching ways.

Fig. 3 going down the ways.

The width necessary to erect staging around vessel should be added to extreme width of vessel, and the width required for handling material should be measured from outside of staging supports.

Always leave ample room between adjacent slips for the operation of hoist and handling the largest pieces of material.

9e.   INCLINATION OF KEEL BLOCKING

Keel blocking is the name given to the blocks upon which a vessel's keel is laid and weight of vessel carried until it is transferred to the launching ways immediately before launching. The height of keel blocks must be such that bottom of vessel's keel and frame will be sufficiently high above the ground of slip, or slip floor, for the workmen to do the necessary construction work, and the inclination relative to slip and launching ways must be such that the forefoot of vessel will clear the lower end of slip by at least 10 inches when vessel is being launched. Bear in mind that the inclination of top of keel blocks determines the inclination keel will have during launching, and that the keel of vessel does not have to be at the same inclination as launching ways or building slip floor.

To determine the required height and inclination of keel blocks proceed in this manner:

Lay out on a piece of drawing paper, to proper scale, lines to indicate correct length and inclination of slip floor and inclination that you intend the launching ways to have. Next mark points on these lines where forefoot, midship section and stern-post of vessel will be located during construction. The height that keel of vessel must be above ground to insure ample working space under vessel for the men who will do the construction work must next be determined, and it is best to determine this height for the midship section position because that will be flattest and widest point of bottom of vessel.

Having determined the height keel must be above slip floor at midship section, measure off this height on drawing, and also measure off at lower end of slip a distance of at least 10 inches above the floor of slip line.

A line drawn through these two points will indicate the correct inclination for keel blocking measured in a straight line, and if the bottom of keel does not extend

Fig. 59. Canibas, 10,000-Ton Freighter Launched From the Texas S. S. Company's Yard at Bath, Me.

below this line you can be sure that there will be ample clearance above slip during launching.

To insure that you understand this explanation I have drawn Fig. 60.

On this illustration I show a longitudinal outline of vessel. The line B.L. is drawn horizontal and only for the purpose of insuring that inclined lines are marked at correct inclinations to the horizontal.

The line S.S. indicates top of slip floor and is drawn at correct slip inclination.

The line W.W. indicates inclination of launching ways and is drawn at their proper inclination and height relative to line S.S.

The line S.K.F. indicates selected height and inclination of keel blocks, S being the location of stern, K the midship section position, and F the position of forefoot of vessel during construction. The line S.K.F. is continued past end of launching ways and if it nowhere falls below the line W.W. and the line W.W. is nowhere nearer to S.S. than 10 inches, the forefoot of vessel will clear end of building slip when vessel is launched. By

measuring from S.S. to S.K.F. at proper intervals height of keel blocks to a straight line can be ascertained.

9f. KEEL BLOCKING

During construction the entire weight of a vessel is carried on a row of temporary building blocks placed immediately under keel at the proper inclination. These keel supporting blocks are generally placed about 4 feet apart, and each block is built of pieces of timber placed one on top of another until the desired height is obtained. When the vessel is not exceedingly heavy, or the keel blocks not excessively high each keel block can consist of pieces of timber placed on top of each other, the lowest one being placed immediately on a cross cap of slip foundation; but when the vessel is heavy or keel blocks have to be erected to a height that would make

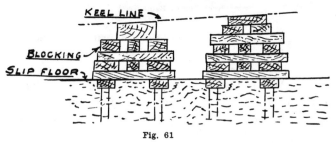

Fig. 61

it difficult to keep single blocking in position, cribbing is resorted to and each keel block is placed on the center of a crib of timber resting on at least two of the cross timbers of the slip foundation and built up of pieces of timber laid alternately lengthways and athwartships. The whole structure of each keel block must be securely fastened together, and as all of the keel-supporting blocking must be removed before vessel can be launched, the blocks or cribbing must be erected in such a manner that they can be removed from below the keel after the entire construction work is completed.

Fig. 61 shows illustration of keel blocking set up on a building slip, a portion of the blocking being cribbed.

9g. LAUNCHING APPARATUS

The launching apparatus may be divided into two principal parts—the launching ways and the cradle or

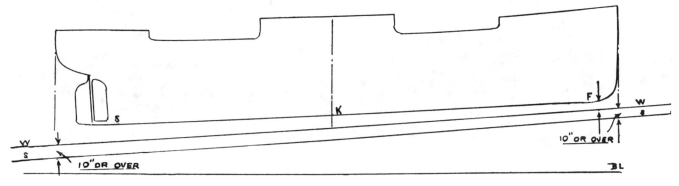

Fig. 60

Keel Blocks Being Laid

temporary framework which slides down the launching ways and supports vessel during its movement down the ways. The launching ways consist of two continuous runways of hard wood (oak, maple or hard pine), planed perfectly smooth and laid at such an inclination that vessel will move freely down the ways as soon as she is free to do so. If the inclination of launching ways is greater than inclination of building slip floor, the ways must be securely supported on blocking or cribbing placed on top of slip foundation timbers. Of course the launching ways must be securely fastened and shored to prevent them moving sideways or lengthways during launching.

The determining factors for inclination are:

1st.—The weight of vessel. The smaller the weight the greater the inclination should be.

2d.—The speed in feet per second that vessel is wanted to move at during launching. The available width of channel and depth of water where vessel will take the water must be carefully considered and a launching speed selected that will be sufficiently great to insure that vessel will take water properly and not so great as to cause vessel to travel too great a distance after she is water-borne.

In practice it has been found that one-half inch to a foot is a dangerously slow inclination for even the largest vessels.

Five-eighths of an inch to the foot will give a moderate and easily controlled safe launching speed for vessels weighing between 800 and 1,200 tons.

An inclination of three-quarters of an inch to a foot will give a good, safe, free launching speed for moderate weight vessel, or a speed that will be sufficient to insure freedom from danger of sticking, and if there is sufficient width of channel to allow this inclination it is an excellent one to select.

Seven-eighths of an inch to a foot will deliver a vessel into the water at a high rate of travel and should not be used except in cases when it is necessary that vessel move very fast, or there is danger of the weight of vessel forcing the lubricating grease out from between the launching and sliding ways.

The following particulars of launching speeds will prove of value as a guide:

TABLE OF LAUNCHING DATA

Length of Vessel in Feet	Launching Weight in Tons	Inclination of Launching Ways per Foot Inches	Launching Speed Feet per Second
200	250	5/8	12*
225	350	3/4	15
250	560	9/16	15
275	675	5/8	16
310	875	5/8	17
325	1,200	9/16	16
350	1,800	9/16	18

*Too slow.

A velocity of 12 feet per second is very slow; one of about 15 feet per second is a good speed to use in cases where it is desired to control the launching or stop vessel gently; 16 to 18 feet per second is an excellent speed for use when width of launching channel is sufficient to allow vessel to move a little distance out before being stopped.

Schooner G. A. Somerville, Designed by Cox & Stevens, Ready For Launching

Fig. 62

Schooner G. A. Somerville Afloat

Above 18 feet per second should not be used unless there is ample room for launching or it is necessary to have vessel move very swiftly down the ways.

9h. BREADTH OF SURFACE OF LAUNCHING WAYS

The width of surface of launching ways must always be proportioned to weight of vessel because the whole of launching weight of vessel must be carried on launching ways, and if weight per unit of surface is too great the lubricating materials placed between launching and sliding ways will be forced out and vessel may stick on ways.

The width of launching ways should be such that maximum pressure on each square foot of surface that is beneath the sliding ways does not exceed 2½ tons.

Suppose, for instance, that launching weight of a certain vessel is 800 tons, the length of launching cradle surface that will bear on ways is 200 feet, and we desire that pressure per square foot during launching does not exceed 2 tons.

As there are two launching ways the weight each must support is 400 tons, and as length of each sliding way is 200 feet a surface of 2 feet is sufficient to carry the weight without exceeding the named pressure per square foot.

9i. DISTANCE TO PLACE LAUNCHING WAYS APART

A distance of about one-third the extreme breadth of vessel from center to center of ways, measured at their upper end, will give excellent results for vessels of ordinary form of cross section. The lower end of ways must be 2 or 3 inches further apart than the upper ends, this increase of distance being necessary to take care of the slight spreading of cradle that occurs when weight of vessel is transferred from keel blocks to cradle, and to insure that the cradle will move freely down the ways.

In addition to this, the upper surfaces of the launching ways should be inclined inwards about ½ inch to a foot for the purpose of reducing the danger of ways being forced outwards when weight is transferred to them.

When a vessel moves along the launching ways there is always a tendency to slide sideways, as well as towards the water, the side tendency being due to the outward pressure on bilge ways which is always present, though not dangerous unless it should happen that one of the launching ways is placed slightly higher than the other or the bilge blocking of cradle is not wedged up alike on both sides. Perfection in these matters cannot be obtained, so, by giving the ways a slight inclination of surface inward, and spreading them a little at the lower

Fig. 63. Launching of a Motorship at the St. Helens Yards, Near Portland, Ore. Another One Hundred and Fifty of These 3,000-Ton Vessels Have Been Ordered. They Are Fitted With Heavy-Oil Engines

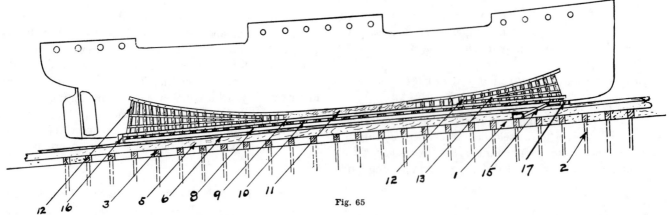

Fig. 65

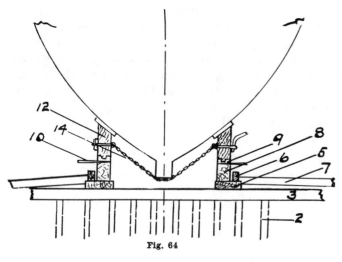

Fig. 64

ends, danger from these two causes is reduced to a minimum.

I will now illustrate and explain the launching apparatus used when launching a moderately sized vessel stern first.

Fig. 64 shows a cross section of launching apparatus placed in position under vessel. I have selected a section through one of the forward sections and show the vessel resting on cradle.

Fig. 65 shows longitudinal view of same vessel and one side of cradle in position ready to wedge up.

9j. Descriptive Explanation of Figs. 64 and 65

No. 1 indicates top of slip floor (already described).

No. 2 indicates supporting piles (already described).

No. 3 indicates athwartships caps placed on piles (already described).

No. 4, keel blocking upon which vessel rests during construction (already described).

No. 5. *Launching Ways* placed in position for launching.

No. 6. *Launching Ribbands* that run full length of launching ways to prevent the sliding, or bilge, ways from sliding sideways. These ribbands are strips of oak or hard wood bolted to launching ways. The butts of ribbands should not coincide with butts of launching ways.

No. 7. *Ribband Shores* placed at frequent intervals along outside of launching ways. Their use is to hold launching ways in place and prevent the ribbands being torn off. Note that one end of shores rests partly against ribband and partly against launching way, and the other is firmly braced against side of slip or piles driven into ground for that purpose.

The abovenamed pieces form the lower line of supports and are the fixed portion of the launching apparatus.

The upper, or movable, portion of the launching apparatus forms a cradle for the vessel to rest in and a carriage that will glide smoothly along the launching ways and convey vessel from the slip to the water.

No. 8. *Sliding, or Bilge, Ways.* These are oak, or yellow pine logs that rest on launching ways. Two or more logs are required on each launching way, and the surface that rests on launching ways must be planed perfectly smooth, and ends of each log slightly rounded to prevent their catching in launching ways should there be a slight irregularity at any joint. The pieces of sliding ways butt against each other and are usually fastened together with rope, or chain lashings passed through holes bored in ends of each piece. The sliding ways form a base for the cradle upon which the whole weight of vessel is carried while being launched. The length and width of sliding ways must be such that pressure on their under surface does not exceed 2½ tons per square foot. The sliding ways must be slightly longer than cradle and should not be less than three-quarters of the length of vessel. The lubricating material is placed between launching and bilge ways. Note that when vessel rests on cradle the outer edge of bilge ways does not bear hard against the launching ribbands. There is about ¾ inch between.

No. 9. *Sole Piece.* Planks of hard wood that extend from end to end of cradle to form a bearing surface for the large wedges that are used to raise vessel off keel blocks immediately before launching. The sole piece planks are fitted so that when their inner edge rests firmly upon the sliding ways the outer edge is about ¾ inch open. This opening is for the purpose of giving a good bearing surface for the wedges. The sole piece planks are made the width sliding ways.

Fig. 66. Coyote, Wooden Ship Built by the Foundation Company. She Is 281 Ft. Long and Is the First of a Big Fleet Building at This Company's Plant on the Passaic River

No. 10. *Slices,* or *Large Wedges,* placed between sliding ways and sole piece planks.

No. 11. *Packing* or *Filling,* that fills space from top of sole piece plank to bilge along the middle length of vessel. The quantity and length of this filling depends upon shape of vessel. This filling is the width of sole plank.

No. 12. *Poppets* are upright pieces of timber placed abaft and before the packing. The packing extends forward and aft to points where the distance between bilge and sole plank becomes too great for the use of solid packing. From these points bilge of vessel is supported by means of logs of timber, called poppets, which are placed about 15 inches apart and stand upright or at a slight rake. The lower ends of poppets rest upon the sole planks and their upper ends against planks that are fitted snugly against the vessel's planking, and both ends of poppets are securely fastened to these planks and held in position by cleats, bolts and tenons. You will note that the extreme forward and after poppets stand at a rake. This helps to resist the upsetting tendency.

No. 13. *Poppet Ribbands.* The poppets are held together, fastened to the packing, and braced longitudinally by pieces of planks called poppet ribbands. One is generally placed near bottom and one near top of poppets, though when poppets are short a single wide ribband is sufficient. The ribbands extend well onto the planking, are let into both filling and poppets and securely fastened

with bolts, thus tying filling and poppets together and making one firm structure, longitudinally, of each side of cradle.

No. 14. *Poppet Chains, or Lashings.* To prevent the upper ends of poppets working outwards when weight of vessel is transferred to cradle, chains are passed under the keel of vessel, one end of each chain being fastened to a poppet on one side of vessel and the other end fastened to corresponding poppet on the other side. The number and size of chains to use depends upon size and shape of vessel's underbody. The greater the deadrise the greater the tendency will be for the hull to wedge cradle outwards and therefore the greater the number of chains required to keep cradle in place. For a vessel of moderate size with normal deadrise there should be at least two chains secured to forward poppets, two to ends of packing and two to the after poppets. Of course the chains must be brought up taut against under side of keel before they are fastened, and it is always advisable to place a piece of hardwood packing between chain and keel to prevent chain cutting into keel when strain is put on chains during launching. Very often it is advisable to make one end of each chain fast with a removable pin extending above water, thus insuring that the chains can be quickly loosened and cradle separated should it be found difficult to remove cradle from under vessel after she is afloat.

No. 15. *Dog Shore.* This is a shore that prevents the

Fig. 67. Chetopa Plunging Into the Water, and Alcona Waiting For Her Turn

sliding ways and cradle moving between the time vessel is raised off keel blocking and time of launching. This shore is placed at the upper end of ways, its lower end resting against the launching ribband (6) and its upper end against a cleat securely fastened to the side of sliding ways. The under side of the cleat that is fastened to bilge ways *must* be kept well above the top of launching ribband, because it must pass over and clear of ribband during launching.

No. 16. *Sole Piece Stops.* These are pieces of hard wood bolted to sliding ways for the purpose of preventing side and end movement of sole piece planks. The top of these stops must be a sufficient distance below top of sole piece plank to enable wedges to be driven.

No. 17. *Holes* bored in ends of sliding ways to receive ropes which are led on board to secure bilge ways when they float after vessel is launched.

I will now briefly describe the preparations for launching a vessel.

The launching ways are first set in position and secured, then ribbands and ribband shores are placed and fastened. When placing launching ways it is well to bear in mind that if their upper surface is given a camber of about 2 inches per 100 feet of length the danger of vessel sticking, should ways settle, will be greatly lessened.

Next the sliding ways, sole pieces, sole piece stops, packing, poppets and poppet ribbands are fitted in place, and poppet chains, lashings, wedges, and dog shores got ready. Everything is fitted and fastened properly, and ropes or chains for removing cradle from under vessel

after she is afloat are led and arranged. For this purpose wire ropes or chain, of sufficient length to extend from upper end of building slip to the point in water where vessel will be fully water-borne, are fastened to upper ends of bilge ways, the other ends of ropes being fastened to an anchor or piles set into ground at upper end of slip.

These ropes or chains are led inside of the sliding ways and stopped up out of the way with rope yarn. As the ropes are only sufficiently long to allow cradle to move freely until vessel is water-borne, they will stop the cradle when that point is reached, and as the vessel can still continue to move she will leave the cradle and thus allow it to float clear.

When everything is fitted and fastened properly, the cradle is removed from under vessel and sliding ways are turned bottom side up and clear of launching ways. The surfaces of launching ways and sliding ways are next thoroughly covered with tallow and soft soap; the tallow being to fill the pores of wood and give it a smooth surface, and the soft soap to lubricate the surface. Oil is added to the soap to insure more perfect lubrication. Several coats of hot tallow are applied, time being given to allow each coat to soak well into the wood.

The sliding ways are next placed back in position and the exposed surfaces of launching ways covered with boards to protect the tallow and soap from dirt until time of launching arrives.

The dog shores are next placed and secured and additional temporary stops placed against lower ends of ways.

Fig. 68. Lake Silver. at the Great Lakes Engineering Works at Ecorse, on the Ways Ready For Her Sideways Plunge

Next the pieces of cradle are put back into position and refastened, and ends of wedges entered between sole plank and sliding ways and driven up until the cradle rests firmly against hull.

The poppet chains and lashings are now placed and everything prepared for transferring the weight of vessel from keel blocking to cradle.

The weight of vessel still rests upon the keel blocks and should rest there until immediately before the time set for launching, when gangs of men are arranged along each side of vessel, and at a given signal the wedges are driven home evenly and weight of vessel gently transferred from keel blocks to cradle. Every other keel block and bilge shore is first removed and blocking moved clear of keel, and when this has been done the wedges are again driven and the remainder of keel blocks and shores are taken down.

The whole weight of vessel now rests on sliding ways and the vessel should be released as soon as possible, because if launching is delayed there is danger of the pressure due to vessel's weight forcing the tallow and soap out from between the ways and thus reducing its lubricating value.

The temporary stops are removed immediately after the men are clear of the bottom of vessel, and then, by simply cutting or releasing the dog shore, vessel will be free to move by its own gravity toward the water.

In all cases it is well to make provision for starting vessel, should she refuse to start immediately the dog shore is released. For this purpose air or hydraulic rams, jack screws, or balks of timber handled by gangs of men can be used. The most important thing to remember is, never to delay a moment if vessel refuses to start, and to make sure that the rams, screws, or balks of timber are applied simultaneously and with equal force to each side of vessel.

Of course proper provisions must be made for stopping vessel when she is afloat. This is usually done by means of drags, weights or anchors operated from on board the vessel.

9k. Concluding Remarks

In all cases it is necessary to insure that damage will not result to hull from excessive strains that occur during launching. The easiest way to do this is to place shoring inside of hull near the places where excessive strains are likely to arise.

As vessel enters the water, the water that surrounds it exerts a supporting force that will lift stern clear of ways just as soon as the total buoyancy becomes greater than the total weight. If the length of ways is sufficient to support the whole length of cradle until buoyancy of water acting on immersed portion of hull is sufficient to lift vessel clear of cradle there will be no tipping moment, but the force of buoyancy will cause a great pressure on the fore poppets and portions of hull and ways that is nearest to them, and if the structure of poppets, hull and ways is not sufficiently strengthened at this point one of three things may happen:

Either the ways may spread out;

Or the fore poppets may collapse;

Or the hull may be forced in and severely strained.

Accoma, Wooden Ship Built by the Foundation Company, Sliding Down the Ways Into the Passaic River

Fig. 70. A Broadside Launching at the Ecorse Yard, Great Lakes

Fig. 69. Launch of the Mexoil, a 3,000-Ton Vessel, Built by the Alabama-New Orleans Transportation Company at Violet, La., For the Mexican Petroleum Company

If, however, the ways are so short that the longitudinal C.G. of hull and cradle weight will pass beyond their ends before buoyancy is sufficient to cause a lifting moment in opposite direction, there will be a tipping moment, and it is clear that the ends of launching ways will become a fulcrum, and if they are not sufficiently strong to support the strain and weight caused by tipping, the ways may give way or they may spread out. If the ways are able to stand the strain and the inclination of ways and depth of water is sufficient to allow vessel to sink deep into water before lifting, the bow of vessel may lift clear of cradle and immediately afterward the up force of buoyancy may be sufficiently strong to bring the bow down onto the launching ways with considerable force. So in this case also it is necessary to insure against damage to hull by placing internal shores and braces along the portion of hull that is near to fore poppets.

91. BROADSIDE LAUNCHING

In many yards on the Great Lakes vessels are constructed with their keels parallel with water front and therefore it is necessary to launch sideways in place of endways as is usual along the coast. When a vessel has to be launched sideways or "broadside" ways are evenly distributed under the whole length of vessel and launching cradle rests on these ways at right angles to their line of direction.

On Fig. 68 launching ways and cradle is clearly shown and on Fig. 70 Lake Janet is shown just entering the water.

Chapter X

Building a Ship

Having described each principal part of a vessel's construction, I will in this chapter describe the proper way to build a vessel in a modern shipyard. By building a vessel I mean management and supervision as well as the actual construction and equipment work.

10a. EXPLANATORY

To become successful as a builder of wooden vessels one must have a thorough knowledge of ship construction, of what constitutes a fair day's labor and of material; and in addition to this, the ability to plan work ahead of requirements, and to manage and supervise men is of prime importance. It is not necessary that all of this knowledge and ability be possessed by one man but it is very necessary that the one or more men who direct work and manage the yard be fully competent in the things I have mentioned. It is an error to imagine that success in building a vessel largely depends upon the mechanic's ability to do work properly. Unless properly managed and someone with brains directs them, the most competent workmen are more likely to make a failure than less competent men managed and directed in a proper manner.

So I will commence at the beginning and explain some of the fundamental essentials for success in ship-building. Ship-building is a business that calls for coordination of the work of men in many trades and the use of many different kinds of material. In addition to this, the building of a ship covers a period of several months at least, and any failure, during this whole period, to have material on hand when required, to supervise and plan properly, or to have the proper number of men at work and work done in proper order, is very likely to cause delays and increase cost.

For the purpose of this explanation I will suppose that a certain vessel owner desires to have a wooden vessel built. The owner can do one of two things. He can either go to a naval architect, explain his ideas and have a set of plans and specifications prepared and then get builders to submit prices for building the vessel in accordance with the architect's plans and specifications, and under his supervision, or he can go to a builder, or to several builders, and get him, or them, to submit prices for building the vessel from their own plans and specifications and under the supervision of an inspector appointed by the owner.

It is a point of controversy as to which is the better method, but this much has been definitely settled—*it is much less costly and more satisfactory if the vessel's plans and specifications are properly prepared and approved before construction work is commenced.* Therefore, even if the owner adopts the second method he should insist upon plans being prepared and specifications being properly drawn up before work is commenced.

Plans are for the purpose of conveying to workmen the owner's intentions as to shape, construction and finish, and by preparing all of the plans beforehand, it is possible to convey to the builder, his superintendents, his foremen, and workmen, a clear picture of the whole building problem, and thus they learn, before work is commenced, what has to be done and the way it is intended it shall be done.

In a book of this kind it will be out of place to enter into a long explanation of the preparation of plans, but as it is necessary that you understand what is meant by Plans and Specifications, I will briefly describe the plans and specifications prepared by naval architects.

Peninsula Shipbuilding Company's Plant at Portland, Ore.

10b. Plans and Specifications Briefly Described

A set of Plans and Specifications prepared by a naval architect generally consist of:

(a) Lines drawing, or drawing to show the *shape* of vessel. This drawing shows profile, cross-section and half-breadth water-line, views of vessel's shape, and has attached to it a table of measurements, called Offset table, from which the mould loftsman can obtain measurements for "laying down" the lines full size.

(b) Construction drawings, or drawings that show the designer's intentions regarding the way structure is to be fitted and fastened together. There are usually several construction drawings, each being devoted to illustrating some particular part of the structure. In general one drawing shows the longitudinal views of framing of keel, keelsons, frames, decks, etc.; another shows transverse views of framing, another the general arrangement of cabins, another longitudinal and transverse views of the completed vessel, another the details of machinery and its piping, another the installation of sanitary piping, etc.; another the electrical wiring and installation, and another rigging, spars and details of fittings pertaining to them. Of course, each drawing is to scale and has marked on it sufficient measures and written explanations to enable the builder to fully understand the designer's intentions. It is impossible to write all necessary explanations and measurements on the plans, therefore, the designer always attaches to them a complete, clearly written explanation of every essential construction detail. This written explanation is called the Specifications.

On Fig. 200 illustration is shown the lines drawing of a large schooner prepared by Crowninshield and on Fig. 201 is shown a number of the construction detail drawings of a large motor-driven vessel prepared by Cox & Stevens.

An examination of these drawings will serve to explain, more clearly than can be done in words, the proper way to prepare drawings of wooden vessels.

Now, I will assume that the drawings have been prepared and contract signed for the construction of a wooden vessel of about 250 feet in length.

The first and really one of the most important things the manager of yard should consider is whether the equipment of his plant is ample to enable vessel to be built at low cost and in the available time, and the next is the proper planning of supervision, of building methods, of methods for keeping track of costs and progress of work, of obtaining materials and workmen, and of financing the job from the day it is started until the day vessel is delivered to owner and contract completed.

Many present-day failures and shipyard difficulties can be traced to some mistake in planning, or neglect to give proper and careful consideration to management details.

Assuming that the builder has the ways ready, and a certain amount of machinery and material on hand, he should, during the time the contract is being discussed, carefully consider these things and map out some definite plan of procedure to follow in case the contract is given to him.

1st.—He should determine whether the machinery in his plant is sufficient to enable vessel to be built economically and as rapidly as necessary.

2d.—He should go over available facilities for receiving material and handling it after it is received, and determine whether they are adequate.

3d.—He should carefully estimate the approximate quantities of material required, the approximate dates for delivery, and it is also advantageous to find out tentatively, where materials can be obtained and their approximate prices.

4th.—He should ascertain whether methods of keeping track of materials, progress of work, and costs, are adequate and sufficiently simple to enable every employee to keep informed of the things he must know, and the things he is responsible for. Bear in mind that all these things should be considered *before* it is even certain that contract will be awarded.

To the man who is used to doing work in a haphazard manner or without properly planning it beforehand it may seem wasteful of time to plan every detail before

The Plant of the Traylor Shipbuilding Company at Cornwells, Pa.

work is commenced, but I can assure you that the most successful builders of wooden vessels are the men who carefully think out the whole building problem before beginning work.

Before proceeding further, I will more fully explain the four items referred to above.

(1st.)   *Machinery in Shipyard*

In these days, machinery is universally used in all modern shipyards, and the better and more complete the machinery equipment is the greater the speed of production and the lower cost will be.

While machinery requirements of each yard will vary, it is safe to say that these machine tools are necessary in a modern shipyard used for the building of wooden vessels, and of course there must be ample power to drive the machines under the most adverse conditions of service. When figuring upon power requirements, do not make the mistake of underestimating. This is a common fault, due largely to the builders of the machines forgetting that the average shipyard woodworking machine tools must work on rough and heavy timbers and the mechanics running the tools are more likely to force them to the limit of speed and power than the mechanic handling a similar tool in a joiner shop.

Here is a list of tools that are considered essential in a modern shipyard. I have listed them under three headings: Shipyard Proper, Joiner Shop, and General, and against each is marked the approximate amount of power required to drive under normal service conditions.

SHIPYARD

48″ Band-saw, shipyard type with beveling arrangement..	20
38″ Band resaw	10
Automatic cut-off saw	15
Self-feed circular rip saw	25
Four-sided timber planer	45
Double surfacer	17
Beveling and edging machine—Shipyard type	25
Band-saw 38″ ordinary type	10
Rip-saw ordinary type	10
Planer single surfacer	7

JOINER SHOP — 184

Band-saw 36″	10
Small rip-saw	15
Universal bench-saw	5
Planer and matcher	25
Joiner	10
Four-sided moulder	20
Buzz planer	5
Single planer or surfacer	12
Tenoner, Mortiser	20
Sander	10
Hollow chisel mortiser	4
Chain mortiser	4
Wood lathe, Saw sharpener and gummer, Band-saw setter and filer, Emery wheels, Grindstone	5

GENERAL — 145

Air compressor, air coupling, air hose	
Air compressor, air piping, air hose	
Six 90-℔ air hammers	
Two extra heavy air hammers	
Six air-driven wood boring machines	
Six electrical drills	
Fifty Hydraulic jacks of various sizes	
Power bolt cutter	10
Hand bolt cutters	
Bolt header	10
Two or more Hoisting Engines with wire cables, manila ropes, blocks and falls	
One or more Traveling Hoist with tracks laid to slipways and woodworking machine shops	
Shaving exhaust blower	35 to 50
Portable forges	
Power punch	10
Additional tools that can be advantageously used:	
Portable electrically driven timber planer	
Portable electrically driven deck planer	5
Air-driven caulking tools for caulking decks	

Three Wooden Cargo Carriers on the Ways at the Yards of the St. Helens Shipbuilding Co. at St. Helens, Oregon. The S. T. Allard is in the Center and the City of St. Helens on the Left

Fig. 71. A Squadron of Electric Carriers at the Yard of the Peninsula Shipbuilding Company. These Handy Vehicles Are Wonders in the Way of Time-Saving and Transportational Flexibility

This list is merely a general one for the purpose of giving information about tools that should be available in a modern shipyard. The powers given are taken from actual installations of electrically driven tools installed in a modern shipyard. It should be remembered that, while it is only occasionally that more than 50% of the tools will be in operation at one time, it is not safe to assume that the total power required will ever fall below the actual total for all tools. As a modern shipyard is frequently called upon to do machine work on metals, a few metalworking machine tools should be installed. Below I give list of power required to drive modern metal-working machine tools:

56″ x 56″ x 12′ planer will require	20
42″ x 42″ x 20′ planer will require	15
30″ x 30″ x 8′ planer	10
24″ x 24″ x 6′ planer	5
10′ boring mill	20
7′ boring mill	15
50″ boring mill	7
62″ lathe	10
48″ lathe	5
32″ lathe	4
24″ lathe	3
18″ lathe	2
5′ radial drill	5
Four spindle gang drill	7
40″ vertical drill	2
Milling machine	3
No. 6 Niles bending rolls	35
Double punch and sheers	10
Angle sheers (double)	10
12″ straightening rolls	15
No. 4 punch	10
No. 2 punch	5
18″ shaper	5
Milling machine	3-5
Grinding machine	3-6
22′ bending rolls driving	35
lifting	10

Regarding installation of machinery. Electrically driven tools are preferable to belt driven, especially in woodworking shops, and in all cases the location of tools should be chosen with a view to every tool being accessible and available for use without it being necessary to stop one tool to enable material to be properly handled at an adjacent one. In addition to this, every tool should be so located that the largest timbers can be machined and finished without excessive handling being necessary. The entering end for rough timber should always be located nearest to receiving end of yard and exit end nearest, or in the direction of assembling and erecting end of yard.

Labor-saving devices for handling timbers, such as portable rollers, tables, and cranes, should be available for use at every machine where heavy timbers will be handled.

(2d.) *Facilities for Handling Material*

If a shipbuilder attempts to handle material by hand he is almost certain to make a failure of the job because costs will be so high that it will become impossible for him to do business at a profit. About 1,250,000 feet of timber has to be handled three or more times during the construction of a 275-foot wooden vessel. First, from the vessel or cars, that delivers it to yard, to the assorting and piling locations; second, from the timber piles to saw-mill; third, in the sawmill, and then from sawmill to assembling and working platforms or stations, and from there to the vessel for erection in position. You can readily understand how labor cost will mount and delays occur when the handling and routing of material has not been properly thought out and planned beforehand. Here are a few suggestions that have proved of value: First, carefully consider the possible locations of receiving and storage points and select those which will enable the materials to be handled the minimum number of times and routed from receiving point through sawmill to assembling point and from there to building slip in the most direct manner.

The first sorting or grading of lumber for parts it can be best utilized for, and for quality, should be done at the receiving point when material is received. By doing this much confusion and unnecessary handling of material, after it is piled, will be avoided.

Second, carefully consider how the materials can be best handled over every point of this routing and the means you will adopt for handling it. For handling timbers from a vessel's hold, or from a car, by lifting power-operated derrick booms are useful, or if the timbers have to be unloaded from a vessel through bow cargo ports, it may be that a large portion of the cargo can be most economically handled by means of a power-operated portable winch and wire rope passed through ports, the timbers being hauled endways from vessel and onto timber trucks that will haul it to storage piles or sawmill. In either case it is very necessary that the conveyors used for moving timbers from vessel or car to its first stopping place be power-driven. Electrically driven timber trucks running on light steel rails or a traveling steam-driven hoist can be used advantageously, so also can auto timber trucks. Bear in mind that this handling of material from vessel to the piling points requires, in a majority of cases, the handling of full loads. For the second handling from the piling points to the sawmill, lighter trucks can be utilized because in the majority of instances partial loads will be hauled and delivered from piles of material that has already been sorted for quality and dimensions. Light motor or electrically driven timber carriers are wonderful labor-savers for transporting material to sawmills and from them to the assembling and erecting points. On Fig. 71 is shown some of these vehicles.

For the actual handling of material in sawmill, there are many very satisfactory devices available, some being power driven and others calling for the use of manual labor while the piece of timber is actually being machined.

For the handling of heavy straight materials through saws and beveling machines, the best kind of devices are those which operate by power and have both vertical and horizontal movement, capable of adjustment for speed, height and direction. For the less weighty materials, and for handling timber through band-saws, moulders and planers, plain rollers and tables that can be quickly adjusted in position are best. When possible to do so, the materials should be handled direct from machine through which it passes, onto the truck or conveyance that will move it to assembling or erecting points. To allow material to be piled on floor of sawmill and then handled a second time from floor to truck or conveyor is wasteful of time and adds to expense, therefore a number of light trucks or conveyors is preferable to ones only adapted for carrying heavy loads.

At the assembling platforms for frames at points where the heavier timbers will be shaped and fastened by the shipbuilders, and at the slipway where vessel is being erected, means should be provided for handling materials economically and rapidly, and I do not know of a better way to do this than by using light, portable steam-driven hoists or cranes that travel on rails. The rails can be laid along the most desirable routes and the hoists can pick up and move the finished pieces in the shortest possible time and with a minimum of hand labor.

Hoists of the kind referred to are clearly shown in operation on tracks shown on Fig. 72.

From this brief description you can readily understand the importance of carefully planning the handling and routing of materials as a means for reducing labor costs and speeding up production.

I do not know of anything that looks more inefficient than to see a large number of workmen handling and hauling material by hand power, and the men assigned to do this kind of work are neither satisfied with their job or efficient workmen. In addition to this the sight of men moving along at low speed tends to slow up work of other and more efficient workmen.

Before passing to my next explanation I want to emphasize this point: It is very necessary that after you have planned the method of handling and routing material you should take pains to make every foreman and workman clearly understand your plan and the *reason for having it,* and of course the plan should be made as simple as possible because the simpler it is the more quickly the average workman will understand it.

(3d.) *Estimating Amounts of Materials Required*

Estimating, if done accurately, is a great saving of time and labor. By estimating, I mean determining quantities, kinds and dimensions of material needed for constructing and outfitting the entire vessel; and if the estimate is prepared in a proper manner and with a view to it being of greatest value, each piece of material should be listed. First, for kind, dimensions, quality and quantity, and second, in the order in which it is needed. The kind, dimensions, quantity and quality list is generally prepared by the estimator, and the order in which material is needed list under the immediate direction of superintendent, and on this list should be clearly stated the dates each piece of material should be in the shipyard ready for use.

I have generally found that if the second list is prepared with a view to using it in all departments for keeping track of available material, it will prove a valuable aid to checking materials and eliminating delays due to non-delivery of materials. How this is done can best be explained by describing the way one shipbuilding firm prepares the list and uses it to check the purchasing

Fig. 72. **Traveling Hoists and Tracks in Shipyard**

department's work and deliveries. In yard referred to a clerk, under the direction of superintendent, prepares a list of materials, on which is listed the quantities of materials required for each principal part of vessel and the date each item should be in the yard. On this list there is placed against each item three blank spaces, or squares, onto which is pasted different colored pasters. When an item of material is ordered a blue paster is fastened in the first square opposite item, and on it is marked three dates—the first indicating date ordered, the second date delivery of material is promised, and the third a safe date when material should be shipped for delivery on date promised. In second blank square, against an item a red paster is fastened whenever shipment date arrives and material has not been shipped. The safe date for shipment is usually several days ahead of actual date shipment must be made, thus allowing time for making inquiries. In third blank space, against each item is fastened a brown paster when materials are in yard ready for use. Thus by having a boy paste the necessary colors against each item at the beginning of each day, it is possible, at a glance, for each head of a department to see if materials are ordered, are shipped in time to insure delivery, or are in yard ready for use. This system is so simple that the smallest yard can use it and it is capable of being advantageously used in the largest yards.

It is unwise and unsafe to try and build a vessel without using some system for keeping track of material that has been ordered, and the system should always be one that will enable the purchasing department and heads of construction to keep track of deliveries and requirements, and the superintendent and men in charge to keep check on purchasing department and on materials in yard.

(4th.) *Methods of Keeping Track of Materials, Progress of Work, Etc.*

These should be adequate and sufficiently simple to enable the heads of departments to keep posted upon every detail of work progress. One of the best methods to use in a small shipyard is the combined numeral and color method. Before work on a vessel is started a tabulated list of each principal part of the work is made out, each item is given a number, and against each item is left four blank columns, or spaces, similar to the ones left on estimating sheets.

The heading of blank columns being:

> 1st column—Material in yard.
> 2d column—Work on material started.
> 3d column—Assembling in ship started.
> 4th column—Assembling in ship finished.

When list is prepared the superintendent enters in each blank space dates that he estimates it is necessary to have materials in yard, work started, assembling begun, and assembling finished.

This list now becomes the yard's prime estimate for work completion, and track is kept of progress of work by pasting various colored pasters in the squares left against each item. When material is in yard a brown paster is fastened in first column, but if there is danger of material not being delivered in yard on date entered against any item, then a *red paster* is fastened in space. It is the same with each stage of progress as indicated by headings above columns. Should date when work on

Fig. 72a.   Meacham & Babcock's Wooden Shipyard at Seattle.   Four 3,500-Ton Ships Under Construction

any piece of material arrive, and work not be started, a red paster is fastened in the space and this remains until work is started, when its place is taken by a paster having one half blue and the other brown—the blue indicating that work was started late. Of course on each paster is written dates to indicate start and completion. Thus by looking at the itemized sheet, it is possible for anyone interested in keeping track of work to see at a glance just how work on the vessel is progressing. A line of brown pasters in fourth column will indicate that all work is finished, and if pasters are partly brown and partly blue they will indicate that while work is finished it was not finished on date estimated.

I mentioned that each principal item or division of work is given a numeral. This serves the double purpose of enabling each part to be quickly traced through each department or stage of work and kept track of by marking its numeral on the piece, and it also enables workmen to indicate on their time cards (if cards are used), by using numbers, the pieces they have worked on during each day. This facilities cost-keeping.

At the beginning of this chapter I mentioned Management and Supervision, so perhaps it will be advisable for me to explain my meaning of these things.

10c. Management and Supervision

Proper and adequate yard management and supervision of workmen and the work is very essential. The manager of a shipyard should have a sufficient knowledge of ship-building and management of men to plan every detail of the work of supervision, and his knowledge should be such that he can fairly judge whether his sub-ordinates are properly attending to their duties and the work is progressing at estimated rate.

I am now referring only to the production management. I have found that the only way to keep proper track of progress of work and costs is to have reports made daily and to have each superintendent and foreman meet at least once a week for discussion of the various problems that arise from time to time. No manager can achieve success by trying to run his yard as a one-man problem, or without sincerely cooperating with his assistants and keeping them fully informed of his plans and intentions.

The manager of a yard should carefully plan each and every detail of management and supervision *beforehand,* and having planned should explain everything to his assistants and insist that the management plan be adhered to.

Some of the daily records that will be found of value are:

1.—Records of number of men at work in yard and on each job of work.

2.—Records of foremen in charge of work on each job and number of men under each.

3.—Records of daily production of work in yard and progress of work on each job.

4.—Records of materials in yard and on order.

5.—Records of amount of material erected and cost.

6.—Daily averages of production, of cost per unit, and of cost compared with selling price.

7.—Records of men available for work should it be necessary to increase force.

8.—Records of wasted material, and mistakes made in the various departments.

The S. T. Allard Ready For Launching

In planning management details, I have found it advisable to let each department keep their own records and then to have their records used as a base to actually check every item. The simpler records are, and the more direct the information they give is, the more valuable they will prove.

The superintendents of work should not only know the manager's intention but they should also be kept informed as to progress of work and its actual cost. Information of this kind should come direct from the manager's office and should be in such form that it can be used by the superintendent to check his prime records and figures. It is very important that superintendents keep in close touch with foremen in charge of work and see that the essential orders of yard are obeyed. One record that will prove very valuable to a superintendent is a short one giving the number of men used for handling material by hand power, the amount of material so handled and reason why it is necessary to use men instead of machine power.

Another record that is of great value is one containing suggestions for improvements. Every man in the employ of a firm should be encouraged to make suggestions, and if any suggestion is of sufficient value to warrant it being adopted the maker of the suggestion should receive an adequate reward. It is very necessary that superintendents take the time and trouble to instruct foremen and leading men in charge of work as to their duties and methods of increasing output. Very few foremen have any fixed ideas regarding methods of directing men and laying out work, and for this reason every superintendent should help foreman to learn the best methods of directing the men and planning work. One very necessary essential is to see that every one in charge of work is kept posted on progress and cost, and if there is combined with this figures taken from a preliminary estimate of cost in labor for each principal part of the work, each foreman will know whether he is ahead or behind the schedule. I have always found it valuable to have this information given to each foreman at least once a week. Management and supervision of work is a comparatively easy matter for the man who knows how to use his brains. Many foremen and superintendents forget that a few moments of thought given to each problem will often expedite work and lessen cost.

10d. Actual Construction Work

I will now begin my explanation of actual construction work. Immediately after plans are ready, or received, they are sent to the mould loft and laid down full size; the mould loftsmen and their assistants then make the necessary full-sized template and patterns for the builders.

Laying down a vessel's lines is enlarging them to full size, and making full-sized templates is making full-sized patterns of parts of vessel and pieces of construction material that have to be shaped in the sawmill or by workmen. On Fig. 73 is shown some of the templates made and work done in a mould loft.

The laying-down and template work required for the construction of a wooden vessel is about as follows:

(a) Lines must be laid down full size and faired.

(b) The shape of each frame of vessel must be laid down full size and templates of the various futtocks and floors made.

(c) The construction details of keel, keelson, stem, stern and other principal parts of the structure must be laid down and templates must be made of the pieces.

(d) Accurate bevels must be taken of every frame and of every necessary detail.

(e) Essential details of joiner work must be laid down full size and templates of the details made or detail rods laid out.

(f) From time to time during the actual construction work, it will be found necessary to refer to the full-sized construction and detail plans, therefore, it is advisable to keep details on mould loft floor until construction has progressed sufficiently to insure that they will not be needed.

Just as soon as the mould loft templates are made and full-sized framing details are ready the work of construction can begin.

When constructing a vessel it is usual to begin work on keel, stem, stern and frames simultaneously and then as the work progresses, the other pieces of material are got out in their proper order and sufficiently ahead of requirements to insure that they will be ready when needed.

In this description I will follow the usual construction procedure and describe each principal part of the work in the order in which it is usually done.

10e. Keel Blocks

Arranging blocks to receive keel is really a part of the construction work. These blocks are set out at proper

Fig. 73. Mould Loft Work

Fig. 74. Assembling a Frame

intervals along center of building slip and they must be arranged correctly as to location and height. The essential things to remember when arranging keel blocks is to have them sufficiently high at lowest keel block to enable workmen to work under vessel, and at the same time their inclination must be in accordance with plans, and correct for the inclination of building slip and launching ways. In chapter on Launching Ways this is explained more fully.

10f. KEEL

This is the principal longitudinal timber of a vessel and is the first timber to put in position. It extends from stem to stern and is the timber upon which the whole structure is erected. The dimensions of keel, and in fact of every piece of timber in a vessel, is usually stated in Construction Specifications. In almost every instance dimensions selected are the ones stipulated in Lloyd's rules. In selecting keel material these rules should govern:

(a) The material should be durable when immersed in water, should be in as long lengths as possible, and scarphs should be located in such positions that they will receive the maximum support from other pieces of timber.

(b) Scarphs of keel should always be nibbed and it is advantageous to use coaks in keel scarphs.

(c) Fastenings of keel scarphs should always be sufficient in number and of proper size. Never use a fewer number of fastenings than is called for by Lloyd's rules.

(d) The material used for a keel should be well seasoned and free from knots and defects that lessen strength. Sapwood should not appear on any keel timber.

When getting out keel timbers it is usual to omit cutting rabbet at ends, because this portion of rabbet can always be more accurately cut after stem and stern posts are in place.

On Fig. 29 a keel is shown being set in position on building blocks.

The location of every frame, obtained from mould loft floor drawing, must be clearly marked on keel, and the fastenings of keel scarphs should be located in positions clear of all frame fastenings. In a modern shipyard, keel timbers are obtained slightly larger than required dimensions and run through a four-sided plane to smooth surfaces and reduce the timber to proper dimensions.

The scarphs can be partly cut on a shipyard bandsaw, providing proper carriers for the keel timbers are used, and the saw is installed in a position that will allow room for keel to swing to right and left. In all cases it will be found necessary to complete the fitting of keel scarph by hand, and it is always advisable to paint or treat the surface of scarphs before fastening them together. After keel pieces are placed in position on blocks they are fastened together by driving the scarph bolts and then the keel is aligned and secured in position on blocks. It is very necessary to have keel timber absolutely straight from end to end.

While keel timbers are being got ready, work on stem, stern, deadwood, keelson timbers, floors and frames is proceeding and just as soon as keel is set in position the frames, and then the stem, stern, deadwood and keelsons can be erected and fastened.

10g. GETTING OUT THE FRAMES

The frames of a wooden vessel are always composed of several pieces of timber, sawed to required shape and fastened together to form the frame. The lowest piece of each frame, called the floor timber, fits across and is notched over keel, and each succeeding piece from keel up is named a futtock and has a numeral added to indicate location relative to keel. Thus the piece next the floor timber is termed the first futtock, the piece next above, the second futtock, and so on upwards until the last piece is reached. The last or upper piece of each

Fig. 75. Assembling a Midship Frame

Fig. 76. Setting Up a Frame

frame is called the top timber. On Fig. 28 each futtock is indicated.

The method of fastening futtocks together is by doubling, allowing their ends to lap, and then bolting the doubled pieces together. On Fig. 28 is shown the various joinings of the piece and bolts that fasten them together. Frames built up in this manner are called *double* because the material is doubled in thickness by the lapping of joints. Thus a 6-inch sided doubled frame is practically 12 inches sided measure.

The shape of each frame is obtained from full-sized mould loft drawing, the templates and bevels being used by the millmen when they saw the pieces of material to proper shape. In a modern shipyard each and every piece of a vessel's frame is accurately beveled and shaped, inside and outside, in the sawmill, and all that the ship carpenters have to do is to assemble the pieces and place cross spalls in position to prevent frame getting out of shape during the erection work.

On Fig. 74 is shown some workmen assembling the pieces of a forward frame. Note the bevel of outer edge and how the bolt holes are being drilled at an inclination from perpendicular, also on Fig. 75 is shown a midship body frame being assembled on one of the assembling platforms. Note the cross spalls. In some shipyards frames are assembled on platforms located some distance from the vessel, and in others they are assembled just ahead or aft of a vessel and then moved to their proper location and erected.

There seems to be a preference for beginning the erection of a vessel's frame at or near to amidships and then working both aft and forward.

I will describe the work of erecting a frame in position.

A timber runway or platform is placed each side of keel at a proper height and distance from center of keel line to enable workmen to use platform or runways for

working on. On Fig. 76 such a runway is shown and on Fig. 77 men are shown moving the platform timbers. A frame is moved to its location on keel and laid down on platform, then by means of a derrick it is hoisted upright and placed in position. When in position on keel it is necessary to plumb and secure the frame against moving. This work is done in the following manner: On the upper cross spall a center line is marked and when frame is in position, but before it is secured to keel, a plumb is dropped from center mark on spall. If the point of plumb bob strikes center longitudinal line marked on top of keel it indicates that frame is set plumb in one direction (transversely). To find out whether frame is plumb in longitudinal direction, measure distance at keel between plumb bob and frame and also distance from cross spall to keel; then, knowing the inclination that keel is set on keel blocks and these two measures, it is an easy matter to calculate whether frame is properly plumbed or not. Of course measurements at keel and cross spall must be made from the same edge of frame.

When frame is plumbed it must be secured against movement by placing shores against it, and then it can be secured to keel by driving one of the frame to keel fastenings.

Bear in mind that the majority of keelson fastenings go through frames into keel and serve to secure both keelson and frames to keel, therefore, as it is undesirable to bore a large number of fastenings holes through frames, only the minimum number of fastenings should be driven when frames are first erected. After the first frame is set in place, the other frames are placed in position, the men working towards both bow and stern and regulating each frame by making measurements to

Fig. 76a. Erecting a Midship Frame

Fig. 77. Moving a Framing Platform

prove that "room and space" between frames is correct and frames properly set and "horned". The usual method of proving that a frame is horizontally square with keel is to "horn" it, or prove its accuracy by measuring from a point on keel, some distance ahead (or aft) of frame being horned, out to sheer line marked on each side of top timber of frame. If the frame is set correctly the distance from point on keel to starboard top timber sheer line on a frame will be identically the same as the measure from same point to port top timber sheer line. Of course plumb bob can also be used to prove accuracy in a transverse direction.

As each frame is erected and secured, it is shored and held in position by fastening it to the adjoining frame with short cleats, and after several frames are erected they are regulated, faired, and held in position by fastening ribband battens near to bilge, to sheer, and along bottom. On Fig. 78 bilge ribband batten is shown shored in position.

While the frames of middle body are being erected, other gangs of men can be putting forward and after deadwoods in place and erecting the stem and stern posts, so that by the time cant frames are ready to erect the deadwood will be in position to receive them.

I have already explained that cant frames are erected at varying angles to the perpendicular and are located at and near to bow and stern. On Fig. 80 the forward cant frames are clearly shown. Cant frames are shaped, assembled, and erected in the same manner that the square frames are, but it is usual to use harpin ribbands forward for the purpose of holding forward cants in position while being fastened, and to run in some short stern ribband aft to hold after cants in position.

Cant frames are generally mortised into deadwood and fastened to deadwood or stem, or stern by means of bolts that pass through frames, deadwood, stem, or stern.

In large vessels strength is added to the bottom framing by inserting filling frames between the regular tim-

bers of the frame. If you will turn to plans of vessel shown on Fig. 205, you will note that there is an open space between each frame. This open space is filled with floors or short frames that extend from keel to about the turn of bilge, the purpose of these being to strengthen the bottom of vessel and prevent dirt accumulating in open spaces between frames. In the days before iron and steel were used for ship-building it was usual to have the filling frames extend well above turn of bilge, to fit and wedge them closely against frames and then to properly caulk all the seams between frames, thus making the whole bottom of a vessel absolutely watertight before the planking was put on, and greatly adding to strength to resist hogging and sagging strains. In these days, however, the use of steel diagonal straps and arches has, to a large extent, done away with the necessity for using filling frames as a means for strengthening the structures of small and moderate sized vessel. Filling frames should be used in large vessels.

10h. The Stem, Apron and Deadwood

The shapes of these are obtained from mould loft, and by using the templates and bevels made in mould loft the various pieces of material can be properly shaped, beveled, and partially finished in sawmill. The stem is usually composed of several pieces of material fastened together with through bolts in the manner designated on plans. Stem is assembled, rabbeted to receive plank-

Fig. 78. Erecting a Stem

Fig. 79. Stem, Deadwood and Frame Set Up

ing, then raised to its position, plumbed and properly fastened.

Now a word about fastening the large timbers of a vessel such as keel, stem, deadwood, frame, etc.

In a modern shipyard nearly all hand drilling for fastening has been replaced by air-operated machine drilling, and it is very necessary to remember that the old hand drilling for fastenings rules do not give satisfactory results if followed when holes are drilled by air-operated machines. With hand-operated augers the practice is to use an auger that is one-eighth smaller than fastening, and this rule is satisfactory because the hole bored by a hand-operated auger is never very much larger than the actual size of auger and, the metal used for fastening

being slightly in excess of designated size, the fastening will drive tightly and hold securely. But when air-machine augers are used the high speed of rotation, combined with the difficulty of holding drilling machine perfectly steady and the necessity for withdrawing auger a number of times while boring a hole for a long fastening, usually causes the auger to bore an oblong hole that is materially larger than auger. It therefore is essential that a smaller size of auger be used when boring holes with an air-operated machine than is called for by the hand-operated auger requirements. I believe the size of auger should be not less than 3/16-inch under fastening, and I have found it sometimes necessary to use an auger 1/4-inch smaller. Much depends upon the skill of operator and the care with which he withdraws and inserts auger while hole is being drilled.

On Fig. 81 and Fig. 81a air-operated augers are shown in operation.

A fastening that will drive easily into its hole is worthless and aside from its insecurity is liable to leak. The old practice of having the fastening hole so small that fastening will head perfectly while driving is an excellent one to follow and the old rule that required each fastening to drive not over 1/4 inch under each of the last six *full blows* is also a most excellent one to adhere to.

Many present-day defects in wooden vessel construction are due to insecurity of fastenings, through the holes into which they are inserted being too large.

Fig. 80. Wooden Ship-Building on the Pacific Coast. The City of St. Helens in Frame at the Yard of the St. Helens, Ore., Shipbuilding Company

Fig. 81. The Little David Pneumatic Boring Machine Makes Light Work of the Deep Holes Required in the Giant Keelsons. The Operator Has to Have Only a Straight Eye and a Steady Hand, For His Task Is But to Guide the Tool

Continuing Remarks About Stem

On Figs. 78 and 79 a stem is shown in position and on Fig. 36 is shown two construction details of forward deadwood and stem of wooden vessels.

10i. STERN-POST AND AFTER DEADWOOD CONSTRUCTION

The shape of stern-post, its deadwood, and the counter timbers for stern is obtained from templates made in mould loft and, as in the case of stem and its deadwood, the various pieces of material are sawed into shape and partly fashioned in the sawmill. The erection of stern-post and its adjoining timbers is done in this manner: First the stern-post and its knee is plumbed and secured in place and then the deadwood and counter timbers are placed in position and fastened. On Fig. 37 is shown the construction details of stern of a vessel and on Fig. 82 is shown photographs of stern-post framing. After stem and stern with their deadwoods are erected the cutting of rabbet is completed and then the whole frame is proved and regulated.

Fig. 90 shows a vessel in frame ready for planking.

10j. THE KEELSON CONSTRUCTION

While the stem and stern-post are being erected and fastened, the lower keelson timbers should be got ready to fasten in place and just as soon as the frame is properly erected and faired, the keelsons can be fastened in place. Keelson timbers are generally got out in sawmill in the same manner that keel timbers are got out, and scarphs should be nibbed ones. It is advantageous to coak all keelson scarphs.

When laying out locations of keelson scarphs, it is essential to locate them in positions that are not too close to keel scarphs and to make scarphs extend over at least three frames. In addition to this scarphs of the rider keelson should be widely separated from those of keelson proper.

It is advantageous to let keelson into floors for about one inch, because by doing this the keelson obtains a firmer base to rest upon and is strengthened against side movement.

On illustrations Nos. 201, 202, 205, 206, 212 are shown details of three kinds of keelson construction.

Fig. 201 shows the most advanced type of construction, consisting of a combination of steel and wood arranged in such a manner that the maximum of resistance against longitudinal strains is obtained with a minimum weight of material.

The Fig. 201 keelson as you will note is a built-up *I* beam having its lower members secured to floors and its upper member fastened to steel plating that rests on, and is fastened to the ceiling of floor. The pieces of ceiling next to keelson fit against and edge-bolt through the steel plate web, thus tying the whole structure together. On Fig. 84 is shown another type of steel keelson construction, consisting of a top steel plate riveted to built-up side members composed of angles and plates. On Fig. 84a cross-section details of a keelson of this kind are shown. The keelson construction shown on Fig. 202 cross-section view is an all-wood keelson composed of three lower and three upper pieces of timber securely fastened together and to the floors of vessel. You will note by referring to the longitudinal view that both the upper and lower center keelson timbers extend from bow to stern and are properly scarphed into and securely fastened to deadwood forward and extend aft to form a portion of after deadwood. It is most important to have keelsons extend the whole length of a vessel and fasten them to forward and after deadwoods in such a manner

Courtesy of Ingersoll-Rand Company

Fig. 81a. The Pneumatic Drift Bolt Driver Hammering Home a Long 1¼-In. Bolt Through a Deck Beam and Its Supporting Sturdy Sill. The Bolt Disappears Into Its Hole With Astonishing Rapidity

that there will not be any weakness of structure at points of termination of keelsons.

On Figs. 205 and 206 are shown longitudinal views of large vessel keelson construction similar to the one shown on Fig. 202. In this construction the keelsons are composed of three tiers of timbers, instead of the two shown on Fig. 202, and you will note that the two lower tiers are put in place before stemson and after deadwood is, and that the upper tier of timbers rests on and is fastened to stemson forward and deadwood aft. On Figs. 36 and 37 are shown details of another method of scarphing upper piece of keelson to stemson and deadwood.

On Fig. 212 is shown cross-section and longitudinal views of another type of wood keelson construction suitable for a large vessel. This construction is composed of two lower tiers of timbers each of which is composed of three members edge-bolted together as well as being fastened securely to the floors. On top of these is fastened three additional tiers of timbers each being composed of one timber. Thus the whole keelson makes a solid structure of an inverted T shape all members of which extend from stem to stern. Under hatch openings it is usual to secure an additional short piece of timber on top of keelson and then cover the portion of keelson under opening with steel plates, for the purpose of protecting it against damage when loading and unloading cargo.

The essentials in keelson construction are:

(a) To have the keelson sufficiently deep to with-stand longitudinal strains tending to hog or sag the whole structure.

(b) To fasten keelson securely to keel frame, stemson and to after deadwood, thus making keelson and all parts mentioned above one longitudinal member of the ship's structure, and at the same time adding strength to transverse members of structure.

10j[1]. OTHER METHODS OF KEELSON CONSTRUCTION

In some of the larger sailing vessels now being constructed the keelson structure, in place of being straight on top, as shown on Fig. 212, is formed in the shape of an arch. In a keelson of this kind the three lower tiers of timber extend from stem to stern in manner shown on Fig. 212, and after these are secured an arch is built up on top of keelson by forming several timbers and bending them in place on top of the lower tiers. Each succeeding timber of the arch is longer than the one below, and the last, or upper, timber reaches to the stemson forward and deadwood aft, and is scarphed to these structures. On Fig. 85 is shown details of this kind of keelson construction.

One objection to this kind of keelson construction is the large amount of material required for its construction, and another is the weakness at point of junction of forward end of arch with stemson.

This arch construction is a development of the center line longitudinal bulkhead construction that has been tried out in several vessels.

Fig. 82. Setting Up the Stern

Fig. 84. Steel Keelson

I will now describe and illustrate the most advanced development of the arch type of keelson.

On Fig. 86 is shown details of a longitudinal trussed keelson composed of wood and steel. Keelson of this kind has the advantage of possessing the maximum of strength with a minimum weight. Of course the members must be properly fitted and the whole structure securely fastened to keel, frame, stemson and stern framing. For a structure of this kind it is advantageous to revert to old timber bridge construction methods and use steel tie-rods and straps, details of a number of which are shown on Fig. 86a.

Another advanced development of keelson construction is an all-steel trussed keelson to which hold stanchions deck beams and transverse framing are secured as well as the longitudinal members of the ship's structure. This type of keelson construction is shown on Fig. 87 and possesses many advantages over the wood keelson for large sailing vessel construction.

Still another development is the reinforced concrete keelson. Deep keelson construction of the types referred to above are not suitable for vessels in which machinery

is installed unless the top of machinery foundation is located sufficiently high to allow keelson to pass below engines and boilers without reduction of its height above keel. In the case of the steel trussed keelson the trussing along machinery foundation space can be arranged to allow machinery foundation timbers to be fastened to and strengthened by the keelson structure, and in one instance as keelson approaches the machinery space it is divided into two members which pass each side of machinery foundation space at a proper distance to allow the steel foundation to be members fitted between the two keelson members.

Details of this kind of construction are shown on Fig. 43b.

10k. STEEL STRAPPING OF FRAME

When frame is regulated it is faired inside and outside by dubbing off irregularities and then, if steel diagonal straps or arch straps are to be used, they are fitted and fastened in place.

In all vessels built of wood there is a continual tendency for the longitudinal members of structure to alter their shape and, especially in large vessels, no amount of additional wood material is capable of resisting this tendency to alter longitudinal shape as efficiently as steel straps will. It, therefore, has become usual to insert steel diagonal straps outside the frames of all wood vessels, and in larger ones these are supplemented by steel arch straps fastened inside or outside the frames.

Method of crossing diagonal straps outside of frames is shown on Fig. 49 and on Fig. 88 is shown details of method of fastening straps to frames, at crossing points and to longitudinal sheer strap.

Fig. 25 also shows steel diagonal strap locations marked by dotted lines, and on Table 3A (page 21) is given dimensions of steel straps used on vessels of named sizes.

Section 39, Lloyd's rules, specifies that proportion of breadth to length and depth to length shall regulate the

Fig. 83. Motorship James Timpson, Built by the G. M. Standifer Construction Company at Portland, Ore. A Correctly-Shaped Elliptical Stern Designed by Cox & Stevens

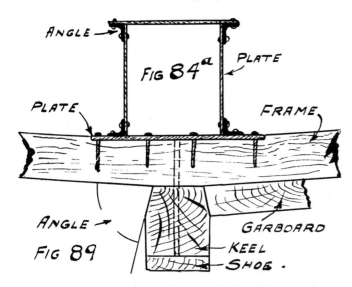

number of straps, that tonnage shall regulate the dimensions of straps, that lower ends of straps must reach to, at least, halfway between long floor heads and first futtocks and upper ends to upper tier of beams. All straps must be let in flush with outside edge of frames by removing a proper depth and width of wood from each frame at point where strap crosses. The steel strap arch is also let in and fastened to every frame it crosses. This arch should begin at stemson forward, rise in a fair sweep until it reaches the upper deck line near to the midship section, and from this point it should drop in a fair sweep until it reaches after deadwood a short distance ahead of stern-post.

You can readily understand that a vessel strapped with both diagonal and arch straps has a greater power of resistance against longitudinal strains than one constructed in the old manner with caulked filling timbers for its entire length and a large number of wooden riders or iron. It is very essential to have tension of *every* strap as nearly alike as possible and to have all strap fastenings properly driven into frames.

When straps are let into frames and fastened the work of planking can begin, and at the same time the ceiling, the deck beams and pieces that compose the deck framing can be got ready.

101. PLANKING

I have explained in Chapter VIII that planking is the name given to outside covering of frame, and that it is put on in planks called strakes, that run in fair curves from bow to stern. For thickness of planking to use see Tables given in Chapter III (page 21), and I also refer you to cross-sections of plans Nos. 201, 202, 212, 213, on which are clearly marked the general dimensions of planking at various points from keel to sheer. When planking a vessel the garboard is the first plank to fit and fasten in place.

101[1]. LAYING A GARBOARD

As the lower edge of garboard must fit snugly into the rabbet of keel it is necessary that the rabbet cut along keel, stem, deadwood and stern be properly faired before a garboard can be laid. The ship-carpenters usually fair this rabbet before taking measurements for garboard (called spiling), and when rabbet is fair garboard measurements are taken, a template made, if it is necessary to do so, and garboard planks got out to shape and fitted in place.

The width of available material usually determines the width that garboard will be at its widest point, and as it is essential that width of garboard and of all planking strakes be properly proportioned from end to end, it is advisable that width marks for each plank be laid off at several frames before any planking is got out. This is done by carefully measuring from rabbet of keel to sheer *around outside* of midship frame and dividing this measurement by the number of strakes the plans specify that vessel's planking shall consist of. The widths of strakes at midship section are very often given on cross-section plan of vessel's construction (see Fig. 202, cross-section) and may vary at different points, but the essential thing to remember when laying out planking marks is to have the proper number of strakes at midship (widest) section. The planking marks are scribed across outside face of midship frame and when this has been done each line indicates where upper edge of each strake of planking must reach to at midship section.

When midship section planking lines have been laid out measurements are taken around several frames located at equal intervals between midship, stem and stern, care being taken to have the same number of marks on all frames (except in cases where a strake of planking terminates before it reaches one of the marked frames). Thus when the selected frames have been measured and

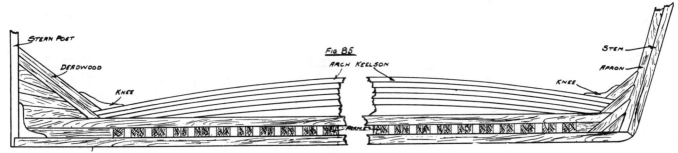

Fig. 85. Arched Wood Keelson

plank marks scribed across their outside faces, a series of lines appear on the outside of frames and each line indicates where a seam of planking will be located.

Some shipbuilders make a practice of going still further and by means of battens and chalk lines they run each plank line and, when they have proved its accuracy, scribe it across the outside face of *every* frame. This is a most excellent plan and will sometimes enable greater planking speed to be made, because planking can be spiled well ahead of planking gang's requirements.

To take the shape, or "spiling" for a plank all that is necessary is to tack a thin plank of material (about ¼-inch thick), that is sufficiently wide to prevent its bending edgeways, along the outside of frames and as near as possible to position where plank will fill. For garboard this thin plank would be fastened with its lower edge an inch or so out from rabbet, then the ship-carpenter sets a pair of dividers to a width that will allow one point of dividers to rest against rabbet of keel and other point on pattern material, and without changing set of dividers he marks a series of points along the pattern material, always holding one point of dividers against rabbet of keel and marking point on material with other. Frame numbers, the width of plank at each frame, and setting of dividers, are marked on pattern material, before taking it to sawmill, for use when getting out the plank. Width of planking measure referred to is obtained by measuring distance from keel rabbet out to mark, on outside of frames, that indicates line upper edge of plank will follow.

Of course a bevel board, on which is marked bevels that lower edge of plank should have, must accompany plank spiling batten. The bevels for lower edge of plank are obtained by placing an adjustable bevel along frame and adjusting it to fit properly against bevel of rabbet in manner shown on Fig. 89. Planking is usually marked out in the sawmill, and if bevels are indicated by degrees at each point the planks can be sawed to shape with properly beveled edges by using an adjustable beveling shipyard saw or one of the modern shipyard adjustable beveling heads.

When garboard plank is shaped, its edges are finished by hand and then it is placed in the steam-box, well steamed to permit it to be bent readily in place, and then

hung in position, bent to fit snugly against the frames and secured by means of fastenings, wedges, jackscrews, and planking clamps. All of the wedges, screws, and clamps are allowed to remain in position until plank is "set" and fastenings are driven.

Garboard strakes should have vertical scarphs all of which should be some distance, longitudinally, from keel and keelson scarphs, and at least three frame spaces away from any mast step. Scarphs of garboards must be edge-bolted to keel.

Regarding the fastening of garboards. Garboards are fastened with at least one *Clinch*-bolt, or bolt riveted on washer, through every second frame timber in addition to the usual double treenail fastenings laid down in building rules. If a garboard strake is over 4 inches in thickness it must be edge-bolted to keel in every second frame space, and if the garboard is over 7 inches in thickness a second (garboard) strake, 1 or 1½ inch less thickness than first garboard, must be used, and this strake must be edge-bolted to first garboard in each alternate frame space. In large wooden vessels a third and sometimes a fourth garboard strake is used.

In all cases the excess thickness over and above that of bottom planking, that shows along edge of garboard strakes, is "dubbed off" even with bottom planking at stem and stern, and sometimes for the whole length of garboard. On Figs. 202 and 212 the garboard is "dubbed off" for its full length and on Fig. 213 is "dubbed off" at bow and stern only. Note difference in appearance of edges on midship section views.

101². Sheer Strake Wales and Other Planking

The plank that follows sheer line of a vessel, named the *sheer* plank, is usually got out and fitted in place at same time that garboard is being fitted. The "spiling" is taken in the same manner as for garboard. Bear in mind that, as covering board (on deck) extends to outside of planking, the upper edge of sheer plank must be beveled to same crown that deck frame has.

The butts of sheer plank should be nibbed scarphs edge-bolted in manner shown on Fig. 43.

On Fig. 90 is shown a vessel framed and ready for sheer strake, and on the ground alongside of vessel is shown some of the sheer strake planks scarphed ready to

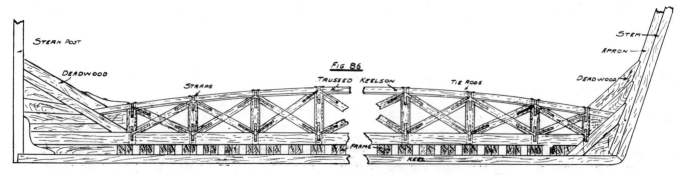

Fig. 86. Trussed Wood Keelson

hang in place. Sheer planks are sawed to shape, beveled, hung and fastened in manner explained in garboard paragraph.

The wales, as you will note by referring to Figs. 28 and 201 and Table 3E (page 22), are somewhat thicker than bottom planking. The proper vertical extent of wales on vessels of usual proportion of depth to length is about one-third of vessel's depth of hold, but when a vessel is eight or more depths in length it is usual to increase vertical depth of wales to about two-fifths of depth of hold. Method of getting out and fastening wales is similar to that of balance of planking.

In all cases the outside planking of a vessel must be put on in as long lengths as possible, because butts tend to weaken longitudinal strength of planking. While I am referring to butts, I will mention some safe rules to following in locating butts.

1st.—All planking butts should come on middle of a frame and should be cut accurately and fastened securely.

2d.—Butts of adjoining planks should not be nearer each other, in a longitudinal direction, than three frames, and two butts should not come on the same frame unless at least three full strakes of planking are between.

It is advisable when a vessel is planked with fir or yellow pine to make the after hoods of planks along the "tuck" and the forward hoods of bow planks that will require a great deal of twisting to get them in place, of white oak. Another detail of importance is to get out all planks with the required curvature, and thus do away with any necessity of having to "force" the planks edgeways in order to make them fit snug against the adjacent plank. "Edge-setting" a plank is a detriment and will sometimes result in the plank breaking *after it has been fastened* in place.

101³. Fastenings of Planking

The number, sizes, and kinds of planking fastenings to use are given on Tables 3B, 3C, 3D, 3E, 3F (pages 20 to 23), and methods of fastening are shown on Figs. 45 and 46.

Three kinds of fastenings are used for securing outside planking of a vessel's frame. *Wood treenails, through bolts with nuts* and *clinch bolts* (bolts whose ends can be clinched or riveted over clinch rings or washers).

Number of planking fastenings should always be proportioned to width of strake of plank.

Planks above 11 inches must have at least two fastenings into each frame, called double fastening. Planks over 8 inches and up to 11 inches must have alternate double and single fastenings; that is, have two fastenings in one frame and one fastening in adjacent one.

Planks under 8 inches in width can be single fastened; that is, have one fastening driven through each frame.

All butts of planks must be fastened with at least *two* bolts going through the timber on which butt is cut and one bolt through each adjacent timber. These butt bolts must be riveted or have nuts set up on washers.

Treenails used for fastening planking must be made of straight-grained well-seasoned hardwood (locust or other approved kind) and must be driven into holes that are sufficiently small to insure the treenail having a maximum of holding strength. After treenails are driven their ends must be cut flush with outside of planking and inside of frame (or ceiling) and then wedged across grain with hardwood wedges.

When fastening planking it is very necessary to give proper consideration to the relative positions of fastenings of outside planking, inside ceiling and of all knee and other fastenings that must pass through frame timbers, because if this is not done many fastenings may pass through a frame so close to each other that wood of frame will be cut away and both strength of frame and holding power of fastenings reduced.

These rules should govern fastening of planking and ceiling:

(a) Not less than two-thirds of treenail fastenings should go through outside planking, frame and inside ceiling or clamps.

(b) At least one fastening in each frame should be of metal, clinched or riveted on inside of frame timber.

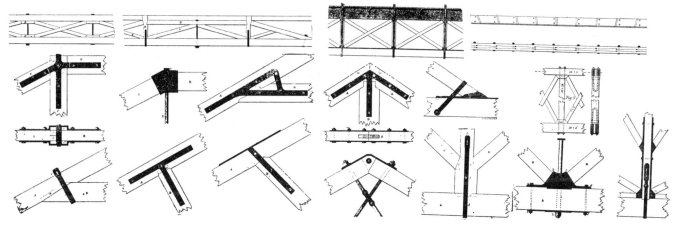

Fig. 86a. **Tie-Rods and Straps**

In a number of present-day wooden vessels defects in planking fastenings are apparent, and these defects are in some cases so serious that the structural strength of vessel is much below requirements. Some of the more serious defects are due to

(a) The use of augers that are too large for fastening diameter.

(b) The use of an improper number and size of fastenings (usually too few and too small).

(c) The use of unseasoned planking material and improper spacing of fastenings.

(d) Improper location of butts and improper butt fastening.

(e) The omission of edge fastenings, especially through garboards.

(f) Imperfect wedging of treenail fastenings.

(g) Failure to properly clinch, or rivet, metal fastenings of planking.

The augers used for plank fastenings should be sufficiently smaller than diameter of fastening to insure that fastening will require exceptionally hard blows to drive them. In my explanation of keel fastenings, I mentioned proper sizes of augers to use. The number of fastenings driven into each frame timber should not be less than mentioned in this paragraph and their diameters should never be less than given in table below:

PLANKING FASTENING

Thickness of Planking	Diameter of Bolts	Diameter of Treenails
1″	½″	⅞″
2½″	⅝″	1″
3-3½″	¾″	1⅛″
4-4½″	⅞″	1¼″
5-5½″	15/16″	1⅜″
6″ or over	1″	1½″

All planking material should be properly seasoned, because unless it is the natural shrinkage of wood during and aften construction will cause seams to open, caulking to loosen, and thus leaks will develop and strength of vessel be greatly reduced. It is folly to use "green" planking material. While air-drying is best, it is better to resort to smoke or steam-drying than to use unseasoned material and in fact if properly and carefully done smoke or steam-drying does not detract from strength and durability of planking material.

Butts should always be located according to rules mentioned in this chapter. Edge fastenings should always be used along garboards, at butts of sheer and along sheer strake.

Another method of fastening planking of vessels is when the plank is being put in place to use a sufficient number of spikes, "dump bolts," and treenails, to properly hold the planks in place and after the ceiling has been wrought to, complete the fastening by putting in the balance of treenails and all the through bolts. The first fastenings, to hold planks in place, go through planking and into frame timbers, and the second fastenings through planking, frame timbers and ceiling. And still another, older method is to use a minimum number of spikes and some temporary fastenings (bolts with nuts) for the first fastenings, and when the ceiling is being put in place to withdraw the temporary fastenings, continue the boring of these fastenings holes through ceiling, and then put in the permanent planking fastenings through planking, frame timbers and ceiling.

The principal things to bear in mind are:

(a) To consider the fastenings of ceiling and planking as being one and to so space the fastenings of both planking and ceiling that the maximum number will serve the double purpose of securing both planking and ceiling to the frame timbers.

(b) To so space all fastenings that there will be a minimum number of holes bored through the frame timbers. If the frame timbers are weakened too much by having an excessive number of fastening holes bored through them, the frames will not properly hold the fastenings and are also liable to break under the strains that are put on them when a vessel works in a sea.

Space fastenings properly, bore the proper sized holes for every fastening, drive and rivet or wedge each fastening properly, and use the proper number of fastenings and the vessel will have the maximum amount of strength. Figs. 46, 47 give illustrations of proper spacing methods for plank fastenings.

Continuing Planking

After garboards and sheer strake are fastened the balance of planking is got out, and as there is now an upper and a lower strake of planking in position (garboard and sheer) planking can proceed from sheer strake down and from garboard strake up.

All planks are "spiled" in manner that garboard is, and as each plank is fitted in place it should be tightly wedged against the next plank before any fastening is driven. Of course all seams of planking must be perfectly tight inside, and open, for caulking, on outside, and care should be taken to have upper edge of each plank follow the line laid out for it.

The last strake of planking to put in place is the

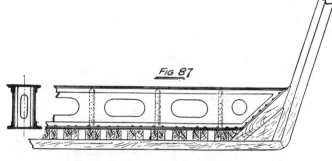

Fig 87

Fig. 87. Trussed Steel Keelson

shutter strake, so called because it "shuts" or closes the last space that planking has to fill. On Fig. 91 the shutter strake opening is clearly shown.

After planking is completed and fastenings all secured, planking is ready for roughing off caulking and smoothing, but this work should be delayed until the last moment in order to give planking time to properly dry out.

101[4]. DOUBLE PLANKING (FORE AND AFT)

The foregoing explanation refers to single planking put on in the usual manner. There are, however, two other accepted planking methods that I will now explain.

The first of these methods is the double fore-and-aft method of planking. In this method all planks run from stem to stern and are shaped in exactly the manner that the usual single thick planking is; but in place of planking being put on in one thickness it is divided into two, the combined thickness of the two being slightly less than the normal thickness of single planking. Thus if the single planking of a vessel is 4 inches, for a double-planked vessel the inner, or plank nearest to frame, would be 1¾ or 1½ inches and the outer planking would be 2 inches.

A vessel is double-planked in this manner:

The garboard and sheer strakes are got out of single thickness material in the usual manner, except that the upper edge of garboard and lower edge of sheer is rabbeted to a depth that leaves standing part along edge of same thickness as inner planking and about 2 inches in width. These planks are then fastened in place and spiling taken for inner planking. The inner planking is got out and fastened to frames with short fastenings sufficient in number and length to hold planks securely in place.

The seams of inner planking are next caulked, surface of planking smoothed and then outer planks are got out in such a manner that their seams will run along middle fore-and-aft lines of all inner planks. Of course

at garboard and sheer the outer plank fits into rabbet already cut. The fastenings of outer planking go through both outer and inner planks and are secured in the usual manner. It is necessary to thoroughly paint or fill outer surface of inner planks and inner surface of outer planks before they are fastened. Bitumastic paint or one of the many wood preservations are used for this. After outer planking is in place, seams are caulked and planking smoothed in the usual manner. It is evident that, as no seams go directly through from outside to inside of a plank, the double planking offers greater resistance to longitudinal strains than single planking, but it is more expensive to lay and for this reason is not very often used.

On Fig. 91a I show a sketch of a midship section outline and portion of profile with details of double planking clearly shown.

101[5]. DOUBLE DIAGONAL AND SINGLE FORE-AND-AFT PLANKING

This method of planking calls for the laying of two thin inner layers of planking diagonally from sheer to keel and one thick outer layer of planking fore-and-aft.

For this method of planking, filling timbers must be added to frame to fill space between frame timbers along sheer and at keel. These additions are necessary because ends of diagonal planks terminate along keel and sheer, and there must be solid wood at these places to receive and hold the fastenings.

The filling timbers that fill space between frame timbers need not extend more than a foot or so out from keel, or down from sheer.

The two inner layers of planking are made of relatively thin material, the total thickness of the two being slightly more than one-third thickness required for single thick planking. Thus if single thickness of planking laid planking should be about ¾-inch. The outer fore-and-aft planking thickness should be somewhat less than

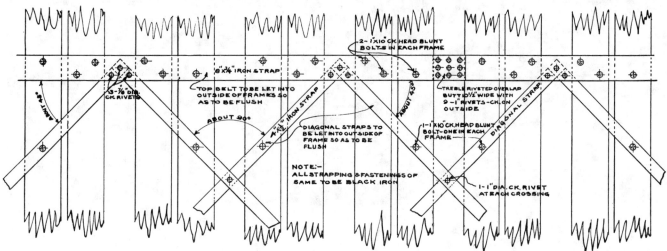

—DETAIL OF IRON STRAPPING—

Fig. 88

one-half the total thickness of planking required for single thick planking method, or about 1¾ inches thick if 4 inches is thickness of single planking.

When planking a vessel in this manner the diagonal planking is got out in planks about 8 or 9 inches wide and the first layer of diagonal planking is laid diagonally across frames, beginning at keel and extending to sheer at an inclination of about 45°. The planks are laid with tight seams and fastened with nails to every frame they cross. Where a butt comes an additional filling piece is secured between the frames and to this filling piece and its adjacent frame the butt end of plank is secured. When the whole frame is covered with one layer of the diagonal planking the planks are smoothed, seams caulked and surface painted.

The second layer is now put on diagonally *in an opposite direction* thus crossing inner layer at right angles. Outer diagonal layer of planking fastenings goes through inner layer into frames, and after this layer of planking is put on its seams are caulked and surface smoothed.

The outer fore-and-aft planking is got out and put on in exactly the manner that single thick planking is, except that the fastenings of outer planking go through both diagonal plankings into frames. After outer fore-and-aft planking is laid, the three thicknesses of planking are fastened together between frame timbers by means of short nails driven from inside into outer fore-and-aft planks or by means of nails driven from outside through the three thicknesses of planks and clinched; thus bringing all planks in close contact and adding strength to the planking structure. Of course the seams of outer planking are caulked and planking smoothed and finished in usual manner.

All fastenings of double and triple planking should be of metal properly riveted, or clinched.

On Fig. 91b I show details of this method of planking. As regards strength of construction the combined diagonal and fore-and-aft method of planking possesses great strength, but it is costly to plank a vessel in this manner.

Fig. 90. Framed Ready For Sheer

10m. CEILING—EXPLANATORY

During the time a vessel is being planked ceiling material can be got ready and when a sufficient portion of bottom and topside planking is fastened in place workmen can begin to lay and fasten ceiling.

The ceiling in a wooden vessel is for the double purpose of adding to structural strength and preventing dirt getting between frame timbers, it therefore is essential that ceiling be of proper strength, that it be properly laid and securely fastened, and that no openings be left between the seams of ceiling planks.

Ceiling is usually laid in planks that run fore-and-aft, the planks being tightly fitted against each other and fastened to every frame.

You will note by referring to cross-section drawings Figs. 202 and 212 that ceiling planks are thicker along bilges than along bottom and sides. This is usual and proper, because it is along the bilges that frames are weakest and strains are greatest. On Tables in Chapter III, I give proper thickness of ceiling to use at bottom, along side, and at turn of bilge.

It is seldom necessary to make templates or mark a ceiling width scale on inside of frames, because ceiling planks are usually got out as near straight and one width from end to end as it is possible to have them. On Fig. 92 is shown the first planks of bottom ceiling in place.

In a modern shipyard sawmill ceiling planks can be beveled and got ready to fit in place by using an adjustable head beveling machine.

10m¹. LAYING CEILING

The first planks of ceiling laid are those which butt against keelsons unless vessel is to have a *limber* strake,
in which case the first strake of ceiling is laid the width of limber strake out from keelson. On Fig. 212 cross-section limber strake is clearly shown next to keelson, and on Fig. 201 cross-section you will note that there is no limber strake.

10m². EXPLAINING THE REASON WHY A LIMBER PASSAGE IS NECESSARY

Water will find its way into the holds of all vessels and it is necessary that pumps be installed for its removal. These pumps have suctions led to lowest point in each hold or compartment, and open passageways through which the water can freely pass to pump suction are always arranged. In wooden vessels these passageways consist of openings cut across *outside* of frame timbers (these openings are clearly shown on Fig. 212) and as it is necessary to have some method of cleaning out the openings, should dirt fill them, it is usual to either reeve a chain through all openings from bow to stern, leaving the ends in a convenient place for crew to take hold of them, haul chain back and forth and thus clear limber openings of obstructions, or to leave removable boards over the frames and thus by removing a board crew can reach any obstruction in passage and clear it away. The best and most satisfactory method is to use both the chain and loose board.

The passage cut along outside of frame timbers is named the *limber;* the chain that is run through passage is named a *limber chain,* and the boards placed over opening left between ceiling and keelson are named *limber boards.*

The limbers are carefully cut before planking is put on, and limber chain is put in position before the strake

Fig. 91. A 255-Foot Auxiliary Schooner, From Designs by Tams, Lemoine & Crane. Planked Ready For Shutter

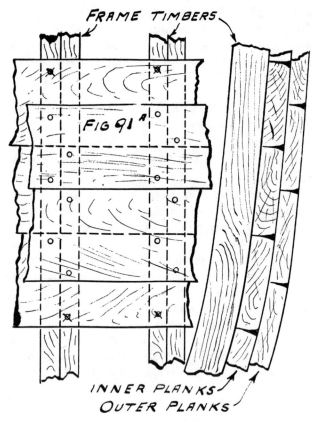

Fig. 91. Double Planking

of planking that covers limber is fastened in place. Of course limber chain must be much smaller than limber, otherwise it would stop flow of water. Dimensions of limbers should not be less than 2½ inches wide by 1½ inches deep and should be cut clear of a plank seam.

10m³. Butts and Fastening of Ceiling

Ceiling planks, especially along the bilges, should be of greatest possible length and all scarphs should be either hooked, nibbed, or locked. When cutting scarphs of ceiling planks consideration must be given to location of butts of outer planks, and all ceiling scarphs must be located some distance away from planking butts.

Each strake of ceiling must be fastened to each frame with at least two (metal) fastenings in addition to the through planking treenail fastenings that have to be driven through outside planking, frame and ceiling.

The bilge ceiling should first be fastened in place with a sufficient number of fastenings, driven into frames only, to hold it in position, and then through each frame and each bilge ceiling plank there should be driven from *outside,* one or two (metal) fastenings, and the inside ends of these fastenings must be riveted over clinch rings.

In addition to this *all* bilge ceiling and a greater portion of bottom and side ceiling must be edge-bolted between frame timbers. On Fig. 212 cross-section view these edge-bolts, or drifts, are clearly marked.

It is very essential that ceiling be laid with tight

seams and that the whole mass of ceiling planks be secured together and to framing in such a manner that it will offer greatest possible resistance to both longitudinal and transverse strains. On Fig. 43b the scarph of a strake of bilge ceiling can be seen on right-hand side, and on left-hand side the ends of fastenings are clearly discernible. A central steel keelson is also very clearly seen in this illustration.

10m⁴. Air Course and Salt Stops

If you will refer to Figs. 202 and 212 cross-section views, you will notice an open space left between strakes of ceiling immediately below the clamps, and you will also see on left-hand side of frame timber immediately above opening in ceiling a piece of wood that extends from inside of planking to outside of ceiling planks. The opening through ceiling is named an *air course* and is placed there to allow air to freely circulate around the spaces between frames. This air course is not a clear opening from bow to stern, but consists of a series of short openings at stated intervals. In other words, portions of the space are filled in and other portions left open. Air courses are usually between 3 and 4 inches wide and their length is equal to the open space between frame timbers. The piece of wood that extends across frame is named a salt stop.

The salt stop consists of short pieces of wood wide enough to reach from inside of planking to outside of ceiling and long enough to fill the open spaces between frame timbers. The purpose for which they are placed

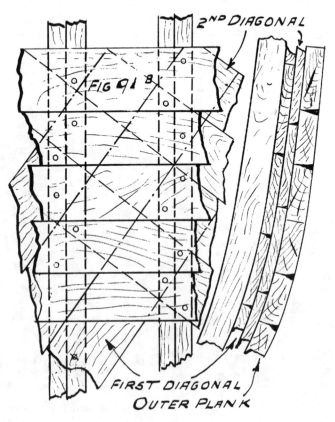

Fig. 92. Ceiling Commenced

there is to hold the salt placed between frame timbers when a vessel is salted.

10m⁵. SALTING

Salting a vessel consists in filling all open spaces between frame timbers, from keel salt stops, with coarse rock salt. Salt is an excellent wood preservative, especially in damp places and where air cannot freely circulate, and it has been found that if all open spaces between the frame timbers of a vessel be filled with salt, the timbers will resist decay longer than unsalted timbers will. For this reason all insurance classification societies will add a named period (usually one or two years) to a vessel's classification if vessel is salted while on the stocks or building ways. When a vessel is to be salted, it is necessary to enclose the space occupied by limbers and chains, otherwise the salt will fill these spaces and clog the openings.

It is advisable to salt a vessel.

10m⁶. DOUBLE AND TRIPLE CEILING

While it is the usual practice to use a single thickness of ceiling put on in manner explained, some of the more advanced builders are beginning to recognize the advantages of using double fore-and-aft ceiling, or triple (two diagonal and one fore-and-aft) diagonal and fore-and-aft ceiling.

By the use of double ceiling the same strength of construction can be obtained by using ceiling having a total thickness of about seven-eighths of single ceiling thickness, and nearly all edge fastenings can be dispensed with. Of course first layer of ceiling planks must be fastened independently, and fastenings of second layer must be spaced to clear inner ceiling fastenings. In addition to the usual fastenings into frame timbers additional short fastenings should be driven along seams

of planks to secure edges of second layer of ceiling to layer below.

Triple ceiling without doubt has greater strength per unit of material than either single or double, and for this reason the total thickness of triple ceiling need not be more than three-quarters or five-eighths of single ceiling thickness.

When triple ceiling is used filling timbers must be fitted to fill open spaces between frame timbers along keelson, along sheer, and wherever a butt of diagonal laid ceiling will come.

The first diagonal layer of ceiling crosses frame timbers at an inclination of about 45° and is fastened to frames with sufficient fastenings to firmly hold the planks in position. The second diagonal layer of ceiling crosses the first at right angles and is fastened securely to first layer and to frames. The third, fore-and-aft, layer is fitted and fastened in the manner explained for single thick ceiling, and as all of its fastenings go through the first and second diagonal layers the whole ceiling structure becomes one solid mass of wood that offers great resistance to both longitudinal and transverse strains.

When triple ceiling is used it is not necessary to increase thickness of bilge ceiling.

When double ceiling is used it is very necessary to thoroughly coat the upper surface of first layer of ceiling and under surface of second layer with a good wood preservative before the second layer is fastened in place. With the triple layer it is necessary to coat surfaces of the three layers of planks, the object being to prevent decay through moisture and stagnant air getting into pores of wood.

Moisture, stagnant air and dirt are the three prime causes of decay in wood.

Fig. 93. Caulking Bottom Planking

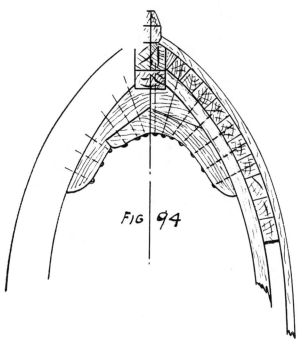

Fig. 94. Breast Hook

10m⁷. CLAMPS AND SHELF PIECES

The clamps, auxiliary clamps, and shelf and lock shelf, is an assemblage of longitudinal timbers firmly fastened to frame timbers, and together, their use being to support deck beams and strengthen the hull along each deck.

On Figs. 201, 202, 212 cross-section drawings, different methods of assembling the pieces are clearly shown, and on Tables in Chapter III is given proper dimensions of materials to use for these parts.

Clamps material is usually got out at the time ceiling material is, and in the same manner.

Clamp and shelf material should be of the greatest possible length and all scarphs must be either locked, hooked, or keyed and edge-bolted, the length of each scarph being not less than six times the width of material. Clamps must be fastened to each frame timber they cross with not less than two through bolts riveted over clinch rings.

The forward end of each clamp usually terminates at apron, and clamps at opposite sides of vessel are connected together by means of knees that are fitted against apron and between the clamps. These knees, called breast-hooks, are secured to apron and also to clamps and frame timbers. On Fig. 94 is shown an excellent method of securing forward ends of clamps by means of wood and steel breast-hook.

The after ends of all clamps that do not merge into the framing of an elliptical stern should also be securely kneed to transom or stern framing. In addition to the clamp breast-hooks at stem there must also be at least one hook in the space between each deck and also at the forward termination of all pointers.

10m⁸. POINTERS

These are built-up assemblages of timber located at bow and stern. The bow pointers begin at after end of apron and stemson, near to forefoot, and run aft and upwards in a diagonal direction until they reach a tier of deck beams. On Fig. 201 interior profile view, two bow and three stern pointers are clearly shown.

At the stern the pointers begin at deadwood at varying distances from keelson and extend upwards and forward.

Pointers are usually constructed of several pieces of oak, or yellow pine, steam-bent to shape and fitted on top of each other, thus forming a solid laminated structure of great strength. The pointers lay on ceiling, are through bolted to ceiling frame timbers and planking, and should extend upwards to most convenient tier of beams and be kneed to clamp of that tier.

Pointers are for the purpose of strengthening the forward and after portions of vessel against a tendency to "hog."

In general pointers should be not over 6 feet apart at points of termination at bow or stern, should be fitted at an inclination of about 45°, and should be fastened to every frame timber they cross with two bolts. The proper dimensions of pointers is given on Tables in Chapter III.

I am of the opinion that pointers of steel channels, or of angles and plates riveted together, are preferable to the wood ones because greater strength can be obtained from a given weight of material.

10n. DECK FRAMING

Deck beams can be sawed to shape and finished in the sawmill of a modern shipyard during the time that vessel's frame is being erected and planking is being put on.

The deck framing of a vessel consists of transverse beams and half-beams, carlins, lodge and hanging knees,

Fig. 95. View of Interior Showing Knees

Fig. 95a. Large Knees Ready For Use

hatch coamings and hatch framing; and in a vessel having more than one deck there must be a properly framed and fastened set of deck beams installed at every deck position. Details of framing of the various decks are always shown on longitudinal profile, and transverse construction plans somewhat in the manner they are shown on Fig. 201 plans.

It is well to remember that in some vessels the lower tier of beams (called hold beams) are merely for the purpose of adding transverse strength and do not carry deck planking.

The sided and moulded dimensions of deck beams vary with width of vessel and not with tonnage; and the spacing of deck beams should always correspond with spacing of frames. In other words, the ends of each deck's beams should bear against a frame timber and rest upon clamp and shelf pieces in one of the ways illustrated on construction drawings of Figs. 201, 202, 212. On Fig. 28 and Fig. 27 are shown details of hatch and mast partner construction with parts marked for identification.

In nearly all vessels it is necessary to support the deck beams along the center line of vessel. This supporting is done by erecting tiers of stanchions, at stated intervals, and fastening their ends securely.

The lower tier of stanchions have their lower ends securely fastened to keelson and their upper ends to lower tier of beams. The next tier of beams are set up immediately over the lower tier ones and have their lower ends secured to deck and deck beam they rest on, and their upper ends secured to beams of deck above. Thus each succeeding stanchion is placed immediately above one below, with the result that the greatest possible support along the longitudinal center line is given to the whole deck structure.

It is very necessary that deck beams be properly crowned on their upper surface. The amount of crown is specified by the designer and is usually much less for lower deck beams than for the upper or exposed deck ones.

If you will turn to Fig. 201 you will note that the ends of both tiers of deck beams are securely kneed to ceiling and framing. This is an excellent method of fastening deck beams, especially if the vessel is a large one. Fig. 95 is an exceptionally clear photograph of hanging deck knees in a vessel built from plans Fig. 201, and on Fig. 95a is shown some natural or root knees sawed to shape.

On Fig. 212 cross-section view is shown another method of securing ends of deck beams. Here there are two shelves and two auxiliary clamps to take the place of the hanging knees, and as one of the shelves is what is termed a *lock* shelf, and the whole structure of shelves, clamps and beam is thoroughly well secured to each other

Fig. 96. View of Main Deck, No. 1 Hatch
From Forward House Looking Aft

Fig. 97. The Pneumatic Hammer Driving Deck Spikes in Holes Which Have Been Drilled and Countersunk at the Same Operation by Another Little David. These Tools Make Short Work of Numerous Tasks

and to frame timbers, the structure is amply strong to withstand strains that tend to separate the pieces.

Now a few words explaining a *lock shelf.*

10n[1]. LOCK SHELF

A lock shelf is a shelf to which the beam is locked by means of a key piece, or coak, or projection that fits into a corresponding depression in underside of beam. If you will look carefully at the Fig. 212 cross-section you will notice (dotted) end of lock piece projecting above upper surface of shelf and let into underside of beam. In my opinion hanging knees are stronger and preferable to the lock shelf and added shelf and clamp timbers.

Bear in mind that lock piece can be used with advantage when hanging knees are used.

Dimensions and number of hanging knees required for vessels of various sizes are given on Table VIII[1] in Chapter VIII.

I have mentioned lodge knees, so I will next explain why they are used.

10n[2]. LODGE KNEES

Lodge knees are used to prevent the deck beams turning on their sides, and for the purpose of strengthening deck framing, near sides of vessel, against fore-and-aft movement.

On Fig. 28 lodge knees are shown in position, and on deck framing of Figs. 201, 206, 207 lodge knees can be seen in position.

10n[3]. KNEE FASTENINGS

Knees of all kinds should be through fastened with bolts passing through knee, clamps, frame, and planking, and through knee deck beam, shelf, the fastenings being driven at inclinations that will enable the knee to resist strain from all directions. On Figs. 201, 202, 212 cross-section views lines of direction are clearly shown by dotted line that indicate fastenings.

10n[4]. HATCH FRAMING

In every vessel that carries cargo there must be a sufficient number of openings through the decks to allow the cargo to be properly and quickly loaded and unloaded, each of the openings must be sufficiently large to permit the most bulky piece of cargo to pass through it, and all of the openings must be arranged to enable the crew to make them absolutely watertight when vessel is at sea.

The openings through decks are named hatchways and it is usual to locate the hatchways in most convenient positions along upper deck and then to have the hatch openings through lower decks come immediately under the upper deck openings. By doing this it is possible to load or unload cargo on any deck or in hold with a minimum of labor. The dimensions of hatch openings having been determined it is necessary to properly frame around the openings, to make removable hatch covers to close the openings, and to have watertight paulins with necessary hatch battens with wedges fitted over the hatch covers and arranged to fasten tightly around the hatch coamings.

Fig. 27 is a detailed drawing of the framing of a hatch and each part is identified by name. On the draw-

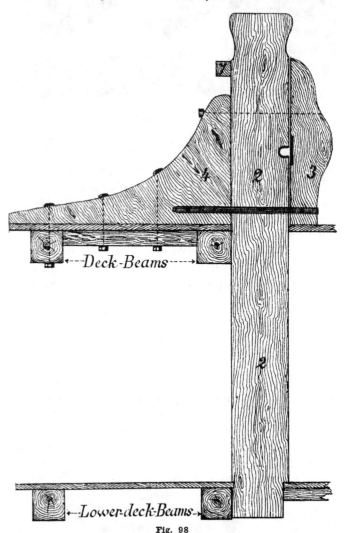

←--*Deck-Beams*--→

←--*Lower-deck-Beams*--→

Fig. 98

Fig. 99. The Caulking Tool Can Be Held in Any Position and Is Able to Deliver 1,500 Taps a Minute. The Oakum Is Fed Mechanically, so That The Work of "Horsing It In" Can Be Done Rapidly and Thoroughly, No Matter Where the Seam Is Located

ing referred to you will notice that the fore-and-aft deck pieces of hatch coaming stop at ends of opening and that the cross pieces are fitted into them. This is the proper method to use for a small sailing vessel, but in large vessels, especially those having a central superstructure or house, it is better to allow the upper deck fore-and-aft timbers of hatch coamings to extend in one piece from forward to aft and to let each cross piece into these fore-and-aft timbers. Then if supporting stanchions are placed directly under these fore-and-aft timbers, the maximum strength, which will, of course, come directly over the under deck fore-and-aft around the hatch openings, is obtained without an unnecessary amount of material being used.

With the construction shown on Fig. 27 there is a slight weakening of structure around hatch openings, but with the continuous fore-and-aft pieces of coaming supported with stanchions there is no weakening. Of course, when the continuous fore-and-aft pieces are used, the deck is practically divided longitudinally into three, and therefore there must be a sufficient number of openings cut in longitudinal timbers, between deck and lower edge of timbers, to allow water to pass freely across the deck and flow into water ways.

On Fig. 96 is shown main deck hatch framing of a schooner and on Figs. 201, 202, 206, 207, 212, 213 are shown details of hatch framing used on vessels constructed from these plans.

On Fig. 201, upper deck plan, you will clearly see the continuous fore-and-aft members of hatch framing, and on Fig. 207, deck framing plan, you will note the continuous under deck fore-and-aft members of the hatch framing.

Chapter XI

Ship Joinery

Ship joinery is the art of cutting, dressing, framing, and finishing wood for the external and internal finishing of a ship. The ship carpenters erect the structure that gives strength to the ship and their work cannot be removed without affecting the strength of structure, while that of the joiners is not intended to add to structural strength and therefore can be removed without affecting strength.

As the finish and appearance of joiner work largely depends upon the care with which the work is done it is essential that woods used for joiner work be thoroughly seasoned, be properly cut, and be of kinds that will not warp or be affected by changes in temperature or by moisture in air.

The best joiner woods available for use in U. S. A. are: Mahogany, teak, Q. S. oak, for natural wood finishes and parts that will be exposed to weather; and white pine, yellow pine, fir, cypress, cedar for parts that will be painted.

While many of the joints and methods of doing work are in common use by both ship carpenters and joiner workers, it is wrong to suppose that a good ship carpenter can do good joiner work because the nature of the work is entirely different. The ship carpenter works on heavy materials and seldom devotes much time to finish of surfaces, while the joiner worker works with light material and has to continually think of finish and appearance of the work when it is completed.

On sheet A joiner work illustration sheet, I show some commonly used joints, or joiner workers' methods of connecting pieces of wood.

11a. Description of Sheet A Joiner Work Illustrations

On this illustration sheet is shown a number of joints used by ship joiners.

Fig. 1 shows a joint formed by planing edges of board perfectly true and inserting wood or iron pins (called dowels) at intervals along joined edges. The pin is shown by dotted line, and such a joint is said to be doweled.

Fig. 2 shows a joint made by grooving edge of one piece of wood and forming a tongue upon another. A joint of this kind is commonly used for uniting pieces of flooring, partitions, etc. The shrinking of wood joined in this manner will cause joint to open, therefore, it is usual to run a bead, or V, along edge of one of the pieces and thus make shrinkage opening less noticeable.

Bead is shown by dotted line on upper edge and V by dotted line on lower edge of Fig. 2.

Fig. 3 is a double-tongued joint, now seldom used.

Fig. 4 is a combined tongue-and-groove joint with rabbet. It is used on tight seamed floors when it is desired to fasten the pieces along their edges.

In Fig. 5 the groove and tongue are angular.

Fig. 6 is a kind of grooving and tonguing resorted to when the timber is thick, or when the tongue requires to be stronger than it would be if formed in the substance of the wood itself. In this mode of jointing corresponding grooves are formed in the edges of the boards, and the tongue is formed of a slip of a harder or stronger wood.

Figs. 7, 8, 9 are examples of slip-tongue joints; the tongue in Fig. 9 is of wrought iron.

Fig. 10 shows dovetail grooves, with a slip tongue of corresponding form, which, of course, must be inserted endways.

Fig. 11 is a simple rebated joint. One-half the thickness of each board is cut away to the same extent, and when the edges are lapped the surfaces lie in the same plane.

Fig. 12 shows a complex mode of grooving and tonguing. The joint is in this case put together by sliding the one edge with its grooves and tongues endways into the corresponding projections and recesses of the other. The boards when thus jointed together cannot be drawn asunder laterally or at right angles to their surface, without rending; but, in the event of shrinking, there is great risk of the wood being rent.

In joining angles formed by the meeting of two boards various joints are used, among which are those which follow:

Fig. 13, the common mitre-joint, used in joining two boards at right angles to each other. Each edge is planed to an angle of 45°.

Fig. 14 shows a mitre-joint keyed by a slip-tongue.

Fig. 15 shows a mitre-joint when the boards are of different thickness. The mitre on thicker piece is only formed to the same extent as that on edge of thinner piece; hence there is a combination of the mitre and simple butt joint.

Fig. 16 shows a different mode of joining two boards of either the same or of different thickness. One board is rebated, and only a small portion at the angle of each board is mitred. This joint may be nailed both ways.

In Fig. 17 both boards are rebated, and a slip-tongue is inserted as a key. This also may be nailed through from both faces.

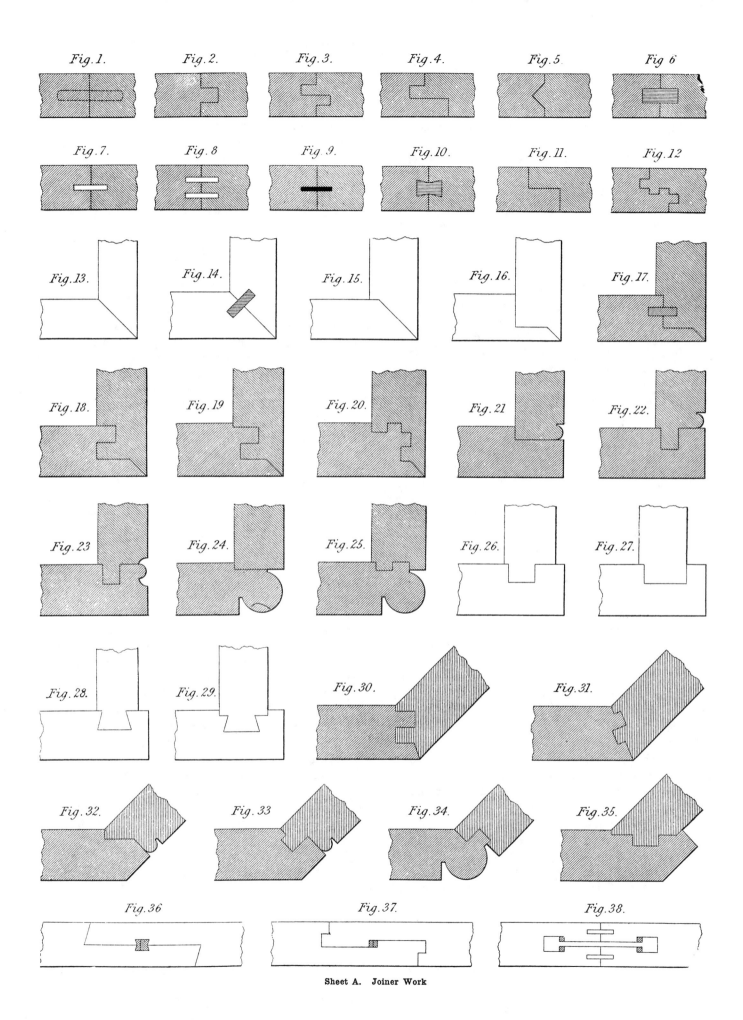

Fig.1. Fig.2. Fig.3. Fig.4. Fig.5. Fig 6

Fig.7. Fig.8. Fig.9. Fig.10. Fig.11. Fig.12

Fig.13. Fig.14. Fig.15. Fig.16. Fig.17.

Fig.18. Fig.19. Fig.20. Fig.21. Fig.22.

Fig.23 Fig.24. Fig.25. Fig.26. Fig.27.

Fig.28. Fig.29. Fig.30. Fig.31.

Fig.32. Fig.33. Fig.34. Fig.35.

Fig.36 Fig.37. Fig.38.

Sheet A. Joiner Work

Figs. 18 and 19 are combinations of grooving and tonguing with the last-described modes. These can be fitted with great accuracy and joined with certainty.

Fig. 20 is a joint formed by the combination of mitring with double grooving and tonguing, shown in Fig. 12. The boards must in this case be slipped together endways, and cannot be separated by a force applied at right angles to the planes of their surfaces.

In all these mitre-joints the faces of boards meet at the angle, and the slight opening which might be caused by shrinkage would be scarcely observable. In the butt-joints which follow, the face of the one board abuts against the face of the other, the edge of which is consequently in the plane of the surface of first board, the shrinkage of which would cause an opening at joint. To make this opening less apparent is the object of forming the bead-moulding seen in the next five figures.

In Fig. 21 the thicker board is rebated from the face, and a small bead is formed on the external angle of abutting board.

In Fig. 22 a groove is formed in the inner face of one board and a tongue on edge of the other.

In Fig. 23 the boards are grooved and tongued as in the last figure. A cavetto is run on the external angle of abutting board, and the bead and a cavetto on the internal angle of other board.

In Fig. 24 a quirked bead run on edge of one board, and the edge of abutting board forms the double quirk.

In Fig. 25 a double quirk bead is formed at the external angle, and the boards are grooved and tongued. The external bead is attended with this advantage, that it is not so liable to injury as the sharp arris.

In Figs. 26 and 27 the joints used in putting together cisterns are shown.

Figs. 28 and 29 are joints for the same purpose. They are of the dovetail form, and require to be slipped together endways.

Figs. 30 to 35 show the same kind of joints as have been described, applied to the framing together of boards meeting in an obtuse angle.

Figs. 36 and 37 show methods of joining boards together laterally by keys, in the manner of scarphing; and Fig. 38 shows another method of securing two pieces, such as those of a circular window frame-head by keys.

The methods of joining timber described are all more or less imperfect. The liability of wood to shrink renders it essential that the joiner should use it in such narrow widths as to prevent this tendency marring the appearance of his work; and, as even when so used it will still expand and contract, provision should be made to admit of this. The groove-and-tongue joint admits of a certain amount of variation, and the grooved, tongued, and beaded joint admits of this variation with a degree of concealment, but the most perfect mode of satisfying both conditions is by the use of framed work.

Framing in joinery consists of pieces of wood of the same thickness, nailed together so as to inclose a space or spaces. These spaces are filled in with boards of a less thickness, termed *panels*.

On sheet B joiner work illustrations is shown method of framing joiner work partitions, doors, etc.

11b. DESCRIPTION OF SHEET B JOINER WORK ILLUSTRATIONS

In Fig. 1b, *a a, b b* shows framing, *c c* raised panel and *c* plain panels. The vertical pieces of the framing *a a* are termed *styles,* and the horizontal pieces *b b* are termed *rails*. The rails have tenons which are let into mortises in the styles. The inner edges of both styles and rails are grooved to receive the edges of panels, and thus the panel is at liberty to expand and contract. Framing is always used for the better description of work. Wide panels should be formed of narrow pieces glued together, with the grain reversed alternately. They should never exceed 15 inches wide, and 4 feet long. These dimensions, indeed, are extremes which should be avoided.

The panels may be boards of equal thickness throughout, in which case the grooves in the styles and rails are made of sufficient width to admit their edges, as in Fig. 2b dotted line. These are termed *flat* panels. *Flush* panels, again, have one of their faces in the same plane as the face of framing, and are rebated round the edges until a tongue sufficient to fit the groove is left. *Raised* panels are those of which the thickness is such that one of their surfaces is a little below the framing, but at a certain distance from the inner edge, all round it, begins to diminish in thickness to the edge, which is thinned off to enter the groove. The line at which the diminution takes place is marked either by a square sinking or a moulding. All these kinds of panels are sometimes combined.

Flush panel framing has generally a simple bead stuck on its edges all round the panel, and the work is called *bead flush*. But in inferior work the bead is run on the edge of the panels in the direction of the grain only, that is, on the two sides of each panel, while its two ends are left plain; this is termed *bead butt*. The nomenclature, however, of the various descriptions of framed, and of framed and moulded work, will be best understood by reference to the annexed figures. Fig. 2b dotted line is the flat panel. In this the framing is not moulded, and is termed *square*. In Figs. 2b and 3b the same framing is shown with a moulding stuck on it. In Fig. 4b the same framing is shown with a moulding *laid in* or *planted* on each side. In Fig. 5b a *bead flush* panel is represented; Fig. 6b a raised panel with stuck mouldings; and Fig. 7b a panel *raised* on one side with *stuck mouldings*.

11c. DOVETAILING

Dovetail-joint.—This joint has three varieties:—1st, the common dovetail, where the dovetails are seen on each side of the angle alternately; 2d, the lapped dovetail, in

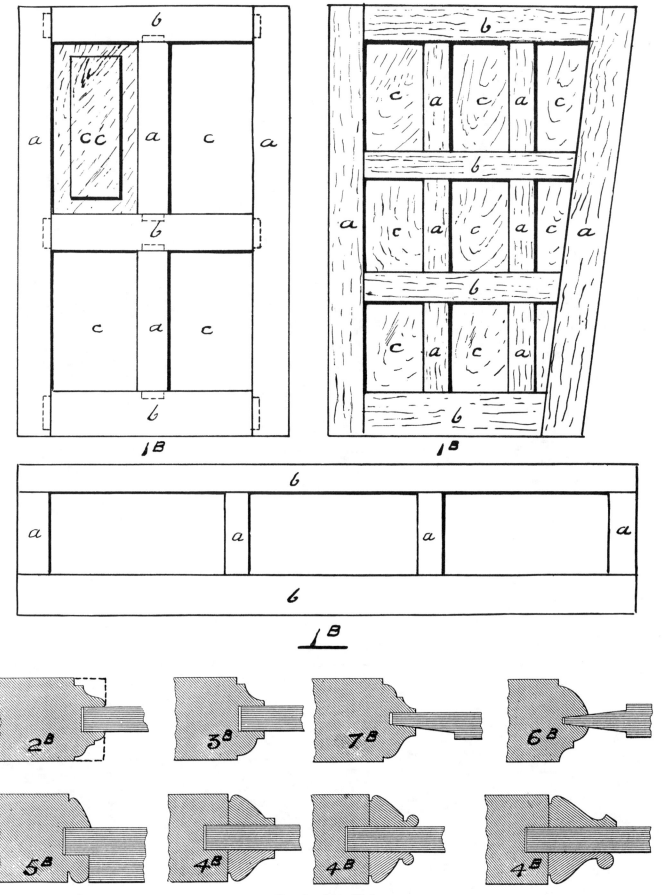

Sheet B. Joiner Work

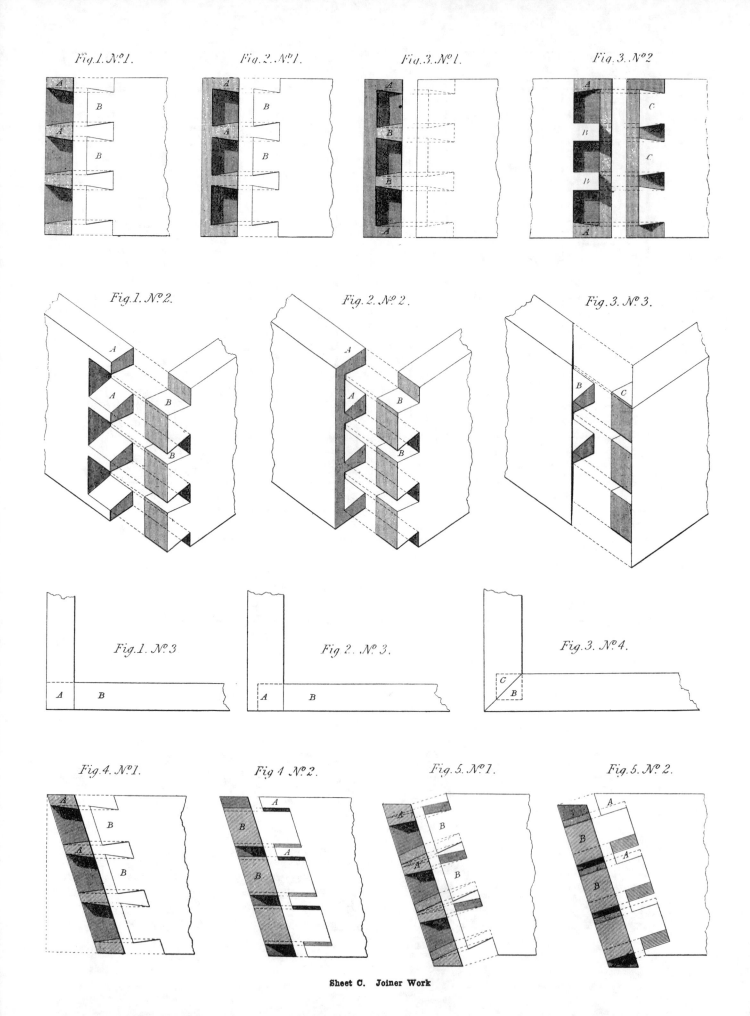

Fig. 1. N.º 1.　　Fig. 2. N.º 1.　　Fig. 3. N.º 1.　　Fig. 3. N.º 2

Fig. 1. N.º 2.　　Fig. 2. N.º 2.　　Fig. 3. N.º 3.

Fig. 1. N.º 3　　Fig. 2. N.º 3.　　Fig. 3. N.º 4.

Fig. 4. N.º 1.　　Fig 1 N.º 2.　　Fig. 5. N.º 1.　　Fig. 5. N.º 2.

Sheet C. Joiner Work

which the dovetails are seen only on one side of angle; and, 3d, the lapped and mitred dovetail, in which the joint appears externally as a common mitre-joint. The lapped and mitred joint is useful in salient angles, in finished work, but it is not so strong as the common dovetail, and therefore, in all re-entrant angles, the latter should be used.

The three varieties of dovetail-joint above enumerated are illustrated on sheet C joiner work illustration.

DESCRIPTION OF SHEET C JOINER WORK ILLUSTRATIONS

Fig. 1, No. 1 is an elevation of the common dovetail-joint; No. 2, a perspective representation; and No. 3, a plan of the same.

In all the figures the pins or dovetails of the one side are marked A, and those of the other side are marked B.

Fig. 2, Nos. 1, 2, 3.—In these the lap-joint is represented in plan, elevation, and perspective projection.

Fig. 3, Nos. 1, 2, 3.—In these figures the mitred dovetail-joint is represented in plan, elevation, and perspective. The dovetails of adjoining sides are marked respectively B and C in all figures.

Fig. 4, Nos. 1, 2 and Fig. 5, Nos. 1, 2, show methods of dovetailing an angle when sides are inclined. The pins of one side are marked A and those of the other B on all figures.

11d. HINGING

Hinging is the art of hanging two pieces of wood together, such as a door to its frame, by certain ligaments that permit one or other of them to revolve. The ligament is termed a hinge.

Hinges are of many sorts, among which may be enumerated butts, rising hinges, casement hinges, chest hinges, folding hinges, screw hinges, scuttle hinges, shutter hinges, desk hinges, back fold hinges, and center-pin or center-point hinges.

As there are many varieties of hinges, there are also many modes of applying even the simplest of them. In some cases the hinge is visible, in others it is necessary that it should be concealed. In some it is required not only that the one hinged part shall revolve on the other, but it shall be thrown back to a greater or lesser distance from the joint.

On illustration sheets D, E, F, joiner work are shown a great variety of hinges and methods of hinging.

DESCRIPTION OF SHEET D JOINER WORK ILLUSTRATIONS

Fig. 1, No. 1, shows the hinging of a door to open to a right angle, as in No. 2.

Fig. 2, Nos. 1 and 2, and Fig. 3, Nos 1 and 2. These figures show other modes of hinging doors to open to 90°.

Fig. 4, Nos. 1 and 2. These figures show a manner of hinging a door to open to 90°, and in which the hinge is concealed. The segments are described from center of hinge g, and the dark shaded portion requires to be cut out to permit it to pass the leaf of hinge g f.

Fig. 5, Nos. 1 and 2, show an example of center-pin hinge permitting door to open either way, and to fold back against the wall in either direction. Draw a b at right angles to door, and just clearing the line of wall, or rather representing the plane in which the inner face of door will lie when folded back against wall; bisect it in f, and draw f d the perpendicular to a b, which make equal to a f or f b, and d is the place of the center of hinge.

Fig. 6, Nos. 1 and 2, another variety of center-pin hinging opening to 90°. The distance of b from a c is equal to half of a c. In this, as in the former case, there is a space between door and wall when the former is folded back. In the succeeding figures this is obviated.

Fig. 7, No. 1. Bisect the angle at a by the line a b; draw d e and make e g equal to once and a half times a d; draw f g at right angle to e d, and bisect the angle f g e by the line c g, meeting a b in b, which is the center of hinge.

No. 2 shows the door folded back when the point e falls on the continuation of line f g.

Fig. 8, Nos. 1 and 2. To find the center draw a b, making an angle of 45° with the inner edge of door, and draw c b parallel to the jamb, meeting it in b, which is the center of hinge. The door revolves to the extent of quadrant d c.

DESCRIPTION OF SHEET E JOINER WORK ILLUSTRATIONS

Fig. 1, Nos. 1 and 2; Fig. 2, Nos. 1 and 2; and Fig. 3, Nos. 1 and 2, examples of center-pin joints, and Fig. 4, Nos. 1 and 2, do not require detailed description.

Fig. 5, Nos. 1, 2, and 3, show the flap with a bead a closing into a corresponding hollow, so that the joint cannot be seen through.

Fig. 6, Nos. 1, 2, and 3, show the hinge a b equally let into the styles, and its knuckle forming a part of the bead on edge of style B. The beads on each side are equal and opposite to each other, and the joint pin is in the center.

Fig. 7, Nos. 1, 2, and 3. In this example, the knuckle of hinge forms portion of bead on style B, which is equal and opposite to the bead on style A.

In Fig. 8, Nos. 1, 2, and 3, the beads are not opposite.

DESCRIPTION OF SHEET F JOINER WORK ILLUSTRATIONS

Fig. 1, shows the hinging of a back flap when the center of hinge is in the middle of joint.

Fig. 2, Nos. 1 and 2, shows the manner of hinging a back flap when it is necessary to throw the flap back from the joint.

Fig. 3, Nos. 1 and 2, is an example of a rule-joint-hinge. The further the hinge is imbedded in the wood, the greater will be the cover of joint when opened to a right angle.

Fig. 4, Nos. 1 and 2, shows the manner of finding the rebate when hinge is placed on the contrary side.

Let f be the center of hinge, a b the line of joint on the same side, h c the line of joint on the opposite side,

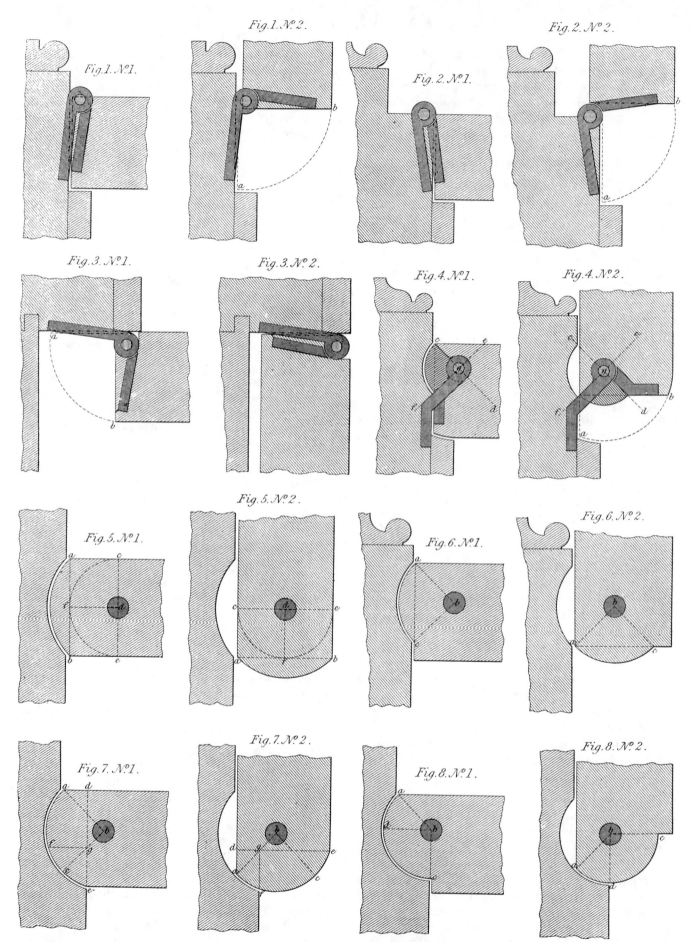

Fig. 1. Nᵒ 1.

Fig. 1. Nᵒ 2.

Fig. 2. Nᵒ 1.

Fig. 2. Nᵒ 2.

Fig. 3. Nᵒ 1.

Fig. 3. Nᵒ 2.

Fig. 4. Nᵒ 1.

Fig. 4. Nᵒ 2.

Fig. 5. Nᵒ 1.

Fig. 5. Nᵒ 2.

Fig. 6. Nᵒ 1.

Fig. 6. Nᵒ 2.

Fig. 7. Nᵒ 1.

Fig. 7. Nᵒ 2.

Fig. 8. Nᵒ 1.

Fig. 8. Nᵒ 2.

Sheet D. Joiner Work Hinging

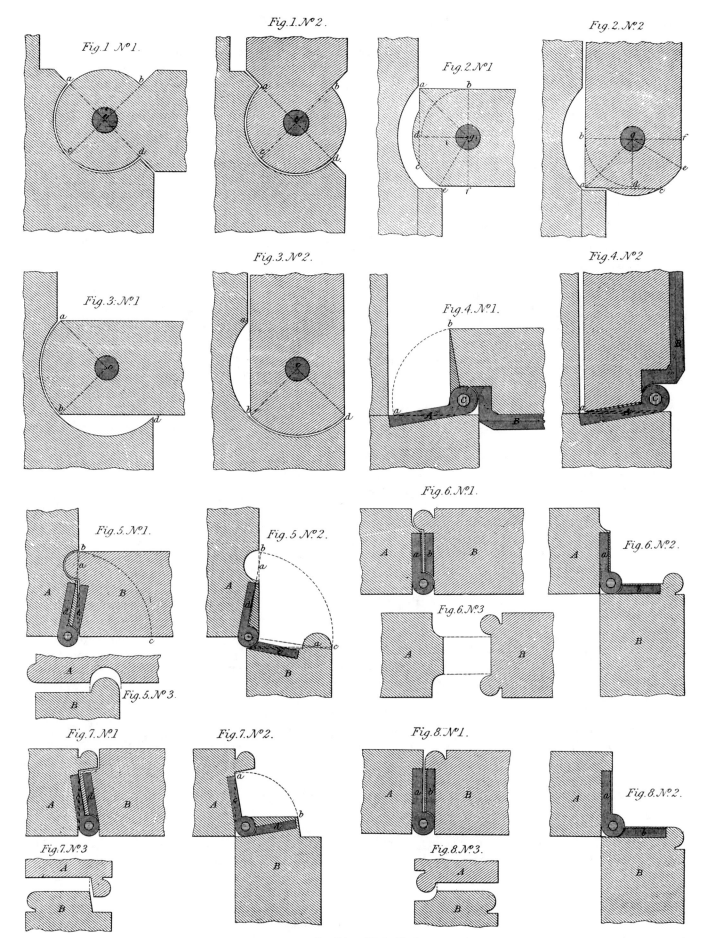

Fig. 1. Nº 1.

Fig. 1. Nº 2.

Fig. 2. Nº 1

Fig. 2. Nº 2

Fig. 3. Nº 1

Fig. 3. Nº 2.

Fig. 4. Nº 1.

Fig. 4. Nº 2

Fig. 5. Nº 1.

Fig. 5 Nº 2.

Fig. 6. Nº 1.

Fig. 6. Nº 2.

Fig. 5. Nº 3.

Fig. 6. Nº 3.

Fig. 7. Nº 1.

Fig. 7. Nº 2.

Fig. 8. Nº 1.

Fig. 8. Nº 2.

Fig. 7. Nº 3.

Fig. 8. Nº 3.

Sheet E.   Joiner Work Hinging

and *b c* the total depth of rebate. Bisect *b c* in *e* and join *e f;* on *e f* describe a semicircle cutting *a b* in *g,* and through *g* and *e* draw *g h* cutting *d c* in *h,* and join *d h, h g,* and *g a* to form the joint.

Fig. 5, Nos. 1 and 2, is a method of hinging employed when the flap on being opened has to be at a distance from the style. It is used to throw the opened flap or door clear of the mouldings of coping.

Fig. 6, Nos. 1 and 2, is the ordinary mode of hinging shutter to a sash frame.

11e. Mouldings

A few of the principal ornamental mouldings used by joiners is illustrated and described in this chapter. The names given to the mouldings are the proper architectural ones and the methods of laying the mouldings out are described in detail.

Grecian and Roman versions of the same mouldings are shown on sheet G joiner illustrations.

Fillet or Listel right-angled mouldings require no description.

The Astragal or Bead.—To describe this moulding, divide its height into two equal parts, and from the point of division as a center, describe a semicircle, which is the contour of the astragal.

Doric Annulets.—The left-hand figure shows the Roman, and the right-hand figure the Grecian form of this moulding. To describe the latter proceed thus:—Divide the height *b a* into four equal parts, and make the projection equal to three of them. The vertical divisions give the lines of the under side of the annulets, and the height of each annulet, *c c,* is equal to one-fifth of the projection; the upper surface of *c* is at right angles to the line of slope.

Listel and Fascia.—(Roman.)—Divide the whole height into seven equal parts, make the listel equal to two of these and its projection equal to two. With the third vertical division as a center, describe a quadrant. (Grecian.)—Divide the height into four equal parts, make the fillet equal to one of them, and its projection equal to three-fourths of its height.

Cavetto or Hollow.—In Roman architecture this moulding is a circular quadrant; in Grecian architecture it is an elliptical quadrant, which may be described by any of the methods given in the first part of the work.

Ovolo or Quarter-round.—This is a convex moulding, the reverse of the cavetto, but described in the same manner.

Cyma Recta.—A curve of double curvature, formed of two equal quadrants. In the Roman moulding these are circular, and in the Grecian moulding elliptical.

Cyma Reversa.—A curve of double curvature, like the former, and formed in the same manner.

Trochilus or Scotia.—A hollow moulding, which, in Roman architecture, is formed of two unequal circular arcs, thus:—Divide the height into ten equal parts, and

at the sixth division draw a horizontal line. From the seventh division as a center, and with seven divisions as radius, describe from the lower part of the moulding an arc, cutting the above horizontal line, and join the center and the point of intersection by a line which bisects; and from the point of bisection as a center, with half the length of the line as radius, describe an arc to form the **upper part of the curve.** There are many other methods of drawing this moulding. The Grecian trochilus is an elliptical or parabolic curve, the proportions of which are shown by the divisions of the dotted lines.

The Torus.—The Roman moulding is semi-cylindrical, and its contour is of course a semicircle. The Grecian moulding is either elliptical or parabolic; and although this and the other Greek mouldings may be drawn, as we have said, by one or other of the methods of drawing ellipses and parabolas, described in the first part of the work, and by other methods about to be illustrated, it is much better to become accustomed to sketch them by the eye, first setting off their projections, as shown in this plate, by the divisions of the dotted lines.

Description of Sheet H Joiner Work Illustrations

The figures in this plate illustrate various ways of describing the ovolo, trochilus or scotia, cyma recta, cyma reversa, and torus.

Fig. 1.—*The Quirked Ovolo.*—The projection of the moulding is in this case made equal to five-sevenths of its height, as seen by the divisions, and the radius of the circle *b c* is made equal to two of the divisions, but any other proportions may be taken. Describe the circle *b c,* forming the upper part of the contour, and from the point *g* draw *g h,* to form a tangent to the lower part of the curve. Draw *g a* perpendicular to *g h,* and make *g f* equal to the radius *d c* of the circle *b c,* join *f d* by a straight line, which bisect by a line perpendicular to it, meeting *g a* in *a.* Join *a d,* and produce the line to *c.* Then from *a* as a center, with the radius *a c* or *a g,* describe the curve *c g.*

Fig. 2.—*To draw an ovolo, the tangent* d e, *and the projection* b, *being given.*

Through the point of extreme projection *b,* draw the vertical line *g h,* and through *b* draw *b c* parallel to the tangent *d e,* and draw *c d* parallel to *g h,* and produce it to *a,* making *c a* equal to *c d.* Divide *e b* and *c b* each into the same number of equal parts, and through the points of division in *c b* draw from *a* straight lines, and through the points of division in *e b* draw from *d* right lines, cutting those drawn from *a.* The intersections will be points in the curve.

Fig. 3.—*To draw an ovolo under the same conditions as before, viz., when the projection* f, *and the tangent* c g, *are given.*

The mode of operation is similar to the last: *f d* is drawn parallel to the tangent *c g,* and *c d* parallel to the perpendicular *a b, d e* is made equal to *c d,* and *d f* and *g f* are each divided into the same number of equal parts.

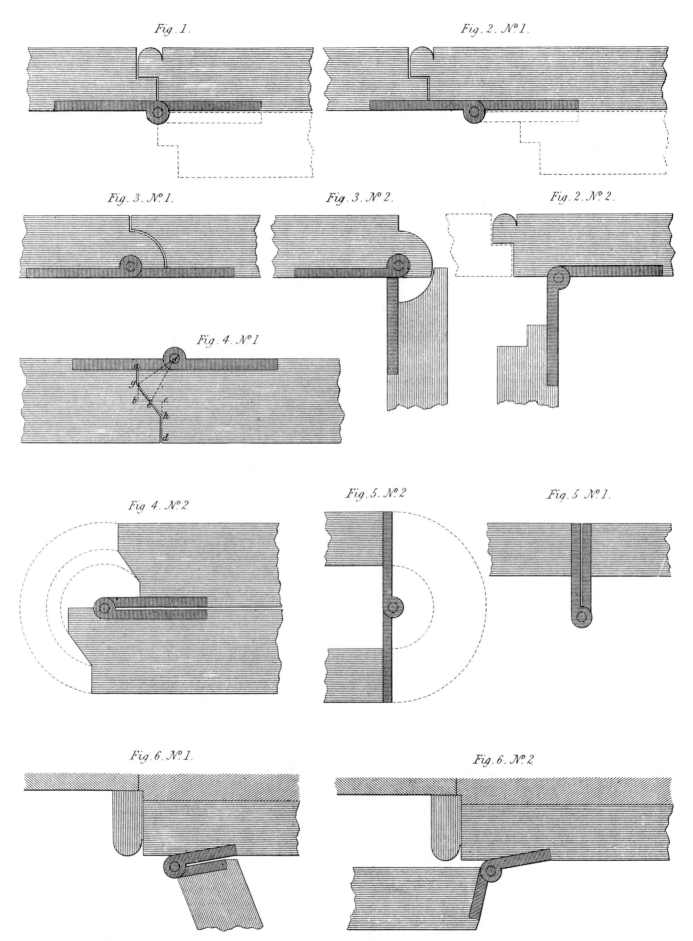

Fig. 1.

Fig. 2. Nº 1.

Fig. 3. Nº 1.

Fig. 3. Nº 2.

Fig. 2. Nº 2.

Fig. 4. Nº 1.

Fig. 4. Nº 2.

Fig. 5. Nº 2.

Fig. 5 Nº 1.

Fig. 6. Nº 1.

Fig. 6. Nº 2.

Sheet F.   Joiner Work Hinging

Roman   Fillet or Listel.   Grecian.

Astragal or Bead.

Doric Annulets.

Listel and Facia.

Cavetto or Hollow.

Ovolo or Quarto Round.

Cyma Recta.

Cyma Reversa.

Trochilus or Scolia.

Torus.

Sheet G. Joiner Work Mouldings

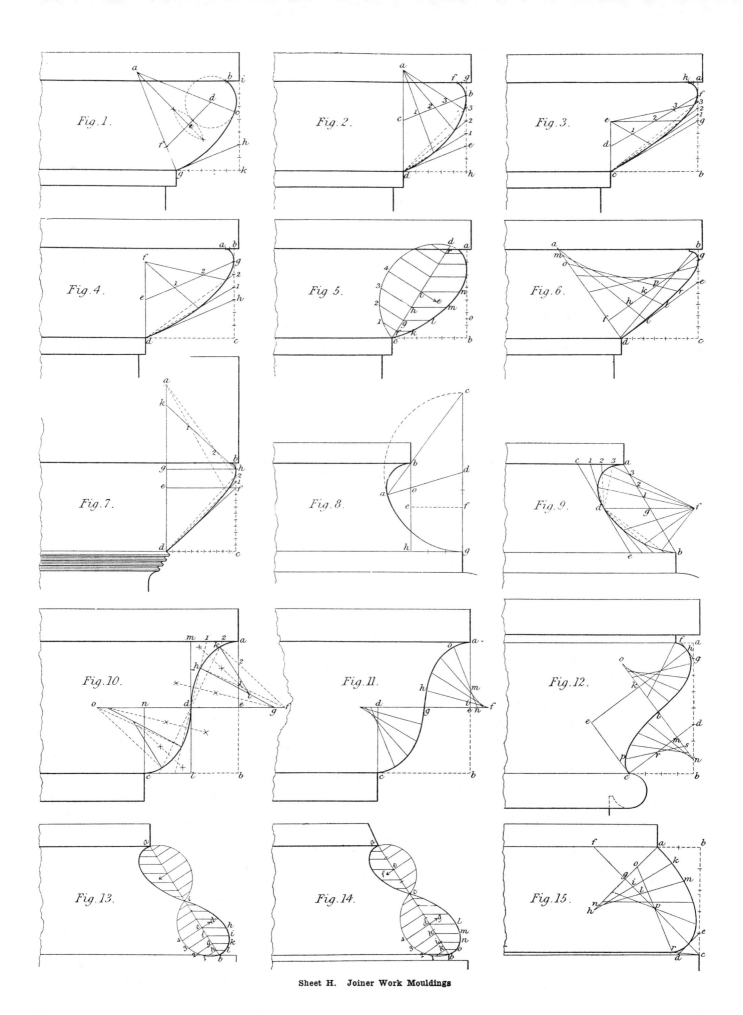

Sheet H.   Joiner Work Mouldings

Fig. 4.—In this the same things are given, and the same mode of operation is followed. By these methods and those about to be described, a more beautiful contour is obtained than can be described by parts of circular curves.

Fig. 5.—Divide the height *b a* into seven equal parts, and make *a r* equal to *b o* 1½ of a division; join *c r,* and produce it to *d,* and make *c d* equal to 8½ divisions. Bisect *c d* in *i,* and draw through *i,* 4 *i* at right angles to *c d,* and produce it to *e;* make *i e* equal to *b o,* and from *e* as a center, with radius *e c* or *e d,* describe the arc *c d.* Then divide the arc into equal parts, and draw ordinates to *c d,* in 1 *f,* 2 *g,* 3 *h,* 4 *i,* etc., and corresponding ordinates *f k, g l, h m, i n,* to find the curve.

Fig. 6.—The height is divided into eight equal parts, seven of which are given to the projection *d c.* Join *d* and the fifth division *e,* and draw *d a* at right angles to *d e.* Make *d f* equal to two divisions, and draw *f g* parallel to *d e,* then *d f* is the semi-axis minor, and *d g* the semi-axis major of the ellipse; and the curve can either be trammelled or drawn by means of the lines *a h, m k, o p,* being made equal to the difference between the semi-axis, as in the problem referred to.

Fig. 7.—*To describe the hyperbolic ovolo of the Grecian Doric capital, the tangent* a c, *and projection* b, *being given.*

Draw *d e g k a* perpendicular to the horizon, and draw *g h* and *e f* at right angles to *d e g k a.* Make *g a* equal to *d g,* and *e k* equal to *d e;* join *h k.* Divide *h k* and *f h* into the same number of parts, and draw lines from *a* through the divisions of *k h,* and lines from *d* through the divisions of *f h,* and their intersections are points in the curve.

Fig. 8 is an elegant mode of drawing the Roman trochilus. Bisect the height *h b* in *e,* and draw *e f,* cutting *g c* in *f;* divide the projection *h g* into three equal parts, make *e o* equal to one of the divisions, and *f d* equal to two of them, join *d o,* and produce the line to *a.* Make *d c* equal to *d g,* and draw *c b,* and produce it to *a.* Then from *d* as a center, with radius *d a* or *d g,* describe the arc *g a;* and from *o* as a center, with radius *o a,* describe the arc *a b.*

Fig. 9 shows the method of drawing the Grecian trochilus by intersecting lines in the same manner as the rampant ellipse.

Fig. 10 shows the cyma recta formed by two equal opposite curves. By taking a greater number of points as centers, a figure resembling still closer the true elliptical curve will be produced.

Fig. 11 shows the cyma recta formed with true elliptical quadrants, or they may be trammelled by a slip of paper.

Fig. 12 shows the cyma reversa, obtained in the same manner. The lines *c d, e h* are the semi-axes major, and the line *o n* is the semi-axis minor, common to both curves.

Figs. 13 and 14 show the cyma recta used as a base moulding, and Fig. 15 the Grecian torus.

11f. STAIRS

Stairs are constructions composed of horizontal planes elevated above each other, forming steps; affording the means of communication between different decks of a vessel.

Definitions.—The opening in which the stair is placed, is called the *staircase.*

The horizontal part of a step is called the *tread,* the vertical part the *riser,* the breadth or distance from riser to riser the *going,* the distance from the first to the last riser in a flight the *going of the flight.*

When the risers are parallel with each other, the stairs are of course *straight.*

When the steps are narrower at one end than the other, they are termed *winders.*

When the bottom step has a circular end, it is called a *round-ended step;* when the end is formed into a spiral, it is called a *curtail step.*

The wide step introduced as a resting-place in the ascent is *a landing,* and the top of a stair is also so called.

When the landing at a resting place is square, it is designated *a quarter space.*

When the landing occupies the whole width of the staircase it is called a *half space.*

So much of a stair as is included between two landings is called a *flight,* especially if the risers are parallel with each other: the steps in this case are *fliers.*

The outward edge of a step is named the *nosing;* if it project beyond the riser, so as to receive a hollow moulding glued under it, it is a *moulded nosing.*

A straight-edge laid on the nosings represents the angle of the stairs, and is denominated the *line of nosings.*

The raking pieces which support the ends of the steps are called *strings.* The inner one is the *wall string;* the other the *outer string.* If the outer string be cut to mitre with the end of the riser, it is a *cut and mitred string;* but when the strings are grooved to receive the ends of the treads and risers, they are said to be *housed,* and the grooves are termed *housings.*

Economy of space in the construction of stairs is an important consideration. To obtain this, the stairs are made to turn upon themselves, one flight being carried above another at such a height as will admit of head room to a full-grown person.

Method of Setting Out Stairs

The first objects to be ascertained are the situation of first and last risers, and the height wherein the stair is to be placed.

The height is next taken on a rod; then, assuming a height of riser suitable to the place, a trial is made, by division, how often this height is contained in the height between decks, and the quotient, if there be no remainder, will be the number of risers. Should there be a remain-

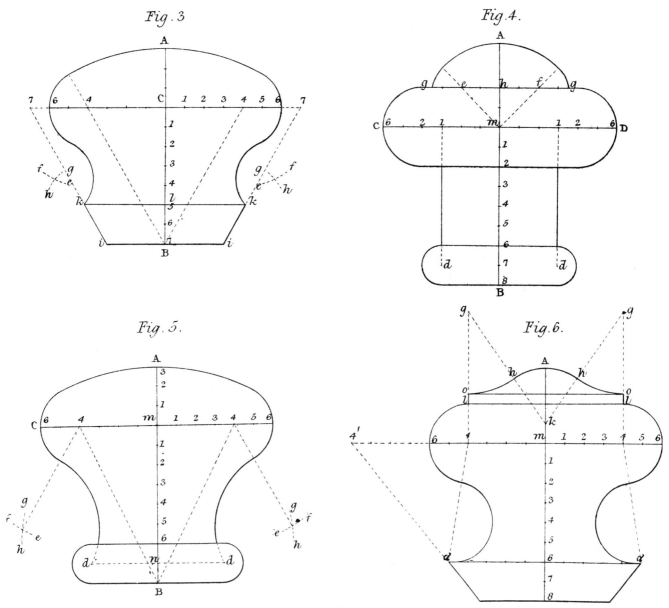

Fig. 3   Fig. 4.   Fig. 5.   Fig. 6.

Sheet I. Joiner Work Handrails

der on the first division, the operation is reversed, the number of inches in the height being made the dividend, and the before-found quotient the divisor, and the operation of division by reduction is carried on, till the height of riser is obtained to the thirty-second part of an inch. These heights are then set off on a measurement rod as exactly as possible.

It is a general maxim that the greater the breadth of a step the less should be the height of the riser; and conversely, the less the breadth of step, the greater should be the height of the riser. Experience shows that a step of 12 inches width and 5½ inches rise, may be taken as a standard.

It is seldom, however, that the proportion of the step and riser is exactly a matter of choice—the room allotted to the stairs usually determines this proportion; but the above will be found a useful standard, to which it is desirable to approximate.

A proportion for steps and risers may be obtained by the annexed method:—

Treads in	Risers in	Treads in	Risers in
5	9	12	5½
6	8½	13	5
7	8	14	4½
8	7½	15	4
9	7	16	3½
10	6½	17	3
11	6	18	2½

Set down two sets of numbers, each in arithmetical progression; the first set showing the width of the steps, ascending by inches, the other showing the height of the riser, descending by half inches. It will readily be seen that each of these steps and risers are such as may suitably pair together.

The landing covers one riser, and therefore the number of steps in a flight will be always one fewer than the number of risers. The width of tread which can be obtained for each flight will thus be found, and consistent with the situation, the plan will be so far decided. A pitch-board should now be formed to the angle of inclination: this is done by making a piece of thin board in the shape of a right-angled triangle, the base of which is the exact going of the step, and its perpendicular the height of the riser.

If the stair be a newel stair, its width will be found by setting out the plan and section of the newel on the landing.

Then mark the place of the outer or front string, and also the place of the back or wall string, according to the intended thickness of each. This should be done not only to a scale on the plan, but likewise to the full size on the rod. Set off on the rod, in the thickness of each string, the depth of the grooving of the steps into the string; mark also on the plan the place and section of the bottom newel.

When two flights are necessary, it is desirable that each flight should consist of an equal number of risers; but this will depend on the form of staircase, situation, height of doors, and other obstacles to be passed over or under, as the case may be.

119. Handrails

The height of the handrail of a stair, as the following considerations will show, need not be uniform throughout, but may be varied within the limits of a few inches, so as to secure a graceful line at the changes of direction. In ascending a stair the body is naturally thrown forward, and in descending it is thrown back, and it is only when standing or walking on the level that it maintains an upright position. Hence the rail may be with propriety made higher where it is level at the landings, the position of the body being then erect, than at the sloping part, where the body is naturally more or less bent.

The height of the rail on the nosings of the straight part of the stairs should be 2 feet 7½ inches, measuring from the tread to its upper side; to this there should be added at the landings the height of half a riser.

In winding stairs, regard should be had, in adjusting the height of the rail, to the position of a person using it, who may be thrown further from it at some points than at others, not only by the narrowing of the treads, but by the oblique position of the risers.

Sections of Handrails.—In Sheet I. some of the usual forms of the sections of handrails are given. To describe Fig. 3, divide the width 6 6 in twelve parts, bisect it by the line A B, at right angles to 6 6; make c B equal to seven, A c equal to three such parts, and B i also equal to three parts; set off one part from 6 to 7, draw the lines 7 i on each side of the figure; set the compasses in 4 4, extend them to 6 6, and describe the arcs at 6 6

to form the sides of the figure; also set the compasses in B, extending them to A, and describe the arc at A to form the top; make l B equal to two parts, and draw the line k l k; take four parts in the compasses, and from the points 4 4 describe the arcs e f, then with two parts in the compasses, one foot being placed in k, draw the intersecting arcs g h; from these intersections as centres, describe the remaining portions of the curves, and by joining k i, k i, *complete figure.*

In Fig. 4 divide the width c D into twelve equal parts; make 6 m equal to 6 parts; 6 B and m h respectively, equal to two parts, and m 1 equal to three parts; make e h and h f respectively, equal to two parts; then in f and e set one foot of the compasses, and with a radius equal to one and a half parts, describe the arcs g g; from the point m, with the radius m A, describe the arc at A meeting the arcs g g, to form the top reed of the figure; from 2 with a radius equal to two parts, describe the side reeds c and D; draw 1 d parallel to A B; and with a radius of one part from the points d d describe the reed d for the bottom of the rail, which completes the figure.

Fig. 5 is another similar section of handrail. The width 6 6 is divided into twelve equal parts as before; the point 4 is the center for the side of the figure, which is described with a radius of two parts; A m is made equal to three parts, and B m to eight parts, and m n equal to seven parts; then will A B be the radius, and B the center for the top of the rail. Take seven parts in the compasses, and from the center 6 in the vertical line A B, describe the arcs g h, g h; take six parts in the compasses, and from the center 4, describe the arcs e f, e f; draw the line d d through the point n; from the intersections at e f g h, as a center, with the radius of four parts, and from 4, as a center, with the radius of two parts, describe the curve of contrary flexure forming the side of the rail; then from d, with the radius of one part, describe the arc at d, forming the astragal for the bottom of the rail.

Fig. 6.—To describe this figure, let the width 6 6 be divided into 12 parts; make m 4 equal to four parts, m 6 equal to 6 parts, and 6 8 equal to 2 parts; make 6 d equal to 5 parts, and draw the dotted lines d 4; also the lines 4 g. On these lines make l 4 equal to two parts, l o equal to half a part, and o g equal to four parts; also make m k equal to one part, and draw the lines g k; from k, as a center, describe the arc at A for the top of the rail; from g describe the arcs h o. At 4 and 4, with the radius of two parts, describe the arcs at 6 for the sides of the rail; then from d set off the distance of two parts on the line d 4, and from this point as a center, with a radius of two parts, describe the curves of contrary flexure terminating in d d, which will complete the curved parts of the figure. Continue the line 6 6 the distance of four parts on each side to the points 4': from these points, and through the points d d, draw the lines d d for the chamfer at the bottom of the rail, thus completing the entire figure.

Chapter XII

Sails

As a builder of ships should have a general knowledge of sails, I have devoted this chapter to illustrating and describing rigs of vessels and boats.

No attempt has been made to do more than give a general description and complete lists of sails of the various rigs. Each rig is illustrated and identifying numbers are marked against each sail.

12a. Ship Sails

Fig. 101 is an illustration of a full-rigged ship, sails being numbered for identification, the name of each sail being listed below with identifying numbers against it.

Fig. 101. Ship

DIFFERENT RIGS OF VESSELS

Ship, Full-Rigged Ship

A three-masted vessel (foremast, mainmast and mizzenmast) each mast is fitted with a topmast, top-gallantmast and royalmast, all are square-rigged, i.e., rigged with yards and square sails. (See Fig. 101.)

Four-Masted Ships

These vessels have either one, two or three of their masts, square-rigged, and those masts not square-rigged are fitted with a topmast only, and carry gaff-sails, like a barkentine, the three foremost masts are named like those in a three-masted ship (foremast, mainmast, mizzenmast) and the hindmost is called a jigger-mast.

Ship Sails (Ship Rig)

1. Flying jib.	8. Royal studdingsail.
2. Standing jib or outer jib.	9. Fore-sail or fore course.
3. Inner or middle jib.	10. Lower-fore topsail.
4. Fore topmast staysail.	11. Upper-fore topsail.
5. Lower studdingsail.	12. Lower-fore topgallantsail.
6. Topmast studdingsail.	13. Upper-fore topgallantsail.
7. Topgallant studdingsail.	14. Fore royal.

15. Fore skysail.	24. Cross-jack.
16. Mainsail or main course.	25. Lower-main topsail.
17. Lower-main topsail.	26. Upper-mizzen topsail.
18. Upper-main topsail.	27. Lower-mizzen topgallantsail.
19. Lower-main topgallantsail.	28. Upper-mizzen topgallantsail.
20. Upper-main topgallantsail.	29. Mizzen royal.
21. Main royal.	30. Mizzen skysail.
22. Main skysail.	31. Spanker.
23. Moonsail.	

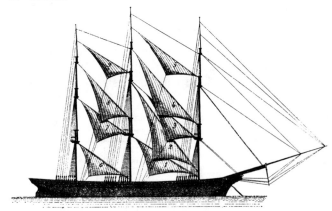

Fig. 102. Staysails

Ship (Staysails)

1. Main staysail.	6. Mizzen staysail.
2. Main topmast staysail.	7. Mizzen topmast staysail.
3. Middle staysail.	8. Mizzen topgallant staysail.
4. Main topgallant staysail.	9. Mizzen royal staysail.
5. Main royal staysail.	

12b. Sails of a Barque

Fig. 103 is an illustration of a barque, her sails being numbered for identification. The name of each sail, with identifying number against it, is listed below.

Barque; Bark (Sails)

A three-masted vessel, (foremast, mainmast and mizzenmast) the two foremost masts are square-rigged, as in a ship, the after or mizzenmast has no yards, being fitted with a topmast only, and carries a gaff-sail (called the spanker) and a gaff-topsail. (See Fig. 103.)

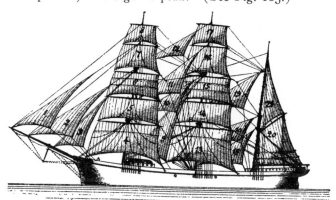

Fig. 103. Barque

1. Flying jib.
2. Jib.
3. Fore topmast staysail.
4. Fore-sail.
5. Lower-top topsail.
6. Upper-top topsail.
7. Fore topgallant sail.
8. Fore royal.
9. Main topmast staysail.
10. Middle staysail.
11. Main topgallant staysail.

12. Main royal staysail.
13. Main sail.
14. Lower-main topsail.
15. Upper-main topsail.
16. Main topgallant sail.
17. **Main** royal.
18. **Mizzen** staysail.
19. Mizzen topmast staysail.
20. **Spanker.**
21. Gaff-topsail.

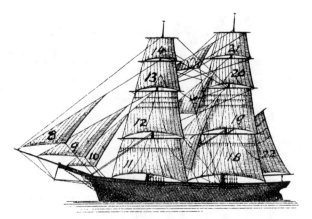

Fig. 105.　Brig

12c.　Sails of a Barkentine

Fig. 104 is an illustration of a barkentine, her sails being numbered for identification. The name of each sail with identifying number against it, is listed below. (No. 1-10 same as on bark. No. 13-16 as on schooner.)

Barkentine

A three-masted vessel, (foremast, mainmast and mizzenmast) the foremast only is square-rigged, the main and mizzen mast are fitted with topmasts, and carry gaff-sails and gaff-topsails.

1. Flying jib.
2. Jib.
3. Fore-topmast staysail.
4. Foresail.
5. Lower topsail.
6. Upper topsail.
7. Top gallantsail.

8. Royal.
9. Main topmast staysail.
10. Middle staysail.
13. **Main** sail.
14. Main gaff topsail.
15. Mizzen or spanker.
16. **Mizzen** topsail.

Brigantine

A two-masted vessel (foremast and mainmast). The foremast is square-rigged, and the after or mainmast (of a greater length than the foremast) carries a boom-sail, called "mainsail," and is fitted with a topmast, carrying a gaff-topsail.　(See Fig. 106.)

8. Flying-jib.
9. Outer jib or main jib.
10. Inner jib.
11. Fore topmast staysail.
12. Fore-sail.
13. Lower topsail.
14. Upper topsail.
15. Topgallant sail.

16. Royal.
17. Main staysail.
18. Middle staysail.
19. Main topmast staysail.
20. Main topgallant staysail.
21. Main sail.
22. Gaff topsail.

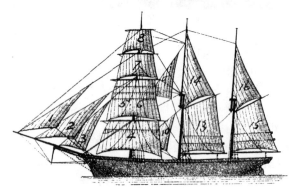

Fig. 104.　Barkentine

12d.　Sails of a Brig

Fig. 105 is an illustration of a brig, her sails being numbered for identification. The name of each sail, with identifying number against it, is listed below.

Brig

A two-masted vessel, (foremast and mainmast), square-rigged, i.e., exactly as the two foremost masts of a full-rigged ship or a barque.

8. **Flying jib.**
9. Outer jib.
10. Inner jib.
11. Fore sail.
12. Fore topsail.
13. Fore topgallantsail.
14. **Fore** royal.
15. Main staysail.

16. Main topmast staysail.
17. Main topgallant staysail.
18. Main sail.
19. Main topsail.
20. Main topgallant sail.
21. Main royal.
22. Spanker.

12e.　Sails of a Brigantine

Fig. 106 is an illustration of a brigantine, her sails being numbered for identification. The name of each sail, with identification number against it, is listed below.

Fig. 106.　Brigantine

12f.　Sails of a Topsail Schooner

Fig. 107 is an illustration of a topsail schooner, her sails being numbered for identification. The name of each sail, with identifying number against it, is listed below.

Topsail Schooner

A two-masted vessel (foremast and mainmast) with long lower masts. The foremast is fitted with yards and square sails, which are lighter than those of a brigantine, and carrying a loose square foresail (only used when sailing before the wind) the main- or after mast is rigged like the after mast in a brigantine.　(See Fig. 107.)

1. Flying jib.
2. Outer jib.
3. Inner jib.
4. Fore topmast staysail.
5. Fore sail.

6. Fore topsail.
7. Upper fore topsail.
8. Main topmast staysail.
9. Main sail.
10. Main gaff topsail.

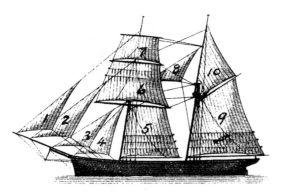

Fig. 107. Topsail Schooner

THREE-MASTED TOPSAIL SCHOONER

A three-masted vessel (foremast, mainmast and mizzenmast). The foremast is rigged like the foremast in a topsail-schooner and the two after masts are fitted with boom sails and gaff-topsails, like those of a barkentine.

12g. SAILS OF A FORE-AND-AFT SCHOONER

Fig. 108 is an illustration of a fore-and-aft schooner, her sails being numbered for identification. The name of each sail, with identifying number against it, is listed below.

SCHOONER

A name applied to vessels of fore-and-aft rig of various sizes. Schooners have two or more long lower masts without tops, and are sometimes fitted with light square topsails, especially at the fore; but these are giving way to the fore-and-aft gaff topsails, which are better adapted to the American coast.

Some of the more modern schooners measure 2,000 and 3,000 tons, and carry six and seven masts. (See Fig. 108.)

Fig. 108. Fore-and-Aft Schooner

13.	Flying jib.	18.	Fore gaff topsail.
14.	Jib.	19.	Main sail.
15.	Inner jib.	20.	Main gaff topsail.
16.	Staysail.	21.	Mizzen.
17.	Fore-sail.	22.	Mizzen-gaff topsail.

12h. SCOW

The scow is a vessel used in the shoal waters of nearly all the States, but principally on the lakes.

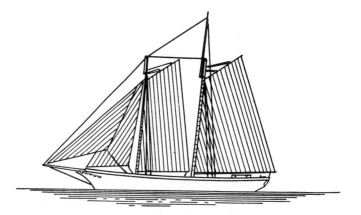

~ SCHOONER ~

Scows are built with flat bottoms and square bilges, but some of them have the ordinary schooner bow. They are fitted with one, two, and three masts, and are called scow-sloop or scow-schooner, according to the rig they carry. Some of them carry bowsprits. The distinctive line between the scow and regular-built schooner is, in the case of some large vessels, quite obscure, but would seem to be determined by the shape of the bilge; the scow having in all cases the angular bilge instead of the curve (futtock) bilge of the ordinary vessel.

12i. CAT

A rig supposed to be derived from the Brazilian catamaran that allows of one sail only, an enormous fore-and-aft mainsail spread by a boom and gaff and hoisted to the one mast stepped near the stem. The cat rig is much employed on Long Island Sound for small coasting and fishing vessels. It is also a favorite rig for pleasure vessels, being easily handled, but is not suited to a heavy sea and rough weather. (See Fig. 109.)

Fig. 109. Cat

12j. YAWL

Resembles the cutter rig, except that it has a jigger-

Fig. 110.   Yawl

Fig. 112.   Cutter

mast at the stern, which carries a small lug-sail, the main boom traversing just clear of it.   (See Fig. 110.)

12k.   SLOOP

The sloop is a vessel with only one mast, and a bowsprit carrying a fore-and-aft mainsail and jib, which, being set on the forestay, is called the foresail.   The sloop is one of the oldest styles of vessel known to the trade of this country, and is (with some local variations in the cut of sails) a rig that is more or less employed in the commerce of the entire globe.   (See Fig. 111.)

12m.   LUGGER

Luggers are vessels generally with one mast (though sometimes two or three), having quadrilateral or four-cornered fore-and-aft sails bent to a hoisting yard, the luff being about two-thirds the length of the after leech. The French chasse-maree or lugger, used for fishing and

Fig. 111.   Sloop

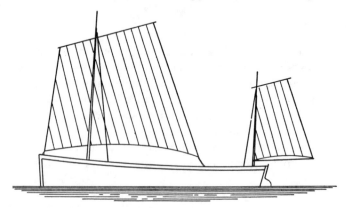

Fig. 113.   Lug-Sails

coasting purposes, carries two or three masts and is of 200 to 300 tons capacity.   In this country the lugger is generally a small vessel with one mast, used for the oyster trade on the Mississippi River and adjacent waters. (See Fig. 113.)

12l.   CUTTER

The cutter carries a fore-and-aft mainsail, stay foresail, flying jib, and topsail.   Large cutters, 400 to 500 tons, have been constructed for naval use and made to carry yards with every sail that can be set on one mast, even to sky sails, moon-rakers, star-gazers, etc.   The modern cutter-yacht generally carries a flying gaff topsail.   The name cutter applies as much to the sharp build of the vessel's hull as to the particular rig.   (See Fig. 112.)

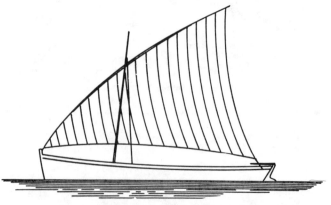

Fig. 114.   Lateen-Sail

12n. Lateen

The lateen rig is similar to the lug rig, excepting that the sail is triangular, a long yard which hoists obliquely to a stout mast forming the luff.

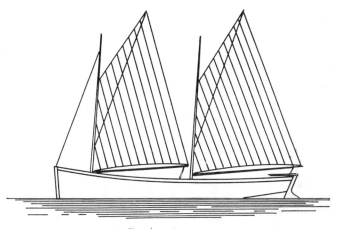

— SPRIT-SAILS —

The lateen rig is much used by small craft in the Mediterranean and in some of the larger size which have more than one mast. The sails brail up in case of need. (See Fig. 114.)

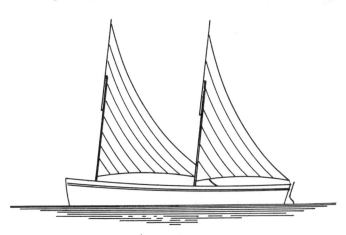

— SLIDING GUNTER —

PARTS AND PARTICULARS OF SAILS (Figs. 115, 116, 117)

Sail

bolt rope of a — (Rope sewed around a sail
bonnet of a —(A removable portion of a sail)
bunt of a square — (*when furled*)
clew or clue of a — 9
spectacle clew, iron clew of a — 9a
clew-rope of a —
cloth of a — 15
cover of a —(Canvas cover put over furled sail to protect them from damage)
cringle of a — 12
earing of a (*square*) — 14

earing cringle of a (*square*) — 13
earing thimble of a (*square*) — (Thimble worked into earing)
eyelet-holes in a — 16
foot of a — 6
foot-band of a —(Band along foot)
foot-rope of a — 6a
girth-band of a — 18
grommets (*for eyelet holes*) of a — (Brass or sewed protection around eyelet holes)
head of a (*square or gaff*) — 1

Sail

head of a (*triangular*) — 1b
head-rope of a (*square*) — 1a
head-rope of a (*gaff*) — 1c
head-rope, stay-rope of a (*triangular*) — 1o
hoist of a — 25
lacing of a —(Line used to lace sail to gaff or boom)
leech of a (*square*) — 8
after leech of a (*triangular or trapezoidal*) — 20
fore-leech or luff of a (*triangular or trapezoidal*) — (*fixed to, or hoisted on a mast*) — 19b
fore-leech, stay or luff of a (*triangular*) — (*hoisted on a stay*) — 19d
leech-lining of a (*square*)
leech-rope of a (*square*) — 8a
after leech-rope of a (*triangular or trapezoidal*) — 20a

fore-leech rope, mastrope of a (*trapezoidal or triangular*) — (*fixed to, or hoisted, on a mast*)
middle band, belly band of a (*top*) — 5
peak of a (*gaff*) — 22
reef in a — (Distance between each set of reef points)
balance reef in a (*gaff*) — 24
reef band of a — 3
reef cringle of a — 12
reef earing of a (*square*) — 14
reef points of a — 4
reef-tackle-cringle of a — 11
reef-tackle piece or patch of a — 10
seam of a — 15a
stopper or roband (*to fasten a sail to a jackstay or to a hank*)
tack of a (*trapezoidal or triangular*) — 21
throat or neck of a (*gaff*) — 23

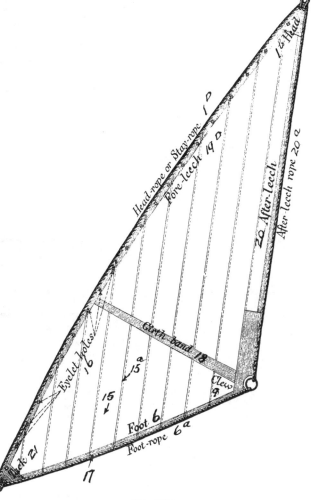

Fig. 115

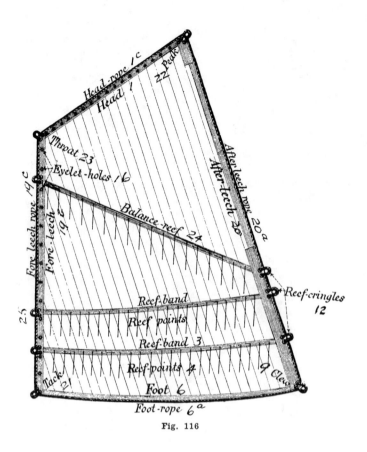

Fig. 116

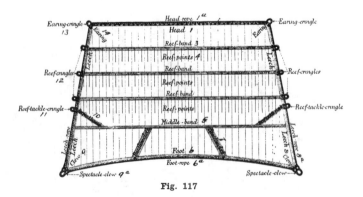

Fig. 117

Chapter XIII

Rigging

Rigging is the name given to all ropes on a vessel employed to support the masts, and raise, lower or fasten the sails. The rigging of a vessel is divided into two classes, one class comprising all standing, or stationary rigging, and the other all running or movable rigging.

13a. STANDING RIGGING DESCRIBED

The standing rigging of a vessel is usually of iron and steel wire rope made of strands of wire laid around a hemp core, the number of strands, varying from 7 to 19, depending upon service rope is put to.

On the accompanying tables I give properties of

TABLES OF WIRE ROPES. 13A

WEIGHT, STRENGTH, ETC., OF EXTRA STRONG CRUCIBLE CAST-STEEL ROPE

Composed of six strands and a hemp center, nineteen wires to the strand

Diameter in Inches	Approximate Circumference in Inches	Weight per Foot in Pounds	Approximate Breaking Strains in Tons of 2000 Pounds	Allowable Working Strains in Tons of 2000 Pounds
2¾	8⅝	11.95	266	53
2½	7⅞	9.85	222	45
2¼	7⅛	8.00	182	36.4
2	6¼	6.30	144	28.8
1¾	5½	4.85	112	22.4
1⅝	5	4.15	97	19.4
1½	4¾	3.55	84	16.8
1⅜	4¼	3.00	72	14.4
1¼	4	2.45	58	11.60
1⅛	3½	2.00	49	9.80
1	3	1.58	39	7.80
⅞	2¾	1.20	30	6.00
¾	2¼	0.89	22	4.40•
⅝	2	0.62	15.8	3.16
9⁄16	1¾	0.50	12.7	2.54
½	1½	0.39	10.1	2.02
7⁄16	1¼	0.30	7.8	1.56
⅜	1⅛	0.22	5.78	1.15
5⁄16	1	0.15	4.05	0.81
¼	¾	0.10	2.70	0.54

SEVEN WIRES TO THE STRAND

1½	4¾	3.55	79	15.8
1⅜	4¼	3.00	68	13.6
1¼	4	2.45	56	11.2
1⅛	3½	2.00	46	9.20
1	3	1.58	37	7.40
⅞	2¾	1.20	28	5.60
¾	2¼	0.89	21	4.20
11⁄16	2⅛	0.75	18.4	3.68
⅝	2	0.62	15.1	3.02
9⁄16	1¾	0.50	12.3	2.46
½	1½	0.39	9.70	1.94
7⁄16	1¼	0.30	7.50	1.50
⅜	1⅛	0.22	5.58	1.11
5⁄16	1	0.15	3.88	0.77
9⁄32	⅞	0.125	3.22	0.64

WEIGHT, STRENGTH, ETC., OF STANDARD WIRE ROPE

Composed of Six Strands and a Hemp Center, Nineteen Wires to the Strand.

Swedish Iron

Diameter in Inches	Approximate Circumference in Inches	Weight per Foot in Pounds	Approximate Breaking Strain in Tons of 2000 Pounds	Allowable Working Strain in Tons of 2000 Pounds
2¾	8⅝	11.95	114	22.8
2½	7⅞	9.85	95	18.9
2¼	7⅛	8.00	78	15.60
2	6¼	6.30	62	12.40
1¾	5½	4.85	48	9.60
1⅝	5	4.15	42	8.40
1½	4¾	3.55	36	7.20
1⅜	4¼	3.00	31	6.20
1¼	4	2.45	25	5.00
1⅛	3½	2.00	21	4.20
1	3	1.58	17	3.40
⅞	2¾	1.20	13	2.60
¾	2¼	0.89	9.7	1.94
⅝	2	0.62	6.8	1.36
9⁄16	1¾	0.50	5.5	1.10
½	1½	0.39	4.4	0.88
7⁄16	1¼	0.30	3.4	0.68
⅜	1⅛	0.22	2.5	0.50
5⁄16	1	0.15	1.7	0.34
¼	¾	0.10	1.2	0.24

CAST STEEL

2¾	8⅝	11.95	228	45.6
2½	7⅞	9.85	190	37.9
2¼	7⅛	8.00	156	31.2
2	6¼	6.30	124	24.8
1¾	5½	4.85	96	19.2
1⅝	5	4.15	84	16.8
1½	4¾	3.55	72	14.4
1⅜	4¼	3.00	62	12.4
1¼	4	2.45	50	10.0
1⅛	3½	2.00	42	8.40
1	3	1.58	34	6.80
⅞	2¾	1.20	26	5.20
¾	2¼	0.89	19.4	3.88
⅝	2	0.62	13.6	2.72
9⁄16	1¾	0.50	11.0	2.20
½	1½	0.39	8.8	1.76
7⁄16	1¼	0.30	6.8	1.36
⅜	1⅛	0.22	5.0	1.00
5⁄16	1	0.15	3.4	0.68
¼	¾	0.10	2.4	0.48

various standard sizes of iron wire and steel wire rope. The size of a wire rope is its diameter, or circumference, as the case may be, and the size required for each piece of standing rigging depends upon working strain that must be withstood, which of course varies with size, type of vessel, rig, and amount of sail that will be carried.

13b. FASTENING OF STANDING RIGGING

One end of each piece of standing rigging is attached

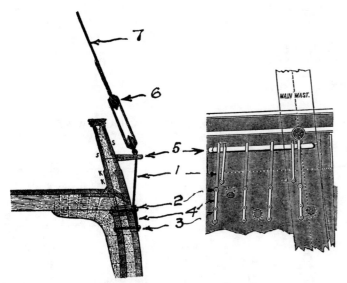

Fig. 118. Chain Plates and Channels

to one of the spars and the other end to one of the chain plates, pad-eyes, or eyebolts fastened to hull, or to another spar.

On Fig. 118 are shown details of chain plate construction and method of fastening chain plates to hull and rigging to chain plates.

No. 1 on the illustration is the chain plate which is attached to hull by chain plate bolt 2 and preventer bolt 3; 4 is a preventer plate, 5 the channel over which the chain plate is led, 6 the dead-eye through which the tightening lanyard is led, and 7 is the strand of rigging attached to chain plate.

The other part of illustration shows profile view of main rigging chain plates. Note that the one channel extends across all chain plates of each set of rigging.

13c. DESCRIBING THE CHANNELS

A channel is an assemblage of oak planks lying horizontally and projecting outwards from side of ship. They are placed near to each mast, with their fore ends slightly ahead of center of mast, and are always sufficiently long to receive and support as many chain plates as necessary. Channels are securely bolted to frames and are frequently shod with iron.

13d. CHAIN PLATES AND THEIR FASTENINGS

Chain plates are made of iron or steel and are usually about 3 or 4 inches broad and from 1 to 1½ inches thick on ships of 1,500 tons. Chain plates are fastened to hull with bolts that pass through planking, frame, ceiling, and are securely riveted in heavy clinch rings inside hull. The main and fore chain plates usually have a preventer plate and bolt as an additional fastening. On Fig. 118 the chain plate fastenings are clearly shown.

Dead-eyes, or turnbuckles, are fastened to the upper end of each chain plate. Turnbuckles are fastened to the chain plates with an iron strap that passes around the dead-eye and is fastened to chain plate with a bolt or link.

Turnbuckles are fastened to chain plates with a bolt that passes through shackle of turnbuckle and hole in upper end of chain plate.

13e. METHOD OF FASTENING STANDING RIGGING TO SPARS, AND TO HULL

The method of fastening standing rigging to spars is by splicing to eyes on bands, by splicing around the spar, or by seizing the end; and the method of fastening to hull is by splicing to turnbuckles or dead-eyes, by splicing around thimbles that are placed in eyebolts and pad-eyes, and by seizing. A large portion of standing rigging is "set up" or tautened by means of either turnbuckles, dead-eyes or lanyards.

All standing rigging must be set taut and securely fastened.

13f. LIST OF A SHIP'S STANDING RIGGING

On the following list are given the names of the principal pieces of a ship's standing rigging, and immediately below the list is an illustration, on which each piece of rigging is marked for identification. Bear in mind that fore and main masts of barks and brigs, and the foremast of a barkentine and a brigantine have standing rigging that is very similar to a ship's.

LIST OF A SHIP'S STANDING RIGGING SHOWN ON FIG. 119

1. Fore skysail stay.
2. Fore royal stay.
3. Flying jib stay.
4. Fore topgallant stay.
5. Jib stay.
6. Fore topmast stay.
7. Fore stay.
8. Main stay.
9. Main topmast stay.
10. Main topgallant stay.
11. Main royal stay.
12. Main skysail stay.
13. Mizzen stay.
14. Mizzen topmast stay.
15. Mizzen topgallant stay.
16. Mizzen royal stay.
17. Mizzen skysail stay
18. Fore rigging.
19. Fore topmast rigging.
20. Fore topgallant rigging.
21. Main rigging.
22. Main topmast rigging.
23. Main topgallant rigging.
24. Mizzen rigging.
25. Mizzen topmast rigging.
26. Mizzen topgallant rigging.
27. Fore topmast backstays.
28. Fore topgallant backstays.
29. Fore royal and skysail backstays.
30. Main topmast backstays.
31. Main topgallant backstays.
32. Main royal and skysail backstays.
33. Mizzen topmast backstays.
34. Mizzen topgallant backstays.
35. Mizzen royal and skysail backstays.
36. Bobstays.
37. Jib boom martingale stay.
38. Flying jib boom martingale stay.
39. Martingale guys or back ropes.
40. Jib flying jib boom guys.

Fig. 119. Ship's Standing Rigging

13g. STANDING RIGGING

Below is listed in alphabetical order the names of each piece of standing rigging used on sailing vessels.

Backstay —(Stays that support topmast, topgallant and royal masts from aft. They reach from heads of their respective masts to the channels at each side of ship.)
preventer —
fore royal — s 29, Fig. 119
main royal — s 32, Fig. 119
mizzen royal — s 35, Fig. 119
fore skysail — s 29, Fig. 119
main skysail — s 32, Fig. 119
mizzen skysail — s — 35, Fig. 119
standing —
fore topgallant — s — 28, Fig. 119
main topgallant — s — 31, Fig. 119
mizzen topgallant — s — 34, Fig. 119
topmast — s (*of a square-rigged mast*) — 20, Fig. 120
fore topmast — s (*of a square-rigged mast*) — 27, Fig. 119

Backstays, fore topmast — s (*of a fore and aft schooner*)
main topmast — s (*of a ship, barque or brig*) — 30, Fig. 119
main topmast — s (*of a barquentine, brigantine or schooner*)
mizzen topmast — s (*of a ship*) — 33, Fig. 119
mizzen topmast — s (*of a barque, barquentine or three-masted schooner*)
weather — s

Bobstay (*usually made of chain*) — 36, Fig. 119

Flemish-horse — 31, Fig. 120

Foot ropes are fitted to all yards (See Rigged Fore-mast) Fig. 120*

Foot ropes
cross-jack —; cross-jack yard —
fore —; fore yard — 28, Fig. 120

Foot ropes
main —; main yard —
topsail —; topsail yard — 29, Fig. 120
topgallant — ; topgallant yard —
royal —; royal yard —
skysail —; skysail yard —
jib boom —
flying jib boom —
stirrup in a — 30, Fig. 120

Guy; Back-rope
boom —
davit —
jib boom —
flying jib boom —
martingale —
lower studdingsail boom—

Man-rope; Ridge-rope of the bowsprit; Bowsprit-horse

Martingale-stay; Martingale
jib boom —
flying jib boom —

Pendant
boom guy —
brace —
fish tackle —
jib sheet —
mast head —
staysail sheet —
topmast head —

Puttock-rigging; Puttock-shrouds
fore —
main —
mizzen — (*of a ship*)
mizzen — (*of a barque, barquentine or three-masted schooner*)

Puttock-rigging, fore topgallant — 23, Fig. 120
main topgallant —
mizzen topgallant —

Ratline — 16, Fig. 120

Rigging
fore —; fore lower — 18, Fig. 119
main —; main lower — 21, Fig. 119
mizzen — ; mizzen lower (*of a ship*) — 24, Fig. 119
mizzen — (*of a barque, barquentine or three-masted schooner*)

Rigging
topmast — (*of a square-rigged mast*) — 22, Fig. 120
fore topmast — (*of a square-rigged mast*) — 19, Fig. 119
fore topmast — (*of a topmast not fitted with any yards*)
main topmast — (*of a square-rigged mast*) — 22, Fig. 119
main topmast — (*of a topmast not fitted with any yards*)
mizzen topmast — (*of a ship*) — 25, Fig. 119
mizzen topmast — (*of a barque, barquentine or three-masted schooner*)
fore topgallant — 20, Fig. 119
main topgallant — 23, Fig. 119
mizzen topgallant — 26, Fig. 119
lower mast — (*all the standing rigging of a lower mast, including stay and mast-head pendants*)
topmast — (*all the standing rigging of a topmast, including backstays and stay*)
topgallant mast — (*all the standing rigging of a topgallant-mast, including backstays and stay*)

Shroud (*)
bowsprit —
fore lower — s
foremost —; Swifter
futtock — s
lower — s
main — s
mizzen — s (*of a ship*)
mizzen — s (*of a barque, barquentine or three-masted schooner*)
preventer —
topgallant — s
topmast — s

(*) A shroud is any one of the ropes—hemp or wire—of which the "rigging", as lower-rigging, topmast-rigging, topgallant rigging, etc., is formed. The bowsprit, futtock, funnel-shrouds, etc., are often made of chain and sometimes of bar-iron.

*Fig. 120 and 133 are alike.

Stay

bumpkin — ; bumpkin-
shroud
fore — 7, Fig. 119
fore — (*of a schooner,
cutter, etc.*)
jib — 5, Fig. 119
flying-jib — 3, Fig. 119
inner-jib — ; middle jib —
Fig. 119
jumping — ; pitching —
main — 8, Fig. 119
middle staysail — Fig. 119
mizzen — (*of a ship*) —
13, Fig. 119
mizzen — (*of a barque,
barquentine or three-
masted schooner*)

Stay

royal —
fore royal — 2, Fig. 119
main royal — 11, Fig. 119
mizzen royal — 16, Fig.
119
skysail — 17, Fig. 119
fore skysail — 1, Fig. 119
main skysail — 12, Fig. 119
mizzen skysail — 17, Fig.
119
spring —
fore topgallant — 4, Fig.
119
main topgallant — 10, Fig.
119
mizzen topgallant — 15,
Fig. 119

Stay

fore topmast — (*of a
square-rigged mast*) — 6,
Fig. 119
fore topmast — (*of a
topmast not fitted with
any yards*)
main topmast — (*of a
square-rigged mast*) — 9,
Fig. 119
main topmast — (*of a
topmast not fitted with any
yards*)
mizzen topmast — (*of a
ship*) — 14, Fig. 119
mizzen topmast — (*of a
barque, barquentine or
three-masted schooner*)

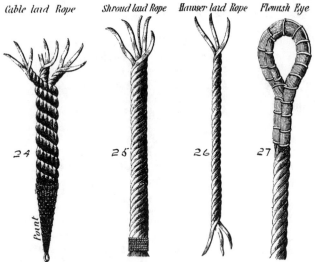

Fig. 121

13h. RUNNING RIGGING

Running rigging is the name applied to all that portion of a vessel's rigging that is used to set, furl, control
and handle the sails. It is usually composed of manila,
hemp, or sizal, cordage, rove through blocks or over
sheaves.

The rope used for rigging is composed of a number
of yarns twisted together to form strands and then a
certain number of these strands are twisted together to
form the rope.

Rope is named according to the manner in which it is
laid and its size is determined by measuring diameter, or
circumference, as the case may be.

Common or plain laid rope is composed of three

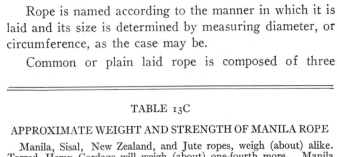

TABLE 13C

APPROXIMATE WEIGHT AND STRENGTH OF MANILA ROPE

Manila, Sisal, New Zealand, and Jute ropes, weigh (about) alike.
Tarred Hemp Cordage will weigh (about) one-fourth more. Manila
is about 25% stronger than Sisal. Working load about one-fourth of
breaking strain.

Circumference in Inches	Diameter in Inches	Weight of 1000 Feet in Pounds	Number of Feet and Inches One Pound		Strength of New Manila Rope in Pounds
			Feet	Inches	
3/4	1/4	23	50	..	450
1	5/16	33	33	..	780
1 1/8	3/8	42	25	..	1000
1 1/4	7/16	52	19	..	1280
1 1/2	1/2	74	11	..	1760
1 3/4	9/16	101	9	..	2400
2	5/8	132	7	..	3140
2 1/4	3/4	167	6	..	3970
2 1/2	13/16	207	5	..	4900
2 3/4	7/8	250	4	..	5900
3	1	297	3	6	7000
3 1/4	1 1/16	349	2	10	8200
3 1/2	1 1/8	405	2	4	9600
3 3/4	1 1/4	465	2	1	11000
4	1 5/16	529	1	10	12500
4 1/4	1 3/8	597	1	8	14000
4 1/2	1 7/16	669	1	5	15800
4 3/4	1 1/2	746	1	4	17600
5	1 5/8	826	1	2	19500
5 1/2	1 3/4	1000	1	..	23700
6	1 7/8	1190	..	10	28000
6 1/4	2	1291	..	9 1/2	33000
6 1/2	2 1/8	1397	..	8 1/2	38000
7	2 1/4	1620	..	7	44000
7 1/2	2 3/8	1860	..	6 1/2	50000
8	2 9/16	2116	..	5 1/2	60000
8 1/2	2 3/4	2388	..	5	63000
9	2 7/8	2673	..	4 1/2	67700
9 1/2	3	2983	..	4	70000
10	3 3/16	3306	..	3 5/8	80000

strands twisted together, the number of yarns in each strand varying with size of rope.

Shroud laid rope has four strands, and *cable* or hawser laid rope consists of three strands laid up as for plain laid rope, and then three of these three-ply strands laid up to form the hawser. Hawser laid rope is twisted together left-handed and, of course has 0 strands as explained above.

There is also a four-stranded hawser laid rope.

On the accompanying Table 13C are given particulars of the most generally used sizes of ropes; on Fig. 121 are shown illustrations of rope, and on Table 13D names of ropes and parts.

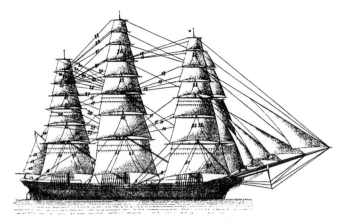

Fig. 122. Ship—Running Rigging

DIFFERENT ROPES SUPPLIED TO A SHIP

Breast-fast; Breast-rope
Cable, spare —
Hawser
   steel —
   wire — (used for towing)
Messenger
Rope
   bolt — (rope used for roping sails)
   cable laid — 24, Fig. 121
   coil of —
   coir —
   common laid —; hawser laid — (see definition)
   heart of a — (the center)
   hemp — (*Europe*) (rope made of hemp)
   manila — (rope made of manila)
   mooring — (rope used for mooring a vessel)
   pointed —; point of a — 24, Fig. 121

Rope
   preventer —
   relieving —
   serving of a —
   shroud laid — 25, Fig. 121
   strand of a — (see definition)
   three-stranded — 26, Fig. 121
   four-stranded — 25, Fig. 121
   tarred — (Hemp rope that has been immersed in tar)
   whip of a —
   white or untarred — (rope made of natural hemp or manila)
   wire — (see Table 13a)
   steel wire — (see Table 13a)
Tow-line; Tow-rope (rope used for towing)

against a number of the items are marked identifying numerals that correspond with similar numerals marked on the running rigging illustrations. By referring to the numeral and illustration entered against any item of running rigging you will learn its location and the purpose it is used for.

NAMES OF RUNNING RIGGING

Bowline
   — bridle
   cross-jack —
   fore —
   lee —
The following bowlines are seldom used:
   main —
   top —
   fore top —
   main top —
   mizzen top —
   topgallant —
   fore topgallant —
   main topgallant —
   mizzen topgallant —
   weather —
Brace
   Cross-jack — 24, Fig. 122
   fore — 9, Fig. 122
   lee —
   main — 16, Fig. 122
   moon-sail — 23, Fig. 122

Brace
   — pendant
   preventer —
   royal —
   fore royal — 14, Fig. 122
   main royal — 21, Fig. 122
   mizzen royal — 29, Fig. 122
   skysail — 30, Fig. 122
   fore skysail — 15, Fig. 122
   main skysail — 22, Fig. 122
   mizzen skysail —
   studdingsail boom —
   topgallant —
   fore topgallant —
   lower fore topgallant — 12, Fig. 122
   upper fore topgallant — 13, Fig. 122
   lower topgallant —
   main topgallant —
   lower main topgallant — 19, Fig. 122

13i. RUNNING RIGGING OF A SHIP (FIG. 122)

1. Flying jib sheet.
2. Jib sheet.
3. Middle jib sheet.
4. Fore topmast staysail sheet.
5. Fore sheet.
6. Main sheet.
7. Cross-jack sheet.
8. Spanker sheet.
9. Fore brace.
10. Lower-fore topsail brace.
11. Upper-fore topsail brace.
12. Lower-fore topgallant brace.
13. Upper-fore topgallant brace.
14. Fore royal brace.
15. Fore skysail brace.
16. Main brace.
17. Lower-main topsail brace.
18. Upper-main topsail brace.
19. Lower-main topgallant brace.
20. Upper-main topgallant brace.
21. Main royal brace.
22. Main skysail brace.
23. Moonsail brace.
24. Cross-jack brace.
25. Lower-mizzen topsail brace.
26. Upper-mizzen topsail brace.
27. Lower-mizzen topgallant brace.
28. Upper-mizzen topgallant brace.
29. Mizzen royal brace.
30. Mizzen skysail brace.
31. Fore buntlines.
32. Fore topsail buntlines.
33. Fore topgallant buntline.
34. Fore royal buntline.
35. Main buntlines.
36. Main topsail buntlines.
37. Main topgallant buntline.
38. Main royal buntline.
39. Cross-jack buntline.
40. Mizzen topsail buntlines.
42. Mizzen royal buntline.
43. Spanker brails.
44. Peak halliards.

13j. FORE-AND-AFT SCHOONER RIGGING (FIG. 123)

23. Fore boom topping lift.
24. Main boom topping lift.
25. Mizzen boom topping lift.
26. Fore peak halliard.
27. Main peak halliard.
28. Mizzen peak halliard.

13k. NAMES OF RUNNING RIGGING

Below is listed in alphabetical order the names of principal pieces of running rigging used on ships, and

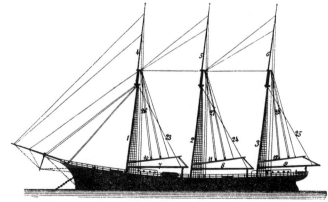

Fig. 123. Fore-and-Aft Schooner Rigging

Halliard
    fore topgallant studding-sail —
    main topgallant studding-sail —
    topmast studdingsail —
    fore topmast studding-sail —
    main topmast studding-sail —
    throat—
    fore-sail throat —
    main throat —
    spanker or mizzen throat —
    topgallant —
    fore topgallant —
    main topgallant —
    mizzen topgallant —
    topsail —
    topsail — (*of a schooner*)
    fore topsail —
    main topsail —
    mizzen topsail —

Inhaul
    spanker —
    trysail —
    fore trysail —
    main trysail —

Jib-heel-rope; Jib-boom-heel-rope

Leech-line
    cross-jack —
    fore —
    main —
    preventer —

Lift
    boom —; boom topping —
    cross-jack —
    fore —
    fore sail boom —; fore boom topping —
    lower — 26, Fig. 120
    lower studdingsail boom topping —
    main —
    main boom —; main boom topping —
    royal —
    fore royal —
    main royal —
    mizzen royal —
    skysail —
    fore skysail —
    main skysail —
    mizzen skysail —
    spanker boom topping —
    mizzen boom topping —
    topgallant —
    fore topgallant —
    main topgallant —
    mizzen topgallant —
    topsail — 27, Fig. 120
    fore topsail —
    main topsail —
    mizzen topsail —

Outhaul
    spanker —
    trysail —
    fore trysail —
    main trysail —

Reef-tackle
    cross-jack —
    fore —
    main —
    topsail —
    topsail — (*of a schooner*)
    fore topsail —
    main topsail —
    mizzen topsail —

Sheet
    boom fore sail —
    brig's boom sail —
    cross-jack — 7, Fig. 122
    fore — 5, Fig. 122
    head — s
    jib — 2, Fig. 122
    flying jib — 17, Fig. 122
    inner jib —; middle jib — 3, Fig. 122
    lee —
    main — 6, Fig. 122
    moon sail —
    preventer —
    ringtail —
    royal —
    fore royal —
    main royal —
    mizzen royal —
    skysail —
    fore skysail —
    main skysail —
    mizzen skysail —
    spanker — 8, Fig. 122
    square sail —
    stay fore sail —
    staysail —
    main staysail —
    middle staysail —
    mizzen staysail — (*of a ship*)
    mizzen staysail — (*of a barque, barquentine or three-masted schooner*)
    main royal staysail —
    mizzen royal staysail —
    main topgallant staysail —
    mizzen topgallant staysail —
    fore topmast staysail — 4, Fig. 122
    main topmast staysail —
    mizzen topmast staysail — (*of a ship*)
    mizzen topmast staysail — (*of a barque, barquentine or three-masted schooner*)
    storm sail —
    studdingsail —
    fore lower studdingsail —
    fore royal studdingsail —
    main royal studdingsail —

Sheet
    fore topgallant studding-sail —
    main topgallant studding-sail —
    fore topmast studding-sail —
    main topmast studding-sail —
    topgallant —
    fore topgallant —
    main topgallant —
    mizzen topgallant —
    topsail —
    topsail — (*of a schooner*)
    fore topsail —
    main topsail —
    mizzen topsail —
    trysail —
    fore trysail –
    main trysail —
    weather —

Slab-line

Span

Spilling-line

Tack
    cross-jack —
    fore —
    gaff topsail —
    jib —
    flying-jib —·
    inner jib —: middle jib —
    main —
    spanker --
    stay fore sail —
    staysail —
    main staysail —
    mizzen staysail —
    main royal staysail —
    mizzen royal staysail —
    main topgallant staysail —
    mizzen topgallant staysail —
    fore topmast staysail —
    main topmast staysail —
    mizzen topmast staysail — (*of a ship*)
    mizzen topmast staysail — (*of a barque, barquentine or three-masted schooner*)
    studdingsail —
    fore royal studdingsail —
    main royal studdingsail —
    fore topgallant studding-sail —
    main topgallant studding-sail —
    fore topmast studding-sail —
    main topmast studding-sail

Tack-tracing-line

Tye or Tie
    topsail — 25, Fig. 120
    topsail -- (*of a schooner*)

Tye or Tie
    fore topsail —
    main topsail —
    mizzen topsail —
    topgallant —
    fore topgallant —
    main topgallant —
    mizzen topgallant —
Topgallant mast-rope
Topping-lift — 23, 24, 25, Fig. 123

Top-rope

Tripping-line

Vang
    — fall; Fall of a —
    pendant of a —
    preventer —
    spanker —
    trysail —
    fore trysail —
    main trysail —

131. Blocks, Tackles and Knots

Blocks are used in a ship either in combination with ropes to increase mechanical power, or to arrange and lead ropes to positions where they can be most conveniently handled or secured.

A block consists of at least four principal parts:

1. The shell or outside.
2. The strap or part of block to which the fastening is secured.
3. The sheave, or wheel over which the rope is run.
4. The pin, or axle, on which the sheave turns.

On Fig. 123A I show the principal parts of a block and several types of blocks used on ships and ashore.

131[1]. Description of a Shell of a Block

Block shells are made of wood, and of metals of various kinds (steel, iron, composition, aluminum).

For the running rigging of ships wood shell blocks are most generally used. These shells are composed of four or more pieces of wood fitted and fastened together with metal dowels and screw pins. On Fig. 8 of illustration sheet 123A is shown the assembled shell of a single block composed of two sides (8b) connected together by top and bottom pieces that keep sides the proper distance apart. The space between sides (8a) is named the score and is always properly proportioned to width and diameter of sheave and diameter of rope that will run

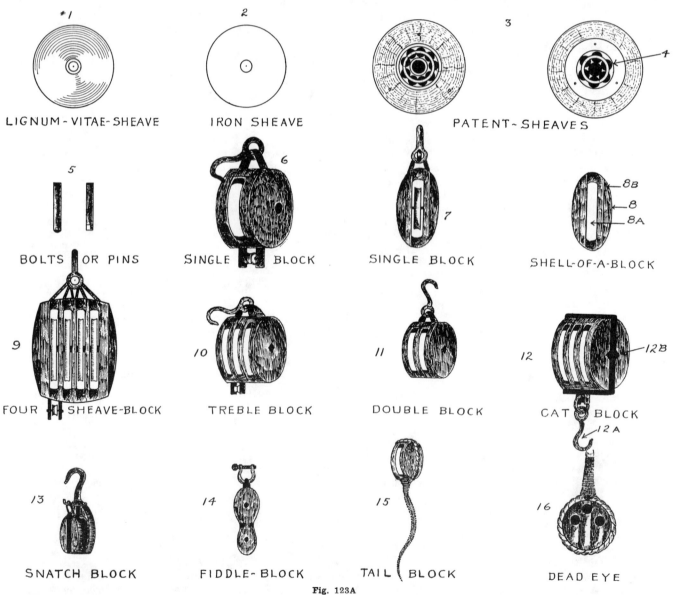

LIGNUM-VITAE-SHEAVE   IRON SHEAVE   PATENT-SHEAVES

BOLTS OR PINS   SINGLE BLOCK   SINGLE BLOCK   SHELL-OF-A-BLOCK

FOUR SHEAVE-BLOCK   TREBLE BLOCK   DOUBLE BLOCK   CAT BLOCK

SNATCH BLOCK   FIDDLE-BLOCK   TAIL BLOCK   DEAD EYE

Fig. 123A

over sheave. All parts of blocks are proportioned to withstand a greater strain than rope rove through it will stand.

The woods most generally used for shells of blocks are: Lignum-vitæ, ash, elm.

Lignum-vitæ is best for small sizes of block shells because it is not liable to split.

For larger sizes of blocks ash and elm are excellent woods.

131². THE STRAP OF A BLOCK DESCRIBED

Block straps are now almost universally made of steel or iron, though for some special uses rope strapped blocks continue to be used. Block straps of iron or steel can be inserted inside of shell or can be fitted outside as shown on Fig. 12b. Inside straps (see Figs. 6, 7, 9) are most frequently used on ships. As you will note by referring to Figs. 6 and 7, the strap passes each side of score and is inserted into grooves cut in shell to receive it. At the upper end of strap a loop is formed for the eye of a hook or other fastenings device (see Figs. 6 and 9).

When it is necessary to fasten the standing end of a rope to a block, it is passed over a thimble fitted between an extension to strap left for that purpose. This extension is clearly shown on Figs. 6, 9 and 10 blocks. Rope straps are spliced around outside of blocks in grooves cut to receive them.

131³. DESCRIBING THE SHEAVE OF A BLOCK

Block sheaves are made of lignum-vitæ, of iron, of composition metal, and a combination of all three.

If a sheave is a wheel with a hole through its center, as shown by Figs. 1 and 2, it is said to be a plain sheave, but if it is composed of one large wheel into which several smaller rollers or balls are inserted, it is called a roller or a patent sheave. Patent sheaves are now in very general use because by their use friction is greatly reduced and less power is required to lift the load.

A sheave is inserted into each score of a block and is held in place by a pin that passes through a hole in each sheave and holes in strap and in shell of block. The pins are generally made of steel, or of composition metal and are shaped as shown on Fig. 5 of illustration sheet 123A.

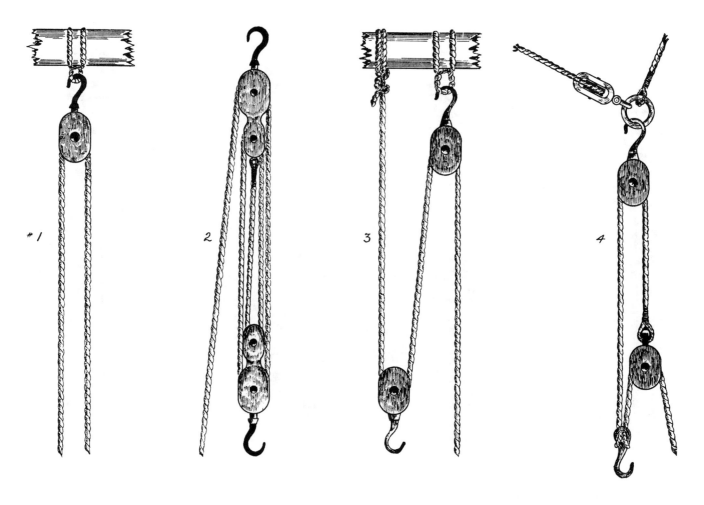

SINGLE-WHIP   LONG-TACKLE   DOUBLE-WHIP   SPANISH-BURTON

Fig. 123B

131⁴. Names of Blocks

Blocks are named according to length of shell, number of sheaves and shape. Thus a block having a shell 6 inches in length is termed a 6-inch block, and if there is one sheave inserted in block it is a 6-inch single block (see Fig. 7); if there are two sheaves it is called a double 6-inch block (see Fig. 11); and if there are three sheaves a 6-inch treble block (see Fig. 10). Blocks are seldom made with more than four sheaves (see Fig. 9).

In addition to this there are many different shapes of blocks each having its special place in a ship, the shape being the one found by experience to be best adapted for the place and purpose.

On illustration sheet 123A, a few shapes of blocks are shown. A dead-eye, while strictly speaking is not a block, is usually classed with them. The lanyards used for setting up standing rigging of a vessel are rove through holes in dead-eyes, one of which is attached to standing rigging and the other to a chain plate on side of vessel.

A fiddle-block is practically two attached single blocks (one over the other); they are used in places where a double block would be liable to split by canting over, such as for top-burtons of a ship. A snatch block is a single block so arranged that a rope can be passed over its sheave without it being necessary to reeve it through the score. This is accomplished by having a cut made through one shell and closing the cut with a hinged metal fastening piece. Both the cut and hinged metal piece are shown on illustration sheet 123A. This kind of block is very useful when it is necessary to lead a rope in a desired direction, such as to a capstan or windlass.

A tail block is a single rope strapped block, to which a tail, or end rope is attached.

Cat-blocks are used when hoisting anchor in position. They are extra heavy blocks fitted with outside iron or steel straps.

Below I list, in alphabetical order, the names of principal blocks used on vessels. The numerals marked against some items indicate that the block, or part of block, against which numeral is placed is identified by that numeral on illustration sheets 123A, B, C.

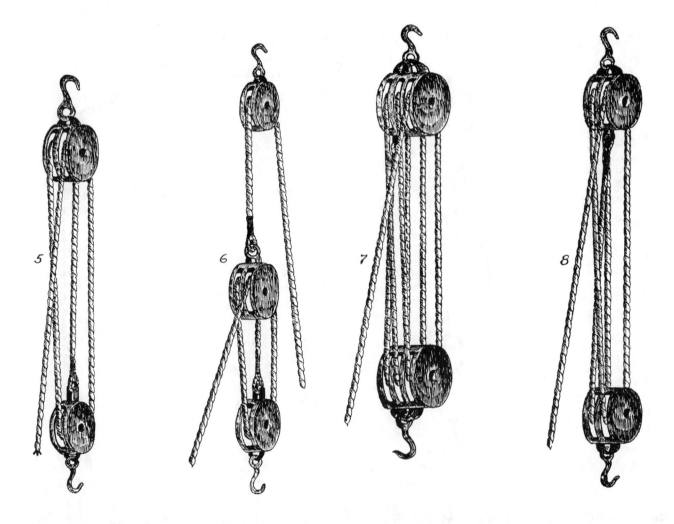

WATCH TACKLE   RUNNER & TACKLE   THREE-FOLD PURCHASE   TWO FOLD PURCHASE

Fig. 123C

NAMES OF BLOCKS

Block, brace —
  brail —
  bunt-line —
  butterfly — (for topsail-sheet at bunt of lower yard)
  cat — ; Cat-hook — 12
  cheek —
  cheek of a — 8b
  clew-garnet —
  clew-line —
  clump —
  dead — (Heart)
  double — 11
  downhaul —
  fiddle — 14
  fish-tackle —
  girtline —
  halliard —
  hook — 12a
  internal bound —
  iron bound — ; iron stropped — 12b
  jeer — (employed for raising a lower yard)
  jewel —
  leading —
  leech-line —
  lift —
  lift purchase —
  nine-pin — s
  pin of a — 5
  purchase —
  reef tackle —
  score — 8a

Block, sheave — 1, 2, 3
  bouching or bush in sheave of a — 4
  sheave-hole or channel of a — 2a
  bottom of a sheave-hole in a —
  lignum-vitæ sheave of — 1
  metal sheave — 2
  sheet —
  shell — 6
  shoe —
  shoulder —
  single — 7
  sister — 14
  snatch — 13
  span —
  strop of a —
  swallow of a —
  swivel —
  tack —
  tackle pendant —
  tail — 15
  tie —
  top —
  topping lift —
  treble — 10
  wheel chain — ; w h e e l rope —
Bull's-eye; Wooden thimble
Dead-eye — 16
Dead-sheave; Half-sheave
Gin; Gin-wheel
Heart (dead-block)

I will now pass to a description of tackles.

13m. TACKLES

When a rope is rove through a single block the combined block and rope is named a single whip, but if the rope is rove through two or more blocks the combination is named a tackle.

There are many different kinds of tackles, each having its use and each increasing the power obtained according to the number of sheaves around which the rope is rove, the manner of reeving the rope and the relative positions of load and of hauling part.

On Figs. 123B and 123C I illustrate a number of commonly used tackles. Fig. 1 shows a single whip, the smallest and simplest purchase in use. Fig. 2 shows details of a long tackle composed of two fiddle blocks with falls rove as shown. Fig. 3 illustrates the way a double whip is rove and Fig. 4 a Spanish-burton. Fig. 5 shows details of a watch tackle composed of a single and a double block, and Fig. 6 a runner and tackle combined. When using the runner and tackle the hook of runner is fixed to object intended to be moved.

A three-fold purchase is composed of two three-sheave blocks. On the illustration the rope is rove off

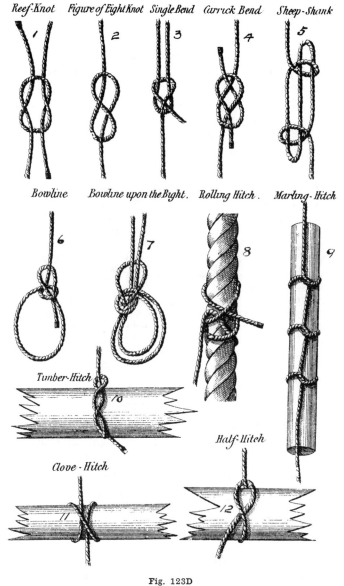

Fig. 123D

from outside to outside thus bringing the hauling part on outside. It is better, I think, to reeve the fall over middle sheave first instead of over an outside one. This

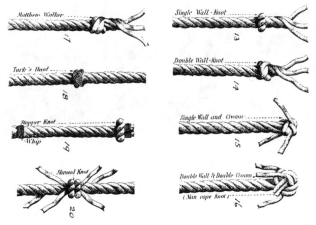

Fig. 123E

will bring a cross in the fall, but it will carry the heaviest strain, which always comes on the fall part, in center of block and will also prevent the block canting. When fall is in middle the block is drawn square with direction of pull and strain is equalized on all sheaves. A two-fold purchase is shown by Fig. 8.

Below I have listed names of a few of the principal tackles used on board ships.

NAMES OF TACKLES

Tackle	Purchase
boom —	gun tackle —
cat — ; Cat ; — for	lift —
fish — for	two-fold — 8
— fall	three-fold — 7
long — 2	four-fold —
luff —	Jigger or Watch-tackle — 5
reef —	boom —
relieving —	bunt —
rolling —	tail —
runner and — 6	Whip, (single) — 1
stay —	bunt —
swifting —	double — 3
tack —	— and runner
— upon tackle	Spanish-burton — 4
yard —	

13n. KNOTS AND SPLICES

As it is necessary that a shipbuilder should know the names of the principal knots used on board ships and in shipyards I have on Figs. 123D and E, illustrated a few of the knots that are in general use, and on Fig. 123F I have shown method of fastening two pieces of ropes together by splicing. The long splice (illustrated) is used when the rope has to pass through a block; you will note that the long splice does not increase diameter of rope, while the short splice does (Fig. 123F).

On list below I give names of a number of commonly used knots and against those illustrated on Figs. 121, 123D and E, I have marked the identifying numeral.

KNOTS, BENDS, HITCHES AND SPLICES

Knot
single diamond —
double diamond —
figure of eight — 2
Matthew Walker — 17
overhand —
reef or square — 1
rope-yarn — 32
shroud — 20
French shroud —
stopper — 19
Turk's-head — 18
single wall — 13
single wall and crown—15
double wall — 14
double wall and crown —
16 — (man-rope knot)

Bend
carrick — 4
double —
fisherman's —
single — 3; sheet — ;
common —
studdingsail halliard —

Clinch
inside —
outside —

Catspaw — 29

Hitch
blackwall — 30
double blackwall —
bowline — 6
bowline on the bight — 7
running bowline
clove — 11
half — 12

Hitch, half — and timber — 10
marling — 9
marling spike —
midshipman's —
rolling — 8
timber — 10
two half — es

Sheep-shank — 5

Splice
cable —
eye — 22
horseshoe —
long — 21
short — 23

Eye
Elliot's —
Flemish — 27

Running Rigging Ready to Reeve Off

TABLE 13D

RECOMMENDED GIRTHS, IN INCHES, OF IRON AND STEEL WIRE LOWER RIGGING, BACKSTAYS, STAYS, AND BOWSPRIT SHROUDS, OF SAILING VESSELS, ALSO SIZES OF BOBSTAYS FOR SAME

TONNAGE OF VESSEL	300		400		500		600		700		850		1000		1250	
	No.	Girth	No.	Girth	No.	Girth	No.	Girth	No.	Girth	No.	Girth	No.	Girth	No.	Girth
Fore and Main Shrouds..........	4	2¾	4	3	4	3¼	5	3½	5	3¾	5	4	5	4¼	6	4½
Fore and Main Topmast Backstays	2	2½	2	2¾	2	3	2	3¼	2	3½	2	3¾	2	4	3	4¼
Fore and Main Top-gallant Backstays....................	1	1¾	1	2	1	2¼	1	2⅜	1	2½	1	2¾	1	2⅞	2	3
Fore and Main Lower Stays.......	2	2¾	2	3	2	3¼	2	3½	2	3¾	2	4	2	4¼	2	4½
Fore and Main Topmast Stays....	2	2½	2	2¾	2	3	2	3¼	2	3½	2	3¾	2	4	·2	4¼
Fore and Main Top-gallant Stays..	1	1¾	1	2	1	2⅛	1	2¼	1	2⅜	1	2½	1	2¾	1	3
Mizzen Shrouds...............	....	....	3	2¾	3	2⅞	3	3	4	3⅛	4	3¼	4	3½	5	3¾
Mizzen Topmast Backstays.......	....	....	1	2⅝	1	2¾	1	2⅞	2	3	2	3⅛	2	3¼	3	3½
Mizzen Top-gallant Backstays....	....	....	1	1½	1	1¾	1	1⅞	1	2	1	2⅛	1	2¼	2	2½
Mizzen Lower Stays.............	....	....	2	2⅝	2	2¾	2	2⅞	2	3	2	3⅛	2	3¼	2	3½
Mizzen Topmast Stays..........	....	....	1	2½	1	2⅝	1	2¾	1	2⅞	1	3	1	3⅛	1	3¼
Mizzen Top-gallant Stays........	....	....	1	1½	1	1⅝	1	1¾	1	1⅞	1	2	1	2⅛	1	2¼
Bowsprit Shrouds...............	2	2½	2	2¾	2	3	2	3⅛	2	3¼	2	3⅜	2	3½	2	3¾
Bobstay Bar, Diameter in Inches..	1¾		2		2⅛		2¼		2⅝		2½		2¾		3	
Bobstay Pin, Diameter in Inches..	1⅜		1½		1⅝		1¾		1⅞		2		2⅛		2¼	
Bobstay Chain, Size in Inches.....	1²⁄₁₆		1²⁄₁₆		1³⁄₁₆		1⁴⁄₁₆		1⁵⁄₁₆		1⁶⁄₁₆		1⁷⁄₁₆		1⁸⁄₁₆	

Steel Wire Rigging may be 12½ per centum less in size than is specified in table.

Hemp Standing Rigging, according to quality, should be from two to two and a quarter times the girth required for iron wire rigging.

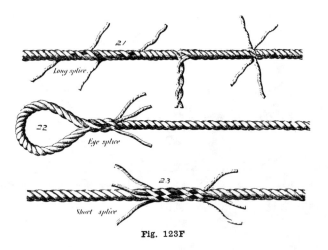

Fig. 123F

Chapter XIV

Masts and Spars

The masts and spars of wooden vessels are usually made of wood. They are rounded for a greater part of their length and stepped in properly prepared mast steps fastened to keelson, though in ships that have a center line propeller, the after mast step cannot extend below top of shaft tunnel.

The location, number and dimensions of mast and all other spars are marked on a spar and rigging plan prepared by designer. Lloyd's and the other classification societies have laid down rules for masting and rigging and have also issued tables of dimensions, and when a designer prepares his plans he generally adheres to the specifications of classification societies.

Mast, or spar making, used to be a separate trade, but at present time most shipyards have their own sparmakers.

14a. Timber Used for Spars

The timbers commonly used in U. S. A. for masts and spars are:

Oregon pine or Douglas fir.
Spruce, Canada red, Yellow and white pine.
Yellow pine.

And in Europe, Riga fir and Norway pine is largely used.

Timber for masts and spars must be absolutely free from sapwood, dead knots and defects likely to lessen

Fig. 125. Making a Spar

strength. In addition to this, it is advantageous to have the smaller pieces of timber delivered to the sparmaker before they are squared, because the sparmaker can then lay out spar in such a manner that center or heartwood of tree is near center of spar.

On Fig. 124 is shown a stick of timber being con-

Fig. 124. Making a Spar

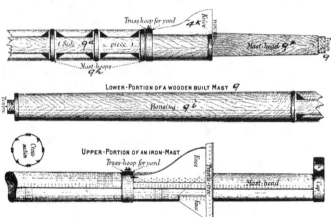

Figs. 126 and 128. Names of Parts of Mast

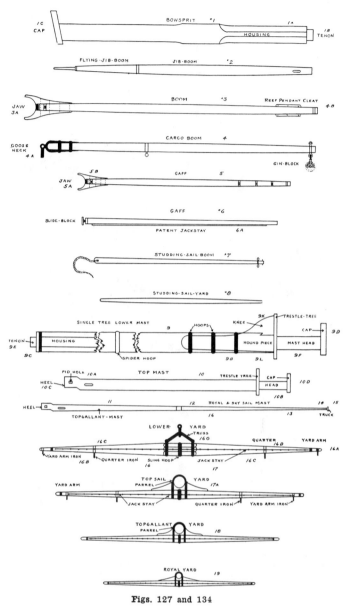

Figs. 127 and 134

has been done, and stick is fair, the sparmaker dubs off the square corners and makes portion of stick that has to be rounded, eight sided. Next he makes it sixteen sided, by again taking off the corners, and after this has been done the stick is rounded and made perfectly smooth. Of course, as spar has a rounding taper from butt to point of greatest diameter, and from this point to top, it is necessary that sparmaker "lay out" longitudinal taper lines very accurately and work to them.

In the case of booms, yards, and other smaller spars, the same method of procedure is followed.

On Fig. 126 is shown details of a ship's mast and on Fig. 127 shapes and names of various spars.

After a spar is shaped, it should be well oiled or painted to prevent wood checking, and then mast fittings and bands should be fitted and fastened in place.

The accompanying illustrations show details of mast head, tops and their fittings, and on each illustration I have listed the name of each detail identified on illustrations by numerals.

14c. MAST STEPS

At the beginning of this chapter I mentioned mast steps. These are generally cast steel shoes, securely

verted into a spar. Note how the center of heart is located at about the center of stick, and on Fig. 125 is shown the same stick of timber converted into a spar.

14b. SPAR-MAKING

A stick of timber is converted into a spar in this manner:

The sparmaker first obtains length and diameter measurements from spar and rigging plans and proceeds to "lay out" the spar on one side of stick of timber, if it is a squared stick; or if it is a round stick of timber, he hews one side to a flat surface upon which the laying out lines can be marked. On a squared stick of timber the "laying off" lines are marked on each face, but if the stick is a round one, it will be necessary to hew to the lines marked on one face before lines can be marked on other faces. The spar is first worked to shape by hewing in the manner shown on Fig. 124 and when this

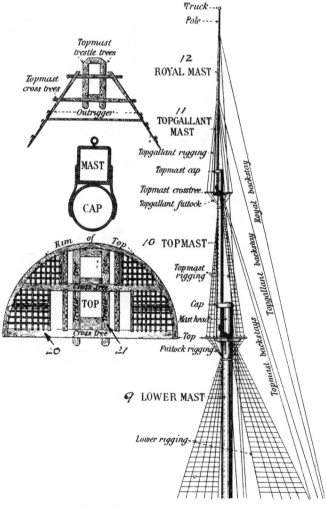

Fig. 129. Spar and Rigging Details

fitted over and bolted to upper keelsons. The upper face
of this casting has a recess of proper size and depth to
receive tenon cut on foot of mast. In the case of
steamers having a single screw and an after mast located
above shaft, it is necessary to step mast on lower deck,
or on a properly prepared step bolted to top of shaft
alley planking and framing. Where a mast goes through
a deck, it must be properly supported and wedged in
place, and of course the deck framing must be sufficiently strong to withstand additional strains that will
come on deck near mast and where rigging is attached to
side of vessel. The manner of framing a deck around a
mast is clearly shown on Fig. 27 and on some of the
drawings of deck framing shown at end of book. On
the drawing No. 28 mast step construction details are
clearly shown.

14d. Masts and Spars of Various Rigs

On the following lists I give names of masts and spars
of principal rigs, each spar being identified by numerals
marked on illustrations.

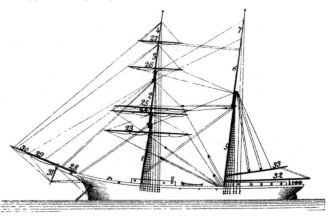

Fig. 131.   Barque Spars

32.	Fore yard.	40.	Main topgallant yard.
33.	Lower-fore topsail yard.	41.	Main royal yard.
34.	Upper-fore topsail yard.	42.	Spanker boom.
35.	Fore topgallant yard.	43.	Spanker gaff.
36.	Fore royal yard.	44.	Bowsprit.
37.	Main yard.	45.	Jib boom.
38.	Lower-main topsail yard.	46.	Flying jib boom.
39.	Upper-main topsail yard.		

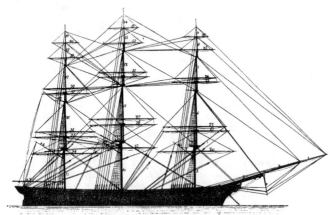

Fig. 130.   Ship Spars

Spars of Ship

1.	Flying jib boom.	24.	Upper-fore topgallant yard.
2.	Jib boom.	25.	Fore royal yard.
3.	Bowsprit.	26.	Fore skysail yard.
4.	Martingale boom.	27.	Main yard.
5.	Fore mast.	28.	Lower-main topsail yard.
6.	Fore topmast.	29.	Upper-main topsail yard.
7.	Fore topgallant mast.	30.	Lower-main topgallant yard.
8.	Fore royal mast.	31.	Upper-main topgallant yard.
9.	Fore skysail mast.	32.	Main royal yard.
10.	Main mast.	33.	Main skysail yard.
11.	Main topmast.	34.	Cross-jack yard.
12.	Main topgallant mast.	35.	Lower-mizzen topsail yard.
13.	Main royal mast.	36.	Upper-mizzen topsail yard.
14.	Main skysail mast.	37.	Lower-mizzen topgallant yard.
15.	Mizzen mast.	38.	Upper-mizzen topgallant yard.
16.	Mizzen topmast.	39.	Mizzen royal yard.
17.	Mizzen topgallant mast.	40.	Mizzen skysail yard.
18.	Mizzen royal mast.	41.	Fore trysail gaff.
19.	Mizzen skysail mast.	42.	Main trysail gaff.
20.	Fore yard.	43.	Spanker boom.
21.	Lower-fore topsail yard.	44.	Spanker gaff.
22.	Upper-fore topsail yard.	45.	Monkey gaff.
23.	Lower-fore topgallant yard.		

Names of Barque Spars

22.	Fore mast.	27.	Main topmast.
23.	Fore topmast.	28.	Main topgallant mast.
24.	Fore topgallant mast.	29.	Main royal mast.
25.	Fore royal mast.	30.	Mizzen mast.
26.	Main mast.	31.	Mizzen topmast.

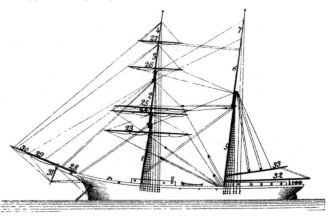

Fig. 132.   Barkentine Spars

23.	Fore yard.	29.	Jib boom.
24.	Lower topsail yard.	30.	Flying jib boom.
25.	Upper topsail yard.	31.	Martingale boom.
26.	Topgallant yard.	32.	Main boom.
27.	Royal yard.	33.	Main gaff.
28.	Bowsprit.		

Foremast and Its Rigging

1.	Lower mast.	18.	Lanyards.
2.	Tap.	19.	Chain plates.
3.	Mast-head.	20.	Topmast backstays.
4.	Lower cap.	21.	Lower futtocks.
5.	Topmast.	22.	Topmast rigging.
6.	Topmast crosstrees.	23.	Topgallant futtocks.
7.	Topmast head.	24.	Sling of lower-yard.
8.	Topmast cap.	25.	Topsail tye.
9.	Lower yard.	26.	Lower lifts.
10.	Topsail yard.	27.	Topsail lifts.
11.	Topmast studdingsail boom.	28.	Lower foot-ropes.
12.	Topgallant studdingsail boom.	29.	Topsail foot-ropes.
13.	Lower rigging.	30.	Stirrups.
14.	Swifter (foremost shroud).	31.	Flemish horse.
15.	Sheer-batten.	32.	Quarter irons.
16.	Ratlines.	33.	Yard-arm irons.
17.	Dead-eyes.	34.	Lift purchase.

Names of Fore-and-Aft Schooner Spars

1.	Fore mast.	7.	Fore boom.
2.	Main mast.	8.	Main boom.
3.	Mizzen mast.	9.	Mizzen boom.
4.	Fore topmast.	10.	Fore gaff.
5.	Main topmast.	11.	Main gaff.
6.	Mizzen topmast.	12.	Mizzen gaff.

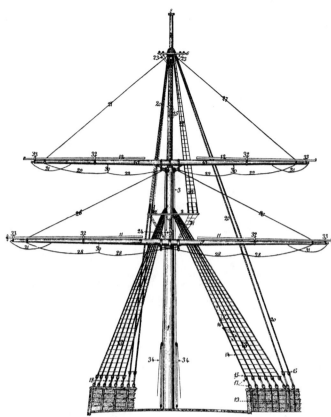

Fig. 133 and 120. Rigged Foremast

List of Masts and Spars of Vessels

Boom, fore topmast studdingsail —
  main topmast studding-
  sail —
Bowsprit — 1, Fig. 127-134
  Parts of Bowsprit:
    bed of —
    bees or cheeks of —
    gammoning of —
    screw-gammoning hoop
    of —
    housing — (*the part in-
    side of stem*) 1a, Fig. 134
    — partners
    running — (*in small ves-
    sels*)
    saddle of —
    steeve of —
    step of —
    tenon of — 1b, Fig. 134
Bumpkin; Bumkin; Boomkin
  quarter —; Outrigger (*for
  main braces*)
Cap is fitted on spars listed below:
    bowsprit — 1c, Fig. 134
    lower 9d, Fig. 134
    fore-mast (*in any vessel*)
    main-mast (*in any vessel*)
    mizzen-mast — (*of a ship*)
    mizzen-mast — (*of a
    barque, barquentine or
    three-masted schooner*)

Boom—Names of parts of:
    — crutch
    gooseneck — 4a, Fig. 127
    jaw or throat — 3a, Fig.
    127
    jaw-rope
    reefing cleat — 4b, Fig. 127
    saddle —
    fore —; gaff-fore sail —
    (*of a schooner*)
    (*square*) fore sail —
    load —; Derrick;
    main — 3, Fig. 127 (*of a
    schooner, brigantine, bar-
    quentine or three-masted
    schooner*)
    main — (*of a brig*)
    main — (*of a sloop or
    cutter*)
    mizzen — (*of a barquen-
    tine or a three-masted
    schooner*)
    ring tail —
    spanker —
    studdingsail — 7, Fig. 127
    studdingsail — (*boom-
    iron*) — on all studding-
    sail booms
    lower studdingsail —;
    swing — (*Ship*)

Boom—Names of parts of:
  royal studdingsail —
  (*Ship*)
  fore royal studdingsail —
  (*Ship*)
  main royal studdingsail —
  (*Ship*)
  topgallant studdingsail —
  fore topgallant studdingsail — (*Ship*)
  main topgallant studdingsail — (*Ship*)
  topmast studdingsail —
  (*Ship*)
Cap, on all top and topgallant
  masts:
    topgallant mast —
    fore topgallant mast —
    main topgallant mast —
    mizzen topgallant mast —
    topmast — 10d, Fig. 127
    fore topmast —
    main topmast —
    mizzen topmast —
Crosstrees — 20, Fig. 129
  Fitted on spars listed below:
    fore mast —; fore lower
    — (*in any vessel*)
    main mast —; main lower
    — (*in any vessel*)
    mizzen mast —; mizzen
    lower — (*of a ship*)
    mizzen mast —; (*of a
    barque, barquentine or
    three-masted schooner*)
    topgallant —
    fore topgallant —
    main topgallant —
    mizzen topgallant —
    topmast —
    fore topmast —
    main topmast —
    mizzen topmast —
Flying jib boom — 1, Fig. 130
Gaff — fitted on vessels rigged
  in manner mentioned be-
  low:
    jackstay on a — 6a, Fig.
    127
    jaw — 5a, Fig. 127
    jaw-rope of a —
    throat bolt — 5b, Fig. 127
    — traveller;
    fore —; boom fore-sail —
    (*of a schooner*)
    main — (*of a schooner,
    barquentine, brigantine or
    three-masted schooner*)
    main —; main boom sail
    — (*of a brig*)
    mizzen — (*of a barquen-
    tine or three-masted
    schooner*)
    monkey — 45, Fig. 130
    trysail —

Yard
  Names of parts of a yard used on square-rigged vessels:
  roller in — arm iron
  — batten
  center, bunt, or sling of a —
  jackstay — 16c, Fig. 127
  parrel of an (*upper*) — 17a, Fig. 127
  quarter — 16d, Fig. 127
  — quarter iron — 16e, Fig. 127
  sheave-hole —
  sling of a lower —
  sling-cleat of a (*lower*) —
  sling-hoop of a (*lower*) — 16f, Fig. 127
  standard or crane of a lower topsail —
  truss of a (*lower*) — 16g, Fig. 127
  truss-hoop of a (*lower*) —
Yards
  Names of yards used on square-rigged vessels:
  Cross-jack-yard — 34, Fig. 130

Fore-yard — 32, Fig. 131
Fore-yard — 20, Fig. 130
Gaff-topsail-yard
Lower-yard
Main-yard — 27, Fig. 130
Royal yard — 19, Fig. 127
  fore — 25, Fig. 130
  main — 32, Fig. 130
  mizzen — 39, Fig. 130
Skysail-yard
  fore — 26, Fig. 130
  main — 33, Fig. 130
  mizzen — 40, Fig. 130
Spritsail-yard
Squaresail yard (*the yard of a schooner or of a sloop, cutter, etc.*)
Studdingsail-yard
  lower — Fig. 130
  royal — Fig. 130
  topgallant — Fig. 130
  topmast — Fig. 130
Topgallant-yard
  fore — 35, Fig. 131
  lower fore — 23, Fig. 130
  upper fore — 24, Fig. 130

Topgallant-yard
  lower —
  main —
  lower main — 30, Fig. 130
  upper main — 31, Fig. 130
  mizzen —
  lower mizzen — 37, Fig. 130
  upper mizzen — 38, Fig. 130
  upper —
Topsail-yard
  (*of a schooner*)
  fore —
  lower fore — 21, Fig. 130
  upper fore — 22, Fig. 130
  lower —
  main —
  lower main — 28, Fig. 130
  upper main — 29, Fig. 130
  mizzen —
  lower mizzen — 35, Fig. 130
  upper mizzen — 36, Fig. 130
Upper-Yards
  upper —

TABLE OF THE FRACTIONAL PROPORTION THAT THE INTERMEDIATE DIAMETERS BEAR TOWARDS THE GIVEN DIAMETER OF MASTS, YARDS, ETC.

SPECIES OF MASTS, YARDS, ETC.	Proportions to the Given Diameter					
	Quarters			Head		Heel
	1st	2nd	3rd	Lower Part	Upper Part	
Standing-Masts	$60/61$	$14/15$	$6/7$	$3/4$	$5/8$	$6/7$
Topmast, Topgallant Masts and Royal-Masts	$60/61$	$14/15$	$9/17$	$9/13$	$6/11$	......
Yards	$30/31$	$7/8$	$7/10$	Arms $3/4$		......
Bowsprit	$60/61$	$11/12$	$4/5$	$2/3$		Outer End $6/7$
Jib and Driver-Booms	$40/41$	$11/12$	$5/6$	Ends $2/3$		......
Main-booms	$40/41$	$12/13$	$7/8$	Fore Ends $2/3$	After End $3/4$	Middle $11/12$
Gaffs	$40/41$	$11/12$	$4/5$	$5/6$		......
Heeling Standing-Masts	Athwart Ship $2/3$	......	......	......	Fore and Aft $1/2$	......
Bowsprit	Athwart Ship $7/12$	......	......	Up and Down $3/4$	......	......

Chapter XV

Description of Types of Vessels

15a. Explaining Division of Vessels into Types and Classes

Vessels are divided into kinds, such as steam, motor-driven, auxiliary and sailing vessels; and each kind of vessel is then divided into types, and each type is sub-divided into classes according to general arrangement of decks, number of decks, and certain structural details.

Steam vessels are generally designated according to purpose for which they are designed. Thus, there are war vessels, passenger steamers, cargo carriers, ferry-boats, fishing vessels, light ships, tugs, steam lighters, wrecking vessels, etc.

Sailing and auxiliary craft are generally designated according to rig. Thus, there are ships, barks, barkentines, brigs, brigantines, schooners, etc.

Vessels are also classed, or named, according to number of decks, structural arrangement of decks and houses, and details of certain parts of their structure, and as it is very necessary that you have a clear understanding of this I have illustrated and briefly described the most important of these details and the various classes of vessels.

15b. One-Decked Vessels

These are small vessels having one completely laid deck-flat, and little depth of hold, say 12 feet or less. When the depth of hold increases to 14 or 15 feet, some hold-beams are inserted.

A one-decked vessel can be either steam or sail driven and, of course, can be used for any purpose it is designed for. Fig. 202 illustrates a one-deck steam trawler, Fig. 203 a one-deck auxiliary schooner, and Fig. 212 a one-deck schooner.

15c. Two-Decked Vessels

These vessels have generally a depth of hold from about 20 to 24 feet, the decks are called upper deck and lower deck, the latter also styled "'tween-deck."

Fig. 205 illustrates a two-deck motor-driven cargo vessel, and Fig. 207 a two-deck schooner.

15d. Three-Decked Vessels

These are vessels having three tiers of beams, with at least two decks laid and caulked; they are sometimes flush decked, in other instances fitted with a poop, bridge-house and a forecastle, or with a shelter deck or shade deck above the upper deck.

The scantlings of materials are of the heaviest description, being regulated by the dimensions of hull, measured to height of upper deck.

This class of vessel is intended for any description of cargo, and for employment in any part of the world.

15e. Spar-Decked Vessels

These are vessels having also three tiers of beams like a three-decked ship, with generally two decks laid and caulked.

They are of lighter construction than the former, the scantlings of materials being principally regulated by the dimensions of hull, measured to the height of middle deck.

This class of vessel is usually constructed for special trades.

15f. Awning-Decked Vessels

These vessels have a superstructure above the main deck, of which the scantlings of material are inferior to the topsides, deck beams, and deck-flat, in a spar-decked vessel of similar dimensions.

An awning deck may be fitted to vessels with either one, two or three decks; and the scantlings of material of hull are regulated by the dimensions of vessel, without reference to the added awning deck.

The space or capacity between the awning deck and the deck below is generally intended for the stowage of light cargo, or for the use of passengers, etc.

15g. Partial Awning-Decked Vessels

These are vessels in which the upper deck is only partially covered by a deck of light construction, having the scantlings of material similar to those in a complete awning-decked vessel.

15h. Shelter-Decked Vessels

These are vessels with exposed (or weather) decks, of a lighter construction than required for awning-decked vessels, the topsides between the upper and shelter decks, are closed-in; but the shelter deck is sometimes fitted with ventilation openings.

15i. Shade-Deck Vessels

These are vessels with a very light exposed or weather deck above the upper deck; this shade deck generally extends over the whole length of upper deck, and is not enclosed at sides above the main rail or bulwark; it is used as a protection from sun or rain.

15j. FLUSH-DECKED VESSELS

These vessels have a continuous upper deck, without poop, bridge-house, or forecastle; spar and awning-decked vessels are generally flush decked (see Fig. 142).

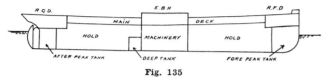

Fig. 135

15k. WELL-DECKED VESSELS

These are vessels having long poops or raised quarter-deck, and topgallant forecastle; the space between these structures forming the well (see Fig. 135).

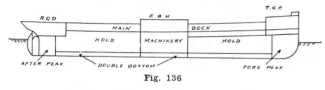

Fig. 136

15l. SHIP WITH A HURRICANE DECK

This is a vessel with a light deck or platform over erections on the upper deck; it has generally a breadth from two-thirds to three-fourths or sometimes the whole breadth of ship, running frequently all fore-and-aft, and is used for a promenade, etc., in passenger ships (see Fig. 137).

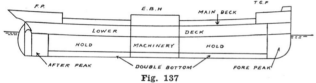

Fig. 137

15m. STRUCTURE AND HOUSE ARRANGEMENTS NAMED

Below I illustrate and describe structural details and deckhouse arrangements that influence type and classification.

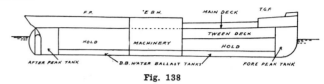

Fig. 138

Fig. 135 is an illustration of a one-deck steamer with short raised quarter-deck, enclosed bridge-house and topgallant forecastle. The illustration shows a vessel without double bottom, but fitted with fore-peak, after-peak and deep tanks.

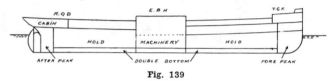

Fig. 139

Fig. 136 shows a similar arrangement of deckhouses but vessel has a double-bottom tank in place of deep tank amidships.

Fig. 137 shows a two-deck steamer with *full* poop, enclosed bridge-houses and topgallant forecastle. This vessel has double bottom and peak tanks.

Fig. 140

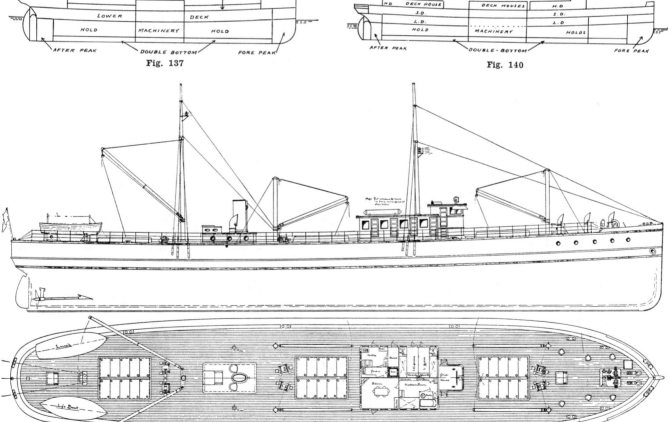

Fig. 142. 200-Foot Flush Decked Oil-Engined Wooden Cargo Vessel From Designs by J. Murray Watts For East India Trade

Fig. 143. Chibiabos, Roy H. Beattie, Milton and Haverhill, Four Ships Built by L. H. Shattuck, Inc., at Portsmouth, at the Dock Fitting Out
With Rigging, Joiner Work, Etc.

Fig. 138 shows a steamship with long full poop deck, enclosed bridge-houses and topgallant forecastle. This vessel has double bottom and peak tanks.

Fig. 139 shows steamship with long raised quarter-deck, enclosed bridge-houses and topgallant forecastle. Double bottom and peak tanks are shown.

Fig. 140 shows a steamer having hurricane deck, shade deck, and lower decks. Double-bottom tanks as well as peak tanks are also shown. This arrangement of decks is generally used in passenger vessels.

Fig. 141

Fig. 141 shows sailing vessel with raised quarter-deck, forecastle, upper and lower decks. Fore and after-peak tanks are fitted, therefore this arrangement of tanks indicates that vessel is of steel construction.

Figs. 143 to 155 are illustrations of various types of vessels.

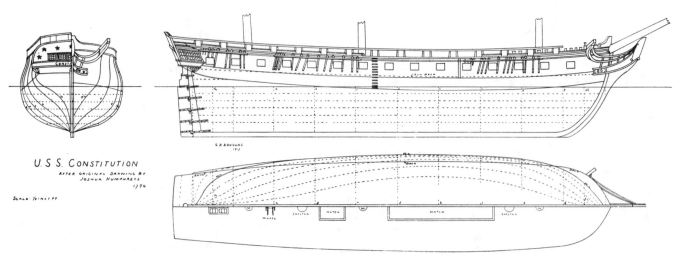

Fig. 144

Fig. 145.   Constitution as She Now Is at the Boston Navy Yard

Fig. 146.   Steam Yacht Vanadis, Built For C. K. G. Billings, Sold to the Russian Government

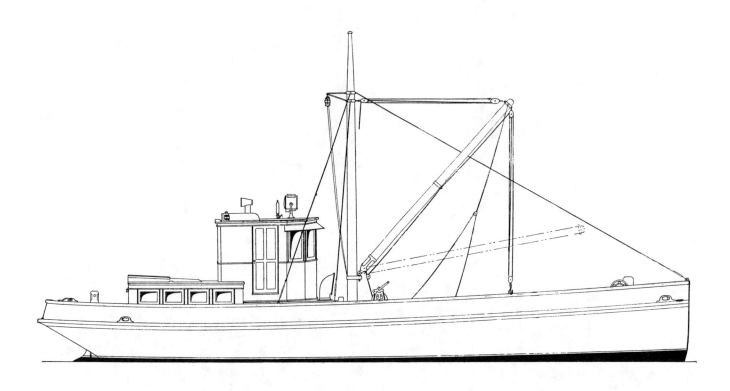

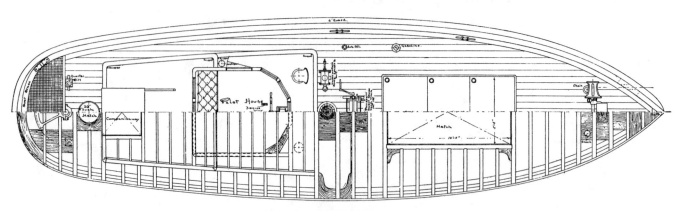

Fig. 146a.   52-Foot Hydro-Aeroplane Tender, Designed by J. Murray Watts

Length .... 52 feet
Breadth .... 14 "

Fig. 147. U. S. S. South Carolina, a Battleship of the Dreadnought Type, Which Mounts Eight 12-Inch Guns and Many Smaller Ones

Fig. 148. U. S. Mine-Sweeper Pelican Built by the Gas Engine & Power Company, Launched June 15, 1918

Fig. 149. Faith, the First Concrete-Built Ocean Steamer, Starting Off From San Francisco for Seattle, Tacoma and Vancouver

Fig. 150. Faith, 5,000-Ton Concrete Vessel, Launched 1918 From the San Francisco Shipbuilding Company's Yard at Redwood City, Cal.

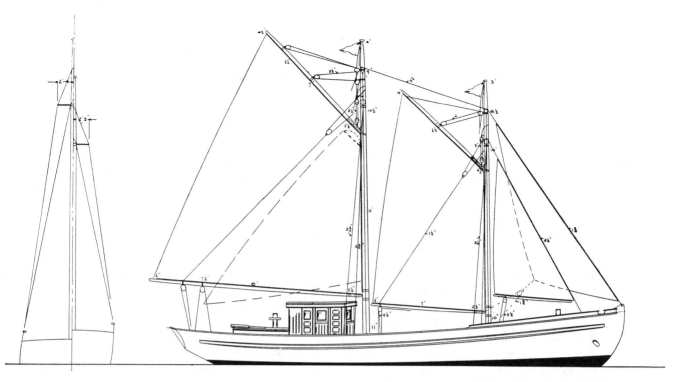

Fig. 151. Iskum, an 80-Foot Fishing Schooner Built From Designs by Edson B. Schock and Fitted With a Corliss Gas Engine

Fig. 152. Northeast End Light Vessel

Fig. 155. Ship Rickmars on the Delaware

Fig. 154. Motorship James Timpson, Built by the Standifer Company,
Designed by Cox & Stevens

Fig. 153. Margaret Haskell

Chapter XVI

Anchor, Chains and Equipment

Every vessel must be properly equipped for sea, and while the amount of equipment necessary varies in each type and size of vessel, the greater part of equipment used on seagoing vessels, as well as the sizes, dimensions and amount of equipment that must be carried on each vessel, has been standardized. Equipment upon which the safety of a vessel or its crew depends, such as anchors, chain, boats and their equipment, navigating and directing instruments, etc., is defined in Government regulations and by rules laid down by classification societies, and no vessel is allowed to put to sea without being equipped in accordance with the rules. Of all equipment, anchors, chains and methods of handling them, the steering apparatus, and navigating instruments are the most important, and next to these comes the lifeboat and its equipment.

16a. Anchors

The number and sizes of anchors that must be carried depends upon size and type of vessel, and the service it will be engaged in. By size of vessel is meant tonnage as computed by rules of the classification societies.

In general it can be said that all seagoing vessels, except the very smallest, must carry three or more anchors and each of these must be of a certain size and type.

On Tables 16A and 16B (page 166) is given lists of weights and kinds of anchors that must be carried on steam and sailing vessels of named tonnage.

As bowers, stream and kedge anchors are mentioned, I will illustrate and describe each kind.

Bowers are the largest and principal anchors carried and they can be either stockless, patent with hinged flukes, or common with wood or steel stock.

Fig. 156 is an illustration of a stockless anchor. (Durkee.)

As this type of anchor is stockless the shank can be housed in hawse pipe and anchor carried in manner shown on Fig. 157. Anchors of this kind are generally used on all modern vessels because they are much easier to handle, stow better and are just as efficient and strong as the older type anchors with stocks.

On Fig. 158 a common bower with wood stock is shown, and on Fig. 159 a patent bower with hinged arm and flukes.

The common bower anchor with wood stock is now seldom used except on sailing vessels, but the bower with iron stock, and bower with hinged arm and fluke is frequently used on smaller vessels. These types of

Fig. 156. Stockless Anchor

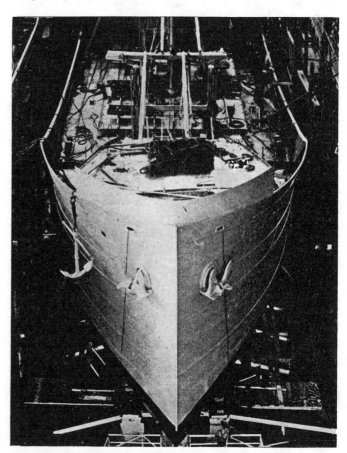

Fig. 157. Stockless Anchor in Place

BOWER (common)

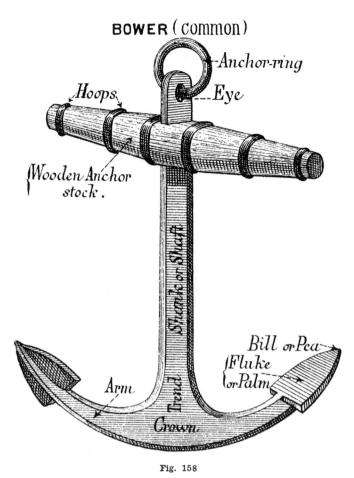

Fig. 158

anchors must be stowed on a properly prepared platform, called a bill board, in the manner shown on Fig. 160, and it is necessary to install proper cat and fish tackles and davits or an anchor crane for hoisting anchor to its stowage position. Anchor davits and falls are shown in position on Fig. 160.

The smaller stream and kedge anchors carried on vessels are similar in shape to bowers. On Fig. 161 anchors of this kind are shown.

16b. HAWSE PIPES

I have mentioned hawse pipes, so I will now describe and illustrate them.

Hawse pipes are fitted at each side of bow, their use being to afford a proper opening for passage of chain cable to which anchors are attached.

In wooden and steel vessels it is necessary to strongly reinforce the framing where hawse pipes pass through framing and planking and to securely bolt hawse pipes to this reinforcing.

Hawse pipes for use with stockless anchors always have opening through them sufficiently large to allow stock of anchor to pass through it. On Fig. 162 the hawse pipes for a pair of stockless anchors are clearly shown in position.

And on Fig. 201, profile view, the direction of lead

of hawse pipes is clearly indicated by dotted lines at bow.

Hawse pipes are made of cast-iron and consist of two pieces, the outer flange with pipe attached, and the inner or deck flange. The outer flange is carefully fitted to planking because it must make a watertight joint, and after pipe is in place the inner flange is fitted around inner end of pipe and joint caulked tight. The outer flange is securely fastened to hull with bolts closely spaced (see bolt holes on Fig. 162) and inner flange is secured to deck in like manner.

As there is considerable wear on flanges and pipe of a hawse pipe, it is necessary that there be ample thickness of metal in casting, especially along lower portion of pipe and outer flange, because it is here that greatest amount of friction occurs when chain is being let out, or hauled up, or vessel is riding at anchor.

On the following table I give diameter of pipe and thickness of metal for hawse pipes of vessels carrying anchors with stock.

TABLE 16C
SIZE AND THICKNESS OF IRON HAWSE PIPE FOR CABLES OF
EACH SIZE

Size of Chain Cable Ins.	Size of Hawse Pipe in the Clear Ins.	Thickness of Iron in the Body of the Pipe and of the Flange Ins.	Size of Chain Cable Ins.	Size of Hawse Pipe in the Clear Ins.	Thickness of Iron in the Body of the Pipe and of the Flange Ins.
2 1/8	21 1/2	1 1/2	1 1/2	13 3/4	1
2	18 3/4	1 3/8	1 3/8	12 1/2	7/8
1 7/8	17 1/2	1 1/4	1 1/4	11 1/2	7/8
1 3/4	15 1/2	1 1/4	1 1/8	10 3/4	3/4
1 5/8	14 1/2	1 1/8	1	9	3/4

For stockless anchors the diameter of opening must be increased considerably but it is not necessary to increase thickness of metal.

The outside diameter of flange should be sufficiently

BOWER (patent)

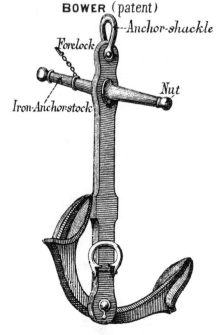

Fig. 159

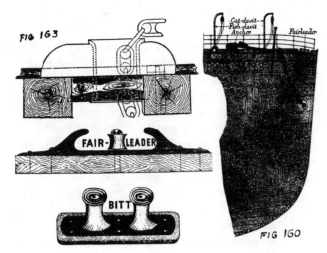

FIG 163

FAIR-LEADER

BITT

Cat-davit
Fish-davit
Anchor
Fairleader

FIG 160

greater than outside diameter of pipe to insure that all fastenings will go into solid wood (or metal).

Do not confuse hawse pipes with the chain pipes that lead from deck to chain locker.

16b¹. CHAIN PIPES

After anchor chain has passed through hawse pipe, it is led around wild-cat of anchor windlass and from there passes through chain pipes, let into deck, into chain locker. On Fig. 163 is shown cross-section view of chain pipe and on Fig. 164 the chain pipes are clearly shown in position under windlass.

16c. ANCHOR CHAIN

Chain is now universally used with anchors for anchoring a vessel. The kind of chain used is stud-linked and diameter of material of which links are made determines size. Each vessel must have a certain specified amount of chain for each anchor, the amount and diameter varying, as with anchors, with tonnage of vessels. On Tables 16A, B, is given diameter and length of chain specified by classification societies' rules, and on Fig. 165 is shown a portion of anchor chain properly shackled and fitted with swivel.

For convenience in handling, anchor chain comes in lengths, several of which are fastened together with shackles to form a cable. The first "shot", or length, is usually a short one and has attached to it a swivel. Anchor is shackled to chain and inboard end of chain is secured to a heavy beam and eyebolt placed in chain locker for that purpose.

16c¹. CHAIN LOCKER

Chain is stowed in a properly prepared locker built in bow of vessel and this locker must be sufficiently large to stow each cable *separately* and there *must be* a division or partition between the chains.

A certain amount of room is required to stow a chain cable, the amount varying with diameter of chain and its length. On Table 16D I give space required to properly stow 50 fathoms of chain of named diameters.

TABLE 16D
SPACE REQUIRED TO STOW ROUGHLY 50 FATHOMS OF CHAIN CABLE

Diameter Ins.	Cubic Feet Required	Diameter Ins.	Cubic Feet Required
2 ¼	89.83	1 ⅜	32.80
2 ⅛	83.84	1 ¼	26.20
2	66.75	1 ⅛	20.96
1 ⅞	60.19	1	17.30
1 ¾	54.01	⅞	14.24
1 ⅝	46.16	¾	11.73
1 ½	39.19	¹¹⁄₁₆	8.26

16d. ANCHOR WINDLASS

An anchor windlass is used to assist in hoisting anchor. This windlass can be operated by power or by hand.

On sailing vessels hand-operated anchor windlasses are installed on forward deck and operated by means of a geared brake lever, or by hand-spikes inserted in openings left for that purpose.

On Fig. 166 is shown three types of hand-operated anchor windlass installed in sailing vessels and on Fig. 167 details of one of the types, with parts marked for identification, are shown.

Below I give list of names of parts of windlass shown on Fig. 167.

HAND-OPERATED ANCHOR WINDLASS

Windlass — carrick-bitts — 1	main piece of —
— side bitts — 2	— pawls — 10
cheeks of carrick bitts — 3	— pawl bitt — 1
standard knees of carrick-	— pawl rim; — pawl
bitts — 4	rack — 11
— connecting rods — 9	— purchase rims — 12
— purchase rods	spindle of —
— crosshead — 8	strong back of a — 7
— ends; — heads — 5	iron whelps on — 6
— hand levers — 13	wood lining on —

16d¹. STEAM-OPERATED ANCHOR WINDLASSES

On Fig. 168 is shown a modern power-operated anchor windlass installed on forecastle deck of a motorship. You will note by referring to illustration (which is a bow view, looking aft) that anchor chains, after passing through hawse pipes (as this is a photo of ship shown on plans Fig. 201, you can see location of hawse pipes by referring to these plans) pass through controllers placed on deck a little distance aft of deck end of hawse pipe. Controllers are for the purpose of con-

STREAM-ANCHOR.   KEDGE.   GRAPNEL.

Fig. 161

Fig. 162.   Hawse Pipes on Agawam

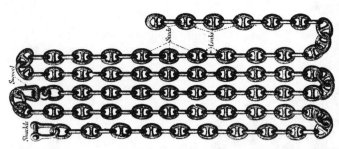

Fig. 165. Anchor Chain

11. Center bitt.
12. Center bitt keep.
13. Chain pipes.
14. Cable relievers.
15. Bedplate.

16. Chain wheel for messenger from steam winch.
17. Clutch for attached strain power.
18. Gearing for steam power.

16e. DECK WINCHES

Modern vessels have power-operated deck winches installed convenient to hatches and booms used for cargo. On Fig. 169 is shown a steam deck winch, principal parts being identified by number, and on deck of vessel shown on Fig. 170 a deck winch can be seen installed in proper location.

Below I give names of parts identified on Fig. 169.

1. Warping ends.
2. Main spur-wheel.
3. Barrel.
4. Barrel shaft.
5. Small spur-wheel.
6. Clutch lever.
7. Cylinders.
8. Steam chest.
9. Stay or tie-rod.
10. Steam pipe.
11. Exhaust pipe.
12. Reversing lever.
13. Base plate.
14. Stop valve.
15. Connecting rod.
16. Piston rod.

A hand-operated deck winch is shown on Fig. 171 and below I give names of parts identified by number on the illustration.

trolling chain should brake on windlass become defective, or when vessel is riding at anchor. From controllers the chain passes over wild-cats of windlass and from thence through chain pipes, placed immediately below wild-cats, into chain lockers.

On Fig. 164 is shown details of one type of steam-operated anchor windlass with principal parts identified by numerals. Below I give names of parts.

1. Hand power levers.
2. Cross-head.
3. Warping ends.
4. Side bitts.
5. Side bitt keeps.
6. Screw brake nut.
7. Cable lifter.
8. Pawl rack.
9. Main cone driving wheel.
10. Cross-head bracket.

Head of Bark Greyhound

Deck of Whaling Brig Viola, Showing Windlass

Deck of Brig Viola

Head of Bark Wanderer

Fig. 166

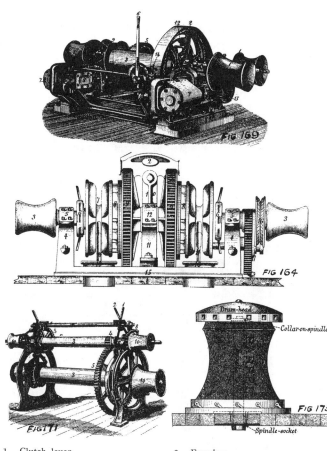

1. Clutch lever.
2. Brake.
3. Barrels.
4. Pinion.
5. Spur wheels.
6. Framing.
7. Ratchet wheel.
8. Pawls.
9. Tie-rod.
10. Warping ends.

16f. HAND PUMP

On Fig. 172 is shown details of hand-operated bilge pump, each principal part being identified by name. Every vessel must be equipped with a proper number of pumps for pumping water out of bilges. In sailing vessels these pumps are generally located on deck, are hand-operated, and of type shown on illustration, but in steam and motor vessels the bilge pumps are located in engine rooms and operated by steam or other power. In all cases the pump suctions are led to properly located wells in which suction boxes with strainers are located. If a vessel is divided into a number of compartments by watertight bulkheads the suction pipes are led through stuffing boxes in bulkheads and each compartment is fitted with a separate suction, and valves to shut off each set of pipes are located in engine room. In the case of a hand pump the water is discharged directly on deck and runs overboard through the scuppers, but all steam and power-operated bilge pumps are fitted with discharge pipes that lead from pump through side of vessel above the water-line.

16g. SOUNDING PIPES

Sounding pipes must be located in every compartment. These pipes extend from upper deck to lowest part of bilge in each compartment, to permit a sounding of amount of water in bilges to be taken without it being necessary to go into hold. The pipes are usually led to upper deck and fitted with a tight flush cap. By removing cap a rod, called a sounding rod, can be lowered through pipe into bilge and if there is any water in bilge, it will wet rod, and by lifting rod and measuring depth of wet portion an accurate estimate can be made of amount of water in bilges.

16h. CAPSTAN

On Fig. 173 is shown hand-operated deck capstans with principal parts marked for identification.

16i. STEERING GEAR

On Fig. 174 is shown details of a hand-operated steering gear and below I give list of parts.

1. Standard.
2. Spindle.
3. Yoke.
4. Nut.
5. Arm.
6. Guide rods.
7. Cross-head.
8. Yoke bolt.
9. Rudder wheel.
10. Spokes.

16j. BOATS AND THEIR EQUIPMENT

The number of boats each vessel must carry, their capacity and equipment, is specified in the regulations governing equipment of vessels which are issued by every government.

Below I give details of equipment that must be carried in lifeboats placed on a seagoing vessel.

Fig. 168. Windlass and Foredeck of the James Timpson

Equipment for Lifeboats

All lifeboats on ocean steam vessels shall be equipped as follows:

A properly secured life-line the entire length on each side, festooned in bights not longer than 3 feet, with a seine float in each bight.

One painter of manila rope of not less than 2¾ inches in circumference and of suitable length.

A full complement of oars and two spare oars.

One set and a half of thole pins or rowlocks attached to the boat with separate chains.

One steering oar with rowlock or becket and one rudder with tiller or yoke and yoke-lines.

One boathook attached to a staff of suitable length.

Two live-preservers.

Two hatchets.

One galvanized iron bucket with lanyard attached.

One bailer.

Where automatic plugs are not provided there shall be two plugs secured with chains for each drain hole.

One efficient liquid compass with not less than a 2-inch card.

One lantern containing sufficient oil to burn at least nine hours and ready for immediate use.

One can containing one gallon illuminating oil.

One box of friction matches wrapped in a waterproof package and carried in a box secured to the underside of stern thwart.

A wooden breaker or suitable tank fitted with a siphon, pump, or spigot for drawing water and containing at least one quart of water for each person.

Two enameled drinking cups.

A watertight receptacle containing 2 ℔ avoirdupois of provisions for each person. These provisions may be hard bread. The receptacle shall be of metal, fitted with an opening in the top not less than 5 inches in diameter, properly protected by a screw cap made of heavy cast brass, with machine thread and an attached double toggle, seating to a pliable rubber gasket, which shall insure a tight joint, in order to properly protect the contents of the can.

One canvas bag containing sailmaker's palm and needles, sail twine, marline, and marline spike.

A watertight metal case containing twelve self-igniting red lights capable of burning at least two minutes.

A sea-anchor.

A vessel containing one gallon of vegetable or animal oil, so constructed that the oil can be easily distributed on the water and so arranged that it can be attached to the sea-anchor.

A mast or masts with one good sail at least and proper gear for each (this does not apply to power lifeboat), the sail and gear to be protected by a suitable

Fig. 170. Deck Views of Motorship James Timpson, Built From Designs by Cox & Stevens

canvas cover. In case of a steam vessel which carries passengers in the North Atlantic, and is provided with a radio-telegraph installation, all the lifeboats need not be equipped with masts and sails. In this case at least one of the boats on each side shall be so equipped.

All loose equipment must be securely attached to the boat to which it belongs.

Lifeboats of less than 180 cubic feet capacity on pleasure steamers are not required to be equipped as above.

On the following list is given names of principal types and parts of boats carried on vessels:

DIFFERENT KINDS OF BOATS

Cutter
Gig
Launch
Steam Launch
Lifeboat
Longboat
Pinnace
Whaleboat

DETAILS AND APPURTENANCES OF BOATS

Boat
— awning
back-board in a —
— bailer
carvel-built —
clinch-built —

Boat
— chock
— chock skids
— compass
— cover
— davit
— davit tackle
foot grating in a —
— gripe
— hook
tank of a (*life*) —
— mast
— oar
—'s painter
plug of a —
rowlock of a —
row port of a —

Boat
— rudder
— rudder tiller
— rudder yoke
— rudder yoke-line
— sail
— skids
swifter of a —
thole-board of a —
thole-pin of a —
thwart of a —
wash-board of a —

DAVIT

Davit, anchor — ; cat —
boat —
fish —
— guy
— socket

16k. EQUIPMENT

For the convenience of the reader I list below names of a large number of pieces of equipment generally carried on seagoing vessels:

Accommodation ladder; Gangway ladder
Anemometer
Awning
boat's — ;
— boom
bridge — ; bridge house —
crowfoot of an —
curtain of an —
forecastle —
lacing of an —
lacing-holes of an —
main-deck —
poop —
quarter-deck —
ridge of an —
ridge lining of an —
ridge rope of an —
— stanchion
Axe; — handle
Ballast
Barometer; Aneroid —
Belaying-pin; Jack-pin; Tack-pin
Bell
— cover

Bell
— crank
— rope
Berth
Binnacle
— cover
— lamp
Blue-light
Boatswain's chair
Buckets
— fire
— rack
Bunk (*sailor's*)
Bunting
Buoy
anchor —
cork —
life —
— sling
sounding —
Burgee
Can-hooks
Canvas
Cask
Cat-head stopper
Caulking

Caulking
— iron
— mallet
Chain-hook
Chair
Chart
— case; — chest
Chinsing-iron (*caulker's tool*)
Chisel
hollow —
mortise —
Chronometer
— chest
Clock; Time-piece
Compass
azimuth —
variation —
boat's —
— box
polinarus
standard —
steering —
Cork-fender
Cover
capstan —
skylight —
ventilator —

Cover
    wheel —
    winch —
Crow-bar
Dogs; Cant-hooks
Dunnage; — wood
Ensign
Fair-leader
Fender
    rope —
    wooden —
Fid (*sailmaker's*)
    splicing —
    turning —
Fish-hook
Flag; Colors
    — chest
    — staff
Foghorn
Fore-lock; Key
Gimblet
Grating
Grindstone
Grommet
Hammock
Hand-cuffs
Hand-hook
Hand-spike
Hank
Harness cask
Hatchet
Hen-coop
Hinge
Holystone
Horsing-iron (*caulker's tool*)
Hose
    canvas —
    deck wash —
    india rubber —
    leather —
    scupper —
Hose-wrench
Ladder
    forecastle —
    hold —
    poop —
    raised quarter-deck —
    rope — ; side —
Lamp
Lantern
    globe —
    signal —
Lead (*sounding*)
    deep-sea —
    hand —
    — line
    — line marks and deeps
Leather; — pump —
Life-belt; Life-buoy

Light, anchor — ; Anchor-
    lantern
    mast-head —
    — masthead lantern
Lightning-conductor
Line
    furling —
    hambro —
    hauling —
    heaving —
    house —
    life —
Lizard
Log
    — board
    — book
    — glass
    ground —
    — line
    — line runner
    patent —
    — reel
    — ship
Making-iron (*caulker's tool*)
Mallet; serving —
Manrope (*of bowsprit*)
Manrope (*on a yard*)
Manropes (*of gangway*)
Marline
Marline spike
Maul
Medicine chest
Mop
Nails
Nautical almanac
Needle
    bolt rope — ; roping —
    sail —
Night-glass; Night-telescope
Oakum
    thread of —
    twisted —
Padlocks
Paint brush
Palm (*sailmaker's tool*)
Parbuckle
Parcelling
Pennant
Pitch
    — ladle
    — mop
    — pot
Plane
Plug
Pricker
Provisions
Raft; saving —
Rasp; wood —
Ratline; Ratline stuff
Rave-hook; Meaking-iron
    (*caulker's tool*)

Reeming-iron (*caulker's tool*)
Ridge-rope (*life-line stretched
    along a deck during bad
    weather*)
Rigging-screw
Ring
Roller (*over which ropes are
    led, to prevent chafing*)
Rope-yarn
Sail-hook; — twine
Sand-glass
Saw; hand —
Scoop
Scraper
Screw-jack
Scrubber; Hand-scrubber
Seizing
    cross —
    flat —
    racking —
    rose —
    tail —
    throat —
Sennit
    common —
    french —
    round —
    square —
Serving-board
Sextant
Shackle
    anchor —
    — bolt
    fore-lock of a — bolt
    joining —
    mooring —
    patent —
Shears; Sheers
Shovel
Side-light; Side lantern
    — screen
    — screen stanchion
Signal
    distress —
    fog —
    international code of —s
    night —
    rocket —
Sling; chain —; rope —
Sounding-rod
    — machine
Spanish windlass
Speaking trumpet
Spike
Spunyarn
Spy-glass
Squillgee
Stage; triangular —
Standard
Staple

Stove
Stopper
Strop; selvagee —
Swab
Swinging tray
Swivel; chain —
    mooring —
Tank; bread —
    fresh-water —
Tar
    — barrel
    — bucket

Tar
    — brush
Tarpaulin
Telescope
Thermometer
Thimble
Toggle
Traverse-board
Truck
    fair lead —
    parrel —
Tub

Turtle-peg
Twine
Vane; — spindle
Varnish; black —
    bright —
Ventilator; — cowl
    — socket
Water-cask
Weather-board
Weather-cloth
Wedge
Wind-sail

161. Stowage of Various Cargoes

Below is given average space in cubic feet required to stow named kinds of cargo. By stowage space is meant the actual number of cubic feet in *hold* of vessel that a ton of named cargo requires. This is always more than actual bulk of a ton of the named material because some space is taken up by containers, and in addition to this there is always some space left between packages.

List of Hold Space Required to Stow Cargo

	Cubic Ft. to the Ton Stowed
Wool	98
Hemp, loosely packed	100
Hemp, compressed in bales	65
Cotton	115
Cotton, compressed in modern compressors	105
Rice in bags	48
Oats in bags	65
Linseed	58
Potatoes in bags	70
Refined sugar in bags	50
Tea	90
Grain in bulk	46
Butter in kegs	58

TABLE 16B
ANCHORS AND CHAINS FOR SAILING VESSELS
MINIMUM WEIGHTS OF ANCHORS; SIZES AND LENGTHS OF CHAIN CABLES

Tonnage	Number Bowers	Number Stream	Number Kedges	Bowers Without Stock Lbs.	Bowers Admiralty Test Tons	Stream Lbs.	Kedge Lbs.	2nd Kedge Lbs.	Stud Chain Cable Minimum Size Ins.	Stud Chain Cable Lengths Fat'ms	Stream Chain Inches
100	2	1	1	700	8	200	110	…	7/8	105	1/2
150	2	1	1	900	10	280	140	…	1	120	9/16
200	2	1	1	1100	12	400	200	…	1 1/8	120	5/8
300	2	1	1	1450	14	500	250	125	1 1/4	135	11/16
400	2	1	1	1850	17	600	300	155	1 5/16	150	3/4
500	2	1	1	2125	20	775	400	195	1 7/16	165	13/16
600	3	1	1	2450	22	900	450	225	1 1/2	180	7/8
700	3	1	1	2800	24	1000	500	250	1 9/16	180	7/8
800	3	1	1	3125	26	1125	615	280	1 5/8	180	15/16
900	3	1	1	3350	28	1225	650	310	1 11/16	180	15/16
1000	3	1	1	3575	29½	1250	675	335	1 3/4	180	1
1200	3	1	1	3800	31	1450	725	360	1 7/8	180	1
1400	3	1	1	4000	32½	1550	780	395	1 15/16	180	1 1/16
1600	3	1	1	4250	34	1600	840	420	2	180	1 1/16
1800	3	1	1	4500	35½	1800	900	450	2	180	1 1/8
2000	3	1	1	4700	37	1900	950	500	2 1/16	180	1 1/8
2500	3	1	1	5000	39	2100	1120	560	2 1/8	180	1 3/16
3000	3	1	1	5400	41	2350	1230	615	2 3/16	180	1 1/4
3500	3	1	1	5800	43½	2600	1300	650	2 1/4	180	1 1/4

Two of the Bowers Anchors must not be less than the weight named; but for the third a reduction of 15 per cent will be allowed. No reduction will be permitted in the lengths of cables.

TABLE 16A
ANCHORS AND CHAINS

Vessels Tonnage Tons	Number Bowers	Number Stream	Number Kedges	Bowers Without Stock Lbs.	Bowers Test Tons	Stream Lbs.	Kedge Lbs.	2nd Kedge Lbs.	Stud-Chain Cables Minimum Sizes Ins.	Stud-Chain Cables Length Fat'ms	Stream Chain Size
100	2	1	…	392	5.9	112	…	…	11/16	105	1/2
150	2	1	…	504	6.9	200	…	…	13/16	120	9/16
200	2	1	…	672	8.8	225	…	…	14/16	120	9/16
250	2	1	…	840	9.7	280	…	…	15/16	120	5/8
300	2	1	…	1008	11.	300	…	…	1	120	5/8
350	2	1	…	1176	12.2	336	…	…	1 1/16	135	11/16
400	2	1	1	1344	13.5	530	250	…	1 2/16	135	3/4
450	2	1	1	1512	14.8	560	280	…	1 3/16	150	3/4
500	2	1	1	1680	16.	675	335	…	1 4/16	150	13/16
600	2	1	1	1848	17.2	730	360	…	1 5/16	165	13/16
700	2	1	1	2016	18.8	790	390	…	1 6/16	165	7/8
800	2	1	1	2184	20.3	900	450	…	1 7/16	180	7/8
900	2	1	2	2380	21.7	1000	500	225	1 8/16	180	15/16
1000	2	1	2	2600	23.5	1120	560	250	1 9/16	180	15/16
1200	2	1	2	2850	25.2	1175	580	280	1 10/16	180	1
1400	2	1	2	3100	26.9	1230	615	310	1 11/16	180	1
1600	2	1	2	3350	28.6	1350	675	310	1 12/16	180	1 1/16
1800	3	1	2	3600	30.1	1450	730	335	1 13/16	180	1 1/16
2000	3	1	2	3800	31.6	1500	760	360	1 14/16	180	1 1/8
2300	3	1	2	4100	33.4	1550	785	360	1 15/16	270	1 3/16
2600	3	1	2	4250	34.5	1625	815	390	2	270	1 1/4
3000	3	1	2	4400	35.	1680	850	420	2 1/16	270	1 5/16
3500	3	1	2	4600	37.	1800	900	475	2 2/16	270	1 1/4
4000	4	1	2	4800	38.	1960	950	500	2 3/16	270	1 5/16
4500	4	1	2	5000	39.2	2130	1050	530	2 4/16	270	1 1/4
5000	4	1	2	5200	40.7	2250	1100	560	2 5/16	300	1 5/16
5500	4	1	2	5400	41.5	2400	1170	585	2 6/16	300	1 3/8
6000	4	1	2	5600	42.5	2520	1250	625	2 7/16	300	1 7/16
6500	4	1	2	5800	43.7	2650	1320	660	2 8/16	300	1 8/16
7000	4	1	2	6000	45.	2800	1400	700	2 9/16	300	1 9/16
8000	4	1	2	6300	46.5	3000	1500	750	2 10/16	330	1 10/16
9000	4	1	2	6650	48.2	3250	1620	800	2 11/16	330	1 9/16
10000	4	1	2	7000	50.	3500	1750	870	2 12/16	360	1 10/16

Chapter XVII

Resolution and Composition of Forces

The effects of the different forces which act on a piece of timber at rest are these—extension and compression in the direction of its length, lateral compression, and torsion. To the first, is opposed cohesion; to the second, stiffness; to the third, transverse strength; and to the fourth, the elasticity of torsion. On these resistances of materials, direct experiments have been made, and practical formulæ for calculating them have been deduced.

It is essential that an accurate idea should be formed of the manner in which several forces act when united in their effect, and I shall therefore explain the principles of the composition and resolution of forces.

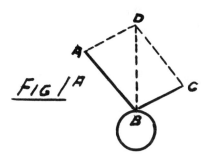

If *a* (Fig. 1a) be a force acting on a body in the direction of line *a b*, and *c* another force acting on the same point in the direction of line *c b*, with pressures in proportion to the length of lines *a b* and *c b* respectively, then the body will be affected precisely in the same manner as if acted on by a single force *d*, acting in the direction *d b*, with a pressure proportioned to the line *d b*, which is the diagonal of a parallelogram formed on *a b*, *c b*, and which is called the *resultant* of the two

forces *a c*. In like manner, if the forces *a*, *c*, *d* (Fig. 2a), act on a body *b*, in the direction of lines *a b*, *d b*, *c b*, and with intensities proportioned to the length of these lines, then the resultant of the two forces, *a* and *d*, is expressed by the diagonal *e b* of the parallelogram, formed on lines *a b*, *d b*, and the resultant of this new force *e*, and the third force *c*, is *f* acting in the direction *f b*, the diagonal formed on *e b*, *c b*; therefore, *f b* expresses, in direction and intensity, the resultant of the three

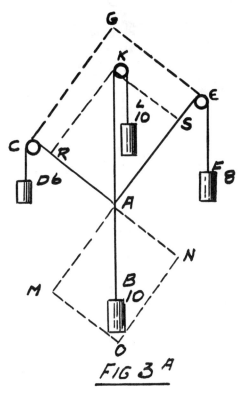

forces *a*, *d*, *c*. A simple experiment may be made to prove this. Let the threads *a b*, *a c d*, *a e f* (Fig. 3a) have the weights *b d f* appended to them, and let the two threads *a c d*, *a e f* be passed over the pulleys *c* and *e;* then if the weight *b* be greater than the sum of *d f*, the assemblage will settle itself in a determinate form, dependent on the weights. If the three weights are equal, the lines *a c*, *a e* of the threads will make equal angles with *a b;* if the weights *d f* and *b* be respectively 6, 8, and 10, then the angle *c a e* will be a right angle, and the lines *c a*, *e a* will be of the respective lengths of 6 and 8; and if we produce *c a*, *e a* to *n* and *m*, and complete the parallelogram *a n o m; a n*, *a m* will also be 6 and 8, and the diagonal *a o* will be 10. The action of weight *b* in the direction *a o* is thus in direct opposition to the combined action of the two weights *d f*, in the

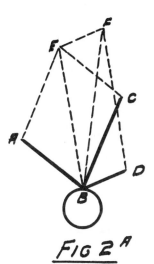

directions *c a, e a;* and if we produce *o a* to some point *k,* making *a r, a s* equal to those weights, we shall manifestly have *a k* equal to *a o.* Now, since it is evident that the weight *b,* represented by *a o,* would just balance another weight *l,* pulling directly upwards by means of the pulley *k,* and as it just balances the two weights *d f,* acting in the directions *a c, a e,* we infer that the point *a* is acted on in the same manner by these weights as by the single weight, and that two pressures acting in the directions and with the intensities *a c, a e* are equal to the single pressure acting in the direction and with the intensity *a k.* In like manner, the pressures *a, s a* are equivalent to *n a,* which is equal and oppo-

site to *r a;* also, *o a, r a* are equivalent to *m a,* which is equal and opposite to *s a.*

In the case of a load w (Fig. 4a) pressing on the two inclined beams *b c, b d,* which abut respectively on the points *c* and *d,* it is obvious that the pressures will be in the directions *b c, b d.* To find the amounts of these pressures, draw vertical line *b e* through the center of load, and give it, by a scale of equal parts, as many units of length as there are units of weight in the load w : draw *e f, e g* parallel to *c b, d b;* then *b g,* measured on the same scale, will give the amount of the pressure sustained by *b c,* and *b f* the amount sustained by *b d.*

The amount of thrust, or pressure, is not influenced by the lengths of pieces *b e, b d.* But it must be borne in mind, that although the pressure is not modified in its amount by the length, it is very much modified in its effects, these being greatest in the longest piece. Hence, great attention must be given to this in designing, lest by unequal yielding of the parts, the whole form of the assemblage be changed, and strains introduced which had not been contemplated.

If the direction of the beam *b d* be changed to that shown by the dotted line *b i,* it will be seen that the pressures on both beams are very much increased, and the more obtuse the angle *i b h* the greater the strain.

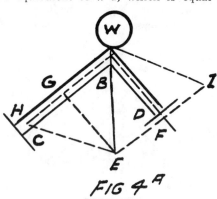

FIG 4ᴬ

Chapter XVIII

Strength and Strain of Materials

The materials employed in vessel construction are exposed to certain forces, which tend to alter their molecular constitution, and to destroy that attraction which exists between their molecules, named cohesion.

The destructive forces in timber may operate in the manners following:

I.   By tension in the direction of fibres of the wood, producing rupture by tearing it asunder.

II.   By compression in the direction of fibres, producing rupture by crushing.

III.   By pressure at right angles to direction of fibres, or transverse strain, which breaks it across, and which, as will be seen, is a combination of the two former strains.

IV.   By torsion or wrenching.

V.   By tearing the fibres asunder.

Every material resists with more or less energy, and for a longer or shorter period, these causes of destruction.

The resistance to the first-named force is called the resistance to extension, or simply, cohesion; to the second, the resistance to compression; and the third, the resistance to transverse force. The measures of these resistances are the efforts necessary to produce rupture by extension, compression, or transverse strain.

Those materials which, when they have been submitted to a certain force less than the amount of their resistance, return to their normal condition when that force is withdrawn, are termed elastic. The knowledge of the elasticity proper to any body gives the means of calculating the amount of extension, compression, or flexure, which the body will sustain under a given force.

For the purposes of calculation, it is convenient to have a measure of the resilience or elastic power of a body expressed either in terms of its own substance, or in weight. This measure is termed the modulus of elasticity of the body.

If we suppose the body to have a square unit of surface, and to be by any force compressed to one-half or extended to double its original dimensions, this force is the modulus of the body's elasticity. No solid substance, it may at once be conceived, will admit of such an extent of compression or extension; but the expression for the modulus may nevertheless be obtained by calculation on the data afforded by experiment. The moduli for various kinds of woods will be found in Table 2, column 7. (See p. 18 for Table 2.)

18a.   I.   *Resistance to Tension.*

Although, mechanically considered, this is the simplest strain to which a body can be subjected, it is yet the one in regard to which fewest experiments have been made, in consequence of the great force required to tear asunder lengthways pieces of timber of even small dimensions. There is, too, a want of agreement sufficiently baffling in the results obtained by different operators. The results of several experiments are given in the table 2, column 4, reduced to a section of one inch square.

Resistance of timber to compression in the direction of the length of its fibres.

18b.   II.   *Resistance to Compression.*

It is not necessary to give rules for the absolute crushing force of timber. Those that follow are applicable to the cases of posts whose length exceeds ten times their diameter, and **which yield by bending.**

To find the diameter of a post that will sustain a given weight.

Rule.—Multiply the weight in ℔ by 1.7 times the value of *e* (Table 2, column 9); then multiply the product by the square of length in feet, and the fourth root of the last product is the diameter in inches required.

Examples.—1.   The height of a cylindrical oak post being 10 feet, and the weight to be supported by it 10,000 ℔, required its diameter.

The tabular value of *e* for oak is .0015—

therefore, $1.7 \times .0015 \times 100 \times 10000 = 2550$

the fourth root of which is 7.106, the diameter required.

By inverting the operation, we find the weight, when the dimensions are given.

To find the scantling of a rectangular post to sustain a given weight.

Rule.—Multiply the weight in ℔ by the square of the length in feet, and the product by the value of *e:* divide this product by the breadth in inches, and the cube root of the quotient will be the depth in inches.

To find the dimensions of a square post that will sustain a given weight.

Rule.—Multiply the weight in ℔ by the square of the length in feet, and the product by 4 times the value of *e;* and the fourth root of this product will be the *diagonal* of the post in inches.

To find the stiffest rectangular post to sustain a given weight.

Rule.—Multiply the weight in ℔ by 0.6 times the tabular value of *e*, and the product by the square of the length in feet; and the fourth root of this product will be the least side in inches: divide the least side by 0.6 to obtain the greatest side.

Let the length of the stiffest rectangular oak post be 10 feet, and the weight to be supported 10,000 ℔, required the side of the post.

$$0.6 \times .0015 \times 10 \times 10 \times 10000 = 900,$$

the fourth root of which is 5.477, the least side, which, divided by 0.6, gives 9.13 as the greatest side.

18c. *III. Resistance of timbers to transverse strain.*

When a piece of timber is fixed horizontally at its two ends, then, either by its own proper weight, or by the addition of a load, it bends, and its fibres become curved. If the curvature do not exceed a certain limit, the timber may recover its straightness when the weight is removed; but if it exceed that limit, although the curvature diminishes on the removal of load, the timber never recovers its straightness, its elasticity is lessened, and its strength is partly lost. On the load being augmented by successive additions of weights, the curvature increases until rupture is produced. Some woods, however, break without previously exhibiting any sensible curvature.

It may be supposed that, in the case of the timber being exactly prismatic in form, and homogeneous in structure, the rupture of its fibres would take place in the middle of its length, in the vertical line, where the curves of the fibres attain their maxima.

In the rupture by transverse strain of elastic bodies in general, and consequently in wood, all the fibres are not affected in the same manner. Suppose a piece of timber, composed of a great number of horizontal ligneous layers, subjected to such a load as will bend it, then it will be seen that the layers in the upper part are contracted, and those in the lower part extended, while between these there is a layer which suffers neither compression nor tension; this is called the neutral plane or axis.

If the position of the neutral axis could be determined with precision, it would render more exact the means of calculating transverse strains; but as the knowledge of the ratios of extensibility and compressibility is not exact, the position of the neutral axis can only be vaguely deduced from experiment. Where the ratios of compression and extension equal, the neutral axis would be in the center of the beam; but experiments show that this equality does not exist. Barlow found that in a rectangular fir beam the neutral axis was at about five-eighths of the depth; and Duhamel cut beams one-third, and one-half, and two-thirds through, inserting in the cuts slips of harder wood, and found the weights borne by the uncut and cut beams to be as follows:

Uncut Beam	⅓ Cut	½ Cut	⅔ Cut
45 ℔	51 ℔	48 ℔	42 ℔

Results which clearly show, that less than half the fibres were engaged in resisting extension; and it has been long known that a beam of soft wood, supported at its extremities, may have a saw-cut made in the center, half-way through its thickness, and a hard wood piece inserted in the cut, without its strength being materially impaired.

The transverse strength of beam is—
Directly as the breadth,
Directly as the square of the depth, and
Inversely as the length;
or substituting the letter b for the breadth,
d for the depth, and
l for the length,
and placing the ratios together, the general expression of the relation of strength to the dimensions of a beam is obtained as follows:—

$$\frac{b \times d^2}{l}$$

But this forms no rule for application, since beams of different materials do not break by the application of the same load; and it is therefore necessary to find by experiment a quantity to express the specific strength of each material.

Let this quantity be represented by S, and the formula becomes—

$$\frac{b \times d^2 \times S}{l} = \text{breaking weight.}$$

By this formula experiments can be reduced so as to give the value of S. It is only necessary to find the breaking weight of a beam whose dimensions are known, and then by transposition of the equation—

$$\frac{l \times \text{breaking weight}}{b \times d^2} = S.$$

S thus becomes a constant for all beams of the same material as the experimental beam.

When the value of S for various kinds of wood is determined, the formula may be used for computing the strength of a given beam, or the size of a beam to carry a given load. For any three of the quantities, l, b, d, **W**, being given, we can find the fourth thus:—

I. When the beam is fixed at one end and loaded at the other, and when

$$\frac{l\,W}{b\,d^2} = S.$$

The length, breadth, and depth being given, to find the weight—

$$W = \frac{S\,b\,d^2}{l}.$$

The weight, breadth, and depth being given, to find the length—

$$l = \frac{S\,b\,d^2}{W}.$$

The weight, length, and depth being given, to find the breadth—

$$b = \frac{l\,W}{S\,d^2}.$$

The weight, length, and breadth being given, to find the depth—

$$d = \sqrt{\frac{l\,W}{b\,S}}.$$

When the section of a beam is square, that is, when $b = d$; then b or $d = \sqrt{\dfrac{l\,W}{S}}$.

The table 1a column 12 contains the results of experiments on transverse strength of various kinds of wood, with the value of S, calculated according to the formula $S = \dfrac{l\,W}{4\,b\,d^2}$.

In any beam exposed to transverse strain, it is manifest that there must be some certain proportion between the breadth and depth which will afford the best results. It is found that this is obtained when the breadth is to the depth as 6 to 10. Therefore, when it is required to find the least breadth that a beam for a given bearing should have, the formula is as follows:—

$$\dfrac{l}{\sqrt{d}}\ 0.6 = b;$$

or, expressed in words—

Rule.—Divide the length in feet by the square root of the depth in inches, and the quotient, multiplied by the decimal 0.6, will give the least breadth the beam ought to have.

The nearer a beam approaches to the section given by this rule, the stronger it will be; and from this rule is derived the next.

To find the strongest form of a beam so as to use only a given quantity of timber.

Rule.—Multiply the length in feet by the decimal 0.6, and divide the given area in inches by the product, and the square of the quotient will be the depth in inches.

Example.—Let the given length be 20 feet, and the given area of section 60 inches. Then $\dfrac{60}{20 \times 0.6} = 5.00$, the square of which is 25 inches, the depth required, and the breadth is consequently 2.4 inches.

The *stiffest* beam is that in which the breadth is to the depth as .58 to 1.

18d. Tenacity

As the strength of cohesion must be proportional to the number of fibres of the wood, or, in other words, to the area of section, it follows that the tenacity of any piece of timber, or the weight which will tear it asunder lengthways, will be found by multiplying the number of square inches in its section by the tabular number corresponding to the kind of timber. (Column 4, Table 2.)

Example.—Suppose it is required to find the tenacity of a tie-beam of fir, of 8 × 6 inches scantling.

8 × 6 = 48, which, multiplied by 12,000, the tabular number for fir, gives 576,000 ℔.

This is the absolute tenacity. Practically it is not considered safe to use more than one-fourth of this weight, or 144,000 ℔.

By the rule inverted, the section of the timber may be found when the weight is given, as follows:—

Rule.—Divide the given weight by the tabular number, and the quotient multiplied by 4 is the area of section required for the safe load.

Example.—Required the area of section of a piece of fir to resist safely a tensile strain of 144,000 ℔.

$\dfrac{144000}{12000} = 12 \times 4 = 48$, the section required.

18e. Summary of Rules

I. *Resistance to Tension or Tenacity.*

To find the tenacity of a piece of timber.

Rule.—Multiply the number of square inches in its section by the tabular number corresponding to the kind of timber.

III. *Resistance to Transverse Strain.*

1st. When the beam is fixed at one end and loaded at the other.

To find the breaking weight, when the length, breadth, and depth are given.

Rule.—Multiply the square of the depth in inches by the breadth in inches, and the product by the tabular value of S (Table 2, column 12, page 18), and divide by the length in inches: the quotient is the breaking weight.

To find the length, when the breadth, depth, and breaking weight are given.

Rule.—Multiply the square of the depth by the breadth and by the value of S, and divide by the weight: the quotient is the length.

To find the breadth, when the depth, length, and breaking weight are given.

Rule.—Multiply the weight by the length in inches, and divide by the square of the depth in inches multiplied by the value of S: the quotient is the breadth.

To find the depth, when the breadth, length, and weight are given.

Rule.—Multiply the length in inches by the weight, divide the product by the breadth in inches multiplied by S, and the square root of the quotient is the depth.

To find the side of a square beam, when the length and weight are given.

Rule.—Multiply the length in inches by the weight, divide the product by S, and the cube root of the quotient is the side of the square section.

To find the scantling of a piece of timber which, when laid in a horizontal position, and supported at both ends, will resist a given transverse strain, with a deflection not exceeding $^{1}/_{40}$th of an inch per foot.

1. *When the breadth and length are given, to find the depth.*

Rule.—Multiply the square of the length in feet by the weight to be sustained in ℔., and the product by the tabular number a (Table 2, column 10, page 18); divide the product by the breadth in inches, and the cube root of the quotient will be the depth in inches.

Example.—Required the depth of a pitch pine-beam,

having a bearing of 20 feet, and a breadth of 6 inches, to sustain a weight of 1000 ℔.

The square of the length, 20 feet.. = 400
Multiplied by the weight .... = 1000

And the product 400,000
By the decimal .... .016

Divide the product by the breadth,
6 inches .... = 6400.000
Gives 1066.666

The cube root of which is 10.2 inches, the depth required.

2. *When the depth is given.*

Rule.—Multiply the square of the length in feet by the weight in ℔, and multiply this product by the tabular value of *a*: divide the last product by the cube of the depth in inches, and the quotient will be the breadth required.

Example.—Length of pitch-pine beam 20 feet; depth, 10.2 inches; weight, 1000 ℔.

Then $\dfrac{20 \times 20 \times 1000 \times .016}{10.2 \times 10.2 \times 10\ 2} = \dfrac{6400}{1061} = 6$, the breadth required.

3. *When neither the breadth nor the depth is given, but they are to be determined by the proportion before given, that is, breadth to depth as 0.6 to 1.*

Rule.—Multiply the weight in ℔ by the tabular number *a*, and divide the product by 0.6, and extract the square root: multiply the root by the length in feet, and extract the square root of this product, which will be the depth in inches, and the breadth will be equal to the depth multiplied by 0.6.

To find the strength of a rectangular beam, fixed at one end and loaded at the other.

Rule.—Multiply the value of S by the area of the section, and by the depth of the beam, and divide the product by the length in inches. The quotient will be the breaking weight in ℔.

Example.—A beam of Riga fir projects 10 feet beyond its point of support, and its section is 8 × 6 inches, what is its breaking weight?

Area 8 × 6 = 48, multiplied by the depth 8 = 384. Multiply this by the constant 1108, and divide the product by the length, $\dfrac{1108 \times 384}{120} = 3545$ ℔. The fourth part of this is the safe weight to impose in practice, therefore—

$$\dfrac{3545}{4} = 886 \text{ ℔.}$$

To find the strength of a rectangular beam, when it is supported at the ends and loaded at the middle.

Rule.—Multiply S by 4 times the depth, and by the area of the section in inches, and divide the product by

the length between the supports in inches, and the quotient will be the greatest weight the beam will bear in ℔.

2d. When the beam is *supported* at one end and loaded in the middle.

The length, breadth, and depth, all in inches, being given, to find the weight.

Rule.—Multiply the square of the depth by 4 times the breadth, and by S, and divide the product by the length for the breaking weight.

The weight, breadth, and depth being given, to find the length.

Rule.—Multiply 4 times the breadth by the square of the depth, and by S, and the product divided by the weight is the length.

The weight, length, and depth being given, to find the breadth.

Rule.—Multiply the length by the weight, and the product divided by 4 times the square of the depth multiplied by S, is the breadth.

The weight, length, and breadth being given, to find the depth.

Rule.—Multiply the length by the weight, and divide the product by 4 times the breadth multiplied by S.

When the section of the beam is square, and the weight and length are given, to find the side of the square.

Rule.—Multiply the length by the weight, and divide the product by 4 times S: the cube root of the quotient is the breadth or the depth.

3d. When the beam is *fixed* at both ends and loaded in the middle.

The breadth, depth, and length being given, to find the weight.

Rule.—Multiply 6 times the breadth by the square of the depth, and by S, and divide the product by the length for the weight.

It is not necessary to repeat all the transpositions of the equation.

4th. When the beam is *fixed* at both ends and loaded at an intermediate point.

Rule.—Multiply 3 times the length by the breadth, and by the square of the depth, and by S; and divide the product by twice the rectangle formed by the segments into which the weight divides the beam.

For example, if the beam is 20 feet long and the weight is placed at 5 feet from one end, then the segments are respectively 5 feet and 15 feet, or, in inches, 60 and 180; and the rectangle is 60 × 180 = 10800; and twice this amount, or 21600, is the divisor.

Suppose the beam of Riga fir, fixed at both ends, and its section 8 × 6 inches and the weight placed at 5 feet from one end, required its breaking weight: then, three times the length = 720, multiplied by the product of the breadth into the square of the depth, and by the tabular value of S = 306339840; which divided by 21600, as above, gives 14,182 ℔ as the breaking weight.

5th. When the beam is supported at both ends, but not fixed, and when the load is in the middle.

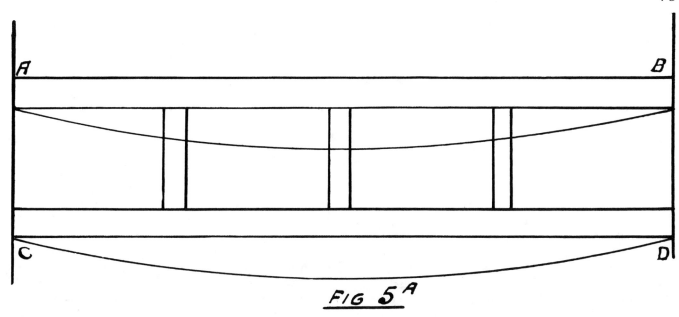

FIG 5ᴬ

To find the weight, when the length, breadth and depth are given.

Rule.—Multiply 4 times the breadth by the square of the depth and by S, and divide the product by the length: the product is the breaking weight.

18f. COMPOUND BEAMS

In any loaded beam, as we have seen, the fibres on the upper side are compressed, while those on the lower side are extended; and within the elastic limits those forces are equal. The intensity of the strain, also, varies directly as the distance of any fibre from the neutral axis.

If the parts of a beam near the neutral axis, which are little strained and oppose but little resistance, could be removed; and if the same amount of material could be disposed at a greater distance from the axis; the strength and stiffness would be increased in exact proportion to the distance at which it could be made to act. Hence, in designing a truss, the material, to resist the horizontal strain, must be placed as far from the neutral axis as the nature of the structure will allow.

Suppose to the single beam *a b* (Fig. 5a) we add another *c d*, and unite them by vertical connections, then it might be supposed that we were doing as above suggested; that is, making a compound beam by disposing the material advantageously at the greatest distance from the neutral axis. But it is not so. There are only two beams resisting with their individual strength and stiffness the load, which is increased by the weight of the vertical connections, and they would sink under the pressure into the curve shown by the dotted lines. It is necessary, therefore, to use some means whereby the two beams will act as one, and their flexure under pressure be prevented. This is found in the use of braces, as in Fig. 6a; and we shall proceed to consider what effect a load would produce on a truss so formed.

The load being uniformly distributed, the depression in the case of flexure will be greatest in the middle, and the diagonals of the rectangles *a b, c d,* will have a tendency to shorten. But, as the braces are incapable of yielding in the direction of their length, the shortening cannot take place, neither can the flexure. A truss of this description, therefore, when properly proportioned, is capable of resisting the action of a *uniform* load.

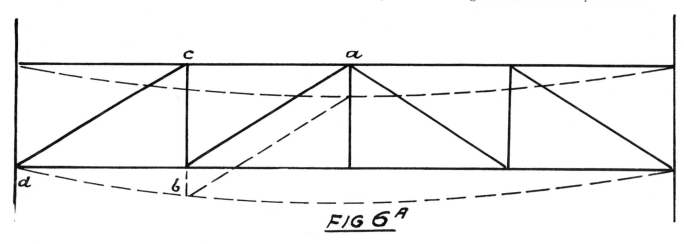

FIG 6ᴬ

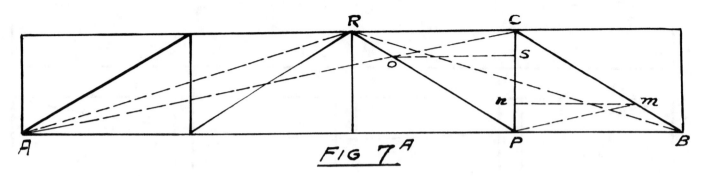

FIG 7ᴬ

If the load is not uniformly distributed, the pressures will be found thus:—Let the weight be applied at some point c (Fig. 7a), and represented by c p. Now resolve this into its components in the direction c a, c b, and construct the parallelogram p m, c o, then c m will represent the strain on c b and c o the strain in the direction c a. By transferring the force c m to the point b, and resolving it into vertical and horizontal components, the vertical pressure on b will be found equal to c n and that on a equal to n p. That is, the pressures on a and b are directly proportional to their distance from the place of the application of the load.

In the same manner, if the load were at r, it would be discharged by direct lines to a and b.

The effect of the oblique force c a acting on r is to force it upwards, and the direction and magnitude of the strain would be the diagonal of a parallelogram constructed on a c, c r.

The consequence of this is, that in a truss a weight at one side produces a tendency to rise at the other side, and, therefore, while the diagonals of the loaded side are compressed those of the unloaded side are extended.

Hence, while the simple truss shown in the last two figures is perfectly sufficient for a structure uniformly loaded, because the weight on one side is balanced by the weight on the other, it is not sufficient for one subjected to a variable load.

For a variable load, it is therefore necessary either that the braces should be made to resist extension by having iron ties added to them, or that other braces to resist compression in the opposite direction should be introduced; and thus we obtain a truss composed of four elements, namely, chords a b and c d (Fig. 8a), vertical

ties e f, g h, k m, braces e c, g f, g m, k d, and counter-braces a f, e h, k h, b m, or, in place of the latter, tie-rods added to the braces.

It has been shown that in any of the parallelograms of such a truss as has been described, the action of a load is to compress the braces a d, a b, and to extend the counter-braces a b, a c. Suppose (Fig. 9a) that the counter-braces have been extended to the length a m, and the braces compressed to an equal extent; then if a wedge be closely fitted into the interval a m, it will

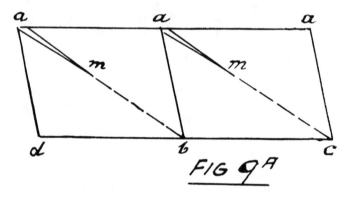

FIG 9ᴬ

neither have any effect on the framing, nor will itself be affected in any way so long as the weight which has produced the flexure continues. But on the removal of the weight, the wedge becomes compressed by the effort of the truss to return to its normal condition. This effort is resisted by the wedge, and there is, consequently, a strain on the counter-brace equal to that which was produced by the action of the weight. The effect of the addition of a similar weight, therefore, would be to relieve the strain on the counter-brace, without adding anything to the strain on the brace a d.

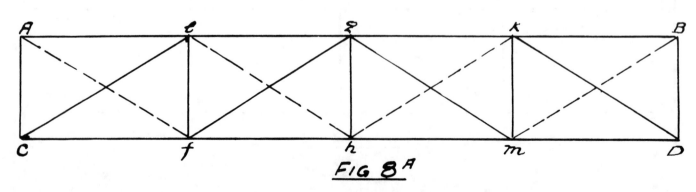

FIG 8ᴬ

Here is listed in alphabetical order the names of principal parts of a wooden ship, the greater number of parts being either defined under proper headings or described and illustrated in one of the chapters.

PARTS OF A WOODEN HULL INCLUDING THE WOODEN PORTIONS OF A COMPOSITE HULL

Air-course

Amidship

Apron

Beam
    after —
    breast —; collar — (of a poop, forecastle, etc.)
    — carling
    deck —
    awning deck —
    between deck —
    forecastle deck —
    lower deck —
    main deck —
    middle deck —
    poop deck —
    raised-quarter deck —
    spardeck —
    upper deck —
    — end
    foremost —
    half — (in way of hatch-ways)
    hatchway —
    hold —
    intermediate —
    mast —
    midship —
    moulding of — s (depth)
    orlop —
    paddle —
    rounding or chamber of a —
    scantling of — s
    siding of — s (breadth)
    — scarph
    spacing of — s
    spring —, sponson — (of paddle-steamer)
    spur — (of paddlewalks)
    tier of — s
    transom —

Bearding-line

Bilge
    — keelson
    — logs
    — planks
    — strakes
    thick strakes of —
    turn of —
    lower turn of —
    upper turn of —

Binding-strake

Bitt
    cross piece of —
    gallow —
    — head
    lining of —
    riding —

Bitt
    standard to —
    step of —
    top sail sheet —
    windlass — (see windlass)

Body (of a ship)

Chock, bow —
    butt — (of timbers)
    corner — (over the stem seam in way of hawse bolster)
    cross —
    dowsing — (breasthook above a deck)
    floor head —

Cable-stage; Cable-tier

Careening

Carling (Beam-carling)
    hatchway —
    mast — (fore and aft partners of mast)

Carvel-built

Carvel-work

Casing

Cat-head
    supporter of —

Cat-tail

Caulking

Ceiling
    between deck —
    close —
    flat —, floor —
    hold —
    — plank
    thick stuff of —

Chain-locker

Chain-plate
    backstay —
    — bolt
    fore —
    main —
    mizzen —
    preventer —
    preventer bolt

Channel
    fore —
    — knee
    lower —
    main —
    mizzen —
    — ribband
    upper —

Cheek

Chess-tree

Chock

Clamp
    deck beam —
    awning deck beam —
    forecastle deck beam —
    lower deck beam —
    middle deck beam —; main deck beam —
    poop —
    spardeck beam —
    upper deck beam —
    hold beam —

Cleat
    sheet —; kevel —
    shroud —
    snatch —
    step of a —
    stop —
    thumb —

Clincher-built

Clinched-work

Coach (quarter-deck cabin)

Coak or dowel

Coal-hold

Coat

Combing; Coaming
    hatchway —
    house —

Companion
    — way

Compartment

Copper
    — fastened

Counter
    lower —
    upper —

Covering-board

Crane

Crew-space

Cross piece (floor)

Crutch (hook in after peak)

Crutch

Curve

Cutwater

Dead-eye

Dead-flat

Dead-light

Dead-rising

Dead-wood

Dead-work

Deck
    awning —
    entire awning —
    partial awning —
    between — ('tweendeck)
    — dowel
    — ends
    first, second and third —

Deck
    flat of —
    flush —
    fore —
    forecastle —
    — hook
    — house
    — light
    lower or orlop —
    middle —, main —
    — plank
    quarter —
    raised quarter — or half
    poop —
    — seam
    shade —
    sheer of —
    shelter —
    spar —
    stage or preventer —
    tonnage —
    upper —
    weather —
    well —

Depth
    — of hold
    moulded—(*measured from top of keel to top of midship beam*)

Diagonal
    — iron plates or riders (*on frames*)

Diminishing stuff; Diminishing planks

Door

Doubling
    diagonal —

Dove-tail
    — plate

Dowel; Coak
    deck —
    floor —

Draught

Draught-mark

Eking

Entrance (*of a vessel*)

Erection (*on deck*)

Escutcheon (*that part of the stern, where the name is written*)
    knee —

Fair leader

Fashion-piece
    toptimber of a —

Fastening
    copper —
    double — (*in planks*)
    iron —

Fastening
    metal —
    single — (*in planks*)
    through —

Faying surface (*of timbers, planking, etc.*)

Felt (*under metal sheathing*)

Figure-head
    fiddle —

Filling; Filling piece

Floor
    aftermost —
    cant — Double futtock
    double —
    flat —
    foremost —
    half —
    — head
    — head chock
    long armed —
    midship or main —
    moulding of — s (*depth*)
    rising of — s
    seating of a —
    short armed —
    siding of — s (*breadth, thickness*)
    top of — s

Forecastle
    — beam
    — coveringboard
    — deck
    — rail
    — skylight
    monkey — (*small height*)
    sunk —
    topgallant —

Frame
    after balance —
    fore balance —
    diagonal — ; trussing —
    flight of — s
    foremost —
    main or midship —
    moulding of — s
    — riders, diagonals on — s
    siding of — s
    spacing of — s
    spacing between — s
    square —
    stern —

Freeboard

Futtock
    first — ; lower —
    second —
    third —
    fourth —
    fifth —
    sixth —
    double —
    — head

Futtock, — heel

Gallery

Galley

Gallows; Gallows-bits

Gangway
    Entering port

Gangways (*under deck*)

Garboard
    outer —
    — plank
    — seam
    — strake

Girder

Girth (*of a ship*)

Gripe (*of stem and keel*)

Groove

Gunwale

Gutter
    — ledge (*of·hatchway*)

Hatch (*cover of a hatchway*)
    — bars
    — battens; Hatchway battens
    — batten-cleat
    booby — ; Booby hatchway
    — carling
    — house

Hatchway (*also called hatch*)
    after or quarter —
    cargo —
    — carlings
    — combing
    lower deck —
    main deck —
    upper deck —
    fore —
    fore and after in a
    — grating
    — headledge
    hood of —
    main —
    thwartship piece, half beam in a —
    wing boards in — (*for grain cargoes*)

Hawse; Hawse-hole
    — bag
    — bolster
    — plug

Hawse-pipe
    — flange

Hawse-timber

Head (*of a vessel*)
    beak of the —
    bluff —
    Knee of the head (`)
    — boards
    bob-stay piece of the —

Head (of a vessel)
    cheeks of the —
    cheek-fillings of the —
    lower cheeks of the —
    washboards under the lower cheeks of the —
    upper cheeks of the —
    filling chocks of the —
    — grating
    independent piece of the —
    lace piece or gammoning of the —

Head, standard knee of the —
    — rail
    berthing rail of —
    main rail of —
    small or middle rail of —
    stem furr of the —
    — timbers

Head-ledge (of a hatchway)

Heel

Helm

Helm-port (the hole in the counter, through which the head of the rudder passes.)

Hogging; Sagging

Hold
    after —
    fore —
    lower —
    main —

Hood
    (of the crew-space)
    after — s (of planking)
    fore — s (of planking)
    — ends; Wood-ends

House; Deck-house

Ice-doubling; Ice-lining

Intercostal

Iron
    bar —
    galvanized —
    plain —
    — rod; Iron-horse
    — work

Keel
    bilge —
    camber of—; hogging of—
    center line—; middle line—
    false — ; safety —
    length or piece of —
    main —
    moulding of —
    lower — ; upper false —
    — rabbet
    — scarph
    stopwater (in keel scarph)
    — seam (garboard-seam)
    side —
    siding of —
    skeg of —
    sliding —
    upper or main —

Keelson
    bilge —
    main —
    middle line —; center —
    rider —
    scarph of —
    sister — ; side —

Kevel; Kevel-head

Knee
    beam arm of a —
    dead wood —
    diagonal —
    hanging — ; vertical —
    heel — (of sternpost and keel)
    hold beam —
    iron —
    lodging —
    lower deck beam —
    middle deck beam —
    upper deck beam —

Knee, — rider
    standard —
    staple —
    throat of a —
    transom —
    wooden —

Knight
    of the fore-mast
    of the main-mast
    of the mizzen-mast

Knighthead

Launching (of a ship)

Lazarette

Leak

Lee-board (used by small flat bottomed vessels)

Lee-flange (iron horse)

Length (of a ship)
    extreme — (from fore-part of stem to afterpart of sternpost)

Lengthening (of a ship)

Limbers; Limber-passage (*)

Limber-boards

Limber-hole

Limber-strakes

Lining

Listing

Load-line
    deep —

Lobby

Locker

Locker-seat

(*) A passage over the floors or holes in same to allow water to reach the pumps; The space between the floors extending a short distance on each side of the middle-line, is also called "Limbers".

Manger
    — board

Mast-carling (fore and aft (partners of mast)
    — hole

Mess-room

Middle-line; Center-line

Midship-section

Mooring-pipe

Moulding

Moulding (of a piece of timber)
    breech —
    cable —

Name-board

Naval-hood (hawse pipe bolster)

Pad

Paddle beam

Paddle box
    framing of —

Paddle walks (extension of the paddle boxes)

Panel-work

Panting (of a ship)

Pantry (steward's room)

Partner
    bowsprit —
    capstan —
    mast —
    fore and aft mast — (mast-carling)

Peak
    after —
    fore —

Pin-rack

Plank
    boundary —; margin — (of a deck)
    shifting of — s

Planking
    bilge — (outside)
    bilge — (inside)
    bottom —
    bow —
    bulwark —
    buttock —
    deck —
    diagonal —
    fastening of —
    inside —
    outside —
    stern —
    topside —

Planksheer

Platform

Pointer

Poop
    — beam
    — bulkhead
    — frame
    full —
    half — (*or raised quarter deck*)
Port
    air —
    ballast —
    — bar
    bow —
    cargo —; gangway — (*in bulwark*)
    entering —
    flap of —
    freeing —; water — (*in bulwark*)
    — hinges
    — lid
Port, quarter —
    raft —
    — ring
    sash —
    side —
    — sill; — cill
Quarter (*after end of a ship*)
    — deck
    raised — deck
    — pieces
Rabbet
    back —
    keel —
    — line
    stem —
    sternpost —
Rail
    boundary —
    counter — s
    cove —
    fife — (*around raised quarter deck*).
    fife — (*around masts*)
    forecastle —
    hand —
    main —; roughtree —
    poop —
    sheer —
    taff —
    topgallant —; monkey —
Ranger (*side pin-rack*)
Ribs (*frames*)
Rider (*hold rider*)
    floor —
    futtock —; top —
Roof
Rubbing-strake
Rudder
    back pieces of —
    balanced —
    — boards (*of inland vessels*)
    — brace; — gudgeon
    — bushes (*bushes in rudder braces or around pintles*)

Rudder
    — coat
    gulleting of a —
    — head
    coning of the — head
    — heel
    rounded heel of —
    — horn (*an iron bar on back of rudder, to which the pendants are shackled*)
    — irons
    jury —; temporary — main
    piece of —
    — mould
    — pendant
    — pintle
    — pintle score
    rake of a —
    sole piece of a —
Rudder tell-tale of a —
    — tiller or tillar
    — trunk
    — woodlock (*to prevent the rudder being unhung*)
Run (*of a vessel*)
    clean —
    full —
Sail-room
Samson-post (*of heavy piece of timber used for different purposes*)
Scantling
Scarph; Scarf
    flat —
    hooked —
    horizontal —
    lip of a —
    dovetail —
    vertical —; side —
Score
Scupper; Scupper hole —
    — leather
    — pipe
    — plug
    — port; Freeing port (*in bulwark*)
Scuttle (*small opening in the ship's side or deck*)
    cable-tier —
    deck —
Seam
    butt —
    longitudinal —
Sheathing
    bottom —
    copper —
    metal —
    wood —
    wood — (*of bottom*)
Sheathing zinc —
Sheer (*of a ship*)
Sheerstrake

Shelf
    deck beam —
    awning deck —, awning deck beam —
    forecastle deck —; forecastle deck beam —
    lower deck —; lowerdeck beam —
    main or middle deck —; main deck beam —
    poop —; poop beam —
    spar-deck —; spar-deck beam —
    upper deck —; upper deck beam —
    hold beam —
Shift of planking.
    after — of planking
    fore — of planking
Shifting-boards (*in hold for grain-cargoes*)
Ship-building
Shore
Side (*of a ship*)
    lee —
    port —
    starboard —
    top —
    weather —
Side-light; Side scuttle
Sill; Cill
Skeleton (*of a ship*)
Skids; Skid-beams
Skin
Skylight
    cabin —
    dead lights of a —
    forecastle —
    — guards
Sounding-pipe (*of pump*)
Spirketting
    deck beam —; deck —
    awning deck —
    forecastle deck —
    lower deck —
    main- or middle deck —
    poop —
    spar-deck —
    upper deck —
    hold beam —
Spur
Spur-beam
Stanchion
    bulwark —
    deck —; deck beam —
    main deck —
    upper deck —
    deck — cleats
    fixed —
    hold —; hold beam —
    loose —
    quarter —

Stanchion
  roughtree —
  step of —
  topgallant bulwark —
State-room
Stealer; Drop-strake
Steerage
Steering-apparatus
  patent —
Steering-wheel
Stem
  moulding of — (*breadth*)
  rake of —; inclination of —
  boxing of — and keel
  siding of — (*thickness*)
  up and down — (*stem forming no cutwater*)
Stemson
Step
  — butted (*planking*)
Stern (*extreme after part of a ship*)
  elliptical —
  — frame
  moulding of —
  pink —
  — pipe
  — port
  round —; circular —
  square —
  — timber
  — window
Sternpost; Rudder post; or Main post
  heel of —
  heel knee of —
  inner — (*inner post*)
  rake of —
  tenon of —
Sternson
Stirrup (*strap on foot of stem and fore-end of keel*)
Stop
Store-room
  boatswain's —
Stowage
Strake; Streak (*of planking*)
Strake, adjoining —
  bilge —

Strake
  binding —
  black —
  bottom —
  intermediate —
  side —
  topside —
Stuff, diminishing —
  short —
  thick —
Thick-strakes (*of ceiling*)
  (*of outside planking*)
Tiller; Tillar (*rudder*)
  quadrant —
  — rope
Timber
  alternate —
  butt of — s
  cant —
  counter —
  side counter —
  — dowel
  filling —
  floor —
  hawse —
  — head
  heel of a —
  horn — (*middle timber of stern*)
  knuckle —
  moulding of — s (*thickness*)
  post — s (*stern timbers in round or elliptical stern*)
Timber, quarter — s
  scantling of — s
  set of — s (*a frame*)
  shift of — s
  siding of — s (*breadth*)
  and space
  space between — s
  square — s
  top —
Tonnage
  — under deck
  gross —
  register —; net —
Tonnage-deck
Topgallant-forecastle (*Forecastle*)

Topside (*of a vessel*)
Topside-planking
Trail-board (*between the cheeks of the head*)
Transom
  deck —
  filling — s
  — knee
  wing — (*in square stern ships*)
Treenail
  — wedge
Treenailing
Trunk
Trussing, internal —
Tuck; Buttock
Waist (*the deck between forecastle and poop*)
Wales
  channel —
Ward-room
Water-closet
Water-course (*limbers*)
Water-line
  light —
Water-way
  inner —
  lower deck —
  main deck —
  outer —
  upper deck —
Well; Pump-well
Wheel (*steering-wheel*)
  barrel of —
  — chain
  — house
  — rope
  — spindle
  — spokes
  — stanchion
Whelp (*of a capstan or windlass*)
Wing (*of the hold*)
Wood-flat
Wood-lining
Work, upper —; Dead work

Chapter XIX
256-Foot Commercial Schooner

The principal dimensions are:

    Length o. a. .... 292 feet
    Length at water-line, loaded .... 256 "
    Length, keel .... 244 "
    Breadth .... 48 "
    Depth .... 23.75"
    Tonnage .... gross, 2,114; net, 1,870

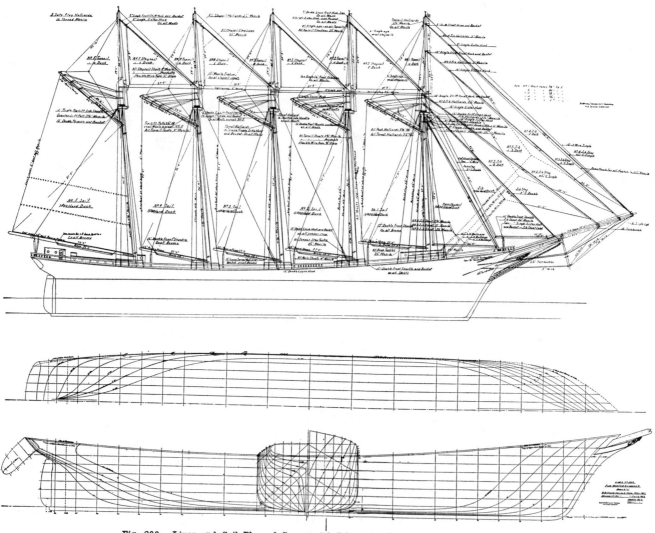

Fig. 200. Lines and Sail Plan of Commercial Schooner. Designed by B. B. Crowninshield

5,000-Ton Motorship

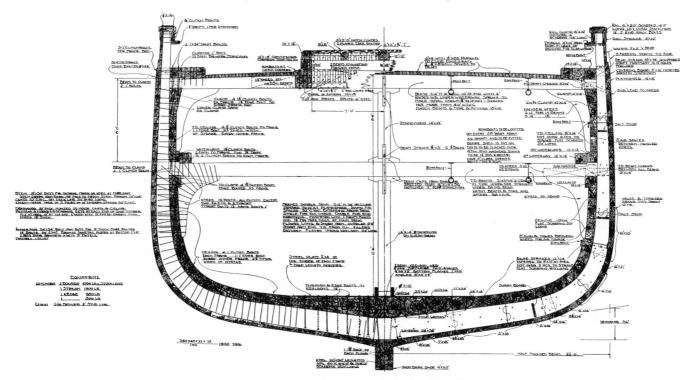

Fig. 201a.   Construction Section of Wooden Motorship

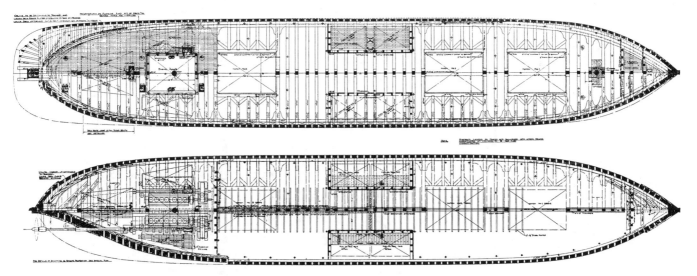

Fig. 201b.   Construction Plan For Hold and Lower Deck

The principal dimensions of this vessel are:

Length o. a.	278 feet	11 inches
Length, A.B.S. rule	260 "	0 "
Length, l.w.l	267 "	0 "
Breadth, extreme	45 "	0 "
Breadth, moulded	44 "	0 "
Depth, moulded	25 "	0 "
Depth of hold	21 "	0 "

Deadrise	36 feet	0 inches
Draught, loaded	22 "	0 "
Draught light, forward	10 "	0 "
Draught, light, aft	16 "	6 "
Displacement	5,087 long tons	
Total D.W.	3,100 long tons	
Net D.W.	2,550 long tons	
Lumber capacity	1,500,000 board feet	

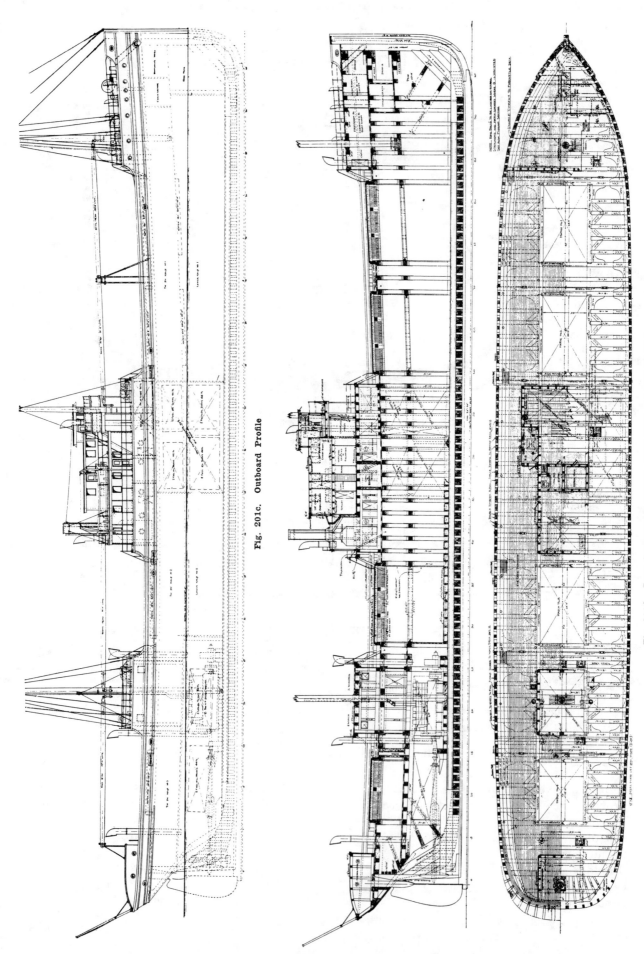

Fig. 201c. Outboard Profile

Fig. 201d. Long Construction Section, Main Deck and Breadth Plan

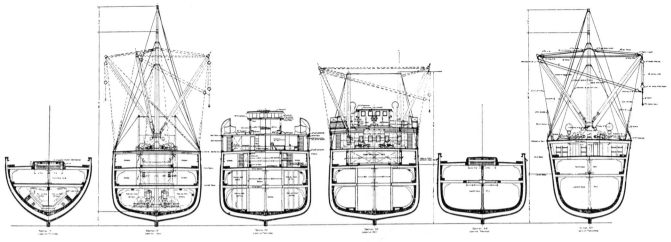

Fig. 201e. Typical Sections

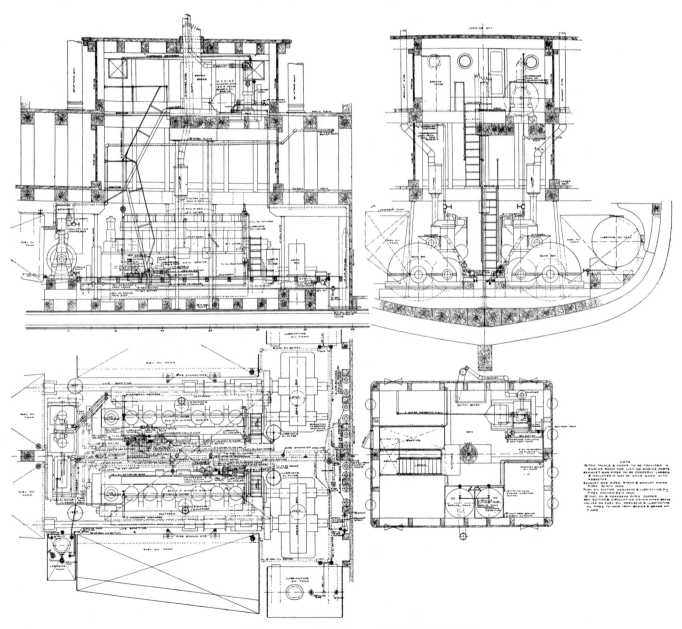

Fig. 201f. Arrangement of Machinery and Piping of Engine Room

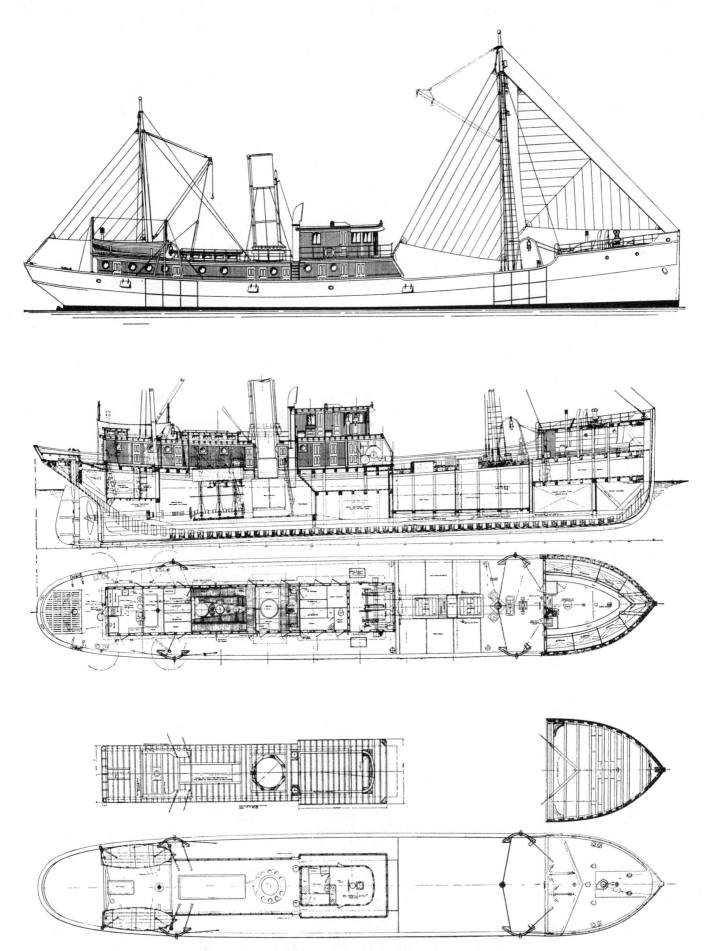

Fig. 202. Profile, Construction and Deck Plans of Steam Trawler, Built From Designs by Cox & Stevens For the East Coast Fisheries Company

The Trawl Ready to Lower Over the Side of the Vessel

Forward Deck House

Kingfisher on the Ways of the Portland Shipbuilding Company Ready For Launching

Steam Trawler Kingfisher on Her Trial Trip at Portland, Me.
Fig. 202a

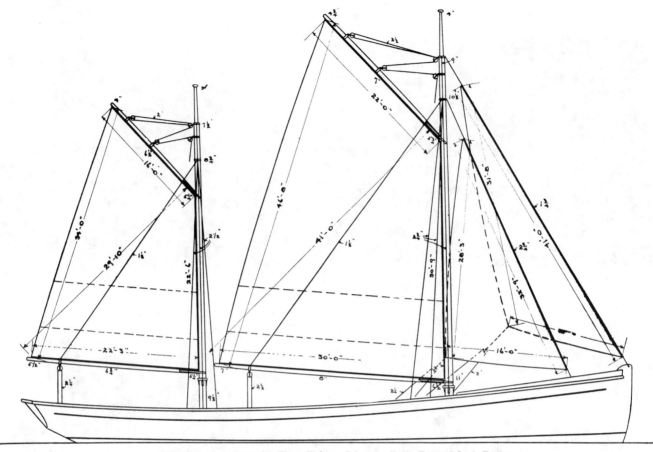

Sail Plan of 80-Foot Auxiliary Fishing Schooner Built From Schock Designs

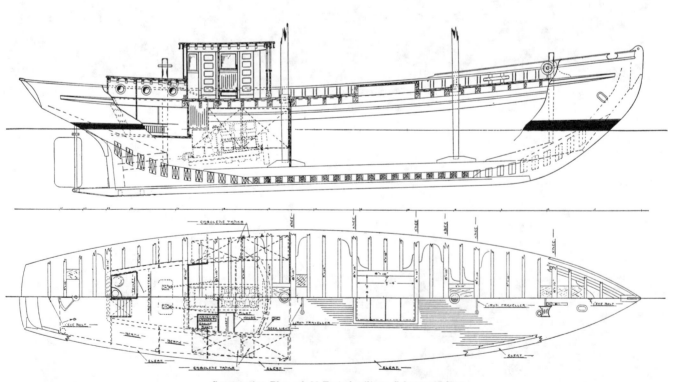

Construction Plan of 80-Foot Auxiliary Schooner Iskum

Fig. 203

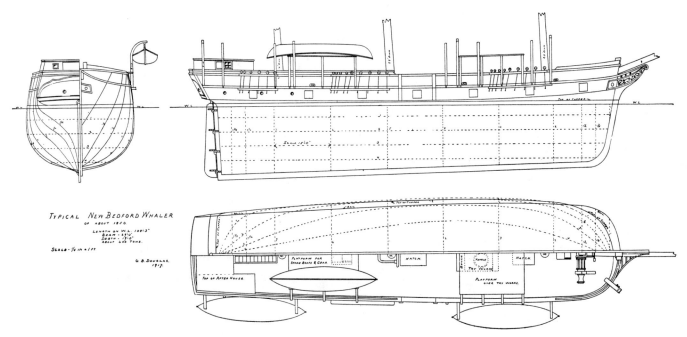

TYPICAL NEW BEDFORD WHALER
OF ABOUT 1850.

LENGTH ON W.L. 108'-3"
BEAM - 28'-0"
DEPTH - 17'-6"
ABOUT 400 TONS.

SCALE - 1/16 IN. = 1 FT.

G. B. DOUGLAS.
1917.

Half Deck Plan and Longitudinal Lines of a Whaler

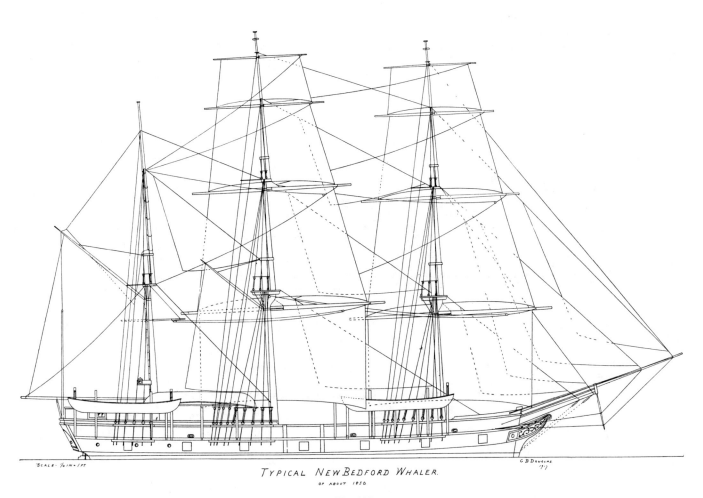

SCALE - 1/16 IN. = 1 FT.

G. B. DOUGLAS.
'17.

TYPICAL NEW BEDFORD WHALER.
OF ABOUT 1850

Fig. 204

270-Foot Cargo Carrier

A 270-foot full-powered cargo vessel, from designs by Edson B. Schock. This vessel has two full decks and about 3,200 tons deadweight carrying capacity.

It is built to the highest class, and is driven by twin McIntosh-Seymour Diesel engines of 500 h.p. each. The estimated speed is 9.5 knots. Fuel capacity 1,000 barrels, carried in four tanks. The auxiliary machinery consists of direct-connected generating outfits for lighting, heating and operating electric winches, of which there are four, and an electric windlass.

The general dimensions are:

Length .... 270 feet
Breadth .... 46 "
Depth moulded .... 26 "

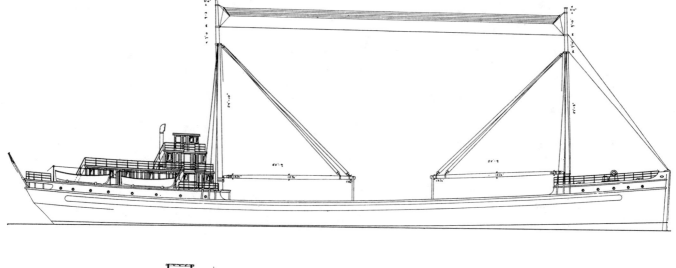

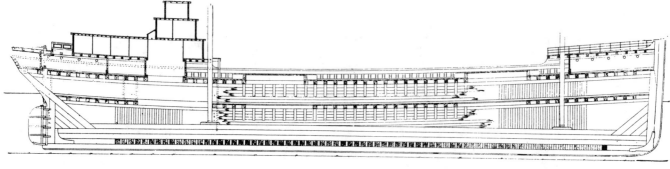

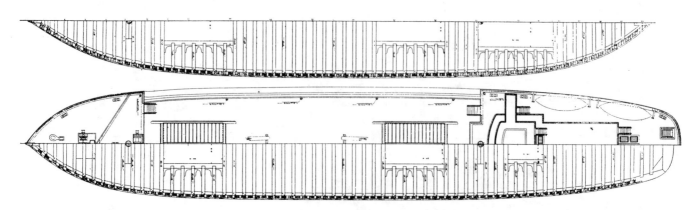

Fig. 205. Plans of a 270-Foot Cargo Carrier, Built From Designs by Edson B. Schock; Equipped With McIntosh-Seymour Diesel Engines

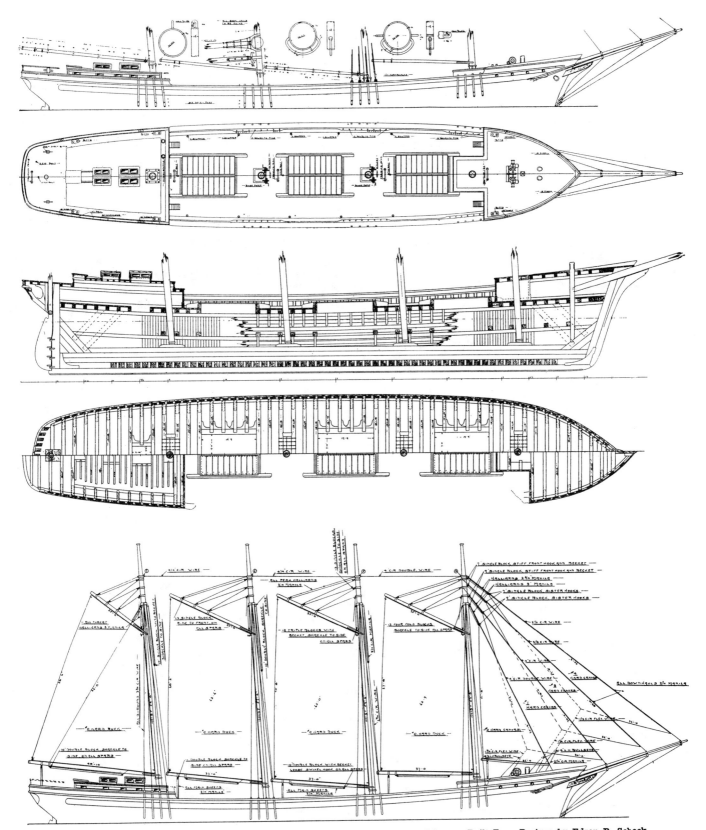

Fig. 206. Profile, Deck, Construction and Sail Plans of 220-Foot Auxiliary Schooner Built From Designs by Edson B. Schock

Length o. a. 220 feet
Breadth . . . . 42 "
Depth moulded . . . . 21 "
Carrying capacity . . . . 1,800 tons

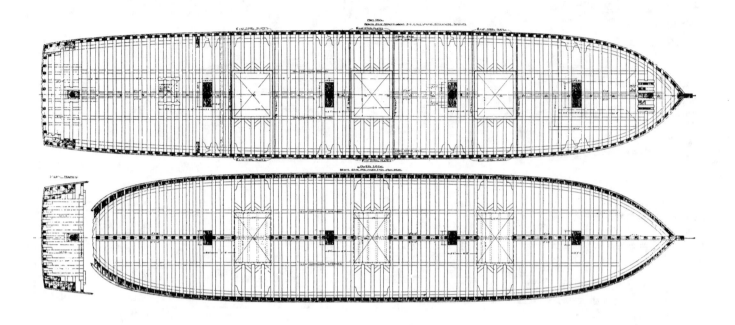

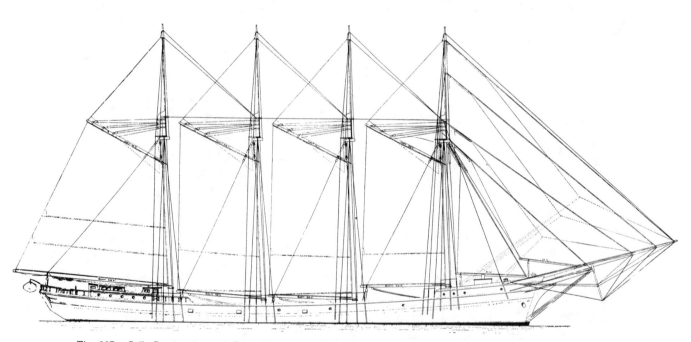

Fig. 207. Sail, Construction and Deck Plans of 223-Foot Auxiliary Schooner, Built From Designs by Cox & Stevens

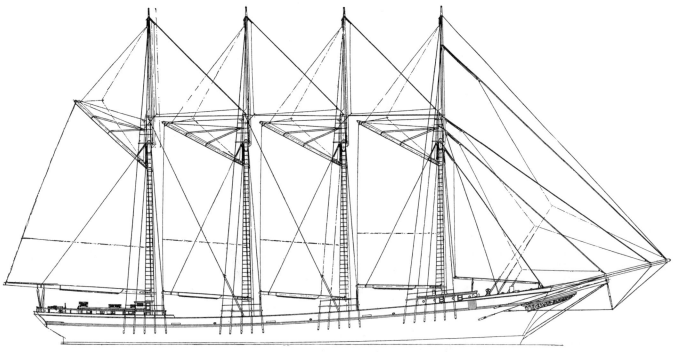

Fig. 209. 235-Foot Auxiliary Commercial Schooner, Designed by J. Murray Watts

235-Foot Auxiliary Schooner

The accompanying plans show a four-masted auxiliary schooner, designed by J. Murray Watts. This vessel is 235 feet over all, 217 feet registered length, 40 feet breadth and 18 feet depth.

Plans and specifications conform with the American Bureau of Shipping.

Power, oil engines of 320 h.p.

Cargo capacity, 2,000 tons.

224-Foot Auxiliary Schooner

A four-masted auxiliary schooner, designed by Edson B. Schock, of Seattle, Wash. The construction is according to the requirements of the American Bureau of Shipping. Teh capacity of this vessel as usually expressed on the West Coast is 1,400,000 feet of lumber.

Length o. a. .... 224 feet 0 inches
Length l. w. l. .... 200 " 0 "
Breadth .... 43 " 6 "
Depth .... 20 " 0 "

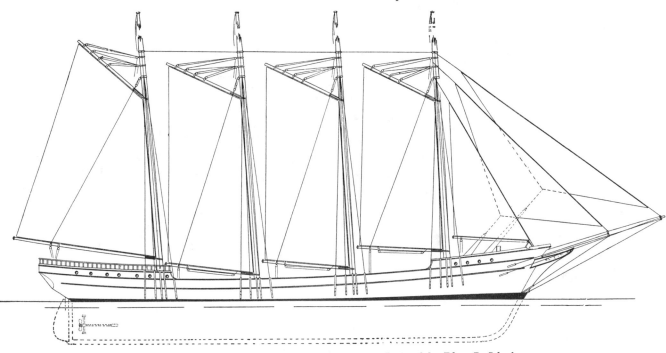

Fig. 208. 224-Foot Auxiliary Commercial Schooner, Designed by Edson B. Schock

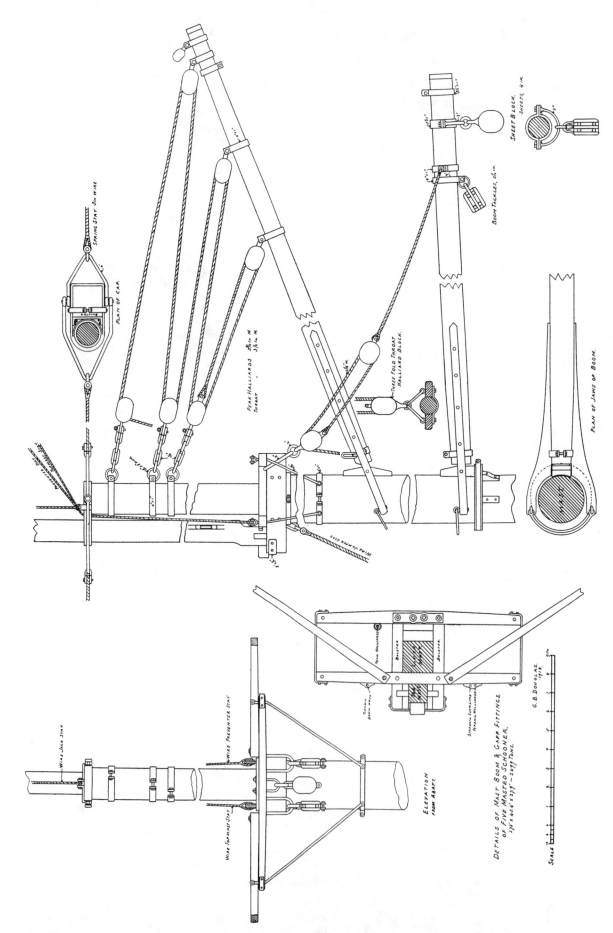

Fig. 210. Details of Mast, Boom and Gaff Fittings of a Five-Masted Schooner, 2,500 Tons, by G. B. Douglas

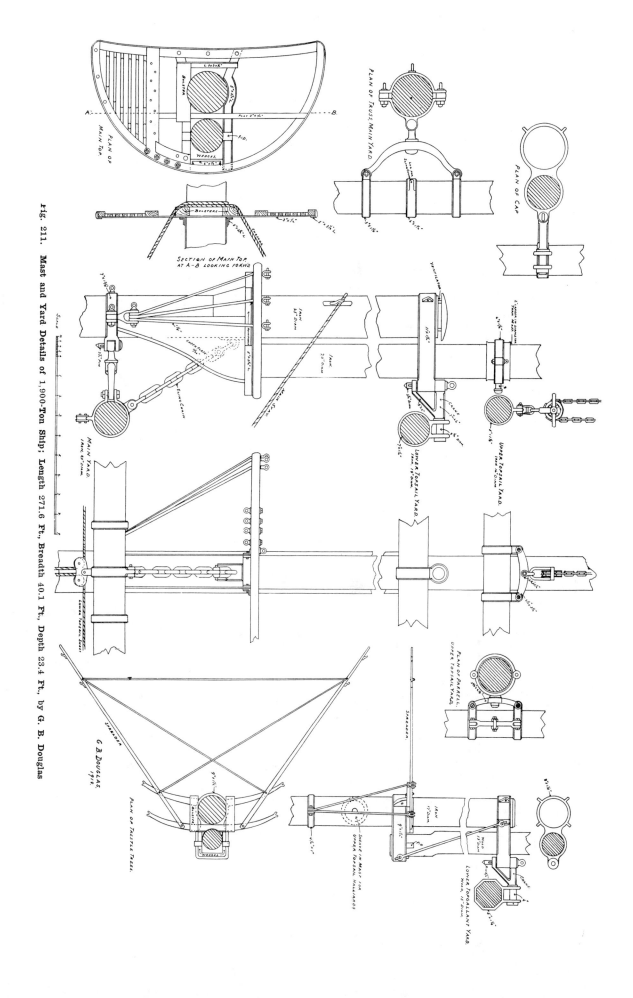

Fig. 211. Mast and Yard Details of 1,900-Ton Ship; Length 271.6 Ft., Breadth 40.1 Ft., Depth 23.4 Ft., by G. B. Douglas

200-Foot Schooner

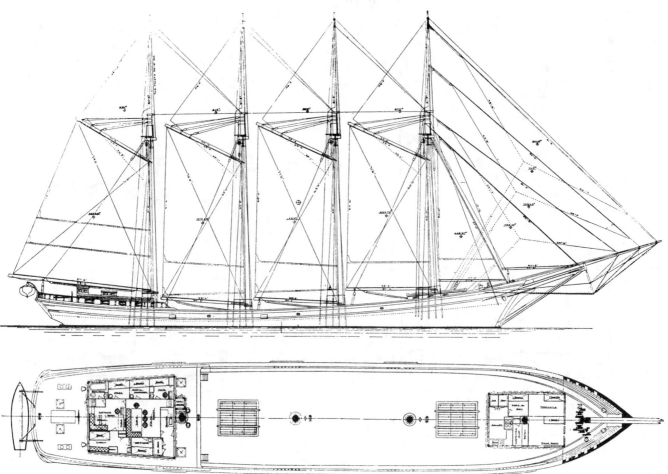

Fig. 212. Profile, Sail and Deck Plans of 200-Foot Four-Masted Schooner Building For J. W. Somerville, Gulfport, Miss., From Designs by Cox & Stevens

This vessel is a four-masted schooner built under the classification of the American Bureau of Shipping and rated A-1 15 years. She is built of long-leaf yellow pine and her spars are of Oregon pine. Her general dimensions are: 200 feet long over all, 177 feet water-line, extreme breadth 36 feet 8 inches, depth of hold 15 feet, depth of side 17 feet 11 inches, draught loaded 16 feet 6 inches. She will displace 1,942 tons and carry 1,240 tons deadweight. The area of the lower sails is 10,794 square feet.

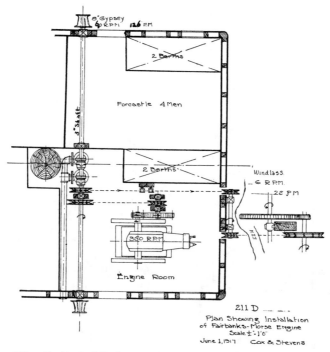

Fig. 212a. Engine Installation For Working Windlass and Capstan

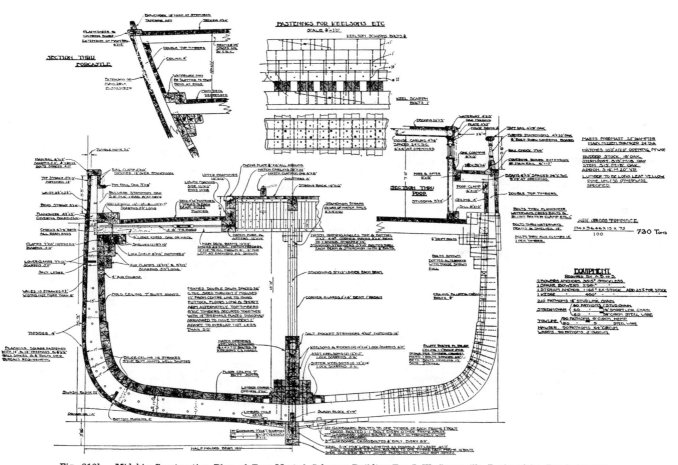

Fig. 212b. Midship Construction Plan of Four-Masted Schooner Building For J. W. Somerville, Designed by Cox & Stevens

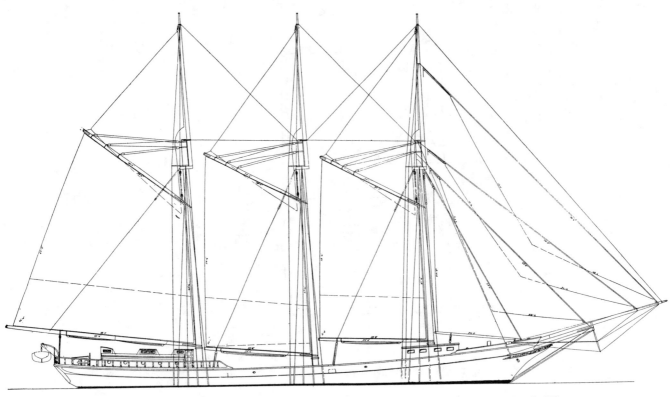

Fig. 213a. Sail Plan of 152-Foot Auxiliary Schooner, Now Building From Designs by John G. Alden

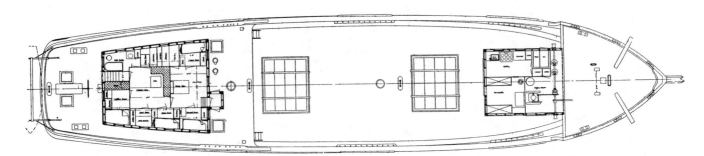

Deck and Arrangement Plan of 152-Foot Cargo Carrier, Building by Frank C. Adams, East Boothbay, Me.

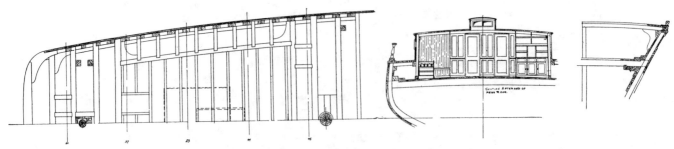

Sections of Auxiliary Schooner, Building From Alden Designs

152-Foot Auxiliary Schooner

An auxiliary schooner, 152 feet long on deck, is being built by Frank C. Adams, of East Boothbay, Me., from designs by John G. Alden. The vessel is to be used as a sailing craft because of the difficulty in obtaining engines, but as soon as the engine builders can furnish the power it will be installed. This is only one instance of the trouble shipbuilders are experiencing with engines and it is because of the great demand for engines which the manufacturers are at present unable to meet. With the great building program of the shipping interests in this country only just put in operation there is coming an era of prosperity for all engine men.

This vessel is most attractive in appearance and has all the earmarks of Mr. Alden's careful work. The plans show a vessel with unusual freight capacity for one of her size. There is a house forward, in which are the quarters for the crew, a galley and the engine space. In the after house is the captain's cabin, 10 feet square, a messroom of the same size, the captain's stateroom, 10 feet 6 inches by 6 feet 2 inches, a bathroom, a chartroom,

storeroom, spare room, and rooms for the mate and steward.

With the present shortage of timber this vessel, being smaller than is usual for cargo carriers, can be built in comparatively short time and made to pay enormous profits. It will carry about 700 tons dead weight and be operated offshore with a crew of seven men, and on the coast, especially in Summer, with five men.

There are many yards which are capable of building vessels of the size of this schooner but which could not handle larger vessels. Such craft at present rates of freight would very soon pay for themselves and would always be useful for coasting or for short voyages.

The vessel is rigged with three masts, which are 113 feet from deck to truck. The bowsprit is 48 feet outboard.

The general dimensions are:

Length on deck .... 152 feet
Length, registered .... 142 "
Breadth .... 33 "
Depth of hold .... 12½ "

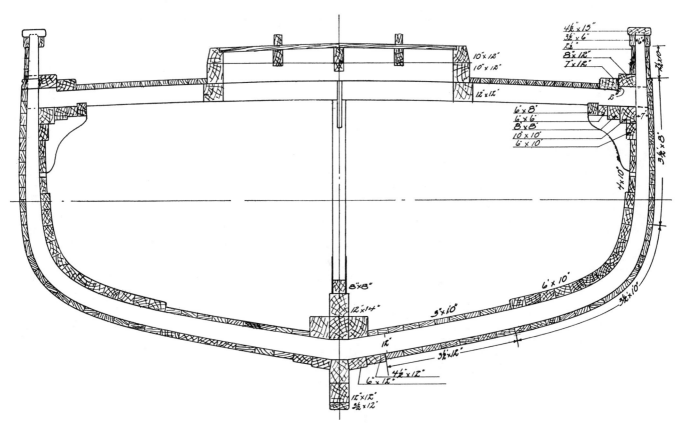

Fig. 213b. Midship Section of Auxiliary Schooner, Designed by John G. Alden

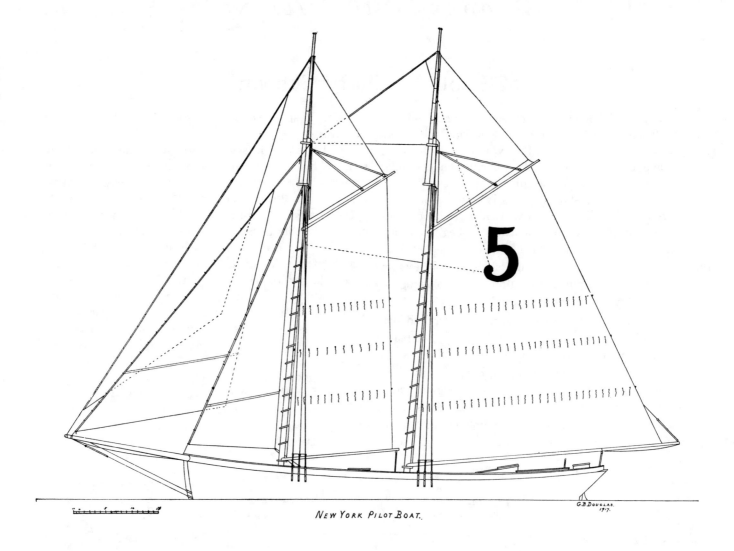

NEW YORK PILOT BOAT.

G.B.Douglas.
1917.

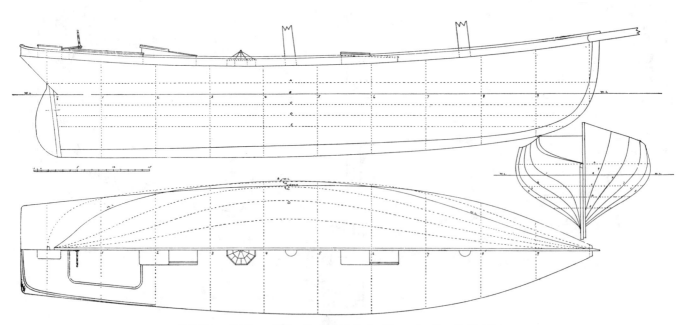

Sail Plan and Lines of New York Pilot Boat.   Drawn by Geo. B. Douglas

Fig. 214

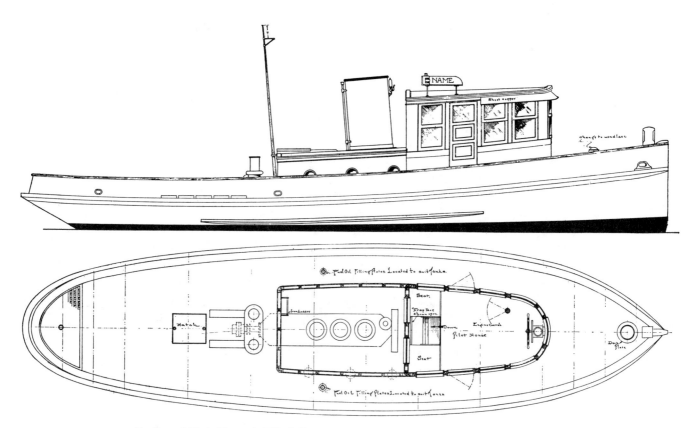

Profile and Deck Plans of 47-Foot Tug.

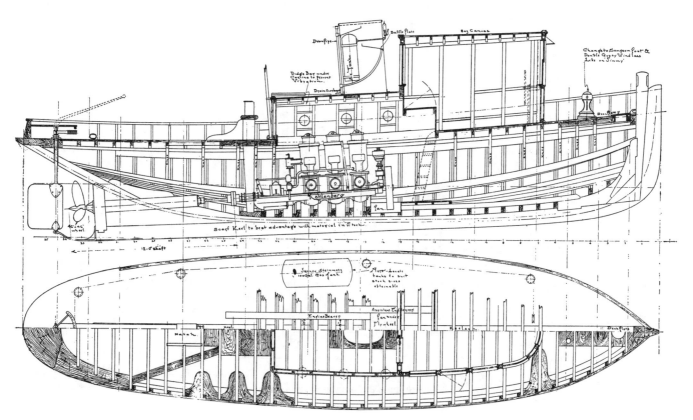

Construction Plan of 47-Foot Tug For South American Service, Equipped With a Kahlenberg Heavy-Oil Engine of 90-100 H.P.

Fig. 215

Length .... 47 feet 0 inches
Breadth .... 12 " 0 "
Draught, running .... 4 " 8 "

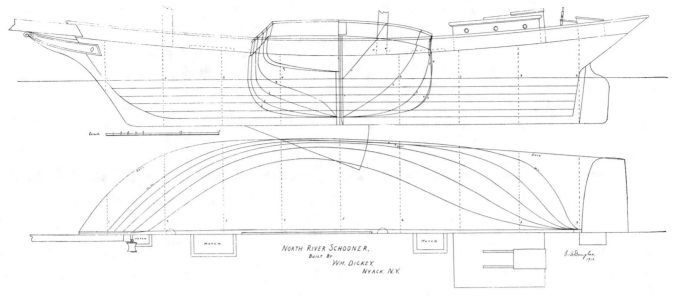

Lines and Sections of 77-Foot North River Schooner

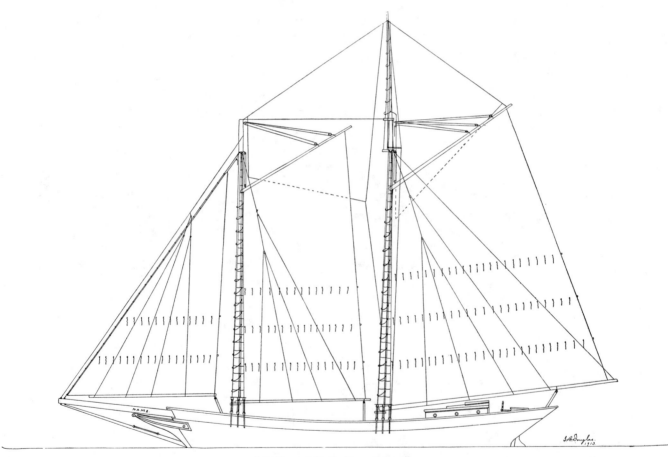

Sail Plan of North River Schooner

Fig. 217

Length o. a.	77 feet	Main topmast, o. a.	27 feet
Length on w. l.	64 "	Boom, main	48 "
Breadth	24 "	Boom, fore	27 "
Draught	7 "	Gaff, main	29 "
Foremast, deck to cap	59 "	Gaff, fore	26 "
Main mast, deck to cap	69 "	Bowsprit, outboard	24 "

Chapter XX

Definitions of Terms Used by Shipbuilders and of Parts of Wooden Ships

Note.—Items marked * are clearly shown on one or more of the illustrations.

Abut.—When two timbers or planks are united endways, they are said to *butt* or *abut* against each other.

Adhesion of surfaces glued together. From Mr. Bevan's experiments it appears that the surfaces of dry ash-wood, cemented by glue newly made, in the dry weather of summer would, after twenty-four hours' standing, adhere with a force of 715 ℔ to the square inch. But when the glue has been frequently melted and the cementing done in wet weather, the adhesive force is reduced to from 300 to 500 ℔ to the square inch. When fir cut in autumn was tried, the force of adhesion was found to be 562 ℔ to the square inch. Mr. Bevan found the force of cohesion in solid glue to be equal to 4,000 ℔ to the square inch, and hence concludes that the application of this substance as a cement is capable of improvement.

Adhesive Force of nails and screws in different kinds of wood. Mr. Bevan's experiments were attended with the following results :—Small brads, 4,560 in the pound, and the length of each 44/100 of an inch, force into dry pine to the depth of 0.4 inch, in a direction at right angles to the grain, required 22 ℔ to extract them. Brads half an inch long, 3,200 in the pound, driven in the same pine to 0.4 inch depth, required 37 ℔ to extract them. Nails 618 in the pound, each nail 1¼ inch long, driven 0.5 inch deep, required 58 ℔ to extract them. Nails 2 inches long, 130 in the pound, driven 1 inch deep, took 320 ℔. Cast-iron nails, 1 inch long, 380 in the pound, driven 0.5 inch, took 72 ℔. Nails 2 inches long, 73 in the pound, driven 1 inch, took 170 ℔; when driven 1½ inch they took 327 ℔, and when driven 2 inches 530 ℔. The adhesion of nails driven at right angles to the grain was to force of adhesion when driven with the grain, in pine, 2 to 1, and in green elm as 4 to 3. If the force of adhesion of a nail and pine be 170, then in similar circumstances the force for green sycamore will be 312, for dry oak 507, for dry beech 667. A common screw 1/5 of an inch diameter was found to hold with a force three times greater than a nail 2½ inches long, 73 of which weighed a pound, when both entered the same length into the wood.

Adze.—A cutting tool for dubbing, much used by shipwrights.

Afloat.—Borne up by, floating in, the water.

After-Body.—That part of a ship's body abaft midships or dead-flat.

After-Hoods.—The after plank of all in any strake, outside or inside.

After Timbers.—All timbers abaft the midships or dead-flat.

* *Air Course.*—An opening left between strakes of ceiling to allow air to circulate around frames. (Fig. 28.)

Air-Ports.—Circular apertures cut in side of a vessel to admit light and air to state-rooms, etc. Closed with a light of glass, set in a composition-frame and turning on a hinge, secured when closed by a heavy thumb-screw.

Amidships.—Signifies the middle of ship, as regards both length and breadth.

Anchor Chock.—A chock bolted upon the gunwale for the bill of sheet-anchor to rest on.

Anchor-crane is employed for taking anchors in board, thus replacing cat-heads, cat-davits and fish-davits.

* *Anchor-Lining.*—Short pieces of plank, or plate iron fastened to sides of ship to prevent the bill of anchor from wounding the ship's side when fishing the anchor.

Anchor Stock, To.—See *"To Anchor Stock."*

An-End.—The position of any mast, etc., when erected perpendicularly on deck. The topmasts are *an-end* when hoisted up to their stations. This is also a common phrase for expressing the forcing of anything in the direction of its length, as to force one plank to meet the butt of the one last worked.

Angle-Bracket.—A bracket placed in an interior or exterior angle, and not at right angles with the planes which form it.

Anvil.—A block of iron on which shipsmiths hammer forgework.

* *Apron.*—A timber conforming to shape of stem, and fixed in the concave part of it, extending from the head to some distance below the scarph joining upper and lower stem-pieces. (Fig. 25.)

Ballast, heavy substances placed in the hold of a ship to regulate the trim, and to bring the center of gravity of ship to its proper place. It is distinguished as metal and shingle. Metal is composed of lead or iron.

Batten, thin and narrow strips of wood. Grating battens unite the ledges that form the covering for the hatchways. (*See Grating.*) Battens to hatchways are battens used for securing tarpaulins over hatchways to prevent the sea from finding a passage between the decks.

Baulk.—A piece of whole timber, being the squared trunk of any of the trees.

Bearing.—The space between the two fixed extremes of a piece of timber; the unsupported part of a piece of timber; also, the length of the part that rests on the supports.

* *Half Beams* are short beams introduced to support the deck where there is no framing, as in places where there are hatchways. (Fig. 27.)

The Midship Beam is the longest beam of ship, lodged between the widest frame of timbers.

* *Bearding-Line.*—A curved line occasioned by bearding the deadwood to the form of the body; this line forms a rabbet for the timbers to step on; hence it is often called the *Stepping-Line.* (Fig. 36.)

Beetle.—A large mallet used by caulkers for driving in their reeming-irons to open seams for caulkings.

Belly.—The inside or hollow part of compass or curved timber, the outside of which is called the *Back.*

**Bends.*—An old name for the frames or ribs that form the ship's body from keel to top of side at any particular station. They are first put together on the ground. That at the broadest part of ship is the *Midship-Bend* or *Dead-Flat.* The forepart of wales are commonly called *bends.*

Between-Decks.—The space contained between any two decks of a ship.

Bevel.—A well-known instrument, composed of a stock and a movable tongue, for taking angles.

Beveling Board.—A piece of board, on which bevelings or angles of the timbers, etc., are described.

Bevelings.—The windings or angles of timbers, etc. A term applied to any deviation from a square or right angle. Of bevelings there are two sorts, *Standing Bevelings* and *Under Bevelings.* By the former is meant an obtuse angle, or that which is *without a square;* and by the latter an acute angle, or that which is *within a square.*

Bibbs.—Pieces of timber bolted to the hounds of mast to support trestle-trees.

Bilge.—That part of a ship's floor on either side of keel which has more of a horizontal than of a perpendicular direction, and on which the ship would rest if on the ground. (Fig. 28.)

Bilge Keels.—The pieces of timber fastened under bilge of boats or other vessels.

Bilgeways.—A square bed of timber placed under the bilge of the ship, to support her while launching.

Bill-Board.—Projections of timber bolted to side of ship and covered with iron, for bills of bower anchors to rest on.

Bill-Plate.—The lining of bill-board.

Binding Strakes.—Thick planks on decks, running just outside the line of hatches, jogged down over the beams and ledges.

Bitts are square timbers fixed to the beams vertically, and enclosed by the flat of deck; they are used for securing the cables to, and for leading the principal ropes connected with the rigging, etc. (Fig. 26.)

Board.—A piece of timber sawed thin, and of considerable length and breadth as compared with its thickness.

Boat-Chocks.—Clamps of wood upon which a boat rests when stowed upon a vessel's deck.

Body.—The body of a ship is the bulk enclosed within the planking of hull and deck. It is a term used by shipbuilders when designing some particular portion of a ship's longitudinal body, as—*Cant Body,* or the portion of ship along which cant frames are placed. *Fore Body,* or portion of ship ahead of square body. *After Body,* or portion of ship aft of square body. *Square Body,* or portion of ship where square frames are located.

Body-Plan.—One of the plans used in delineating the lines of a ship, showing sections perpendicular to length.

Bollard.—A belaying bitt placed on deck.

Bolsters.—Pieces of wood placed on the lower trestle-trees to keep the rigging from chafing.

Bolsters for Sheets, Tacks, etc., are small pieces of ash or oak fayed under the gunwale, etc., with outer surface rounded to prevent sheets and other rigging from chafing.

Bolts.—Cylindrical or square pins of iron or copper, of various forms, for fastening and securing the different parts of the ship. Of bolts there are a variety of different kinds, as *Eye-bolts, Hook-bolts, Ring-bolts, Fixed-bolts, Drift-bolts, Clevis-Bolts, Toggle-bolts, etc.*

Booby Hatch.—A small companion, readily removed; it lifts off in one piece.

Boom-Kin.—A boom made of iron or wood projecting from bow of ship, for hauling down the fore-tack; also from their quarter, for securing the standing part and leading block for the main-brace.

Boom-Irons.—Are metal rings fitted on the yard-arms, through which the studding-sail booms traverse; there is one on each top-sail yard-arm, but on the lower yards a second, which opens to allow the boom to be triced up.

Booms.—The *main boom* is for extending the fore-and-aft main sail; the *spanker boom* for the spanker; the *jib boom* for the jib and the *flying jib boom* for the flying jib. The *studding-sail booms* are for the fore and main lower, top and top-gallant studding-sails and swinging booms for bearing out the lower studding-sails.

Bottom.—All that part of a vessel that is below the wales.

Bottom Rail.—A term used to denote the lowest rail in a piece of framed work.

Bow.—The circular part of ship forward, terminating at the rabbet of stem. (Fig. 26.)

Bows are of different kinds, as the full or bluff bow, bell bow, straight bow, flare-out or clipper bow, wave bow, water-borne bow, tumble-home bow, and the parabolic bow.

Bowsprit.—The use of bowsprit is to secure the foremast and extend the head sails. (Fig. 25.)

Bowsprit Chock.—A piece placed between the knight-heads, fitting close upon the upper part of bowsprit.

Boxing.—The boxing is any projecting wood, forming a rabbet, as the boxing of the knight-heads, center counter timber, etc.

Brace.—A piece of timber in any system of framing extending across the angle between two other pieces at right angles.

Braces.—Straps of iron, or steel, secured with bolts and screws in stern-post and bottom planks. In their after ends are holes to receive the pintles by which the rudder is hung.

Brad.—A particular kind of nail, used in floors or other work where it is deemed proper to drive nails entirely into the wood. To this end it is made without a broad head or shoulder on the shank.

Breadth.—A term applied to some dimension of a vessel athwartships, as the *Breadth-Extreme* and the *Breadth-Moulded.* The *Extreme-Breadth* is the extent of midships or dead-flat, with thickness of bottom plank included. The *Breadth-Moulded* is the same extent, without the thickness of plank.

Breadth-Line.—A curved line of the ship lengthwise, intersecting the timbers at their respective broadest parts.

Break is the name given to the termination of a deck, when interrupted by a raised quarter-deck, sunk-forecastle, etc.; the front-bulkheads placed at such terminations are known as "Break bulkheads". Any elevation of a ship's deck, no matter whether aft, forward or amidships, is also styled a "Break" and the extra capacity gained by such raised portion, is known as the "Tonnage of Break".

Break.—The sudden termination or rise in the decks of merchant ships.

Breaking-Joint.—That disposition of joints by which the occurrence of two contiguous joints in the same straight line is avoided.

Breakwater (on a forecastle, etc.).—A coaming fastened diagonally across forecastle deck to stop water that is thrown on deck when ship is in a sea.

Breast-Hooks.—Large pieces of timber fixed within and athwart the bows of a ship, through which they are well bolted. There is generally one between each deck, and three or four below the lower deck, fayed upon the plank. Those below are placed square to the shape of ship at their respective places. The Breast-Hooks that receive the ends of deck planks are called *Deck-Hooks,* and are fayed close home to the timbers of decks.

Bridge.—A raised superstructure built across deck. Sometimes the bridge is a separate structure, but more frequently it is an enclosed portion of a deck house on which is located the steering wheel, binnacle, engine room telegraphs, chart house, etc.

Bucklers.—Lids or shutters used for closing the hawse-holes, holes in the port-shutters and side-pipes.

Bulkheads.—Transverse, or longitudinal, partitions in a ship. Solid structural bulkheads, known as *water-tight bulkheads,* divide a ship into water-tight compartments. The number and locations of these are designated in building rules of classification societies.

Bulls-Eye.—A thick piece of glass inserted in topsides, etc.

Bulwarks.—A planked railing built around ship above the planksheer. The bulwarks are generally built on a continuation of top timbers called bulwark stanchions. The names of principal parts of bulwarks are: Bulwark freeing port, bulwark rail, bulwark stanchions, bulwark planking.

Butt.—The joint where two planks meet endwise.

Butt-End.—The end of a plank in a ship's side. The root or largest end.

Buttocks.—The after-part of a ship on each side below the knuckle.

Buttock-Lines.—Cut the ship into vertical longitudinal sections, parallel to the center line.

Cabin.—The living space for officers and passengers. The principal room is called the Main Cabin. Entrance to cabin is usually through a raised trunk called a cabin companion trunk, or cabin companionway. Any skylight placed over a cabin is called a cabin skylight.

Camber.—A curve or arch. *Cambered beam,* a beam bent or cut in a curve like an arch.

Cant.—A term signifying the inclination that anything has from perpendicular.

Cant-Ribbands are ribbands that do not lie in a horizontal or level direction, or square from the middle line, as the diagonal ribbands.

Cant-Timbers are those timbers afore and abaft, whose planes are not square with, or perpendicular to, the middle line of ship.

Caps.—Square pieces of oak laid upon the upper blocks on which the ship is built. The depth of them may be a few inches more than the thickness of false keel.

Capstan.—A mechanical device for handling rope. A heaving appliance which takes a rope around its barrel.

Carlings.—Long pieces of timber, above four inches square, which lie fore and aft, from beam to beam, into which their ends are scored. They receive the ends of the ledges for framing the decks.

Carlings, Hatchway, are the fore and aft frame timbers of hatchway framing, mast carlings are the fore and aft partners of mast. (Fig. 27.)

Carvel Work.—Signifying that the seams of bottom-planking are square, and made tight by caulking.

Cathead.—A piece of timber with sheaves in the end, projecting from bow of a ship, for the purpose of raising the anchor after cable has brought it clear of the water. It is strengthened outside from underneath by a knee, called a *supporter.* The cathead is iron-bound, and is braced with knees forward and aft. (Fig. 25.)

Caulking.—Forcing oakum into the seams and between the butts of plank, etc., to prevent water penetrating into ship.

Caulking-Mallet.—The wooden instrument with which the caulking-irons are driven.

Cavil.—A large cleat for belaying the fore and main tacks, sheets, and braces to.

Ceiling.—The inside planks of the bottom of a ship. It is usually designated according to location, thus:—*Hold Ceiling, Between Deck Ceiling, Floor Ceiling, etc.* (Fig. 28.)

Center of Buoyancy, or Center of Gravity of Displacement.—The center of that part of the ship's body immersed in water, and which is also the center of the vertical force that water exerts to support the vessel.

Center of Effort of Sail.—That point in the plane of sails at which the whole transverse force of wind is supposed to be collected.

Chain-Bolts.—The bolt which passes through the toe-links, and secures the chains to side. (Fig. 28.)

Chain-Plates.—Iron plates to which the dead-eyes are secured; they are often substituted for chains, being considered preferable. (Fig. 25-28.)

Chamfer.—To cut in a slope.

Channels.—Flat ledges of white oak plank or steel projecting outboard from the ship's side, for spreading the lower shrouds and giving additional support to masts. (Fig. 25-28.)

Cheek-Blocks.—Blocks placed upon the side of bitts for fair leaders.

Cheek-Knees.—Knees worked above and below the hawse pipes in the angle of bow and cutwater, the brackets being a continuation of them to the billet or figurehead.

Chine.—That part of the waterway which is left above deck, and hollowed out or beveled off to the spirketting.

Chinse.—A mode of caulking any seams or butts.

Clamps.—Strakes of timber upon which the deck beams rest. Clamps are placed immediately below the shelf pieces and serve to support the deck frame. Clamps are placed below each set of deck beams and are designated by affixing the name of deck to the word clamp, thus:—*Forecastle Deck Beam Clamp* supports forecastle deck beams, *Upper Deck Beam Clamp* supports the upper deck beams. *Main Deck Beam Clamps* support main deck beams. *Hold Deck Beam Clamps* support the hold deck beams, etc. (Fig. 28.)

Clamping.—Fastening or binding by a clamp.

Clear.—Free from interruption. *In the clear,* the net distance between any two bodies, without anything intervening.

Cleats.—Pieces of wood having projecting arms, used for belaying ropes to.

Clinch or Clench.—To spread the point, or rivet it upon a ring or plate; to prevent the bolt from drawing out, same as riveting.

Clincher, or Clinker Built.—A term applied to boats built with the lower edge of one strake overlapping the upper edge of the one next below.

Coaking.—The placing of pieces of hard wood, either circular or square, in edges or surfaces of any pieces that are to be united together, to prevent their working or sliding over each other. (Fig. 33.)

Coamings.—The pieces that lie fore-and-aft in the framing of hatchways and scuttles. The pieces that lie athwart ship, to form the ends, are called head-ledges. (Fig. 27.)

Cocking, Cogging.—A mode of notching a timber.

Companion.—A wooden hood or covering placed over a ladderway to a cabin, etc.

Counter.—A part of the stern. (Fig. 25.)

Counter-sunk.—The hollows, to receive the heads of screws or nails, so that they may be flush or even with the surface.

Counter Timbers.—The timbers which form the stern.

Cove.—Any kind of concave moulding.

Cradle.—A strong frame of timber, etc., placed under the bottom of a ship to conduct her steadily till she is safely launched into water sufficient to float her.

Cradle Bolts.—Large ring-bolts in the ship's side, on a line with and between the toe-links of the chain plates.

Crank.—A term applied to ships built too deep in proportion to their breadth, and from which they are in danger of oversetting.

Cross-Grained Stuff.—Timber having the grain or fibre not corresponding to the direction of its length, but crossing it, or irregular. Where a branch has shot from the trunk of a tree, the timber of the latter is curled in the grain.

* *Cross Spalls.*—Planks nailed in a temporary manner to the frames of ship at a certain height, and by which the frames are kept to their proper breadths until the deck-knees are fastened.

Dagger.—A piece of timber that faces on to the poppets of bilgeways, and crosses them diagonally, to keep them together. The plank that secures the heads of poppets is called the *dagger plank.* The word *dagger* seems to apply to anything that stands diagonally or aslant.

Dagger-Knees.—Knees to supply the place of hanging knees. Their sidearms are brought up aslant, to the under side of beams adjoining. Any straight hanging knees, not perpendicular to the side of beam, are in general termed *dagger-knees.*

* *Davits.*—Pieces of steel projecting over the side of ship or the stern, for the purpose of raising boats. *Fish Davits* are used for fishing the anchor.

* *Dead-Eyes.*—Pieces of elm, ash or lignum-vitae, of a round shape, used for reeving the lanyards of standing rigging. (Fig. 28.)

Dead-Flat.—A name given to that timber or frame which has the greatest breadth and capacity in the ship, and which is generally called the *midship bend.* In those ships where there are several frames or timbers of equal breadth or capacity, that which is in the middle should be always considered as *dead-flat.*

* *Deadwood.*—Forward and aft, is formed by solid pieces of timber scarphed together lengthwise on keel. These should be sufficiently broad to admit of a stepping or rabbet for the heels of the timbers, and they should be sufficiently high to seat the floors. Afore and abaft the floors deadwood is continued to the cutting-down line, for the purpose of securing the heels of cant-timbers.

* *Decks.*—The several platforms in ships, distinguished by different names according to their situations and purposes.

* *Deck Planks.*—The flooring or covering of deck beams.

Deck Transom.—A timber extending across the ship at the after extremity of deck, on which the ends of deck plank rests.

Depth of Hold.—One of the principal dimensions of a ship; it is the depth in midships, from the upper side of the upper deck beams, in flush-decked vessels, and from the upper side of the lower deck beams in all others, to the throats of the floor timbers.

Diagonal Lines.—Lines used principally to fair the bodies, shown as straight lines in the *body-plan.*

Dished.—Formed in a concave. *To dish out,* to form coves by wooden ribs.

Displacement.—The volume of water displaced by the immersed body of ship, and which is always equal to the weight of the whole body.

Distribution.—The dividing and disposing of the several parts, according to some plan.

Dog.—A tool (iron) used by shipwrights; it is made of iron having both ends sharpened and one turned over making a right angle. In planking the decks or outside it is first driven a short distance into the beams or frame timbers and wedges introduced between that and the strake's edge to force the plank up to the one last worked.

Door-Case.—The frame which incloses a door.

Door-Post.—The post of a door.

Door-Stops.—Pieces of wood against which the door shuts in its frame.

Doorway.—The entrance into a cabin, or room. The forms and designs of doorways should partake of the characteristics of the finish of room it opens into.

Doubling.—The covering of a ship's bottom or side, without taking off the old plank, a method sometimes resorted to when the plank get thin or worn down.

* *Dove-Tailing.*—Joining two pieces together with a mortise and tenon resembling the shape of a dove's tail.

Dove-Tail Plates.—Metal plates resembling dove-tails in form, let into the heel of stern-post and keel, to bind them together.

Dowel.—To fasten two boards or pieces together by pins inserted in their edges. This is similar to coaking.

Draft of Water.—The depth of water a ship displaces when she is afloat.

Drag.—A term used to denote an excess of draft of water

Drift.—A piece of iron or steel-rod used in driving back a key of a wheel, or the like, out of its place, when it cannot be struck directly with the hammer. The drift is placed against the end of the key, or other object, and the strokes of the hammer are communicated through it to the object to be displaced.

Dubb, To.—To smooth and cut off with an adze.

Entrance.—The forward part of a vessel below the water-aft.

Even-Keel.—When the vessel has the same draught of water forward and aft, she is said to be on an even-keel.

Falling Home or Tumbling Home.—A term applied to the upper part of the topside of a ship, when it falls very much within a vertical line from the main breadth.

* *False Keel.*—A thin keel, put on below the main keel, that it may be torn off without injury to the main keel, should the vessel touch the ground.

* *Fashion Pieces.*—Timbers that give the form or fashion of the after extremity, below the wing transom, when they terminate at the tuck in square-sterned ships.

Fay.—To fit with a close joint.

Feather-Edged Boards.—Boards made thin on one edge.

Felt Grain.—Timber split in a direction crossing the annular layers towards the center. When split conformably with the layers it is called the *quarter grain.*

Felloes.—The arch pieces which form the rim of the steering wheel.

Fid.—A bar of wood or iron used to support the top-mast and top-gallant masts when they are on end.

* *Fid-Hole.*—Mortises in the heels of top-masts and top-gallant-masts.

* *Fife Rail.*—Rails placed around the mast in which the pins are placed to belay the running rigging to. (Fig. 26.)

Fillet.—A small moulding, generally rectangular in section, and having the appearance of a narrow band.

Fillings.—Pieces placed in the openings between the frames wherever solidity is required.

Firrings.—Pieces of wood nailed to any range of scantlings to bring them to one plane.

Fishing, Fished Beam.—A built beam, composed of two beams placed end to end, and secured by pieces of wood covering the joint on opposite sides.

Fit-Rod.—A small iron rod with a hook at the end, which is put into the holes made in a vessel's side, etc., to ascertain the lengths of bolts required to be driven in.

Fishes.—Pieces used in made masts; also cheek pieces carried to sea on board vessels to secure a crippled mast or yard.

Fixed Blocks.—Sheet chocks, or any other chock placed in the side of a vessel to lead a rope through.

Flaring.—The reverse of *Falling* or *Tumbling Home*. As this can be only in the forepart of the ship, it is said that a ship has a *flaring* bow when the topside falls outward from a perpendicular. Its uses are to shorten the cathead and yet keep the anchor clear of the bow. It also prevents the sea from breaking in upon the forecastle.

Flats.—A name given to timbers amidships that have no bevelings, and are similar to dead-flat. *See Dead-Flat.*

Flashings.—In plumbing, pieces of lead, zinc, or other metal, used to protect the joinings of partitions with floor, or where a coaming joins the deck, or around pipes that pass through a deck. The metal is let into a joint or groove, and then folded down so as to cover and protect the joinings.

* Floor.—The bottom of a ship, or all that part on each side of keel which approaches nearer to a horizontal than a perpendicular direction, and whereon the ship rests when aground.

*Floors, or Floor Timbers.—The timbers that are fixed athwart the keel, and upon which the whole frame is erected. They generally extend as far forward as the foremast, and as far aft as the after square timber, and sometimes one or two cant-floors are added.

Flush.—With a continued even surface, as a *Flush Deck*, which is a deck upon one continued line, without interruption, from fore to aft.

* Fore Body.—That part of the ship's body afore midships or dead-flat. This term is more particularly used in expressing the *figure* or *shape* of that part of ship.

* Fore-Foot.—The foremost piece of keel. Also called gripe. (Fig. 25.)

Forelock.—A thin circular wedge of iron, used to retain a bolt in its place, by being thrust through a mortise hole at the point of bolt. It is sometimes turned or twisted round the bolt to prevent its drawing.

Fore-Peak.—Close forward under the lower deck.

Fore-Sheet Traveller.—An iron ring which travels along on the fore-sheet horse of a fore-and-aft vessel.

* Foretop, Trestle, and Cross-Trees.—Foretop, a platform surrounding the foremast-head: it is composed of the trestle-trees, which are strong bars of oak timber fixed horizontally on opposite sides of foremast; and cross-trees, which are of oak, and supported by the cheeks and trestle-trees.

Frame.—A term applied to any assemblage of pieces of timber firmly connected together.

* Frames.—The bends of timber which form the body of a ship, each of which is composed of one *floor-timber,* two or three *futtocks,* and a *top-timber* on each side, which, being united together, form the frame. (Fig. 28.)

* Futtocks.—Timbers of the frame between the floors and top-timbers.

Gain.—1. A beveling shoulder. 2. A lapping of timbers. 3. The cut that is made to receive a timber.

* Garboard Strake.—That strake of bottom which is wrought next the keel, and rabbets therein. (Fig. 25.)

Gauge.—Measure; dimension.

Gauged-Piles.—Large piles placed at regular distances apart, and connected by horizontal beams, called *runners* or *wale-pieces,* fitted to each side of them by notching, and firmly bolted. A gauge or guide is thus formed for the *sheeting* or *filling* piles, which are drawn between the gauged-piles. Gauged-piles are called also *standard piles.*

Geometrical Stairs.—Those stairs the steps of which are supported at one end only by being built into the wall.

Girth.—In practice, the square of the quarter girth multiplied by the length, is taken as the solid content of a tree.

Glass-Plate.—Specific gravity, 2.453; weight of a cubic foot, 153 ℔; expansion by 180° of heat, from 32° to 212°, .00086 inch.

Gore.—A wedge-shaped or triangular piece.

* Goose-Neck.—An iron hinged bolt, with strap to clasp it, used on the spanker, lower and fish booms. The bolt fore-locks below a sort of gudgeon.

Grade.—A step or degree.

Grain-Cut.—Cut across the grain.

Graining.—Painting in imitation of the grain of wood.

* Gratings.—Lattice coverings for hatchways and scuttles.

* Gripe.—A piece of white oak or elm timber that completes the lower part of the knee of head, and makes a finish with fore-foot. It bolts to stem, and is farther secured by two plates of copper in the form of a horse-shoe, and therefrom called by that name.

Grooving and *Tonguing, Grooving* and *Feathering, Ploughing* and *Tonguing.*—In joinery, a mode of joining boards, which consists in forming a groove or channel along the edge of one board, and a continuous projection or tongue on the edge of another board. When a series of boards is to be joined, each board has a groove on its one edge and a tongue on the other.

* Groundways.—Large pieces of timber, which are laid upon piles driven in the ground, across the building slip, in order to make a good foundation to lay blocks on, upon which the ship is to rest.

* Gudgeons.—The hinges upon which rudder turns. Those fastened to ship are called braces, while those fastened to rudder are called pintles. (Fig. 25.)

Gunwale.—That horizontal plank which covers the heads of timbers between the main and fore drifts. Although this term is so commonly employed, there is really not a piece in the present structure, either of an iron or wooden Merchant-vessel, bearing that name.—In *wooden* vessels the upper outer edge of the Planksheer may be considered as the Gunwale.

* Half-Breadth Plan.—A ship-drawing, showing a series of longitudinal transverse sections.

Half-Round.—A moulding whose profile is a semicircle; a bead; a torus.

Half-Timbers.—The short timbers in the cant bodies.

Halving.—A mode of joining two timbers by letting them into each other.

Hance.—The sudden breaking-in from one form to another, as when a piece is formed, one part eight-square and the other part cylindrical, the part between the termination of these different forms is called the hance; or the parts of any timber where it suddenly becomes narrower or smaller.

Handrail.—A rail to hold by. It is used in staircases to assist in ascending and descending. When it is next to the open newel, it forms a coping to the stair balusters.

* Hanging-Knee.—Those knees against the sides whose arms hang vertically or perpendicular. (Fig. 28.)

* Hanging-Knees.—Knees placed vertically under the deck-beams.

Harpins.—A continuation of the ribbands at the fore and after extremities of ship, fixed to keep the cant-frames, etc., in position, until outside planking is worked.

Hawse-Holes.—The apertures forward, lined with iron casings, for the chain cables to pass through. (Fig. 25.)

Hawse-Hook.—The breast hook at hawse-holes.

Hawse-Pipes or Chain-Pipes.—The pipes in deck, through which the chain cables lead to the lockers. (Fig. 25.)

Head.—The upper end of anything, but more particularly applied to all the work fitted afore the stem, as the figure, the knee, rails, etc. A "scroll head" signifies that there is no carved or ornamental figure at the head, but that the termination is formed and finished off by a *volute*, or scroll turning outward. A "fiddle head" signifies a similar kind of finish, but with the scroll turning aft or inward.

Head-Ledges.—The 'thwartship pieces which frame the hatchways and ladderways. (Fig. 27.)

Head-Rails.—Those rails in the head which extend from the back of figure to cathead and bows.

Heart-Wood.—The central part of the trunk of a tree; the *duramen*.

Heel.—The lower end of any timber. To incline.

Helm.—The rudder, tiller and wheel, taken as a whole.

Hogging.—The arching up of the body along its middle, occasioned frequently by the unequal distribution of the weights. Ships hog in launching, unless the after part of vessel is properly water-borne till she is clear of the ways.

Hood.—The foremost and aftermost plank in each strake.

Hooding Ends.—The ends of hoods where they abut in the rabbet of stem and stern-post.

Horse.—The iron rod placed between the fife-rail stanchions on which the leading blocks are rove or secured. Also in fore-and-aft rigged vessels, it is a stout bar of iron, with a large ring or thimble on it, which spans the vessel from side to side just before the foremast, for the fore-staysail sheet; and when required one is also used for the fore and main-boom sheets to haul down to and transverse on.

Horse Shoes.—Straps of composition in the form of a horse shoe, used for securing the stem to keel, placed on opposite sides, let in flush and bolted through; rings are now generally used instead.

Horsing-Irons.—A caulking-iron, with a long handle attached, which is struck with a beetle by a caulker in hardening up oakum in seams and butts, called *horsing-up*.

Hounding.—The length of the mast from the heel to the lower part of head.

Hounds.—Those projections at mast-heads serving as supports for the trestle-trees of large, and rigging of smaller, vessels to rest upon. With lower masts they are termed cheeks.

Housing.—The space taken out of one solid to admit of the insertion of the extremity of another, for the purpose of connecting them.

In-and-Out.—The bolts that are driven through the ship's side are said to be in-and-out bolts.

Incise.—To cut in; to carve.

Indented.—Cut in the edge or margin into points like teeth, as an indented moulding.

Inner Post.—Worked on the inside of the main post running down to the throat of stern-post knee.

Iron-Sick.—The condition of vessels when the iron-work becomes loose in the timbers from corrosion by gallic acid.

Jambs.—The vertical sides of any aperture, such as a door, a window.

Joint of Frame.—The line at which the two inner surfaces of the frame-timber meet.

Keel.—The main and lowest timber of a ship, extending longitudinally from the stem to the stern-post. It is formed of several pieces, which are scarphed together endways, and form the basis of the whole structure. Of course, it is usually the first thing laid down upon the blocks. (Fig. 30.)

Keelson, or, more commonly, Kelson.—The timber, formed of long square pieces of oak, fixed within the ship exactly over keel for binding and strengthening the lower part of ship; for which purpose it is fitted to, and laid upon, the middle of the floor timbers, and bolted through floors and keel. (Fig. 25, 28.)

Kevel.—Large wooden cleats to belay ropes and hawsers to, commonly called *Cavils*.

Key-Pile.—The center pile plank of one of the divisions of sheeting piles contained between two gauge piles of a cofferdam, or similar work. It is made of a wedge form, narrowest at the bottom, and when driven, keys or wedges the whole together.

King-Piece.—Another and more appropriate name for *king-post*.

King-Post.—The post which, in a truss, extends between the apex of two inclined pieces and the tie-beam, which unites their lower ends.

Knee.—A piece of timber somewhat in the form of the human knee when bent.

Knight-Heads.—Timbers worked on each side of the stem and apron. (Fig. 26.)

Knights (*also called "Jeer bitts"*) are small bitts, placed behind the different masts on the upper-deck, in the heads of these are several sheaveholes (*with sheaves*), through which running-rigging for hoisting, etc., is rove; with the exception of some Mediterranean vessels, they are now very rarely found in merchant ships.

Knots in Wood.—Some kinds render wood unfit for the carpenter; some kinds are not prejudicial.

Knuckle of the Stern.—The sudden angle made by the counter-timbers and after cants.

Kyanize, v.—To steep in a solution of corrosive sublimate, as timber, to preserve it from the dry-rot.

Lacing-Piece.—The piece running across the top of head from the backing-piece to the front-piece. (Fig. 25.)

Landing.—First part of a floor at the end of a flight of steps. Also, a resting-place between flights.

Landing Strake.—The upper strake but one in a boat.

Launch.—The slip upon which the ship is built, with the cradle and all connected with launching.

Launching Ribband.—An oak plank bolted to outside of the launching ways, to guide the cradle in its descent in launching.

Lap, v.—To lap boards is to lay one partly over the other.

Lateral Resistance.—The resistance of water against the side of a vessel in a direction perpendicular to her length.

Laying-Off, or Laying-Down.—The act of delineating the various parts of the ship, to its true size, upon the mould-loft floor.

Ledges.—The pieces of the deck frame lying between the beams jogged into the carlings and knees. (Fig. 27.)

Lee Boards.—Similar to center-boards, affixed to the sides of flat-bottomed vessels; these on being let down, when the vessel is close-hauled, decrease her drifting to leeward.

Let-in, To—To fix or fit one timber or plank into another, as the ends of carlings into beams, and the beams into shelf or clamps, vacancies being made in each to receive the other.

Level Lines.—Lines determining the shape of a ship's body horizontally, or square from the middle line of the ship.

Lighter.—A large open flat bottom vessel.

* Limber-Holes or *Watercourses* are square grooves cut through the underside of floor timber, about nine inches from the side of keel on each side, through which water may run toward the pumps, in the whole length of floors. This precaution is requisite, where small quantities of water, by the heeling of the ship, may come through the ceiling and damage the cargo. It is for this reason that the lower futtocks of merchant ships are cut off short of the keel. (Fig. 28.)

* Limber-Passage.—A passage or channel formed throughout the whole length of the floor, on each side of kelson, for giving water a free communication to the pumps. It is formed by the *Limber-Strake* on each side, a thick strake wrought next kelson. This strake is kept about eleven inches from kelson, and forms the passage fore and aft which admits the water to the pump-well. The upper part of limber-passage is formed by the *Limber-Boards* or plates. These boards are composed of iron plates, or else of short pieces of oak plank, one edge of which is fitted by a rabbet into the limber-strake, and the other edge beveled with a descent against the kelson. They are fitted in short pieces, for the convenience of taking up any one or more readily. (Fig. 28.)

Lips of a Scarph.—The thin parts or laps of scarph.

Lockers.—Compartments built in cabins, etc., for various purposes.

Lock.—1. Lock, in its primary sense, is anything that fastens; but in the art of construction the word is appropriated to an instrument composed of springs, wards, and bolts of iron or steel, used to fasten doors, drawers, chests, etc. Locks on outer doors are called *stock locks;* those on chamber doors, *spring locks;* and such as are hidden in the thickness of the doors to which they are applied, are called *mortise locks.* 2. A basin or chamber in a canal, or at the entrance to a dock. It has gates at each end, which may be opened or shut at pleasure. By means of such locks vessels are transferred from a higher to a lower level, or from a lower to a higher. Whenever a canal changes its level on account of an ascent or descent of the ground through which it passes, the place where the change takes place is commanded by a lock.

Lock-Chamber.—In canals, the area of a lock inclosed by the side walls and gates.

Lock-Gate.—The gate of a lock provided with paddles.

Lock-Paddle.—The sluice in a lock which serves to fill or empty it.

Lock-Pit.—The excavated area of a lock.

Lock-Sill.—An angular piece of timber at the bottom of a lock, against which the gates shut.

Locker.—A small cupboard.

Main Breadth.—The broadest part of ship at any particular timber or frame.

* Main-Wales.—The lower wales, which are generally placed on the lower breadth, and so that the main deck knee-bolts may come into them. (Fig. 28.)

Mallet.—A large wooden hammer, used by caulkers.

Manager Board.—A piece of oak plank fitted over deck and running from side to side a short distance abaft the hawse pipes.

Manger.—An apartment extending athwart the ship, immediately within the hawse-holes. It serves as a fence to interrupt the passage of water which may come in at the hawse-holes or from the cable when heaving in; and the water thus prevented from running aft is returned into the sea by the manger-scuppers, which are larger than the other scuppers on that account.

Margin.—A line in ships having a square stern, at a parallel distance down from the upper edge of the wing transom forming the lower part of a surface for seating the tuck rail; it terminates at the ends of the exterior planking, or what is called the tuck.

* Mast Carlings, large carlings on each side of mast; they are placed at equal distances from the middle line, and apart the diameter of mast, and sufficient for wedging on each side; they score and face into the beams, before and abaft mast, and lap on them about two-thirds the breadth of beam, and are bolted with two bolts in each end. (Fig. 27.)

Mast-Coat.—A canvas covering fitted over the upper ends of the mast wedges and nailed to the mast and mast coaming to prevent any leakage around the mast.

* Mast Partners, commonly called cross partners, are pieces placed before and abaft the mast for the wedges to come against; they are let into a double rabbet taken out of mast carlings, and are bolted through these, with two or three bolts in end of each piece. (Fig. 27.)

Mauls.—Large hammers used for driving treenails, having a steel face at one end and a point or pen drawn out at the other. Double-headed mauls have a steel face at each end of the same size, and are used for driving bolts, etc.

Meta-Center.—That point in a ship below which the center of gravity of weight must be placed.

Middle Line.—A line dividing the ship exactly in the middle. In the horizontal or half-breadth plan it is a right line bisecting the ship from stem to stern-post; and in the plane of projection, or body plan, it is a perpendicular line bisecting the ship from keel to height of top of side.

Midships (see *Amidships*).

* Miter or *Mitre,* the mode of joining two solid pieces of timber; the surfaces to be brought together are so formed, that when connected, the joint shall make an angle with the side of each piece that shall be common to both.

Momentum of a body is the product of weight multiplied by the distance of its center of gravity from a certain point, or from a line called the axis of momentum.

* Mortise.—A hole or hollow made in a piece of timber, etc., in order to receive the end of another piece, with a tenon fitted exactly to fill it.

Moulded.—Cut to the mould. Also, the size or bigness of the timbers the way the mould is laid. *See Sided.*

* Moulds.—Pieces of board made to the shape of the lines on mould-loft floor, as the timbers, harpins, ribbands, etc., and used as patterns when cutting out the different pieces of timber, etc., for the ship.

Nail.—A small pointed piece of metal, usually with a head, to be driven into a board or other piece of timber, and serving to fasten it to other timber. The larger kinds of instruments of this sort are called *spikes;* and a long, thin kind, with a flattish head, is called a *brad.* There are three leading distinctions of nails, as respects the state of the metal from which they are prepared, namely, *wrought* or *forged* nails, *cut* or *pressed* nails, and *cast* nails. Of the wrought or forged nails there are about 300 sorts, which receive different names, expressing for the most part the uses to which they are applied, as, *deck, scupper, boat.* Some are distinguished by names expressive of their form: thus, *rose, clasp, diamond,* etc., indicate the form of their heads, and *flat, sharp, spear, chisel,* etc., their points. The thickness of any specified form is expressed by trade terms.

Offset, or *Set-off.*—A horizontal break.

Ogee.—A moulding consisting of two members, one concave and the other convex. It is called also *cyma reversa.*

* *Orlop-beams* are hold-beams, fitted below the lower-deck of two and three-decked vessels; their spacing is greater, and they are therefore generally heavier than the beams in the decks above. (Fig. 28.)

Orlop-deck is the lowermost deck in four-decked ships.

Ovolo.—A moulding, the vertical section of which is, in Roman architecture, a quarter of a circle; it is thence called the *quarter-round.* In Grecian architecture the section of the ovolo is elliptical, or rather egg-shaped.

Panel.—An area sunk from the general face of the surrounding work; also a compartment of a wainscot or ceiling, or of the surface of a wall, etc. In joinery, it is a thin piece of wood, framed or received in a groove by two upright pieces or styles, and two transverse pieces or rails; as the *panels* of doors.

Piles.—Beams of timber, pointed at the end, driven into the soil for the support of some superstructure. They are either driven through a compressible stratum, till they meet with one that is incompressible, and thus transmit the weight of the structure erected on the softer to the more solid material, or they are driven into a soft or compressible structure in such numbers as to solidify it. In the first instance, the piles are from 9 to 18 inches in diameter, and about twenty times their diameter in length. They are pointed with iron at their lower end, and their head is encircled with an iron.

Pile-Driver.—An engine for driving down piles. It consists of a large ram or block of iron, termed the *monkey,* which slides between two guide-posts. Being drawn up to the top, and then let fall from a considerable height, it comes down on the head of the pile with a violent blow.

Pile-Planks.—Planks about 9 inches broad, and from 2 to 4 inches thick, sharpened at their lower end, and driven with their edges close together into the ground in hydraulic works. Two rows of pile-planks thus driven, with a space between them filled with puddle, is the means used to form watertight cofferdams and similar erections.

Pin.—A piece of wood or metal, square or cylindrical in section, and sharpened or pointed, used to fasten timbers together. Large metal pins are termed *bolts,* and the wooden pins used in ship-building *treenails.*

Plank.—All timber from one and a half to four inches in thickness has this name given to it.

* *Planking.*—Covering the outside of a ship's timbers with plank, the plank being the outer coating when the vessel is not sheathed. (Fig. 28.)

* *Plank-Sheers, or Plank-Sheer.*—The pieces of plank laid horizontally over timber-heads of quarter deck and forecastle, for the purpose of covering the top of the side; hence sometimes called covering-boards. (Fig. 28.)

Planted.—In joinery, a projecting member wrought on a separate piece of stuff, and afterwards fixed in its place, is said to be *planted;* as a *planted* moulding.

* *Poppets.*—Those pieces which are fixed perpendicularly between the ship's bottom and the bilgeways, at the fore and aftermost parts of the ship, to support her in launching.

* *Preventer-Bolts.*—The bolts passing through the lower end of the preventer-plates, to assist the chain-bolts in heavy strains. (Fig. 28.)

Preventer-Plates.—Short plates of iron bolted to the side at the lower part of the chains, as extra security.

Pump.—The machine fitted in the wells of ships to draw water out of the hold.

Quarter-Grain.—When timber is split in the direction of its annular plates or rings. When it is split across these, towards the center, it is called the *felt-grain*

Quarter-Round.—The echinus moulding.

Quicken, To.—To give anything a greater curve. For instance, *"To quicken the sheer"* is to shorten the radius by which the curve is struck. This term is therefore opposed to straightening the sheer.

Quick-Work.—A term given to the strakes which shut in between the spirketing and the clamps. By quick-work was formerly meant all that part of a merchant vessel below the level of the water when she is laden.

* *Rabbet.*—A joint made by a groove or channel in a piece of timber, cut for the purpose of receiving and securing the edge or ends of planks, as the planks of bottom into the keel, stem or stern-post, or the edge of one plank into another.

Rag-Bolt.—A sort of bolt having its point jagged or barbed, to make it hold the more securely.

Rails.—The horizontal timbers in any piece of framing.

Rake.—A slope or inclination.

Rake.—The overhanging of the stem or stern beyond a perpendicular with the keel, or any part or thing that forms an obtuse angle with the horizon.

Raking Mouldings.—Those which are inclined from the horizontal line.

Ram-Line.—A small rope or line, sometimes used for the purpose of forming the sheer or hang of the decks, for setting the beams fair, etc.

Razing.—The act of marking by a mould on a piece of timber, or any marks made by a tool called a *razing-knife* or *scriber.*

Reeming.—The opening of the seams of plank for caulking by driving in irons called reeming irons.

Rends.—Large shakes or splits in timber or plank, most common to plank.

Riding-Bitts are bitts to which chain-cables are belayed when a ship is anchored.

Ring-Bolts.—Eye-bolts having a ring passed through the eye of the bolt.

**Room and Space.*—The distance from one frame to the adjoining one.

Rough-Hew.—To hew coarsely without smoothing, as to *rough-hew* timber.

Rowlocks.—Places either raised above or sunk in the gunwale of a boat used to place the oar in when rowing.

Rudder.—The machine by which the ship is steered.

Rudder-Stock.—The main piece of a rudder.

Run.—The narrowing of the after-part of ship; thus a ship is said to have a full, fine, or clean run.

Sagging.—The contrary of hogging.

* *Sampson-Knee.*—A knee used to strengthen riding bitts.

Saucers.—Metal steps bolted to the aft-side of the rudderpost below a brace, so that the plug of the pintle will rest on it, and keep the straps of pintles and braces from coming in contact, thereby lessening the friction to be overcome in turning the rudder. The pintles which rest on these saucers are made with longer plugs, and are called saucer-pintles.

Sap-Wood.—The external part of the wood of exogens, which from being the latest formed, is not filled up with solid matter. It is that through which the ascending fluids of plants move most freely. For all building purposes the sap-wood is or ought to be removed from timber, as it soon decays.

Scantling.—The dimensions given for the timbers, planks, etc. Likewise all quartering under five inches square, which is termed scantling; all above that size is called *carling.*

Scarphing.—The letting of one piece of timber or plank into another with a lap, in such a manner that both may appear as one solid and even surface, as keel-pieces, stem-pieces, clamps, etc.

Scarphs.—Scarphs are called vertical when their surfaces are parallel to the sides, and flat or horizontal when their surfaces are opposite, as the scarphs of keelson and keel. They are hook-scarphs when formed with a hook or projection, as the scarphs of stem; and key-scarphs, when their lips are set close by wedge-like keys at the hook, as the scarphs of beams.

Schooner.—A vessel with two, three or more masts, with fore-and-aft sails set on gaffs. A topsail schooner has a fore-topsail, and sometimes a fore-topgallant sail.

Scuppers.—Holes cut through water-ways and side, and lined with lead, to convey water to the sea.

Scuttle.—An opening in deck smaller than a hatchway.

Screw-Jack.—A portable machine for raising great weights by the agency of a screw.

Scribe.—To mark by a rule or compasses; to mark so as to fit one piece to another.

Seams.—The spaces between the planks when worked.

Seasoning.—A term applied to a ship kept standing a certain time after she is completely framed and dubbed out for planking, which should never be less than six months, when circumstances will permit. *Seasoned plank or timber* is such as has been cut down and sawed out one season at least, particularly when thoroughly dry and not liable to shrink.

Seating.—That part of the floor which fays on deadwood, and of a transom which fays against the post.

Sending or 'Scending.—The act of pitching violently into the hollows or intervals of waves.

Setting or Setting-to.—The act of making the planks, etc., fay close to the timbers, by driving wedges between the plank, etc., and a wrain staff. Hence we say, "set or set away," meaning to exert more strength. The power or engine used for the purpose of setting is called a *Sett,* and is composed of two ring-bolts and a wrain staff, cleats and lashings.

Shaken or Shaky.—A natural defect in plank or timber when it is full of splits or clefts, and will not bear fastening or caulking.

Sheathing.—A thin sort of doubling or casing of yellow pine board or sheet copper, and sometimes of both, over the ship's bottom, to protect the planks from worms, etc. Tar and hair, or brown paper dipped in tar and oil, is laid between the sheathing and the bottom.

Sheer.—The longitudinal curve or hanging of a ship's side in a fore-and-aft direction.

Sheer-Draught.—The plan of elevation of a ship, whereon is described the outboard works, as the wales, sheer-rails, ports, drifts, head, quarters, post and stem, etc., the hang of each deck inside, the height of the water-lines, etc.

Sheers.—Elevated spars, connected at upper ends, used in masting and dismasting vessels, etc.

Sheers.—Two masts or spars lashed or bolted together at or near the head, provided with a pulley, and raised to nearly a vertical position, used in lifting stones and other building materials.

Sheer-Strake.—The strake or strakes wrought in the topside, of which the upper edge is the top-timber line or top of side. It forms the chief strength of the upper part of topside, and is therefore always worked thicker than the other strakes, and scarphed with hook and butt between the drifts. (Fig. 25.)

Sheet-Piles, Sheeting-Piles.—Piles formed of thick plank, shot or jointed on the edges, and sometimes grooved and tongued, driven closely together between the main or gauge piles of a coffer-dam or other hydraulic work, to inclose the space so as either to retain or exclude water, as the case may be. Sheeting-piles have of late been formed of iron.

Shelf-Pieces.—A strake worked for deck beams to rest on where iron hanging knees are to be used. (Fig. 28.)

Shift.—A term made use of to denote the position of butts and scarphs of planks and timber.

Shore.—An oblique brace or support, the upper end resting against the body to be supported.

Shoulder.—Among artificers, a horizontal or rectangular projection from the body of a thing. *Shoulder of a tenon,* the plane transverse to the length of a piece of timber from which the tenon projects. It does not, however, always lie in the plane here defined, but sometimes lies in different planes.

Sirmarks.—Stations marked upon the moulds for the frame timber, etc., indicating where the bevelings are to be applied.

Skeg.—The after-end of the keel. The composition piece supporting the heel of an equipoise rudder.

Skew, or *Askew.*—Oblique; as a *skew*-bridge.

Snaping.—Cutting the ends of a stick off beveling so as to fay upon an inclined plane.

Sny or Hang.—When the edges of strakes of plank curve up or down, they are said to *sny* or *hang;* if down, to hang; if up, to sny.

Specific Gravity.—The relative weight of any body when compared with an equal bulk of any other body. Bodies are said to be specifically heavier than other bodies when they contain a greater weight under the same bulk; and when of less weight, they are said to be specifically lighter.

Spiles.—Wooden pins used for driving into nail-holes. Those for putting over bolt-heads and deck-spikes are cylindrical, and are called plugs.

Spirketting.—The strakes of plank worked between the lower sills of ports and waterways. (Fig. 28.)

Sprung.—A yard or mast is said to be sprung when it is cracked or split.

Square Framed.—In joinery, a work is said to be *square framed* or *framed square,* when the framing has all the angles of its styles, rails, and mountings square without being moulded.

Square-Body.—The square body comprises all those frames that are square to the center line of ship.

Squaring Off.—The trimming off of the projecting edges of the strakes after vessel is planked.

Stanchions.—Upright pieces of wood or iron placed under deck beams to support them in the center. (Fig. 27.)

Standards.—Knees placed against the fore-side of cable or riding-bitts, and projecting above the deck.

Staples.—A bent fastening of metal formed as a loop, and driven in at both ends.

Start-Hammer.—A steel bolt, with a handle attached, which is held on the heads of bolts, and struck with a double-header to start them in below the surface.

Stealer.—A name given to plank that fall short of the stem or stern-post, on account of the amount of sny given sometimes in planking full-bowed ships.

Stem.—The main timber at the fore part of ship, formed by the combination of several pieces into a curved shape and erected vertically to receive the ends of bow-planks, which are united to it by means of a rabbet. Its lower end scarphs or boxes into the keel, through which the rabbet is also carried, and the bottom unites in the same manner. (Fig. 25.)

Stemson.—A piece of timber, wrought on after part of apron, the lower end of which scarphs into the keelson. Its upper end is continued as high as the middle or upper deck, and its use is to strengthen the scarphs of apron, and stem. (Fig. 25.)

Step.—One of the gradients in a stair; it is composed of two fronts, one horizontal, called the *tread,* and one vertical, called the *riser.*

Steps for the Ship's Side.—The pieces of quartering, with mouldings, nailed to the sides amidship, about nine inches asunder, from the wales upward, for the convenience of persons getting on board.

Steps of Masts.—The steps into which the heels of masts are fixed are large pieces of timber. Those for the main and foremasts are fixed across the keelson, and that for the mizzenmast upon the lower deck-beams. The holes or mortises into which the masts step should have sufficient wood on each side to accord in strength with the tenon left at the heel of mast, and the hole should be cut rather less than the tenon, as an allowance for shrinking. (Fig. 25.)

Stern Frame.—The strong frame of timber composed of the stern-post, transoms and fashion-pieces, which form the basis of the whole stern.

Stern-Post.—The principal piece of timber in stern frame on which the rudder is hung, and to which the transoms are bolted. It therefore terminates the ship below the wing-transom, and its lower end is tenoned into keel. (Fig. 25.)

Stiff.—Stable; steady under canvas.

Stiving.—The elevation of a ship's cathead or bowsprit, or the angle which either makes with the horizon; generally called steeve.

Shoe, Anchor.—A flat block of hard wood, convex on back, and scored out on flat side to take the bill of anchor; it is used in fishing the anchor to prevent tearing the plank on vessel's bow, and is placed under the bill of it, and is hauled up with it.

Stoppings-Up.—The poppets, timber, etc., used to fill up the vacancy between the upper side of the bilgeways and ship's bottom, for supporting her when launching.

Straight of Breadth.—The space before and abaft dead-flat, in which the ship is of the same uniform breadth, or of the same breadth as at dead-flat. *See Dead-Flat.*

Strake.—One breadth of plank wrought from one end of the ship to the other, either within or outboard.

Strut.—Any piece of timber in a system of framing which is pressed or crushed in the direction of its length.

Stub-Mortise.—A mortise which does not pass through the whole thickness of the timber.

Tabling.—Letting one piece of timber into another by alternate scores or projections from the middle, so that it cannot be drawn asunder either lengthwise or sidewise.

Taffarel or Taff-Rail.—The upper part of the ship's stern, usually ornamented with carved work or mouldings, the ends of which unite to the quarter-pieces.

Tasting of Plank or Timber.—Chipping it with an adze, or boring it with a small auger, for the purpose of ascertaining its quality or defects.

Templet.—A pattern or mould used by masons, machinists, smiths, shipwrights, etc., for shaping anything by. It is made of tin or zinc plate, sheet-iron, or thin board, according to the use to which it is to be applied.

Tenon.—The square part at the end of one piece of timber, diminished so as to fix in a hole of another piece, called a mortise, for joining or fastening the two pieces together.

Tenon.—The end of a piece of wood cut into the form of a rectangular prism, which is received into a cavity in another piece, having the same shape and size, called a *mortise.* It is sometimes written *tenant.*

Thickstuff.—A name for sided timber exceeding four inches, but not being more than twelve inches in thickness.

Tholes, or Thole-Pins.—The battens or pins forming the rowlocks of a boat.

Throat.—The inside of knee at the middle or turn of the arms. Also the midship part of the floor timbers.

Thwarts.—The seats in a boat on which the oarsmen sit.

Tiller.—An arm of wood or iron fitted into the rudder-head to steer a ship or boat by.

Timber.—That sort of wood which is squared, or capable of being squared, and fit for being employed in house or ship-building, or in carpentry, joinery, etc.

Timber.—(*Material for ship-building.*).—Timber is generally distinguished into rough, square or hewn, sided and converted timber. *Rough timber* is the timber to its full size as felled, with lop, top and bark off. *Hewn timber* is timber squared for measurement. *Sided timber* is the tree of full size, one way, as it is felled, but with slabs taken off from two of its sides. *Converted timber* is timber cut for different purposes.

Timber-Heads.—Projecting timbers for belaying towing lines, etc.

To Anchor Stock.—To work planks by fashioning them in a tapering form from the middle, and working or fixing them over each other, so that the broad or middle part of one plank shall be immediately above or below the butts or ends of two others. This method, as it occasions a great consumption of wood, is only used where particular strength is required.

Tonnage of Capacity.—The capacity which the body has for carrying cargo, estimated at 100 cubic feet to the ton.

Tonnage of Displacement.—The weight of the ship in tons with all on board; found by computing number of cubic feet of the immersed body to the deep load line and dividing by 35.

Top and Half Top-Timbers.—The upper timbers of the frame. (Fig. 28.)

Top-Rail.—An iron rail at the after part of ship's tops.

Top-Rim.—The circular sweep or the fore-part of a vessel's top and covering in the ends of cross-trees and trestle-trees, to prevent their chafing the topsail.

Topside.—That part of the ship above the main wales. (Fig. 28.)

To Teach.—A term applied to the direction that any line, etc., seems to point out. Thus we say, "Let the line or mould *teach fair* to such a spot, raze," etc.

Trail-Boards.—The filling pieces, sometimes carved, placed between the brackets on the head.

Transoms.—Transverse timbers in square-sterned ships, connected and placed square with the stern-posts.

Tread.—The horizontal surface of a step.

Tread of the Keel.—The whole length of the keel upon a straight line.

Treenails.—Cylindrical oak pins driven through the planks and timbers of a vessel, to fasten or connect them together. These certainly make the best fastening when driven quite through, and caulked or wedged inside. They should be made of the very best oak or locust, cut near the butt, and perfectly dry or well-seasoned.

Trimming of Timber.—The working of any piece of timber into the proper shape, by means of the axe or adze.

Truss.—A combination of timbers, of iron, or of timbers and iron-work so arranged as to constitute an unyielding frame. It is so named because it is *trussed* or tied together.

Trussed Beam.—A compound beam composed of two beams secured together side by side with a truss, generally of iron, between them.

The Tuck.—The after part of ship, where the ends of planks of bottom are terminated by the tuck-rail, and all below the wing-transom when it partakes of the figure of the wing-transom as far as the fashion-pieces.

Tuck-Rail.—The rail which is wrought well with the upper side of wing-transom, and forms a rabbet for the purpose of caulking the butt ends of planks of bottom.

Upright.—The position of a ship when she inclines neither to one side nor the other.

Veneer.—A facing of superior wood placed in thin leaves over an inferior sort. Generally, a facing of superior material laid over an inferior material.

Wales (by some also called *Bends*) (*Wooden Vessels*).— The thickest outside planking of a ship's side, about midway between the light water-line and the plank sheer; the breadth of the Wales is generally equal to ¼ or ⅓ of the depth of the vessel's hold. (Fig. 28.)

Wall-Sided.—A term applied to the topsides of the ship when the main breadth is continued very low down and very high up, so that the topsides appear straight and upright like a wall.

Washboards.—Thin plank placed above the gunwale of a boat forward and aft to increase the height.

Water-Lines.—Sections of the vessel parallel to the plane of flotation.

Water-logged.—The condition of a leaky ship when she is so full of water as to be heavy and unmanageable.

Waterways.—The edge of the deck next the timbers, which is wrought thicker than the rest of deck, and so hollowed to thickness of deck as to form a gutter or channel for water to run through to the scuppers. (Fig. 26.)

Wedges.—Slices of wood driven in between the masts and their partners, to admit of giving rake if desired.

Whelps.—The brackets or projecting parts of the barrel of a capstan.

Whole-Moulded.—A term applied to the bodies of those ships which are so constructed that one mould made to the midship-bend, with the addition of a floor hollow, will mould all the timbers below the main-breadth in square body.

Winch.—A machine similar to a windlass, but much smaller, often placed on the fore side of the lower masts of merchant vessels, just above the deck, to assist in hoisting the topsails, etc.

Wind.—To cast or warp; to turn or twist any surface, so that all its parts do not lie in the same plane.

Windlass.—A machine used in vessels for hoisting the anchor.

Wings.—The places next the side upon the orlop.

Wing-Transom.—The uppermost transom in stern frame, upon which the heels of counter-timbers are let in and rest. It is by some called the main-transom.

Wood-Lock.—A piece of elm or oak, closely fitted and sheathed with copper, in the throating or score of the pintle, near the load water-line, so that when the rudder is hung and wood-lock nailed in its place, it cannot rise, because the latter butts against the under side of the brace and butt of score.

Wrain-Bolt.—Ring-bolts used when planking, with two or more forelock holes in the end for taking in the set, as the plank, etc., works nearer the timbers.

Wrain-Stave.—A sort of stout billet of tough wood, tapered at the ends so as to go into the ring of the wrain-bolt, to make the setts necessary for bringing-to the planks or thickstuff to the timbers.

Yacht.—A small vessel (sailing or power-driven vessel) used for pleasure.

USEFUL TABLES

FRACTIONS OF AN INCH IN DECIMALS

Fraction of an Inch	Decimal of an Inch	Fraction of an Inch	Decimal of an Inch	Fraction of an Inch	Decimal of an Inch	Fraction of an Inch	Decimal of an Inch
1/64	.01562	17/64	.26562	33/64	.51562	49/64	.76562
1/32	.03125	9/32	.28125	17/32	.53125	25/32	.78125
3/64	.04687	19/64	.29687	35/64	.54687	51/64	.79687
1/16	.06250	5/16	.31250	9/16	.56250	13/16	.81250
5/64	.07812	21/64	.32812	37/64	.57812	53/64	.82812
3/32	.09375	11/32	.34375	19/32	.59375	27/32	.84375
7/64	.10937	23/64	.35937	39/64	.60937	55/64	.85937
1/8	.12500	3/8	.37500	5/8	.62500	7/8	.87500
9/64	.14062	25/64	.39062	41/64	.64062	57/64	.89062
5/32	.15625	13/32	.40625	21/32	.65625	29/32	.90625
11/64	.17187	27/64	.42187	43/64	.67187	59/64	.92187
3/16	.18750	7/16	.43750	11/16	.68750	15/16	.93750
13/64	.20312	29/64	.45312	45/64	.70312	61/64	.95312
7/32	.21875	15/32	.46875	23/32	.71875	31/32	.96875
15/64	.23437	31/64	.48437	47/64	.73437	63/64	.98437
1/4	.25000	1/2	.50000	3/4	.75000	1 inch	1.00000

INCHES AND FRACTIONS IN DECIMALS OF A FOOT

Parts of Foot in Inches and Fractions	Decimal of a Foot	Parts of Foot in Inches and Fractions	Decimal of a Foot	Parts of Foot in Inches and Fractions	Decimal of a Foot	Parts of Foot in Inches and Fractions	Decimal of a Foot
1/16	.00520	3 1/16	.25520	6 1/16	.50520	9 1/16	.75520
1/8	.01040	3 1/8	.26040	6 1/8	.51040	9 1/8	.76040
3/16	.01562	3 3/16	.26562	6 3/16	.51562	9 3/16	.76562
1/4	.02080	3 1/4	.27080	6 1/4	.52080	9 1/4	.77080
5/16	.02600	3 5/16	.27600	6 5/16	.52600	9 5/16	.77600
3/8	.03125	3 3/8	.28125	6 3/8	.53125	9 3/8	.78125
7/16	.03640	3 7/16	.28650	6 7/16	.53640	9 7/16	.78650
1/2	.04170	3 1/2	.29170	6 1/2	.54170	9 1/2	.79170
9/16	.04687	3 9/16	.29687	6 9/16	.54687	9 9/16	.79687
5/8	.05210	3 5/8	.30210	6 5/8	.55210	9 5/8	.80210
11/16	.05730	3 11/16	.30730	6 11/16	.55730	9 11/16	.80730
3/4	.06250	3 3/4	.31250	6 3/4	.56250	9 3/4	.81250
13/16	.06770	3 13/16	.31770	6 13/16	.56770	9 13/16	.81770
7/8	.07290	3 7/8	.32290	6 7/8	.57290	9 7/8	.82290
15/16	.07812	3 15/16	.32812	6 15/16	.57812	9 15/16	.82812
1 inch	.08330	4 inches	.33330	7 inches	.58330	10 inches	.83330
1 1/16	.08850	4 1/16	.33850	7 1/16	.58850	10 1/16	.83850
1 1/8	.09375	4 1/8	.34375	7 1/8	.59375	10 1/8	.84375
1 3/16	.09900	4 3/16	.34900	7 3/16	.59900	10 3/16	.84900
1 1/4	.10420	4 1/4	.35420	7 1/4	.60420	10 1/4	.85420
1 5/16	.10937	4 5/16	.35937	7 5/16	.60937	10 5/16	.85937
1 3/8	.11460	4 3/8	.36460	7 3/8	.61460	10 3/8	.86460
1 7/16	.11980	4 7/16	.36980	7 7/16	.61980	10 7/16	.86980
1 1/2	.12500	4 1/2	.37500	7 1/2	.62500	10 1/2	.87500
1 9/16	.13020	4 9/16	.38020	7 9/16	.63020	10 9/16	.88020
1 5/8	.13540	4 5/8	.38540	7 5/8	.63540	10 5/8	.88540
1 11/16	.14062	4 11/16	.39062	7 11/16	.64062	10 11/16	.89062
1 3/4	.14580	4 3/4	.39580	7 3/4	.64580	10 3/4	.89580
1 13/16	.15100	4 13/16	.40100	7 13/16	.65100	10 13/16	.90100
1 7/8	.15625	4 7/8	.40625	7 7/8	.65625	10 7/8	.90625
1 15/16	.16150	4 15/16	.41140	7 15/16	.66150	10 15/16	.91150
2 inches	.16670	5 inches	.41670	8 inches	.66670	11 inches	.91670
2 1/16	.17187	5 1/16	.42187	8 1/16	.67187	11 1/16	.92187
2 1/8	.17710	5 1/8	.42710	8 1/8	.67710	11 1/8	.92710
2 3/16	.18230	5 3/16	.43230	8 3/16	.68230	11 3/16	.93230
2 1/4	.18750	5 1/4	.43750	8 1/4	.68750	11 1/4	.93750
2 5/16	.19270	5 5/16	.44270	8 5/16	.69270	11 5/16	.94270
2 3/8	.19790	5 3/8	.44790	8 3/8	.69790	11 3/8	.94790
2 7/16	.20312	5 7/16	.45312	8 7/16	.70312	11 7/16	.95312
2 1/2	.20830	5 1/2	.45830	8 1/2	.70830	11 1/2	.95830
2 9/16	.21350	5 9/16	.46350	8 9/16	.71350	11 9/16	.96350
2 5/8	.21875	5 5/8	.46875	8 5/8	.71875	11 5/8	.96875
2 11/16	.22400	5 11/16	.47400	8 11/16	.72400	11 11/16	.97400
2 3/4	.22920	5 3/4	.47920	8 3/4	.72920	11 3/4	.97920
2 13/16	.23437	5 13/16	.48437	8 13/16	.73437	11 13/16	.98437
2 7/8	.23950	5 7/8	.48960	8 7/8	.73960	11 7/8	.98960
2 15/16	.24480	5 15/16	.49480	8 15/16	.74480	11 15/16	.99480
3 inches	.25000	6 inches	.50000	9 inches	.75000	12 inches	1.00000

AREAS AND CIRCUMFERENCES OF CIRCLES

Diameter	Area	Circumference	Diameter	Area	Circumference
1	.7854	3.1416	51	2042.8206	160.2212
2	3.1416	6.2832	52	2123.7166	163.3628
3	7.0686	9.4248	53	2206.1834	166.5044
4	12.5664	12.5664	54	2290.2210	169.6460
5	19.6350	15.7080	55	2375.8294	172.7876
6	28.2743	18.8496	56	2463.0086	175.9292
7	38.4845	21.9911	57	2551.7586	179.0708
8	50.2655	25.1327	58	2642.0794	182.2184
9	63.6173	28.2743	59	2733.9710	185.3540
10	78.5398	31.4159	60	2827.4334	188.4956
11	95.0332	34.5575	61	2922.4666	191.6372
12	113.0973	37.6991	62	3019.0705	194.7787
13	132.7323	40.8407	63	3117.2453	197.9203
14	153.9380	43.9823	64	3216.9909	201.0619
15	176.7146	47.1239	65	3318.3072	204.2035
16	201.0619	50.2655	66	3421.1944	207.3451
17	226.9801	53.4071	67	3525.6524	210.4867
18	254.4690	56.5487	68	3631.6811	213.6283
19	283.5287	59.6903	69	3739.2807	216.7699
20	314.1593	62.8319	70	3848.4510	219.9115
21	346.3606	65.9734	71	3959.1921	223.0531
22	380.1327	69.1150	72	4071.5041	226.1947
23	415.4756	72.2566	73	4185.3868	229.3363
24	452.3893	75.3982	74	4300.8403	232.4779
25	490.8739	78.5398	75	4417.8647	235.6194
26	530.9292	81.6814	76	4536.4598	238.7610
27	572.5553	84.8230	77	4656.6257	241.9026
28	615.7522	87.9646	78	4778.3624	245.0442
29	660.5199	91.1062	79	4901.6699	248.1858
30	706.8583	94.2478	80	5026.5482	251.3274
31	754.7676	97.3894	81	5152.9974	254.4690
32	804.2477	100.5310	82	5281.0173	257.6106
33	855.2986	103.6726	83	5410.6079	260.7522
34	907.9203	106.8142	84	5541.7694	263.8938
35	962.1128	109.9557	85	5674.5017	267.0354
36	1017.8760	113.0973	86	5808.8048	270.1770
37	1075.2101	116.2389	87	5944.6787	273.3186
38	1134.1149	119.3805	88	6082.1234	276.4602
39	1194.5906	122.5221	89	6221.1389	279.6017
40	1256.6371	125.6637	90	6361.7251	282.7434
41	1320.2543	128.8053	91	6503.8822	285.8849
42	1385.4424	131.9469	92	6647.6101	289.0265
43	1452.2012	135.0835	93	6792.9097	292.1681
44	1520.5308	138.2301	94	6939.7782	295.3097
45	1590.4313	141.3717	95	7088.2184	298.4513
46	1661.9025	144.5133	96	7238.2295	301.5929
47	1734.9445	147.6549	97	7389.8113	304.7345
48	1809.5574	150.7964	98	7542.9610	307.8761
49	1885.7410	153.9380	99	7697.6874	311.0177
50	1963.4954	157.0796	100	7853.9816	314.1593

WEIGHT OF A SQUARE FOOT OF CAST AND WROUGHT IRON, COPPER, LEAD, BRASS AND ZINC FROM 1/16 TO 1 INCH IN THICKNESS

Thickness Inch	Cast Iron Lbs.	Wrought Iron Lbs.	Copper Lbs.	Lead Lbs.	Brass Lbs.	Zinc Lbs.
1/16	2.346	2.517	2.89	3.691	2.675	2.34
1/8	4.693	5.035	5.781	7.382	5.35	4.68
3/16	7.039	7.552	8.672	11.074	8.025	7.02
1/4	9.386	10.07	11.562	14.765	10.7	9.36
5/16	11.733	12.588	14.453	18.456	13.375	11.7
3/8	14.079	15.106	17.344	22.148	16.05	14.04
7/16	16.426	17.623	20.234	25.839	18.725	16.34
1/2	18.773	20.141	23.125	29.53	21.4	18.72
9/16	21.119	22.659	26.016	33.222	24.075	
5/8	23.466	25.176	28.906	36.923	26.75	
11/16	25.812	27.694	31.797	40.604	29.425	
3/4	28.159	30.211	34.688	44.296	32.1	
13/16	30.505	32.729	37.578	47.987		
7/8	32.852	35.247	40.469	51.678		
15/16	35.199	37.764	43.359	55.37		
1	37.545	40.282	46.25	59.061		

NOTE.—The wrought iron and the copper weights are those of hard-rolled plates.

FRESH WATER
UNITED STATES GALLON

Tons = gallons
268.365

Tons = cubic feet
35.883

Pounds = cubic feet × 62.425
Gallons = cubic feet × 7.48
Pressure = height in feet × .4335
Height in feet = pressure × 2.3093

Logarithm
1 ton contains 35.883 cubic feet............................... 1.55489
1 ton contains 268.365 gallons................................ 2.56628
1 ton weighs 2240 pounds..................................... 3.35025
1 gallon contains 231 cubic inches............................ 2.36361
1 gallon contains .833 imperial gallon........................ 2.92065
1 gallon weighs 8.33 pounds.................................. 1.92065
1 quart weighs 2.08 pounds................................... .31806
1 pint weighs 1.04 pounds.................................... .01703
1 gill weighs .26 pound...................................... 9.41497
1 cubic foot weighs 62.425 pounds............................ 1.79536
1 cubic foot contains 7.48 gallons............................ .87390
1 cubic foot contains 1728 cubic inches....................... 3.23754
1 cubic inch weighs .036125 pound............................ 8.55781
12 cubic inches weighs .4335 pound........................... 9.63699
27.71 cubic inches weighs 1 pound............................
27.71 cubic inches, height 2.3093 feet........................ .36348

METRIC CONVERSION TABLE

Inches	Millimeters	Inches	Millimeters	Inches	Millimeters
1/16	1.59	2 5/16	58.74	6	152.40
1/8	3.17	2 3/8	60.33	6 1/4	158.75
3/16	4.76	2 7/16	61.91	6 1/2	165.10
1/4	6.35	2 1/2	63.50	6 3/4	171.45
5/16	7.94	2 9/16	65.09	7	177.80
3/8	9.53	2 5/8	66.67	7 1/4	184.15
7/16	11.10	2 11/16	68.26	7 1/2	190.50
1/2	12.70	2 3/4	69.85	7 3/4	196.85
9/16	14.29	2 13/16	71.44	8	203.20
5/8	15.87	2 7/8	73.03	8 1/4	209.55
11/16	17.46	2 15/16	74.61	8 1/2	215.90
3/4	19.05	3	76.20	8 3/4	222.25
13/16	20.64	3 1/8	79.37	9	228.60
7/8	22.23	3 1/4	82.55	9 1/4	234.95
15/16	23.81	3 3/8	85.73	9 1/2	241.30
1	25.40	3 1/2	88.90	9 3/4	247.65
1 1/16	26.99	3 5/8	92.08	10	254.00
1 1/8	28.57	3 3/4	95.25	10 1/4	260.35
1 3/16	30.16	3 7/8	98.43	10 1/2	266.70
1 1/4	31.75	4	101.60	10 3/4	273.05
1 5/16	33.34	4 1/8	104.78	11	279.40
1 3/8	34.92	4 1/4	107.95	11 1/4	285.75
1 7/16	36.51	4 3/8	111.13	11 1/2	292.10
1 1/2	38.10	4 1/2	114.30	11 3/4	298.45
1 9/16	39.68	4 5/8	117.48	12	304.80
1 5/8	41.27	4 3/4	120.65	13	330.20
1 11/16	42.86	4 7/8	123.83	14	355.60
1 3/4	44.44	5	127.00	15	381.00
1 13/16	46.03	5 1/8	130.18	16	406.40
1 7/8	47.62	5 1/4	133.35	17	431.80
1 15/16	49.21	5 3/8	136.53	18	457.20
2	50.80	5 1/2	139.70	19	482.60
2 1/16	52.39	5 5/8	142.88	20	508.00
2 1/8	53.97	5 3/4	146.05	———	
2 3/16	55.56	5 7/8	147.25	39.3708	1. Meter
2 1/4	56.15				

1 Kilogramme = 2.2046 Lb.
50,8 Kilogrammes = 1 Cwt.
100 Kilogrammes = 1,96 Cwts.
1000 Kilogrammes = 19,68 Cwts.
1016,06 Kilogrammes = 1 Ton.
1.0 Cubic Meter = 35,317 Cubic Feet

WEIGHTS OF ENGINES IN POUNDS PER H.P. FOR VARIOUS VESSELS

Comp	Compound	Triple	Quadruple
Steam Launches........................	17-33		
Small Cargo Steamers..................	132-187		
Torpedo Boats.........................		5-36	
Small Cruisers........................		36-70	
Large Cruisers........................		57-110	
Cargo Steamers.......................		143-210	
Cargo Steamers.......................			154-242
Passenger Steamers...................		92-143	110-176

WEIGHTS OF SINGLE PARTS OF ENGINES

Designation of Parts	Cargo Steamer 2460 H. P. Lbs.	Cargo and Passenger Steamer 2000 H. P. Lbs.
Cylinders and Valve Boxes.........................	1.76	1.780
Cylinder Cover and Other Joints...................	.24	.251
Covers and Faces of Valve Chests.................	.11	.167
Stuffing Boxes, Safety Valves......................	.05	.053
Screw Bolts..	.025	.031
Foundations, Col's, Bearings with Guides..........	1.84	1.837
Thrust Blocks, Complete..........................	.24	.217
Pistons..	.18	.253
Piston Rods..	.092	.114
Crossheads..	.077	.143
Connecting Rods...................................	.264	.354
Valves...	.121	
Valve Rods and Eccentrics.........................	.337	.220
Reversing Gear, including Reversing Shaft..........	.128	
Crank Shaft and Shafting..........................	2.068	2.640
Condenser...	.946	.814
Driven Air Pump...................................	.528	.414
Driven Circulating Pump...........................	.198	.132

WEIGHTS OF STATIONARY AND MOVING PARTS OF MARINE ENGINES

	I. H. P.	Moving Parts Lbs.	Fixed Parts Lbs.	Condenser, Pumps, Piping, Including Water Lbs.	Total Lbs.
1	520	31.2	59.6	9.6	100.4
2	1040	23.3	49.5	1.9	74.7
3	1200	60.5	99.0	5.8	165.3
4	1470	101.0	145.0	10.2	256.2
5	1670	88.0	143.0	4.8	235.8
6	1880	44.0	74.1	5.4	123.5
7	1880	53.6	107.6	7.3	168.5
8	2000	72.2	101.0	51.8	225.0
9	2100	78.5	118.0	36.1	232.6
10	2500	72.6	114.0	7.8	194.4
11	6600	66.5	88.0	28.8	183.3
12	2000	67.9	68.0	21.7	157.6

NOTE.—Since the weights will vary with the design, the above values can only be used as an estimate and their limitations appreciated. Weights are from actual calculations and checked by scale weights.

PARTICULARS OF MARINE BOILERS—SCOTCH TYPE

Rules	Working Pressure	Shell Diameter	Shell Length	Shell Thickness	Furnaces Number	Furnaces Diameter In.	Furnaces Thickness	No. Combustion Chambers	Tubes Number	Tubes Diameter	Tubes Length	Surface Square Feet	Total Heating Surface, Square Feet	Weight Boiler, Tons	Weight Water, Tons	Weight Total Tons	Wt. per 100 Sq. Ft. Boiler, Tons	Wt. per 100 Sq. Ft. Water, Tons	Wt. per 100 Sq. Ft. Total Tons	Sq. Ft. Heating Surface, per Ton Boiler
Board Trade	190	16'5"	17'10"	1 11/32	8	40 3/4	19/32		848	2 3/4"	7' 2"	4293	5112	83.0	47.0	130.0	1.62	0.92	2.54	61.6
Board Trade	180	16'4"	17'6"	1 1/2	8	40 5/8	9/16		840	2 3/4"	7' 0 1/2"	4170	4572	79.5	45.5	125.0	1.74	0.99	2.73	57.5
Board Trade	210	15'6"	19'6"	1 13/32	6	44	11/16		852	2 5/8"	7' 10 5/8"	4540	5210	83.0	46.7	129.7	1.59	0.91	2.50	62.7
Board Trade	192	15'3"	18'6"	1 15/32	6	43 1/2	5/8		826	2 5/8"	7' 6"	4180	4830	73.8	42.7	116.5	1.52	0.88	2.40	65.6
Board Trade	214	14'5"	19'10"	1 9/32	6	40 1/16	21/32		740	2 1/2"	7' 11"	3760	4415	75.5	41.7	117.2	1.71	0.95	2.66	58.5
Board Trade	200	14'3"	19'6"	1 18/32	6	42	9/16	3	730	2 1/2"	7' 7 1/2"	3578	4575	68.5	40.5	109.0	1.50	0.88	2.38	66.8
Board Trade	216	14'2"	19'6"	1 9/32	6	38	17/32	3	612	2 3/4"	8' 0"	3460	4071	72.5	40.5	113.0	1.78	1.00	2.78	56.1
Lloyds	180	12'9"	18'0"	1 3/16	4	42	19/32	3	616	2 3/4"	6' 6"	2826	3415	41.0	30.1	71.1	1.20	0.88	2.08	83.3
Board Trade	190	11'6"	18'9"	1 5/16	3	45	19/32	3	496	2 3/4"	8' 0"	2494	3000	43.2	22.5	65.7	1.44	0.75	2.19	69.4
Board Trade	180	15'0"	11'6"	1 7/32	3	44	19/32	3	409	3 1/2"	7' 1 5/8"	2355	2860	45.0	26.0	71.0	1.57	0.91	2.48	63.5
Board Trade	200	14'3"	11'6"	1 5/16	3	38	17/32	3	238	3 1/2"	8' 0"	1067	2138	37.8	19.6	59.6	1.90	0.89	2.79	52.6
Board Trade	160	13'0"	11'0"	1 1/16	3	46	9/16	3	240	3 1/4"	8' 1 1/2"	1756	2232	34.8	17.2	52.0	1.70	0.88	2.58	56.3
Lloyds	200	13'0"	10'6"	1 1/16	3	40	19/32	2	234	3 1/4"	7' 6"	1492	1907	26.5	16.5	43.0	1.82	0.90	2.72	54.8
Lloyds	180	11'6"	11'3"	1 1/8	2	37 3/4	1/2	2	176	3 1/4"	6' 3"	1067	1335	27.3	13.8	41.9	1.92	1.24	3.16	50.4
Lloyds	200	11'0"	9'6"	1	2	36	5/8	2	172	3 1/4"	7' 7"	1088	1327	18.8	10.5	29.3	2.14	1.04	2.95	50.0
Lloyds	160	11'0"	9'6"	15/16	2	35	9/16	2	132	3 1/4"	6' 3"	761	1000	17.6	10.2	27.8	1.91	1.19	3.33	46.7
Lloyds	200	10'0"	9'6"	15/16	2	35	1/2	2	146	3 1/4"	5' 5 1/2"	686	880	17.3	8.8	26.1	1.76	1.02	2.78	56.8
Lloyds	180	10'0"	9'9"	15/16	2	32	9/16	1	118	3 1/4"	6' 5 1/2"	650	820	16.4	8.8	25.2	2.11	1.67	2.78	47.4
Bureau Veritas	180	8'9"	9'9"	27/32	2	32	11/16	1	82	3 3/4"	6' 9"	561	600	13.4	7.5	20.9	2.23	1.24	3.47	44.8

PARTICULARS OF VESSELS OF NAMED DIMENSIONS AND TYPES

Elements	T.S.S.	S.S.S.	S.S.S.	S.S.S.	S.S.S.	S.S.S.	S.S.S.	S.S.S.	S.S.S.	S.S.S.	T.S.S.	T.S.S.	S.S.S.
Length Between Perpendiculars	120.0	200.0	330.0	250.0	255.0	310.0	319.0	320.0	392.0	420.0	460.0	469.0	426.0
Beam Extreme	21.0	30.0	41.0	32.0	34.5	37.0	34.0	40.0	39.0	48.0	52.0	56.0	54.25
Draught, Mean	7.10	12.1	24.4	12.6	9.2	17.3	17.8	18.33	21.3	18.8	26.7	24.5	24.0
Displacement, Tons	282	1285	6880	1740	1420	3600	3445	4720	5767	8160	13080	13895	11556
Area Midship Section, Square Feet	150	324	925	355	285	590	526	664	738	828	1322	1315	1250
Wetted Surface, Square Feet	4508	8628	25210	11184	10164	18099	19245	21102	26235	31196	42423	43389	37798
Length of Fore Body, Feet	54	61	70	79	80	96	90	71	118	75	110	99	102.5
Prismatic Coefficient	.550	.695	.788	.684	.700	.690	.712	.771	.698	.821	.753	.789	.760
Speed in Knots per Hour	9.20	10.8	10.5	11.94	11.3	11.97	11.59	11.79	12.05	11.8	12.05	12.0	12.51
Indicated Horse Power	192	661	1372	962	816	1655	1194	1788	1758	2086	3382	3780	3305
Admiralty Constant	174	228	305	255	223	244	297	258	320	276	276	264	303
Midship Section Constant	608	617	780	627	504	613	686	670	735	560	690	607	744
I. H. P. ÷ Displacement	0.680	0.514	0.200	0.553	0.574	0.534	0.347	0.375	0.305	0.255	0.256	0.272	0.286

Elements	T.S.S.	T.S.S.	T.S.S.	T.S.S.	T.S.S.	T.S.S.	T.S.S.	Naval T.S.S.	Naval T.S.S.	Naval T.S.S.	Naval T.S.S.
Length Between Perpendiculars	300.0	302.0	311.5	270.0	290.0	470.0	685.0	200.0	210.0	300.0	360.0
Beam Extreme	34.5	38.0	36.0	34.0	38.0	58.0	68.0	19.5	20.5	36.5	60.0
Draught, Mean	13.78	13.5	11.5	10.5	11.92	20.5	29.91	5.5	5.67	13.9	20.6
Displacement, Tons	2200	2400	1780	1350	2100	9650	25910	263	320	2235	6100
Area Midship Section, Square Feet	425	460	392	311	416	1100	1922	77	91	445	1059
Wetted Surface, Square Feet	14043	14472	12628	10253	13170	35912	72208	3890	4323	14083	25545
Length of Forebody, Feet	129	119.4	152.5	118.0	113.3	163	213	80	87.0	124	158
Prismatic Coefficient	.603	.604	.514	.563	.609	.653	.690	.600	.586	.586	.561
Speed in Knots per Hour	18.20	18.57	18.70	19.3	20.34	20.2	20.8	27.6	30.5	20.8	20.96
Indicated Horse Power	4398	5241	4000	3750	5820	16200	26500	3628	6017	7275	10646
Admiralty Constant	246	219	240	207	236	230	297	237	220	212	288
Midship Section Constant	556	563	641	596	599	560	652	419	428	551	915
I. H. P. ÷ Displacement	2.00	2.18	2.25	2.78	2.77	1.68	1.02	13.8	18.3	3.26	1.74

Elements	S.S.S.	S.S.S.	S.S.S.	T.S.S.	S.S.S.	T.S.S.	S.S.S.	T.S.S.	S.S.S.	S.S.S.	S.S.S.	T.S.S.	S.S.S.
Length Between Perpendiculars	300.0	402.0	380.0	550.0	460.0	204.0	240.0	420.0	340.0	400.0	425.0	530.0	300.0
Beam Extreme	42.0	43.0	43.0	63.0	50.0	34.0	32.0	50.0	41.0	45.2	51.0	59.0	38.0
Draught, Mean	11.2	18.51	18.6	29.92	26.7	10.33	15.4	21.1	17.0	18.6	23.2	23.5	13.10
Displacement, Tons	2502	5670	5685	22589	12720	1080	2040	9070	4120	5842	9950	14206	2506
Area Midship Section, Square Feet	401	700	712	1779	1270	300	450	980	620	747	1126	1225	453
Wetted Surface, Square Feet	14683	25694	24956	60090	41058	7929	12022	33065	20128	26063	36448	46391	14596
Length of Fore Body, Feet	81.4	118.5	100	106	110	78	81.3	96	107.4	126.3	116	124	107
Prismatic Coefficient	.729	.708	.737	.809	.761	.617	.661	.771	.684	.684	.767	.765	.643
Speed in Knots per Hour	12.23	12.28	12.4	12.75	12.95	13.20	13.23	13.90	14.36	14.79	14.8	14.7	15.33
Indicated Horse Power	1511	2101	2329	4790	3950	1018	1584	3908	2884	3742	4512	6118	2602
Admiralty Constant	223	279	260	345	299	240	235	306	262	280	299	305	255
Midship Section Constant	484	616	581	768	698	685	658	670	633	645	648	637	629
I. H. P. ÷ Displacement	0.604	0.371	0.410	0.213	0.310	0.942	0.776	0.430	0.700	0.645	0.452	0.430	1.04

Elements	T.S.S.	T.S.S.	T.S.S.	S.S.S.	S.S.S.	S.S.S.	T.S.S.	S.S.S.	S.S.S.	T.S.S.	T.S.S.	T.S.S.	T.S.S.
Length Between Perpendiculars	280.0	290.0	300.0	315.5	420.0	450.0	220.0	388.0	466.0	600.0	680.0	570.0	269.0
Beam Extreme	31.0	38.0	34.5	33.5	43.0	45.17	28.0	43.0	52.0	65.0	75.0	64.0	33.0
Draught, Mean	13.4	11.92	13.78	15.0	18.4	23.6	9.0	17.6	20.1	30.01	30.0	27.5	8.75
Displacement, Tons	1940	2100	2200	2480	5906	8500	736	4315	8124	23630	30020	19150	1237
Area Midship Section, Square Feet	350	416	425	422	698	926	204	615	980	1810	2094	1629	266
Wetted Surface, Square Feet	12582	13170	14043	15200	26699	32578	6841	22330	28511	63977	76440	56195	9678
Length of Forebody, Feet	86	113.3	129.0	107.5	124	129	94	142	176	143	178	168	106.3
Prismatic Coefficient	.693	.609	.603	.658	.705	.714	.573	.632	.622	.762	.738	.723	.605
Speed in Knots per Hour	15.03	15.00	15.34	15.34	15.10	15.05	16.50	16.82	16.52	16.01	16.20	17.25	18.9
Indicated Horse Power	2373	2157	2358	2243	4437	4900	1405	4660	6347	10508	12491	11035	3231
Admiralty Constant	223	257	259	295	253	289	261	269	287	321	329	332	246
Midship Section, Constant	501	650	650	678	543	642	654	626	696	707	712	760	556
I. H. P. ÷ Displacement	1.22	1.03	1.07	0.90	0.75	0.58	1.90	1.08	0.78	0.44	0.42	0.57	2.61

Thetis, a Sea-Nymph—Wooden Figurehead

Paragraph Reference Index

Alphabetical Index

Index to Illustrations

Plans